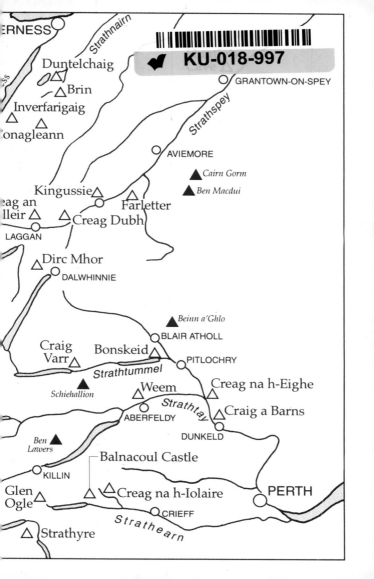

Highland Outcrops

By Kevin Howett

*With contributions by
Gary Latter, Andy Nisbet,
Grant Farquhar, George Ridge,
Ben Ankers, Ed Grindley
and Graham Little*

Series Editor: Roger Everett

SCOTTISH MOUNTAINEERING CLUB
CLIMBERS' GUIDE

Published in Great Britain by the Scottish Mountaineering Trust, 1998
Copyright © the Scottish Mountaineering Club

British Library Cataloguing in Publication Data
ISBN 0 907521 54 1

A catalogue record of this book is available from
The British Library

Diagrams drawn by Kevin Howett
Production by Scottish Mountaineering Trust (Publications) Ltd
Typeset by Elliot Robertson, Westec, North Connel
Printed by St Edmundsbury Press, Bury St Edmunds and
GNP Booth Ltd, Yoker, Glasgow
Bound by WBC, Glamorgan, Wales

Distributed by Cordee, 3a DeMontfort Street, Leicester LE1 7HD

The compilation of this guidebook has been the work of several contributors and has been co-ordinated by the principal author, Kevin Howett, and the editor of the SMC's Climbers Guidebooks, Roger Everett. Individual contributions have been as follows:-

Kevin Howett	*Glen Lednock, Glen Ogle, Lower Cave Crag, Newtyle Quarry, Binnein Shuas, Dirc Mhor and others.*
Gary Latter	*Glen Nevis, Lochaber and Argyll outcrops*
Andy Nisbet	*Strathnairn, Strathspey, Creag Dubh*
Grant Farquhar	*Creag Dubh, Upper Cave Crag*
George Ridge	*Weem Crags, Glen Ogle*
Ben Ankers	*Polney Crag*
Ed Grindley	*Glenfinnan area*
Graham Little	*Mallaig crags*

Contents

List of Illustrations

List of Diagrams

Acknowledgements

We, the collective authors, would like to thank all those climbers who documented their routes over the past 50 years. Without this act of altruism we would not have anything to talk about or enjoy. In any event we wish to pay thanks to those who have gone before by faithfully recording their routes, their desires and their achievements.

We would also like to thank the previous authors of guidebooks to the areas covered. Their past work has been invaluable in the compilation of this guide. They are Richard Frere (*Rock Climbs: A Guide to the crags in the neighbourhood of Inverness, 1938*), Jimmy Marshall (*Climbers' Guide to Ben Nevis, 1969*), Klaus Schwartz and Blyth Wright (*Rock Climbs in Glen Nevis, The Polldubh Crags, 1970 and update 1978*) , Colin Stead and Jimmy Marshall (*Rock and Ice Climbs in Lochaber and Badenoch, 1981*), Dave Cuthbertson (*Creag Dubh and Craig-a-Barns, 1983*), Dougie Dinwoodie (*North East Outcrops, 1984*), Ed Grindley (*Rock Climbs, Glen Nevis and the Lochaber Outcrops, 1985*), Rab Anderson and Gary Latter (*Scottish New Routes, 1986*), Doug Rennie (*Creag na h-Eighe, The Secret Crag, 1989*) and Andy Nisbet (*Glenmore Lodge Local Area Guide*).

Thanks are due to Niall Ritchie for organising the selection of illustrations from over 500 slides submitted; to Roger Everett for his helpful advice about routes, grades and descriptions and for keeping the guide on course in his role as Series Editor; and to Donald Bennet whose careful scrutiny of the book during proof-reading and production has resulted in a professional product for the last in the present series of SMC climbers' guides.

Finally, there were many people who helped in some way, be it checking routes, sorting out confusion over first ascents, giving advice or simply persevering with the authors when they needed to climb and check even the most awful routes. They included (in alphabetical order): Rab Anderson, Robin Campbell, Rick Campbell, Melanie Crowther, Dave Cassidy, Dave Cuthbertson, Carol Fettes, Allen Fyffe, Dave Griffiths, Davy Gunn, Janet Horrocks, Lawrence Hughes, Bruce Kerr, Alan Kimber, Dougie Lang, Alan Leary, James McLeod, Duncan McCallum, Rennie McOwan, Andy MacDonald, John Mackenzie, Colin Moody, Neil Morrison, Andy Nelson, Grahame Nicoll, Tom Prentice, Tom Redfern, Clive Rowland, Alex Runciman, Neil Shepherd, Andy Slater, Craig Smith, Simon Steer, Ian Taylor, and Paul Thorburn. Many thanks to them all for their patience and at times stoic enthusiasm.

We also all owe thanks to the many people who contributed their views while at various crags and whose names we could never remember.

Kevin Howett, Gary Latter, Grant Farquhar, Andy Nisbet, Graham Little, Ben Ankers and George Ridge.

Introduction

What you are about to delve into is a mixture of new information and that reincarnated from a number of different sources. These include the 1983 Creag Dubh and Craig a Barns guide, written by the area's most prolific activist, Dave Cuthbertson; the 1985 Glen Nevis guide by Ed Grindley, which spurred on the boom of the late 1980s new routing in Glen Nevis; the Northeast Outcrops of Scotland guide by Dougie Dinwoodie, which curiously included Huntly's Cave; even the 1981 guide to Lochaber and Badenoch by Colin Stead and Jimmy Marshall held the only available information on Binnein Shuas. Other information was only available from local home grown guides (particularly the outcrops around Aviemore which were first collated by the instructors at Glenmore Lodge National Outdoor Training Centre); and even more was hidden amongst the labyrinthine new routes section of over ten years' worth of the Scottish Mountaineering Club Journal.

Now, after several years in the making, it is gathered together, inviting you to taste its delights.

> "Stranger! if e'er thine ardent step hath traced
> The northern realms of ancient Caledon,
> Where the proud queen of wilderness hath placed,
> by lake and cataract, her lonely throne;
> sublime but sad delight thy soul hath known,
> listing where from the cliffs the torrents thrown,
> mingle their echoes with the eagles' cry,
> and with the sounding lake and the moaning sky."
> *Sir Walter Scott*

From the sea-cliffs of Seil Island near Oban to the rugged grandeur of the Mallaig hinterland; from the stunning Glen Nevis, the embodiment of Sir Walter Scott's words, to the tranquil setting of Dunkeld; from the hidden delights of the mountain surprise of Dirc Mhor to the convenient outcrops of rural Aviemore; the breadth of 'sublime delight' to be had, lost amongst the folds of rock described here, will breath fresh life into the most jaded of rockjocks.

On a personal note I now look forward to being able to climb on these crags without fear of earache from frustrated climbers, whose old guides were getting very dog-eared and faded.

Kevin Howett. 1997

Climbers and their Environment

"The soul of the Gael is on the summit of the mountain"
Gaelic Proverb

This lovely proverb forms part of a great mass of Highland and Gaelic cultural material (songs, poems, prayers, blessings and sayings), which emphasises the strong sense of possession the indigenous people had with their environment, and particularly with the mountains that surrounded them. As part of that, they roamed freely in their hills and glens for what today we would consider as 'recreational activities', as a right; not written in law but as a natural part of their lives. More 'commercial' uses were covered by regulations of some kind, such as the sheiling pattern, drove routes and grazing rights. It was only in the relatively recent times of more definitive land ownership that came with the Victorians and the birth of the 'sporting estate' that such freedom became more controlled. The restrictions on access at this period caused much controversy and resentment, and still does to some extent today. But it is the much older heritage of the right to roam the hills that has helped shape the Scottish psyche and which makes people believe that there is no law of trespass in Scotland. Of course there has been such legislation since Victorian times, although it is grey and blurred and argued over. The reality is that people continue to enjoy their hills from the point of view of tradition and moral right, not wishing to harm wildlife and without searching for confrontation with estate staff or hill farmers.

Since early in 1996 a voluntary Concordat has been agreed between access groups and landowners in Scotland which offers a chance to improve relationships over access. This informal agreement beholds both groups of people to acknowledge the legitimate desires and needs of the other. In essence this means that climbers and walkers should expect a welcome onto the hills and crags of Scotland as long as they act sensibly, respect the people who own and work in the hills and have due regard for the plants and wildlife that surrounds them. The four main principles of the Access Concordat are reproduced below.

THE ACCESS CONCORDAT

The parties to the Concordat agree that the basis of access to the hills for informal recreation should be as follows:

- Freedom of access exercised with responsibility and subject to reasonable restraints for management and conservation purposes.

- Acceptance by visitors of the needs of land management, and understanding of how this sustains the livelihood, culture and community interests of those who live and work in the hills.

- Acceptance by land managers of the public's expectation of having access to the hills.

- Acknowledgement of a common interest in the natural beauty and special qualities of Scotland's hills, and of the need to work together for their protection and enhancement.

The Mountaineering Council of Scotland (MCofS) is the body that represents the views of climbers and hill walkers. One of its primary concerns is the continued free access to the hills and crags that we all enjoy and it played an instrumental part in formulating The Access Concordat. Should climbers encounter situations that are contrary to the Concordat then they should contact the MCofS with full details.

The Scottish Mountaineering Club (SMC) and Trust (SMT), who jointly produce this and other guidebooks, wish to impress on all who avail themselves of the information in these books to do so in the spirit of the Access Concordat and so consider the sporting and proprietary rights of landowners and farmers. Always try to follow a path or track through cultivated land and forests, and avoid causing damage to fences, dykes and gates by climbing over them carelessly. Do not leave litter anywhere, but take it down from the hill in your rucksack. Avoid disturbance to sheep during the lambing period (between March and May) and keep dogs under close control at all times.

Climbers should not intentionally disrupt stalking and shooting. These activities are important to the economy of many Highland estates. If climbers *intentionally* disrupt such activities they will be in contravention of the Criminal Justice Act, 1994. More information about this act is available from the MCofS. Deer stalking occurs between the 1st July and 20th October, although the critical period for most estates is much shorter. The grouse shooting season is from 12th August to 10th December. The Act does not preclude access during these times.

Climbers and walkers are recommended to consult the book *HEADING FOR THE SCOTTISH HILLS*, published by the SMT on behalf of the MCofS and The Scottish Landowners' Federation, which gives the names and addresses of estate factors and keepers who may be contacted for information regarding their sporting shooting activities on the hill.

Climbers are reminded that they should not drive along private estate roads without permission, and when parking their cars should avoid blocking access to private roads and land, and should avoid causing any hazard to other road users.

CONSERVATION

With increasing numbers of climbers and walkers going to the hills it is important that every individual does their utmost to reduce any detrimental impact on what is often a special environment. One sign of this increased activity is erosion to footpaths and hillsides, which in some cases is unsightly. Some of the revenue from the sale of this and other SMC guidebooks is used by the Trust to assist financially the work being carried out to repair and maintain hill paths in Scotland. However, it is important for all of us to recognise our responsibility to minimise the erosive effect of our passage over the hills so that the enjoyment of future climbers shall not be spoiled by our own actions.

As a general rule, where a path exists walkers should follow it and even where it is wet and muddy should avoid walking along its edges, the effect of which is to extend erosion sideways. Do not take short-cuts at the corners of zigzag paths. Remember too that the effects are exacerbated when the ground is waterlogged during or after rain.

Although the use of bicycles can often be very helpful for reaching remote crags and hills, the erosion damage caused when they are used 'off road' on soft footpaths and open hillsides is far greater than that caused by feet. It is the editorial policy of the SMC that the use of bicycles in hill country may only be recommended on hard tracks such as forest roads or on private roads following rights of way.

The proliferation of cairns on hills detracts from the feeling of wildness, and may be confusing rather than helpful as regards route finding. The indiscriminate building of cairns on the hills is therefore to be discouraged.

NESTING BIRDS AND CLIMBERS

In England and Wales the British Mountaineering Council has entered into dialogue with the RSPB over voluntary restrictions when rare birds have nested on crags used by climbers. They are very successful. In Scotland, the Mountaineering Council of Scotland has contact with the RSPB. Many of the crags described in this guide are the home for various birds of prey. They include those birds known as Schedule 1 Species, such as Eagles and Peregrine Falcons, which are specially protected by Law. It is an offence to disturb these birds (or any bird) at their nests (with large fines imposed on those convicted of disturbance). As nest sites can vary each year from crag to crag, and some of the sites are monitored under licence from Scottish Natural Heritage by Raptor Study Groups, the MCofS urges climbers to contact them for advice and up-to-date information about any voluntary climbing restrictions that may be necessary. Remember if a site is not being used then there will be no restrictions.

The following general guidance to climbers has been issued by the MCofS in association with the RSPB:

The designation of birds.
Almost all birds, their eggs and nests, are protected by the Wildlife and Countryside Act 1981. Certain rarer or more endangered species are further protected by increased penalties under the 1981 Act and cannot be intentionally disturbed when nesting. These are referred to as Schedule 1 species (S1). These species can only be disturbed at the nest by those in possession of a special licence issued by Scottish Natural Heritage. If a population of a specific bird in the UK is of international importance, is a scarce breeder, is declining in breeding numbers, is restricted in distribution, vulnerable or of special concern it is further classified in the Red Data Books (RD).

The bird species most commonly encountered on crags in Scotland are: Golden Eagle (S1/RD), White Tailed Eagle (Sea Eagle, S1/RD), Peregrine Falcon (S1/RD), Puffin (S1/RD), Guillemot (RD), Razorbill (RD), Fulmar, Kittiwakes, Cormorants, Shags, Buzzards, Kestrels.

A general climbers' principle:
Before starting out on the route of your choice on a certain crag or cliff, it is best to assess whether there is a nesting site that is being used by any bird, but particularly those listed above. The nest site is often quite obvious and it is best to avoid any climbs that directly affect it.

Concerning those species mentioned above, the numbers of peregrine falcons in Scotland is healthy and they nest successfully on many crags that are also enjoyed by climbers, but they should still not be directly disturbed. Often it is possible to continue climbing on parts of the crag well away from the nest site. Eagles are the most important species that climbers may encounter, and they are much more prone to disturbance. The entire crag area should not be disturbed in this case. Both these species are variable in their choice of nest site.

The nesting and restrictions period.
The general time period for seasonal nesting restrictions usually applies between 1st February and the end of July. The area of crag to be avoided can vary depending upon various factors such as the size and extent of the breeding site, the importance of the population, the level of disruption any climbing would cause, the approach routes to the crag and the tolerance of the birds at that site. Some species also vary their choice of nesting site each year either within a crag on between different crags.

Many sites of Schedule 1 species are monitored throughout the nesting period by Raptor Study Groups (licensed by SNH) to ensure they are not disturbed or their eggs or chicks are not stolen.

How you can help.
1. Get up-to-date information: The MCofS has contact with the RSPB in Scotland and, where there are known concerns about breeding birds and climbing routes, they can pass information on including variable nesting sites and if a site is not being used, when there will be no restrictions on climbing.
2. Any climbers witnessing illegal disturbance should report the matter to the Police immediately. All Police forces now have Wildlife Liaison Officers who will deal with such calls. Those licensed to be close to nests should be able to produce the licence when asked. Climbers witnessing other climbers disturbing nest sites should also contact the MCofS.
3. Make a donation to the MCofS Access and Conservation Fund (The Henry Hindmarch Fund) to help maintain free access to Scottish crags and mountains.

For more details and an information leaflet about bird nesting and access, contact the Mountaineering Council of Scotland at : 4a St. Catherine's Road Perth PH1 5SE. Tel. 01738 638 227, Fax. 01738 442 950.

Notes on the Use of this Guide

The Highland Outcrops described here are spread over a vast area. For ease of identification they have been grouped into areas based around the major Glens or Straths that slice through the hills and provide us humans with wheeled access to otherwise remote lands. Relevant information about amenities has been included in the introduction to each area. This includes accommodation, cafes and hostelries and any other general interest for those bored with climbing or encumbered by screaming toddlers.

TERMINOLOGY

In all of the topographical descriptions of crags and routes, the words left and right refer to the climber looking at the crag and facing upwards. Regarding descents, jumping off the top of the crag, or being pulled off when the belay fails, left and right refer to climbers facing downhill. Any other permutation is stated in the text.

DIAGRAMS

As many crag diagrams as possible are included to aid route identification. Where a climb is numbered in the text, it can be found with the corresponding number on a crag diagram, located close to that text. Not all crags and routes are handed on a platter in this way and to successfully locate these will require extra effort. Indeed to fully find your way around the myriad of Polldubh crags in Glen Nevis will take a few visits, but the diagram of the layout of the crags on the hillside will help.

HOW HARD IS IT?

Scottish guide book authors of recent years have attempted to rid Scotland of unwelcome frights, epics, VS leaders getting stuck on the crux of E3s, and chop routes hiding behind innocuous descriptions. There have been some attempts to see Scottish grades brought in line with Welsh grades. As a result many of the routes described in the predecessors to this guide could perhaps be considered to be the last stand of the noble style of sandbagging. The question now of course is have the authors of this guide succumbed to the banal standardisation of grades (the climbing equivalent of the Ecu) or have we left a little bit for the imagination. Well, let's just say that the we hope that we have now prevented the worst epics from occurring, but there still remains a very healthy trend within some of Scotland's activists to outdo any competitors and put the wind up anyone fool enough to try and repeat routes by the simple expedient of grading them lower than their true difficulty. Hence, a small-print health warning may still be applicable - some of us think that there are only two grades - 'piece of duff' (translated as "I can do it, just") and 'desperate' (translated as "I couldn't get off the ground"). So bear this in mind when you set off into what could still be the unknown.

GRADES
There are two kinds of climbs to be found in this guide; Gear and Sport climbs. They have different grading systems that reflect the differing style of the climbs.
Gear climbs:
These climbs rely upon the leader hand-placing 'natural' gear into natural cracks in the rock, which are, hopefully, later removed by the second, thus leaving little trace of either of you passing. Some idea of the difficulty of these climbs can be gleaned by careful study of the combination of the overall (adjectival) grade and the technical grade. When combined with comments in the general route description this subtle system tells a lot about a route and what you can expect in terms of the protection (and difficulty of placing it), the sustained nature of the climbing or the quality of the rock. At least that's the idea. It works reasonably well but is often misused and misunderstood even by those who've used it for years and so should not be taken as gospel. Use your own judgement and see why this kind of climbing is thought by many to be 'adventurous' climbing.

The overall grades go from Easy, Moderate, Difficult, Very Difficult, Severe, Very Severe (VS), Hard Very Severe (HVS), and Extremely Severe. The Extreme grade is divided into E1, E2, E3, E4, E5, E6, E7, (and forever upwards dependent on what else might be achieved in the future). Technical grades have only been used from those found on the harder Severes or easier VSs. These are 4a, 4b, 4c, 5a, 5b, 5c, 6a, 6b, 6c, 7a, etc.

The normal range of technical grades expected on routes of the given overall grades are roughly as follows:
VS - 4a to 5b.   HVS - 4b to 5c.   E1 - 4c to 6a.   E2 - 5a to 6a.   E3 - 5b to 6b.
E4 - 5c to 6c.   E5 - 5c to 6c.   E6 - 6a to 7a.   E7 - 6b to 7a.
Routes with a technical grade at the lower end of the range will be either poorly protected, or sustained with reasonable protection. Those with grades at the upper end of the expected range will have short hard crux sections which are generally well protected.
Sport climbs:
The sport routes are given one overall grade based on the French system. There is no need for anything else as the routes have nice big bolts at regular intervals and should therefore be safe, thus allowing one to concentrate on the technicality and the sustained or strenuous nature of the climbing. Having said that, some of the routes have very necky first or second clips and the less brave (more shifty) climbers have clipped some of these from below by the judicious use of a long stick. Any stick longer than 5m may be considered as an unfair advantage (especially on routes 5m tall!). Removing branches from trees for this purpose is definitely a hanging offence. The grades used are 5, 6a, 6b, 6c, 7a, 7b, 7c, 8a, 8b (the hardest so far in Scotland). The jump from one of these grades to the next actually corresponds to two grade steps, the intermediate being indicated by a + sign. These numbers do not correspond to

the rather similar-looking British technical grades described above. In fact, there is little use in comparing the two types of grade, although foreign visitors may wish to start by thinking of a French 6a+ as equivalent to a well protected E2 5c, and work from there.

ETHICS
It's never a good idea to put a group of climbers together in the evening (with beer or other high energy isotonic liquid) without non-climbers around who can bring sanity to the proceedings. The resulting conversation will inevitably drift from issues of worldly import to the mind-numbingly boring but completely unavoidable issue of climbing ethics, gossip, slander and piss-taking. Here are some thoughts:

BOLTS
More vehemently discussed than politics or sex, and with about as many different viewpoints as both these subjects combined. It has been decided by the authors to give general advice on bolts at this stage and let folk fight out details in the bar. But all climbers should bear in mind that the decision of where and where not to place bolts should be made with due regard to the fact that other climbers will have different opinions and visions of the future of Scottish climbing. Some of the ethics of native North Americans, who feel very close to the land, are applicable to climbers too in this respect:

> "In our every deliberation, we must consider the impact of our decisions on the next seven generations."
> *The great law of the Iroquois*
confederation.

So far most of the venues developed for sport climbing that are described in this guide have been accepted by the majority of Scottish climbers. Those bolts that clearly overstepped the general consensus were removed. No-one active in Scottish climbing wishes to see the indiscriminate use of the bolt destroy future achievements using gear, so we would ask that anyone considering developing sport routes give a great deal of thought, and discussion with others, before becoming the driller-killer of future generations.

Bolting Guidelines for Scotland:
This compromise statement developed from the views of most of the active climbers in Scotland by the Mountaineering Council of Scotland should act as a guideline:
"The MCofS acknowledges that there is a place for bolts in the future development of Scottish climbing. However, to ensure that the highly regarded ethos of, and future development of, traditional climbing (involving leader-placed and second-removed protection) is not threatened, it is felt that the use of bolts should be limited to the production of 'Sport' climbs. There should be no retrospective bolting of established climbs for protection or belays, and there should be no minimalist bolting.

The production of Sport climbs with bolts is acceptable on natural rock only when all the following conditions have been satisfied:

(1) On low-lying cliffs, provided that such development is not against the wishes of the landowner. Bolts are inappropriate on mountain and sea-cliffs.

(2) On routes where natural protection is absent or is inadequate for the repeated falls that such routes necessitate.

(3) Where the rock is steep and provides climbs of a high order of difficulty, at the forefront of developments of the day.

(4) Where there is no anti-bolt ethic.

Concerning quarried rock, it is felt that any future development should be constrained only by points (2) and (4) above. Finally it is felt that bolts should be located to ensure minimum visual impact and should be placed according to current best practices.

It is intended that these principles are not seen as simply restrictive rules, but as a guide to promote the positive development of Scottish climbing, where Sport climbing, rather than becoming a substitute for traditional climbing, grows alongside it."

Mountaineering Council of Scotland, 1991

EQUIPMENT

It is assumed that anyone getting as far as buying this guide will be committed and will have a full range of the most commonly available equipment that is now carried as standard. This includes a full set of nuts, micronuts (most commonly RPs or HBs) and camming devices (including Tri-cams). A lot of the routes in this guide require a substantial set (or sets) of RPs and some require double sets of the smaller Tri-cams to give the maximum amount of available protection.

Skyhooks have also been used for protection, albeit sparingly and most commonly on first ascents, on routes where nothing else existed. They are not designed for such use and they should not be relied upon even when their use is mentioned in the text. Anyone testing the strength of a skyhook and surviving can enter the competition for the luckiest leader fall - the best effort so far being a head-first dive of about 8m ! They are normally secured in place by the use of a third rope and tensioned to a runner at the base of the crag. If that seems ridiculous, Blu-Tack or Sellotape would be another, although less effective, means of securing them. If the skyhook of a first ascent has not been dispensed with on subsequent ascents its use is still indicated in the route description. Whether the regular use of a skyhook (or numerous skyhooks) on all the routes one may climb should be regarded as unethical can be argued about elsewhere, although the authors would be glad to hear opinions.

The placement of a peg is commonly regarded as a last resort on the first ascent of a route and anyone using them on repeat ascents of established routes should regard their ascent as a dismal failure and should take up train spotting where they will cause less damage. Where routes have pegs in place, they should not be relied upon as they all deteriorate over time. Whether it is ethical to remove pegs from a route if it is felt that they are unnecessary (e.g. upon the advent of new, improved 'natural' gear) is another contentious issue, but as they should only be used in the first instance when natural protection is lacking there may be some merit in allowing anarchy to prevail, but remember, damaging the rock by removing them is just as heinous a crime as banging them in 'willy-nilly' in the first place.

The placement of *in situ* wires (usually hammered) should be avoided as they corrode faster than pegs (when they can ruin a placement for the future) and they often fall out during a bad winter anyway.

Finally, remember "rust never sleeps" and even the most bomb-proof looking bolt will have a limited life-span. The bolts used on the routes described here vary in their make and style (expansion and glue-in) and anyone considering falling onto them should make their own assessment of their reliability, based perhaps on their age (both the bolt's and the climber's). The following information is reproduced courtesy of the British Mountaineering Council.

Checking Placements. What to look out for
Corrosion.
In theory if the thickness of an anchor is reduced to less than 75% of its original thickness it should not be used. In practice, judgements on corrosion damage are hard to make and corrosion may be hidden. It is always sensible to back up any anchor.
Fracturing the rock.
If the anchor is in fractured, loose or hollow rock it should not be used. If surface rock has come away around the placement, then at least 90% of the length of the anchor should still be covered for it to be acceptable. Anchors placed less than 20cm (8 inches) from cracks, edges or other anchors should be considered suspect.
Looseness of the anchor.
Always check that the anchor is not loose before weighting it. Resin failure, resin anchor bond failure and fracturing of the rock will lead to dangerously loose anchors. Bear in mind that an anchor that has taken lots of falls may be progressively weakened.

What You Can Do To Reduce The Risk
Never belay away from the base of the crag. Standing more than a few metres out will cause a degree of outward pull on the first runner of the route. You would never let this happen on a gear route - the same applies to bolts.

When getting ready to lower off from the top of a route, never allow yourself to become fully untied from the rope. Clip directly into the belay bolt(s). Take a loop of rope, pass it through the bolt belay and clip it into the belay loop of your harness with a figure of 8 knot and screwgate karabiner. Untie, thread the rope through the belay bolt(s), tie in again, then unclip the bight of rope.

Don't remove the runners on the route unless you are the last person to lower off (this makes good sense when top-roping as it reduces the swing following a fall as well as providing backup to the belay anchor(s). If dogging a route, don't cause unnecessary outward pull onto the runner you are clipped into.

Be wary of any *in situ* karabiners left as lower offs on hangers. If top-roping the line, always do so off your own karabiners. If the *in situ* karabiner looks dangerous, feel free to replace it.

Only you can make judgements on these hidden dangers based on your own experience.

STYLE

The authors have attempted to document honestly the style of the first ascents of the routes in the guide, when they are known, and these are included in the first ascent list. This is done without comment upon the rights or wrongs of whatever tactic was used, but as an important part of the history of the climbs and the evolution of climbing ethics. It must also be remembered that these tactics are not localised events and such activities occur all over the UK but are not always documented. Working on the basis that the perfect ascent (and one we should all strive for) is on sight, in one push, naked, placing ones own natural protection and without falling off or resting on the runners, then any other form of ascent can be regarded as tainted, however slightly. This is said with the full knowledge that it is often only possible for those at the cutting edge to extend the upper limit of difficulty by deviating from the ideal at times, a reality confirmed numerous times in climbing history all over the UK (indeed the world).

In the time scale of this guide such tactics have included yo-yoing (lowering to the ground each time upon falling off), dogging (having a breather on a runner and not lowering to the ground), top-roping or practising the hardest moves, leaving gear in place over several days attempts, clipping the ropes back into the high point from an abseil on a subsequent attempt, practising runner placements, and of course simply cleaning a route gives some knowledge of the holds and protection. There has also been the occasional ball-point ascent (only ever done with a pen and paper). Thus, any successive ascent that was closer to the ideal than that of the first has also been noted for posterity as such an ascent is clearly worthy of praise. Some of the harder routes detailed here have yet to see a repeat. It should also be remembered that many routes, even some of the hard ones, have been done in very pure style, many on-sight.

Of course one is allowed to do any of the aforementioned tactics on a sport route (and anything else that comes to mind as long as it is safe and there is no audience!) but climbers should only claim an ascent after a red-point (all the moves done in one go, usually after lots of practice) or a pink-point (as for a red-point but with all the bolts pre-clipped with extenders). And remember, if the first bolt seems a bit high up, the chances are it was 'stick clipped' on the first ascent or had the clip pre-placed.

There are sport climb 'projects' mentioned in the text as they aid identification of neighbouring routes, but how long that line can be considered the property of the person who pounded in the bolts is another debatable issue. All too often a line is equipped, then left for a long period without any attempts taking place (e.g. The Project Crag in Glen Ogle). In some countries those who equipped the line have one year to climb it before it becomes public property. Would this work in Scotland?

Finally, it goes without saying that the use of a hammer and chisel to ascend a sheet of rock is regarded by most climbers as blasphemous. And leaving anything other than your spirit at the base of crags is very shoddy (there have been instances of old ropes, gear and used containers of Sica left abandoned for years).

First Ascents
A list of first ascent details appears at the back of the guide. It is as complete as possible, bearing in mind that some details have been lost in the mists of time (and some climbers too). Anyone able to throw some light on the omissions should contact the authors. Snippets of general information about the routes is also included here for interest and posterity.

USEFUL ADDRESSES

Scottish Mountaineering Club/Trust
John R. R. Fowler, Secretary, 4 Doune Terrace, Edinburgh, EH3 6DY.
The Club is one of the oldest in Scotland. It produces the definitive climbing guides to Scotland as well as walking and area guides. Membership is open to those individuals resident in Scotland who have shown a commitment to Scottish mountaineering. The Trust helps footpath repair and access work.
The Club's Web Site address (its URL) is: http://www.smc.org.uk/smc/
Information is available at this address about all Club publications and it is a forum for new route information and discussion.

Mountaineering Council of Scotland
4a, St. Catherine's Road, Perth PH1 5SE. Tel. 01738 638 227. Fax. 01738 442 095
The MCofS is the National Body for climbers and walkers in Scotland. It is a voluntary organisation that campaigns for access to the hills and crags, promotes safety, safeguards mountaineering ethos and prevents damaging developments in the hills. Membership is open to clubs, associate groups and individuals. Benefits of membership include regular Newsletters, free liability insurance, use of Member Clubs' Huts throughout Scotland and cheap skills courses. The MCofS Information Service offers information on all aspects of Scotland's climbing and walking, from safety advice, access information, bird restrictions, accommodation, outdoor shops and amenities in all the major mountaineering and climbing areas as well as guide book lists, contacts for mountain guides and indoor climbing walls information.

Loch Linnhe and Loch Leven

Encompassing the area along the shores of the two huge lochs, Linnhe and Leven, between Fort William and Oban (and including the magnificent Glen Nevis under the mighty Ben Nevis, as well as the lower reaches of Glen Coe), the crags detailed here are all easily accessible being virtually at sea-level. None of the bigger crags higher up the hillsides have been included as they are covered by the SMC guides to Glen Coe and Ben Nevis, which include winter climbs as well as summer. There is a selection of contrasting rock types in the area and the crags encompass the full range from mica-schist, kentallanite (a form of limestone with no noticeable effect on the local supermen; pure quartz and granite. Also detailed are the only sea-cliffs in this guide. These are tucked away on Seil Island south of Oban and although very out of the way from other climbing areas they are worth a visit for the adventurous.

ACCOMMODATION

The most convenient accommodation for Glen Nevis is in the area around Fort William. There are a multitude of B&Bs and Hotels. The less expensive bunkhouse alternatives are: Achintee Bunkhouse at the north entrance to Glen Nevis itself near Fort William (Tel. 01397 702240) and The Smiddy Independent Bunkhouse, Corpach (Tel. 01397 772 467). Numerous self-catering accommodation is available (details from magazines and the local Tourist Board office in Fort William) including Calluna (Tel. 01397 700 451) and Drumore (Tel. 01397 702 094), both in the centre of Fort William. Camping can be had either at the official site in Glen Nevis or wild camping is possible further up Glen Nevis below the crags themselves. Please note that this is presently being discouraged.

Equally convenient for this area are a profusion of independent bunkhouses and cheap climbing huts in the area around Glen Coe; Inchree Chalets and Bunkhouse, Onich (Tel. 01855 821 287); Leacantuim Farm Bunkhouse (and The Red Squirrel campsite) on the old road between Glencoe village and The Clachaig Inn (Tel. 01855 811256); The Glen Coe Outdoor Centre in the village (Tel. 01855 811350); Glencoe Mountain Cottages at Gleann-leac-na-muidhe in Glen Coe (Tel/Fax: 01855 811 598); West Highland Lodge (Tel. 01855 831 471) and The Mamore Lodge Hotel Bunkhouse for groups of 10 or more (Tel. 01855 831 213), both in Kinlochleven. The Creag Mhor Hotel in North Ballachulish offers walkers and climbers suitable accommodation.

Finally, There is an independent bunkhouse in Oban, The Jeremy Inglis Hostel (Tel. 01631 565 065), for anyone intent on the exploration of this particular area.

Huts available to MCofS and BMC members are Steall Hut in the Steall area of Glen Nevis, operated by Lochaber Mountaineering Club, the Alex MacIntyre Memorial Hut, adjacent to the Creag Mhor Hotel, North Ballachulish; Manse

Barn, the Lomond Club Hut, beside the Onich Hotel; Blackrock Cottage, the Ladies Scottish Climbing Club hut under the Glen Coe Ski area; and the SMC Lagangarbh Hut below the Buachaille Etive Mor. Contact the MCofS for further details.

AMENITIES
Climbing and mountaineering are integral to the economy of the area, with Ben Nevis and Glen Coe attracting winter climbers from many parts of the world. As a result, Fort William has several outdoor shops; West Coast Outdoor Leisure, Ellis Brigham's and the original Nevisport, which has a good café and climbers' bar and has become a traditional meeting place. The Nevis Bank Hotel lounge bar is used by local climbers and the Grogg and Gruel in the High Street has pushed Fort William cuisine into the 1990s. Other shops in the area include Glencoe Guides and Gear in Glen Coe.

In the weather or the midges get too bad, the climbing wall at the Lochaber Leisure Centre in Fort William is ideal for loosening the limbs and straining tendons. Speaking of which, Kinlochleven may soon have a hill walking and climbing centre. The Clachaig Inn in Glen Coe also offers a climbers bar, café and accommodation.

GLEN NEVIS

Maps : OS Landranger Series 1:50,000 Sheet 41; Outdoor Leisure Series 1:25,000 Sheet 32

This magnificent glen not only ranks as one of the most stunning in the whole of Scotland but also offers a multitude of excellent outcrops of all shapes and sizes, unmatched anywhere in the country. The combination of the dramatic setting between the glistening screes of Sgurr a' Mhaim and the mighty Ben Nevis, and the stands of remaining Caledonian pine, birch and rowan mean that it is a tourist magnet in the summer months, but one of the most pleasing places to climb in the whole UK. That may sound a little over the top to the uninitiated but one visit is enough for complete seduction.

The River Nevis starts life in the Mamore Forest, on the fringe of the wasteland known as Rannoch Moor. It soon gathers momentum as it heads west to fall turbulently through the gorge of Eas-an-Tuill, then descends through the lower glen towards Fort William. The climbing is concentrated near the upper reaches of the glen from a point where the road turns to single track as it crosses the Lower Falls of Nevis at Achriabhach (and then ends at a carpark), up through the gorge of Eas-an-Tuill and into Steall meadow with its stunning Waterfall (An'Steall, the second highest fall in Scotland).

The rock is very clean mica-schist, scoured by glaciers into wrinkled overhanging walls with slabby front faces (known as 'roches moutonnées'). Cracks tend to be small or incipient and many of the harder routes rely entirely on RPs for protection. Few pegs have been used on the modern routes and skyhooks have been employed for dubious psychological protection on the blanker lines.

ACCESS
A small road, signposted to Glen Nevis, leaves the main A82 Trunk road from a roundabout at Nevis Bridge, just on the way north out of Fort William. The road leads, after 10km, to a dead-end at a carpark. There is generally no public transport, but in summer months there is sometimes a bus service for tourists as far as Achriabhach below Polldubh Crags which can prove useful.

HISTORY
Climbing in the glen dates back to the mid-1940s. Brian Pinder Kellet, a pacifist who spent the war working in the forestry in Torlundy, used the crags of Polldubh for training . He would hire a bike and climb solo here in the evenings but he left no details of his routes (unlike the routes he pioneered on the north face of The Ben with which he was obsessed).

After the war a small band of Fort William-based climbers started recording the glen's exploration with Jimmy Ness and Basil Ellison climbing Hangover Buttress Edge (Moderate). Wearing tricounis and using hemp rope, with no runners, Ness went on to add Cavalry Crack, Secretaries' Crack, Sheep Fank Wall and Rib and Pinnacle Ridge. The former two routes have never become popular but Pinnacle Ridge could lay claim to being Scotland's most climbed route and is now polished enough to warrant a Severe grade. At about the same time the first extreme graded routes were being pioneered in Scotland by John Cunningham wearing plimsoles.

There followed a lull when Ness was conscripted, but on his return he resumed action, climbing variously with Jimmy Wynne and Alan Burgeon. Although standards were not yet up to those attained elsewhere, the merits of the Polldubh crags became widely known, mainly due to an article by Ness in the SMC Journal of 1951 entitled 'The rock playground of Lochaber'.

Through the 1950s the only activity came from the RAF Rescue teams during training. Dan Stewart added the middle section of what is now Crag Lough Grooves, R.Wilkinson discovered Scimitar Buttress, and Ian Clough (with Team Leader John Alexander) produced Doomsday and Damnation, both VS, on Styx Buttress. In a 1960 SMC Journal article Clough hailed this as the "advent of hard free climbing". In 1959 Clough and Terry Sullivan, with Eddie Buckley, made the most of a good two month period and produced over thirty routes, most of which have become today's middle grade classics; Storm (HVS with some aid), Phantom Slab, Flying Dutchman, Crag Lough Grooves and Direct Route on Secretaries' Crag.

The first foray into the Steall area came in 1960 with Clough doing two routes on carpark Crag, but on the whole 1960s activity concentrated on difficulty rather than quantity. Allan Austin, on honeymoon with his wife Jenny in 1962, freed Storm but locally-based Ken Johnson was responsible for the first extremes in the glen. He climbed the poorly protected Vampire Direct (E1 5a),

Bitch, and a direct on Tip Toe (E1 5b). Johnson also wrote the first guide to the glen in 1965 but this remained unpublished.

In 1968 Klaus Schwartz took up residence as an instructor at Loch Eil Centre. With fellow instructors Blyth Wright (who co-authored the first published guide to Polldubh in 1970), Alec Fulton, Brian Chambers and Sammy Crymble, and often with students and domestic staff in tow, Schwartz pioneered 90 new routes in the next decade. Fulton climbed Secretaries Super Direct top pitch (E1), Crymble added South Diagonal and John Cunningham paid a fleeting visit to establish Twitch (E1). The longest route in the glen came with Schwartz's ascent of Autobahnausfahrt up all three tiers of High Crag, and on which combined tactics breached the top tier's bulge. Schwartz also made many aided ascents. Perhaps his best free route was the lower pitch of Secretaries' Super Direct in 1973.

During the 1970s aid climbs were made on two of the areas most impressive crags, Creag an Fhitheach Beag ('small crag of the raven', but erroneously named Buzzard Crag), and Steall Hut Crag. Noel Williams and Andrew Wielochowski were responsible for Monster, Groanangasp and Scorpion (all A3), whilst Dud Knowles used bolts to overcome the flared diagonal crack that is the main feature of Steall. It was ten years or more before their free potential was realised. Up until this point the general ethic had been of ground up ascents, but when Williams top-roped two routes prior to leading and Schwartz used a McInnes ice-axe to clean The Gutter, it heralded a definite change in tactics.

The next major activist to come onto the scene was 'Lakelander' Ed Grindley. With competition from Willie Todd, Rab Carrington and Nick Colton, he brought with him the first real jump in standards since the early 1960s. Activity centred around freeing old aid routes such as The Web, Fang and Ascension (all E2). John Taylor also left his mark with the excellent Storm True Finish (E1) which he climbed in 1976 with Schwartz. This activity was publicised by various articles from Schwartz and Williams in Alpinus Magazine, Rocksport and Climber and Rambler and a second edition of the guide appeared in 1978.

In 1976 two young Edinburgh climbers, Dave Cuthbertson and Murray Hamilton, took a rest day from a winter ascent of Orion Face Direct over the other side of the hill, and climbed Chalky Wall (E4) on Pinnacle Ridge - short but nasty. Grindley continued to free Schwartz's aid routes including Foil (E3 6a) and Withering Crack (E3 5c) which he got on the second attempt with wife Cynthia, having failed on an attempt with Allan Austin due to a wet hold.

In the years after 1977, an intense period of development was sweeping Scotland at the hands of an energetic band of Edinburgh-based climbers, including Cuthbertson, Hamilton, Rab Anderson, Alan Taylor and Derek Jamieson. Creag Dubh near Newtonmore and Cave Crag at Craig a Barns were the initial scenes of this rise in standards, whilst Glen Nevis largely remained remote from these dynamic changes. Abseil cleaning and inspection was becoming accepted practice in England at this time and was beginning to influence activities in Scotland, although the majority of routes were still being done on sight, even the harder ones. The standards were being pushed to the limits and as a result the hardest routes were often yo-yoed and some took several attempts over a couple of days or more. By the early 1980s there was a general acceptance of abseil cleaning and inspection by these climbers and they turned their attention to Glen Nevis, aided by the development of RP nuts that played a part in the ability to tackle the often incipient cracks of the glen's mica schist.

The profusion of old aid routes on Polldubh attracted many suitors; Alan Taylor freed Andrea's Visit at E4 6a, Kenny Spence freed Autobahnausfahrt (as Autoroof, E2 6a) and Murray Hamilton bagged Tomag (E4 6a), Wee One (E2 6a), and Black Friday (E5 6a). Cuthbertson became resident in Fort William, working in the Nevisport shop whilst recuperating after a bad fall on the first ascent of Revengence in Glen Coe. His search for routes of a similar style of climbing to Revengence (blank walls with tiny edges) led him to realise the potential of Glen Nevis. He teamed up with Derek Jamieson and together they picked many plum lines including Before the Flood (E4 6a) and Ring of Fire (E5 6a). At the time, all these Scottish climbers were also making regular trips to repeat routes in the English Peak District, and Steve Bancroft's conservative use of the grading system down there influenced the grading used in Scotland. This gave many people attempting early repeats a fright (on both sides of the border!).

Despite the pre-inspection of some routes, on sight ascents were still made of even very hard lines. Of particular note was Jamieson's sight lead of the bold Risque Grapefruit and Lucy Lime, both E4 5c, and Cuthbertson's ascent of Vincent (E3 5c) and the spectacular 45 degree overhanging Sky Pilot (E5 6b) which was significantly harder than anything done before in the glen.

Attention then turned to the area around the gorge. Hamilton, in the company of Lake's activists Alan Murray, Pete Whillance and Dave Armstrong, attacked carpark Crag with wire brushes to produce four fine E2s and one of the best routes in the glen (in some eyes), Quality Street (E3 6a). Grindley was still very much on the scene, indeed he was opening up one of the best crags, now known as Wave Buttress, with First Wave (E1), Ground Zero (E2) and the stunning and photogenic Edgehog (E3 5c and possibly his finest route here).

Cuthbertson meanwhile was pushing standards again, firstly with his free version of Groanangasp on Creag an Fhitheach Beag, renamed Exocet (E6 6b), then with Cosmopolitan on Gorge Crag, rated E5 and thought to be 6c initially. Gorge Crag became the focus with most of the lines falling to Cuthbertson and Latter and culminating with Conscription (E1), an expression of Cuthbertson's fear of being called up for the Falklands War. Development then became confined to the activities of two resident parties, with Grindley and friends adding to Wave Buttress and forgotten areas of Polldubh (one of his pupils from the high school, Ramsey Donaldson, adding the bold Parisian Walkway, E2), whilst Cuthbertson utilised protection from an *in situ* hammered nut to give the sustained and fingery Handren Effect (E6 6b) on Creag an Fhithich Beag.

Whale Rock gained its first route (the excellent Earthstrip, E2 5c) from Dave Armstrong (from Nottingham) who was also active in developing crags around

Glenfinnan the following year with Grindley. Grindley's parting offering on the new routing scene in Glen Nevis was the impressive 3m roof overlooking Steall meadows. Going For Gold, weighed in at a brutal E4 6a, and proved he wasn't quite over the hill (yet). For a short time this was the longest free roof in Scotland.

Through 1984 and (in particular) 1985, there was a dramatic increase in activity, with a dozen new crags opened up and over 70 Extremes climbed. Spence added the first route of 1984 on a small isolated slab left of Gorge Crag, with the short but necky Mother's Day (E4 6a). The race for the remaining lines on Wave Buttress started early. The first of the two most obvious remaining lines gave Spence the serious Walter Wall (E4 6a) whilst the large expanse of untouched rock between First Wave and Ground Zero gave three excellent lines. Hamilton, climbing on sight, followed the obvious vertical crack and bold runnel to give On the Beach, (E5 6a), whilst Cuthbertson climbed two difficult lines either side; Jodicus Grotticus (E5 6c) accepted the challenge offered by the pitted central wall to the right and the very thin diagonal crack above. Climbed on the very rough texture of the rock alone, protection originally consisted of two hammered RP nuts on the bold initial section, followed by a peg runner in the crack. Clipping and passing the peg proved to be the crux - the hammered nuts later fell out; and to the left, Freddie Across the Mersey (E5 6a) climbed a bulging wall with scant protection. Both routes were named after dogs who lived at the Achintee farm at the base of the tourist track up Ben Nevis at the time! Achintee soon became a base and focal point for an active resident group of climbers over the next few years.

After moving north for the 1983/4 winter season, Kevin Howett and fellow climbers from the North-East of England, Alan Moist, Mark Charlton and Calum Henderson stayed on to share in the spoils on Nevis rock. Howetts' first new route was Romancing the Stone (E5) on Wave Buttress with Charlton, whilst three new buttresses were unearthed in the gorge, the biggest and best being The Gorge Wall, a superb 30m wall overhanging the path. Here, Armstrong found Power in the Darkness (E1) and Moist and Henderson opened up the River Walls in the constriction of the gorge with Gawping Grockles (E2) and Sue's Crack (HVS). Cuthbertson added the excellent Just a Little Tease (E5 6b), up the bottomless scoop and ragged cracks in the prow of Whale Rock, with its crucifix move and use of a second belayer to reduce the pendulum of a fall. Soon after he contributed the very bold solos of Sweet Little Mystery, Where the Mood Takes Me and the very committing blank gritstone-like slab in between to give Jahu (E6 6a). Later that year whilst recovering from pulmonary oedema caught on a trip to the Himalaya and finding himself the only climber resident in the glen, he made many on sight solos including Withering Crack, Chalky Wall, Soap Suds, Wee One, Mother's Day and Crackattack. The remaining glaringly obvious possibilities subsequently got lost during the usual Autumn deluge.

Grindley had started building a small climbing wall in the Lochaber High School in 1980 and during a further phase of its development over the winter of 1984/5 invited the current group of activists to try it out. This acted as the stimulus for Howett, Moist and Henderson to stay on after the winter and join Cuthbertson in residence (and party mood) at the convivial Achintee Farm. This guaranteed an enthusiastic start to the years activities, especially when they were later joined by Latter. Despite the following summer being the wettest on record in Scotland, routes fell thick and fast from February onwards with Cuthbertson, Howett and Latter alone accounting for over 40 Extremes - more than double the number of routes of previous years.

During a very cold spell with the glen clothed in snow, Moist discovered Barrel Buttress. After removing the icicles, The Beer Hunter (E4 6b) fell on-sight to Howett and Moist and A-Proper-Kiss-Now (E2 6a) was sight soloed by both. Unseasonably good weather for February allowed an early burst of activity. Moist and Henderson found and developed Bistro Buttress, although it's hardest route (Self Control, E3 5c) was climbed by Nick Sharpe. Howett on sighted Mouseplay (E4 6b) on Hangover Buttress, a line that was the subject of past interest from Grindley to the extent that he modelled the roof in the High School wall around it. Finger fit from the local wall, Howett made a sprint up the tenuous line of Run for Home (E5 6a) on Whale Rock and Easy Pickings (E4 6a), on sight, on The Gorge Wall. These routes just saw inclusion in the new guide written by Grindley and published by Cicerone Press later in 1985. In a matter of months it was resoundingly put out of date as the pace of activity picked up somewhat and whole new buttresses were opened up.

Cuthbertson breached the centre of the hanging slab of The River Walls with Aquarian Rebels (E4 6a). That same day Howett established Hard Station (E5 6a) on Buccaneer Crag, a new buttress high on the slopes of Sgurr a' Mhaim. Cuthbertson boldly climbed, on sight, the first route on the sculptured Meadow Walls with The Mutant (E4 5c). On a busy day in the gorge, Latter forced Rats in Paradise (E5 6b), Howett produced Chimera (E4 6a) across the way and Cuthbertson created The Amusement Arcade (E5 6b), all to a crowd of bewildered tourists. Later Cuthbertson contributed the hard and bold neb of If Looks Could Kill (E5 6b) directly above the path, along with a couple more hard pitches up on Wave Buttress - Washington (E5 6a) and the extremely bold The Edwardo Shuffle (E6). Down at Polldubh both Latter and Cuthbertson led the bouldery Cubsville (E5 6b), freeing a previously pegged crack.

Up on Blade Buttress, Howett's attempt to gain the centre of the pillar initially produced Ugly Duckling, which the next day was transformed by him into The Snowgoose (Flight of), at E6 6b an altogether different beast. This was the first of a number of hard additions to make use of tied down skyhooks for protection rather than resort to pegs or top rope practice. Across the way on Steall Hut Crag, Howett breached the impressive continuously overhanging front face with the hard and serious Lame Beaver, but unfortunately had to resort to rests after completing the necky crux. This was later freed (1987) by Cuthbertson and is now graded E7 6b.

By 1986 Latter was resident in nearby Glen Coe and systematically worked his way through the more obvious remaining lines, especially on Wave Buttress where he established a number of E5s - The Dark Crystal, Nowhere Near the Sea and Straight Thinking. Up on Blade Buttress the stupendous bomb-bay groove became the subject of a race and after a protracted battle succumbed to Latter, to give Cruisability (E5 6b). Howett meanwhile, completed the first route on the nearby Space Face with Dancing on the Edge of Existence (E4 5c) whilst down in Polldubh Mark McGowan made his first contribution with Stage Fright (E5) also using a skyhook for a runner. The big news this year however was Cuthbertson's ascent of Femme Fatal (E7 6c; possibly E8!) on Whale Rock, again using a skyhook for protection. The route remains unrepeated eleven years on.

The following year saw more difficult additions from the now usual bunch of residents whilst significant second ascents of the hard routes occurred. Latter accounted for Ring of Fire, Handren Effect, Romancing the Stone and Run for Home; Hamilton repeated Just a Little tease, The Monster and Cosmopolitan; McGowan sight-soloed Where the Mood Takes Me and Sweet Little Mystery; the talented Colin Gilchrist made stylish second ascents of The Amusement Arcade, Stage Fright and Rats in Paradise, whilst Howett did likewise for Straight Thinking, Freddy Across the Mersey, Black Friday and Washington. Visiting South African Andy de Clerk (working at Loch Eil Outdoor Centre) succeeded on Exocet, Sky Pilot and Jahu and gave his own addition with So Long And Thanks For All The Fish (E5 6b). Soloing continued to be quite in vogue with Cuthbertson making the second ascent, on sight, of Lord of the Midges (E5 5c), a route done by Latter in 1985 and de Clerk soloing Black Friday after having led it.

Gilchrist went on to give the glen one of his own routes, The Nuns of Navarone (E5 6c), and would have undoubtedly contributed many more difficult routes had he not been tragically killed in an avalanche in Glen Coe the next year. McGowan made use of a hammered nut for protection on Frantic Across the Atlantic (E5 6b), then pulled off his best effort on Jodicus Direct (E6 6c). Cuthbertson's main addition this year was the arete of Liminality (E7 6b), to which pegs had been added for protection by another interested party. Late in the autumn Howett succeeded on Centrepiece (E5 6b) on the smooth immaculate rock of Black's Buttress, climbed on sight. A skyhook and poor peg runner (placed by another suitor) accounted for the sole protection on the crux. Latter made the second ascent immediately after. The peg later fell out and it was repeated by Mark Garthwaite in 1994 in its more natural state (E6). In December Dave Griffiths squeezed in the last route of the year with Circus (E4 6a). About this time Latter experimented with the first placement of bolts in the glen to produce a sport route. The action was considered out of place at the time and the line was never climbed.

In 1988 a few remaining big lines fell. Firstly, the three pitch Restless Natives (E5 6a,6a,5b) on carpark Crag, from Latter, Howett and Andy Nelson which had two very bold pitches, one being led using a skyhook and one without to give a very scary crux. A few days later Howett and Andy Nelson's determination produced Chiaroscuro (E7 6b). Success was only achieved on this route after some long falls onto dubious gear that resulted in broken ribs and it remains one of the boldest undertakings in the glen. A number of good crags were unearthed on the lower slopes of Sgurr a' Mhaim. Nelson discovered Tectonic Man (E4 6a) amongst the foliage below Buccaneer Crag, as well as taking a spectacular 10m ground fall from an unfinished line on The Bog Wall (discovered by George Szuca) which scared the belayer more than the leader. Latter also discovered the elusive Phantom Crag and established the powerful finger crack of The First Cut (E6 6b). He later added a harder variation on Dancing on the Edge of Existence at E5.

At Polldubh, Griffiths made a free ascent of the aid route Ethmoid, utilising a blow torch to dry out the holds, renaming the resultant route Hot Spots. A surprising find was the 60m Blaeberry Buttress hidden in the middle of Polldubh. Andy Ravenhill and friends unearthed three routes here, Hedge of Insanatree (E2 5c,5c) being the best.

There was a noticeable slowing in the pace of development over the next few years. A visit by Johnny Dawes saw an impressive on sight flash of Jodicus Direct whilst McGowan soloed the second ascent of The Dark Crystal. He went on to pick two remaining plumbs with Trick of the Tail (E6 6b) on Steall Hut Crag and Move it or Park it (E5 6c) in Polldubh. Also here a small band of strong Fort William-based climbers produced a number of hard routes. Shaun McLean soloed Precious Cargo (E5 6a) after abseil inspection and Craig Smith top roped then led the excellent Evil Eye (E5 6a). Paul Newton added the very powerful People Will Talk (E5 6c), on the closest piece of rock to the road, again after extensive top rope practice. Latter then suffered severe back injuries from a small fall in the gorge but his first route upon emerging back onto the scene was Carpe Diem, a very bold E5 on What Wee Wall, using pegs and a skyhook.

The final bout of activity has centred on the obvious hard potential of Steall Hut Crag but in the process has reopened the debate over style and the use of bolts. Firstly in 1992, Hamilton made a trip from his new home in France and free climbed the old aided diagonal crack line. Hamilton decided to pre-place the natural gear and climb this stunning line in pink point style to produce Leopold (E7 6c). Its neighbouring crack was also attempted by Carol Hamilton, but was left unfinished. In 1993 it was done in red point style by Latter to result in Arcadia (E7 6b). Whilst this was being worked on, other parties were bolting sport projects that crossed both crack lines. The line of bolts passing through Arcadia were removed but the other line still remains and has yet to be climbed. Finally, the immensely powerful and talented Malcolm Smith climbed a line bolted by another party at the right side in one day (on his fourth red point attempt), to give Steall Appeal which at 8b remains the hardest sport route in Scotland and possesses the glen's hardest single move – a technical 7a.

CRAG LAYOUT

The climbing is spread quite a distance along the glen, but it can be considered in three distinct areas: firstly, the extensive myriad of buttresses on the southern flank of Ben Nevis itself, an area called Polldubh; secondly, the crags in the vicinity of the carpark at the road head; and finally a selection of crags around the area of the gorge of Eas-an-Tuill and in the flat area of Steall meadows above Eas-an-Tuill. They are described in this order as approaching up the glen.

GLEN NEVIS

The Polldubh Crags

LOWER TIER - THE ROADSIDE BUTTRESSES

1 West End Crag
2 Sheep Fank Buttress
3 Double Buttress
4 Hangover Buttress
5 Tricouni Buttress
6 Dundee Buttress
7 Cavalry Crack Buttress
8 Pandora's Buttress
9 Repton Buttress
10 Pinnacle Ridge
11 Wall End Crag
12 Road Buttress
13 Upper Road Buttress

THE SECOND TIER BUTTRESSES

14 After Crag
15 Two Pine Crag
16 Tiny Buttress
17 Little Buttress
18 S W Buttress
19 Pine Wall Crag
20 Styx Buttress

THE UPPER TIER BUTTRESSES

21 Ridge Buttress
22 Blaeberry Buttress
23 Hamlet Crag
24 Secretaries' Buttress
25 Nameless Crag
26 King Slab
27 High Crag
28 Crown Buttress
29 Crossbones Crag
30 Crack Buttress
31 Cook's Buttress
32 Black's Buttress
33 Dog's Head Buttress
34 The Block
35 Scimitar Buttress

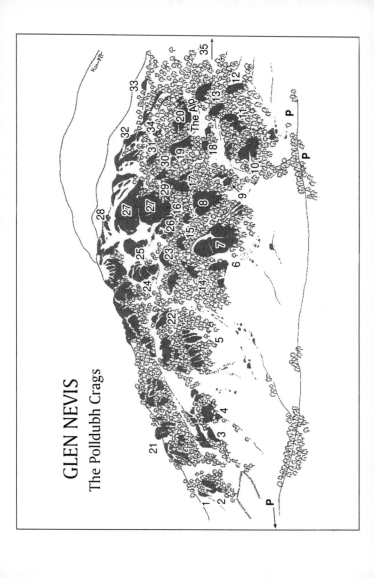

GLEN NEVIS
The Polldubh Crags

CAR PARKING

From Achriabhach and the bridge over the Lower Falls to the road-head carpark, the road is single track. In summer it is very busy so the most convenient parking for the various groups of crags is as follows: The western area of Polldubh crags (West End Crag to Tricouni Buttress) — at the carpark just before the Achriabhach bridge; the main, eastern, section of Polldubh (Cavalry Crack Buttress to Road Buttress) — a layby below Pinnacle Ridge; Scimitar Buttress, Bistro Buttress and Barrel Buttress — at the wooden bridge over the river Nevis near the base of the spur of Mam Beag (Map Ref 158 164); Carpark Crag Area — for dry feet, park at the wooden bridge over the river Nevis near the base of the spur of Mam Beag, otherwise at the road-head carpark; Steall Area — at the road-head carpark.

POLLDUBH

The name Polldubh, (literally the black pool) correctly refers to a pool in the River Nevis, just upstream from the layby at Map Ref 153 685 below Pinnacle Ridge. Common usage has resulted in the frontage of crags on the hillside extending for over 1km from the bridge at Achriabhach being referred to as Polldubh.The crags are many and varied, numbering around 40 in all and varying from mere overgrown boulders a few metres high to fine 60m plus crags with two and sometimes three pitch routes.

The layout is complex. Firstly, there are three areas that can be considered separate. The twin buttresses that are clearly seen nestling alone in the trees on the opposite side of the glen from the road before reaching the bend in the glen at Achriabhach are known as Creag an Fhithich Beag and Creag an Fhithich Mor. Secondly, the Polldubh area itself forms the south side of a distinctive southern spur of Carn Dearg of Ben Nevis called Am Mam Buidhe. The crags lie between the spur of Am Mam Buidhe called Leith Aire on the west (directly above Achriabhach) and the spur of Mam Beag on the east (at a point where the road bends away from the crags to circumnavigate the spur and rejoin the river). The Polldubh crags have been split into three separate tiers for the aid of description and location of the buttresses. The obvious advantage of linking numerous routes within separate tiers is quite apparent, giving up to 300m of vertical rock. Careful reference to the layout diagram and the map, together with scrutiny of the text, should make the location of any particular crag relative to its neighbours possible. Finally, there is Upper Polldubh lying on Carn Dearg itself above Am Mam Buidhe.

CREAG AN FHITHICH BEAG   (Map Ref 145 694)

Known in the past as Buzzard Crag (despite its gaelic name meaning small crag of the raven), this west-facing crag is the first to come into view when driving up the glen and one of the most impressive. The crag is characterised by an impressive overhanging front face broken by several overhangs on its right side. Tree belays well back.

The quickest approach is by crossing the river at a ford at a point about a kilometre downstream from The Lower Falls at Achriabhach (see map). From the other side of the river (north), gain a path on the left and follow this to a stream (Allt na Dubh-ghlaic) just beyond a gate. Cross the stream and cut directly up through the trees by an ill defined ridge to gain the left end of the crag. If the river is too high, or for those with hydrophobia, approach can also be made by starting along the track at Achriabhach bridge (Map Ref 145 685).

Either side of the crag may be used for descent, but the right side (looking down) is more common.

1   Virtual Reality   25m   E5 6b *   (1992)
The thin crack and hanging groove in the left wall of the crag is reasonably well protected, although it is difficult to place.

The following three routes all share a common start, a quartz intrusion on the left arete.

2   Liminality   25m   E7 6c ***   (1987)
A subliminal excursion up the edge of all things, or just a neat little arete? The prominent left-bounding edge of the crag. Climb up on quartz holds, then move left to a ledge on the left side of the arete. Follow the thin crack on the right side (stacked peg runners, backed up by a good RP5), then pull left to a further peg runner and go up the arete to the top.

3   Lepidoptery   25m   E5 6b   (1987)
Good climbing with a bold crux, which used to be protected by a peg. Start up the quartz, then go straight up an obvious shallow groove past a good undercling to reach a large flat hold. Make a hard move up and left to a good hold in the middle of the wall, then continue on better holds to a ledge on top of the arete.

4   Caterpillar   25m   E3 5c *   (1984)
A serious route, high in the grade with some precarious climbing. Climb the diagonal quartz vein, then climb awkwardly up the ramp to finish direct up short steep walls.

5   The Dream of the Butterfly   30m   E6 6b *   (1993)
The horizontal fault emanating from the initial crack of The Handren Effect provides very safe strenuous climbing protected by lots of peg runners. Follow the fault with a difficult section stepping down to better holds leading to the quartz recess on the three previous routes. The choice of finish is yours.

6   The Handren Effect   25m   E6 6b ***   (1983)
One of the best pieces of wall climbing in the glen, bold and sustained at a high standard. Start at an obvious inverted L-shaped crack. Climb this past a pair of peg runners with difficulty to reach a good flake hold in a scoop (RPs behind this; old *in situ* nut in the runnel above). Move up the shallow runnel with hard moves to reach a superb quartz spike at the top of the wall. Stroll easily up the short corner above.

7   The Monster   30m   E5 6a ***   (1975/85)
A strenuous well protected pitch. Start beneath a shallow left-facing scoop, as for Steerpike. Climb directly, firstly on good holds, then go up the wall above to the overhang. Go left to undercuts and good footholds, then climb the wall above, passing a diagonal crack, and step left to ledges. Easier climbing leads up and rightwards to finish.

8   Steerpike   45m   E2 **   (1975/82)
Start just right of the inverted L-shaped crack, beneath a shallow left-facing scoop.
1. 20m 5b   Climb up on good holds past some old pegs to arrange a runner underneath the roof. Cross the gangway on the right until it is possible to move up and left to a stance on a nose at the foot of a quartz groove.
2. 15m 5b   Go up the quartz groove and thin crack directly above and pull rightwards onto a ledge and belay at a tree.
3. 10m 4c   Climb the tree and move right into a chimney, or abseil off.

9   Spring Fever   25m   E3 5c **   (1985)
This provides a fine route when combined with Steerpike. Start from the hanging belay at the top of pitch one of that route. Climb the quartz groove to a slab right of a hanging corner. Step down and swing wildly left for a jug and follow the obvious line leftwards.

10   Exocet   40m   E6 ***   (1975/82)
A direct uncompromising line through the overhanging prow up the steepest section of the crag. The first pitch, although slow to dry, provides a very fine pitch in its own right at E3 6a, and would give an excellent combination with Spring Fever. The section above the roof can also be gained from The Monster, providing a long exposed pitch at no change in the overall grade. Start at the foot of a prominent diagonal crack line up and left of an overgrown left-facing corner crack.
1. 15m 6a   Swing right into the crack and go up this to a hanging belay at the foot of a quartz groove (common to Steerpike).
2. 25m 6b   Undercut the roof leftwards for about 3m (awkward) to a large flat hold above. Attain a standing position on this with difficulty, and follow a line of holds trending leftwards to a resting ledge. Continue up a series of short awkward walls to the top.

11   Dragon   45m   E1 5b   (1975)
Start at the left-facing corner, below and right of the previous routes. Follow it to the left end of the first terrace at 10m, then climb the wall above past a niche, and continue to a large overhang. Turn this on the right, gain a ledge and move up an overhanging groove to the finish of Steerpike.

12   Titus   10m   E1 5c   (1975/70s)
Climb the crack in the short wall about 6 metres right of Dragon, just left of a wider chossy crack.

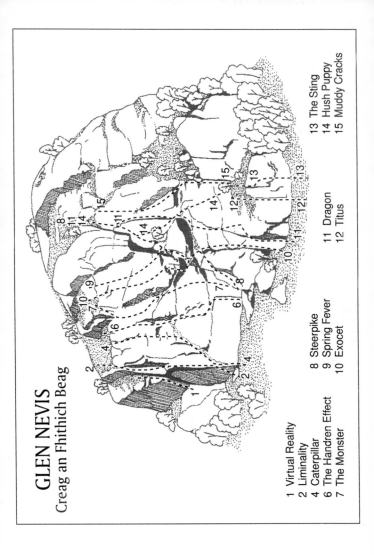

GLEN NEVIS
Creag an Fhithich Beag

1 Virtual Reality
2 Liminality
4 Caterpillar
6 The Handren Effect
7 The Monster

8 Steerpike
9 Spring Fever
10 Exocet

11 Dragon
12 Titus

13 The Sting
14 Hush Puppy
15 Muddy Cracks

13 **The Sting** 8m VS 4c (1975)
Start about 5 metres right of Titus, at a heathery crack. Move up this a short way, then hand traverse left to easier ground at the top of the chossy crack.

14 **Hush Puppy** 35m Hard Severe (1975)
Start from the oak on the first terrace, gained from the right. Go up the wall trending left to the right end of the large overhang. Climb to a ledge, then go up the slab above and move left to join Steerpike. Finish as for that route.

15 **Muddy Cracks** 25m Moderate
Climb up above the oak, with a crack/ramp continuation above the second terrace.

16 **Pete's Corner** 30m Very Difficult (1975)
From the right end of the first terrace, climb up to a corner and follow this to the second terrace. Climb the crack behind two trees, or more easily to the right.

The following shorter routes are on the lower wall, below the left side of the main crag.

Hollow Wall 10m VS 4c ** (1975)
This is the crack near the left end, stepping left near the top.

Titter Ye Not 10m E2 5c (1992)
Climb the flake up the centre of the wall.

Mental Block 6m VS 5a (1975)
The overhanging wall and rounded flake a few metres from the right end of the lower wall.

CREAG AN FHITHICH MOR *(Map Ref 146 695)*

The upper crag is, on closer inspection and despite it name, smaller and much more broken than the altogether more impressive lower crag. It is about ten minutes further up the hillside and further west than the main crag.

Upleft 35m Very Difficult (1976)
Start below the left-hand gully. Climb to the first tree, then hand traverse left to a ledge with a tiny tree. Continue left round corner and move up steep slabs before stepping left into heathery gully and finish up the diedre.

Heather 35m Difficult (1975)
The heather-choked gully above the start of Upleft.

In the centre of the crag is a short steep wall.

Forty Two 10m E4 6a * (1988)
The deceptive, overhanging crack-line at the left end of the short wall. Climb the crack using a good undercling to reach a large flake and nut runners. Move slightly left, then go back right to finish on good holds.

So Long, and Thanks for all the Fish   10m   E5 6b **   (1987)
The fierce, thin overhanging crack above the roof midway up the crag. Climb the
initial awkward crack on the right, as for Green Wellies, and reach left to a good
undercling and PR above. Powerful moves for good holds lead to a superb
Friend slot. Crank past this to a cosmic final jug on top. Finish easily above.

Green Wellies   12m   HVS 5a   (1985)
The crack leading into groove on the right of the short wall. Climb directly up a
vague groove onto a steep slab. Follow the left-hand crack trending slightly
rightwards. Fight through heather jungle to belay at an oak tree.

Sods   35m   Difficult   (1976)
The water-trickle gully on the right-hand section of the cliff.

POLLDUBH – THE ROADSIDE BUTTRESSES

These are described from left to right from Achriabhach to the buttresses above
the layby beside Pinnacle Ridge, the closest crag to the road.

WEST END CRAG

This is the small square wall at the far left end of the hillside, directly above the
lower falls. It is up and left from the Sheep Fank, and to the left of Sheep Fank
Wall at a slightly higher level. The best descent is down the right side of the
buttress.

Showoff   8m   Hard Severe   (1970s)
Climb the left-slanting line at the left edge of the crag, with the crux at the top.

All's Fair   15m   E2 5c *   (1983)
A bold route. Start on top of a small triangular pedestal, about 4m down from the
left side of the crag. Climb slightly leftwards up the wall to good protection below
a small overlap. Break out right and finish up a scoop.
Direct Finish: **Sparkle in the Rain**   E3 6a *   (1986)
Continue directly up from where the normal route pulls out right.

The Principle of Moments   15m   E3 6a **   (1983)
Start in the centre of the crag, at the left-hand of two diagonal cracks. Follow this
until forced to step right (it is also possible direct) above a small overlap. Step
back left and go up the wall (crux) to finish in the scoop at the same point as All's
Fair. Technical.

Shogun   15m   HVS 5b   (1983)
The right-hand crack. Start below a ledge at the bottom right of the crag.

Longboat   12m   Difficult   (1970s)
Midway between West End Crag and Sheep Fank Wall is a smaller buttress
with a flat rock ledge below its right side. Follow the rib left of the ledge.

Digit Midget   14m   E1 5c   (1990)
On the same area of rock is an obvious undercut slab. Pull over the bulge at an obvious hold and continue up the slab.

SHEEP FANK WALL

This buttress lies directly above the bridge (and, not surprisingly, the Sheep Fank!) over the Lower Falls at Achriabhach. A fence leads directly up to the buttress. The crag is composed of a clean slab on the left split by a diagonal crack, and several small roofs in the lower right side. The routes are described from left to right.

Sheep Fank Rib   20m   Moderate   (1947)
The rib 30 metres left of the main buttress.

Unnamed   20m   HVS 5b   (1990)
Start under a bulging rib to the left of Sheep Fank Rib. Move left and go up to a good hold, then climb up and right. Finish up the slab.

Foursome   25m   Very Difficult   (1969)
A recess right of the gully between the main crag and Sheep Fank Rib leads to better climbing higher up. The upper section can also be reached from the start of Gambit Wall or a traverse from near the top of Gambit.

Gambit Wall   30m   Severe   (1960s)
Climb the slab diagonally, crossing Gambit and finishing by a wide crack fault.

The Fuzz   30m   VS 4c   (1984)
Start at a small overhung niche 5 metres left of Gambit. Pull through the niche and move right onto the slab. Follow a line up the slab parallel to and about 2 metres left of Gambit.

Gambit   30m   Severe **   (1960)
The obvious polished diagonal crack splitting the left wall gives a pleasant natural line.
Variation: The vegetatious cracks parallel to and right of the main crack can be climbed at a similar grade.

Fence Edge   35m   Mild Severe   (1960s)
Pleasant and well protected. Start up a crack just left of the toe of the buttress. Continue straight up the slab to finish up an easier angled rib.

Sheep Fank Direct   35m   Hard Severe *   (1960s)
Start at a groove 3 metres right of the lowest point of the crag. Climb the groove, or the next one on the right, to a birch. Traverse left onto the buttress edge a few metres above the tree, and climb this to finish up an easier angled rib, as for Fence Edge.

Tonis   15m   HVS 5a *   (1977/78)
Start just right of a small tree, 5 metres right of the previous route. Move up to an oblong nose, step onto the slab above, then trend left across the bulge. Delicate.

A direct line breaking right through the roof to good holds gives **Pay No Poll Tax**, HVS 5a * (1992).

Bardhinaghi   10m   Hard Severe **   (1960)
The polished brown groove leading to the first stance on Sheep Fank Wall.

Haul   10m   HVS 5a *   (1978)
The right rib of the brown groove, with the crux crossing the roof.

Sheep Fank Wall   45m   Difficult *   (1947)
Good well protected climbing. Climb the slab right of a crack and go into the crack to reach a birch. Continue leftwards up the slab past another tree on the crest to reach a tree terrace. The step left of a gully leads to top.

DOUBLE BUTTRESS

This buttress is situated between Sheep Fank Wall and Hangover Buttress, slightly closer to the latter. The lower crag on the right is slabby with some overhangs. The upper crag on the left has a 20m vertical front wall, and a similarly steep, tapering left wall. The routes are described from left to right, starting on the upper wall.

THE UPPER WALL

The Gaza Strip   10m   E4 6a/b   (1992)
The short, innocuous-looking diagonal crack at the left end of the wall. Climb the bottom wall to ledge, then follow the crack with hard moves near top.

Wall Games   15m   E5 6a *   (1986)
This route takes the wall at the highest point of the left-hand wall, starting up a diagonal crack. Climb this until it starts to fade, and pull directly up the wall on small holds (hidden RP placement). Continue to better holds (crux) to finish up a shallow depression.

Playaway   20m   E2 5b *   (1983)
Start at a large tree below a slab at the foot of the left wall. Move rightwards across the slab and past a small tree to a gangway. Follow this rightwards, then take the left-slanting twin cracks in the rib.

Oak Wall   20m   HVS 5a   (1970s)
Start at the toe of the crag. Enter a groove and move up left to an oak tree. Continue by shallow grooves and traverse right across the wall to finish.

Double or Quits   20m   E1 5b **   (1982)
Start at the same point as Oak Wall. Climb straight up the groove, and go over the bulge to better holds on a slab. Trend right to the rib, then move slightly left to finish.
Direct Finish: 10m   E2 5c **   (1980s)
From above the bulge, climb directly up the wall on pockets. There are easier variations out right near the top.

Double Think   25m   E2 5c *   (1986)
This route gains the blunt central rib of the crag by the initial crack of Andrea's Visit. Climb the crack and pull round the arete to good quartz holds (fragile). Move up on these, then step left and go up the slab to finish up the easy groove out right.

Andrea's Visit   20m   E4 6a *   (1973/81)
A huge block sits beneath the right side of the front face. Just left of this is a thin hand crack. Follow this to the bulge and arrange protection. Cross the wall rightwards on quartz, heading for a hollow block in the hanging groove. Finish more easily up this.

South Crack   20m   E1 5b   (1973/78)
A hard route for its grade. Start on top of the huge block. Climb up on steep flakes to enter a shallow heather-filled groove.

Wee Joe   15m   VS 4c   (1981)
Start just left of Stonetrap. Move left and ascend a shallow groove above the bulges.

Stonetrap   12m   Mild Severe   (1975)
A holly and an oak tree are the sole redeeming features on this line to the right of South Crack.

THE LOWER WALL

Hidden Groove   12m   Hard Severe *   (1970s)
This groove is hidden behind some trees and to the left of the buttress edge. Keep right at the top.

Lower Crag Edge   20m   VS 4c   (1970s)
Starting at the lowest point as the previous route, climb the edge past a ledge, with a deviation to the right.

Cling   15m   Difficult   (1975)
From the ledge 6m up the previous route, move up and right below overhangs and back left above.

HANGOVER BUTTRESS

This is located midway between Sheep Fank Wall and the very distinctive Cavalry Crack Buttress — the most prominent crag in the lower tier of crags above the road, halfway along the Polldubh hillside. Double Buttress lies to its immediate left and Tricouni Buttress to its right. The buttress is distinguished by two prominent roof systems, one on the lower left, the other on the upper right.

1 Barf 12m E3 5b (1988)
The short hanging groove on the wall high up on the left side of the crag. It is possible to protect it with a sling on the tree.

2 Picnic at Hanging Rock 15m E2 5c (1988)
Start below and right of obvious flake, just right of Barf. Climb a flake and go straight up the wall above.

3 Tree Groove 20m Very Difficult (1950s)
Start halfway up the wall on the left. Follow a wide crack past a tree to the groove proper. Exit rightwards at another tree.

A poorly protected eliminate, **Apocalypse the Day Before Yesterday**, HVS 5b (1988) has also been recorded 2 metres to the left of Shag.

4 Shag 10m VS 5a (1960)
Climb the thin strenuous crack starting 5m up left from Hangover Buttress Edge.

5 Fribbles 25m VS 5a (1976)
Climb the initial crack as for Shag, then follow the easy edge to a point level with the oak. Move left and go up a groove to the top.

6 Hangover Buttress Edge 30m Moderate * (1946)
The first recorded route on Polldubh gives a well protected beginner's climb. Climb the rib which comes down to the lowest point of the left roofs. Above an oak at 15m, a groove leads to an easy left-slanting ramp.

7 Route 1 30m Difficult (1950)
Leave the groove about 5m above the Oak on a right-slanting ramp around the buttress edge.

8 Eliminator 15m E1 5a (1988)
From the oak, move up and right up a poorly protected slab, then go left to a good horizontal crack. Step left and follow a good flange leftwards to finish.

9 Route 2 30m Hard Severe ** (1957)
Start 10m up right from Hangover Buttress Edge, under the roof. Climb diagonally left to the left end of the roof, pull up and traverse right between the roofs to gain a chimney. A popular and polished climb.

10 Nuts 12m E3 6a (1975/81)
Beneath the roof on the left side of the buttress is a short innocuous-looking crack which proves strenuous and well protected.

11   Frogs   20m   VS 5a   (1983)
Just right of the previous route is a shorter crack. Climb this to a ledge, step left and pull over the overhang. Climb the easy slab above to the top.

12   Cross 3   30m   Difficult *   (1950s)
Start below the right end of the upper, right-hand roof, and follow the obvious line leftwards below the roof.

13   Friends   10m   E3 5c *   (1975/81)
The fierce fist-wide crack splitting the left side of the roof above Cross 3 gives a brutal climb.

14   Mouseplay   10m   E4 6b **   (1957/85)
The thin crack over the right side of the main roof is very technical.

15   McAlck   20m   E2 5c *   (1975/82)
From a tree stump in a corner at the right side of the roof, traverse right before finishing up easy slabs.

16   Hang   20m   Severe   (1975)
Hand traverse right from the start of Cross 3 to reach a tree. Climb up and left to easier slabs which lead to the top.

TRICOUNI BUTTRESS

At the same height as Hangover Buttress and about 100 metres further right is a large area of rock. A clean wall on its left-hand side comprises two overhangs on the left and a slab bounded by an open left-facing corner. The middle section is more broken. A conspicuous slim vertical slab with a well defined left arete lies on the right-hand side. The routes are described from left to right.

Corner   15m   Mild Severe   (1950s)
This route is on the left side of the crag. Climb a crack formed by a large block leaning against the wall. Step onto the slab and move round the edge on the left to enter a groove between two overhangs.

Tricouni Overhang   10m   VS 5a   (1960s)
The crack right of the overhang, to the right of Corner.

Nails   15m   Severe   (1950s)
The easy left edge of the main slab, with a difficult start.

Dolly's Delight   25m   Difficult   (1950s)
Climb the recess 4 metres left of Tricouni Slab to a crack leading to small tree at 20m. Continue leftwards above.

Tricouni Slab   25m   Very Difficult **   (1950s)
Good climbing up the prominent right-angled diedre. Reach it from the right and climb up almost anywhere on the slab.
Variation Finish: **Latter Day Saint**   VS 4c
Follow the shallow cracked groove in the right wall above.

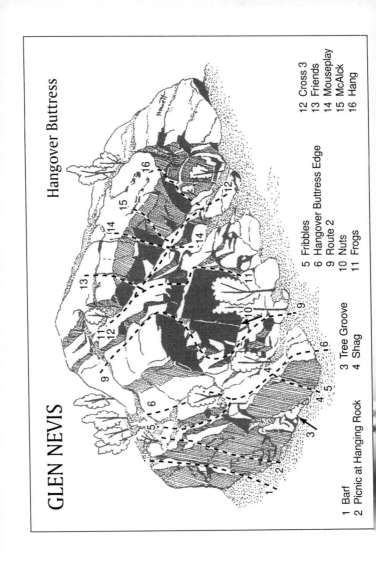

GLEN NEVIS

Hangover Buttress

1 Barf
2 Picnic at Hanging Rock
3 Tree Groove
4 Shag
5 Fribbles
6 Hangover Buttress Edge
9 Route 2
10 Nuts
11 Frogs
12 Cross 3
13 Friends
14 Mouseplay
15 McAlck
16 Hang

Singapore Crack   25m   Severe   (1994)
Climb Tricouni Slab on its right side under the Black Slab Edge for some 12m to
gain an obvious crack at some 50 degrees to the slab. Follow the crack and pull
up on a large pinnacle at the top to finish.

Black Slab Edge   25m   VS 4c   (1960/61)
Climb the steep right edge of the slab by a groove to a step right and finish up
the short wall above.

Black Slab   25m   Very Difficult   (1950s)
Start by a slab 6 metres to the right. Move left onto a hanging slab at about 10m
and finish near Black Slab Edge.

TRICOUNI RIGHT-HAND SLAB

About 50m up and right of the main buttress is a prominent clean slab, clearly
visible from the road.

Reflections   25m   HVS 5a   (1994)
Start 5m up and left of Fly Direct at an obvious corner. Climb leftwards into the
corner which leads to the slab above. From the midway fault in the slab, finish
up either Fly or Parisian Walkway.

Fly Direct   25m   HVS 5a **   (1960s/83)
The edge of the slab, originally gained by traversing across the slab low down,
but much better as described. Start at a small rib below the main edge. Move up
to a small overlap, turn this on the left, then follow easier ground up the edge.

Parisian Walkway   25m   E2 5b *   (1983)
An enjoyable but very serious eliminate up the centre of the slab. Climb past a
thin section to a horizontal break at half-height, step left and continue to the
belay on Fly Direct.

Ant's Walk   25m   VS 4c   (1960/61)
Climb the thin cracks up the right side of the slab, then traverse left to the belay
on Fly, about 3m from the top. A bit dirty.

DUNDEE BUTTRESS

This is the small buttress immediately to the left of Cavalry Crack Buttress,
about 100m above the road. It is distinguished by a niche in its upper half.

Red Wall   12m   Difficult
Climb the left wall of the buttress, with easier and shorter variations to the left.

Weaver's Loom   20m   HVS 5a   (1997)
Start a couple of metres left of Dundee Weaver and climb the left side of the
front face, joining Dundee Weaver at its crux.

Heading for the Howff   20m   HVS 5b   (1997)
This route takes a line crossing Dundee Weaver. Start at the base of Weaver's Loom and climb direct to a grassy ledge on that route. Pull over the bulge above on good layaways to gain the slab above (crux). Move right to finish up the final niche of Promises.

Dundee Weaver   20m   HVS 5a   (1965/68)
A popular route with a tricky crux. Climb the front wall left of the central recess to gain a small platform on the left. Hard moves lead up the crack close to the edge to easier ground. It is not easily protected.

Promises   20m   Hard Severe 4b **   (1960)
Climb straight up to the niche near the top. Finish up the crack in its right side.

An eliminate, **Dark Horse**, E1 5b (1988) takes a line between Promises and Wren's Delight.

Wren's Delight   25m   Difficult
Start 8 metres right of and below the niche. Climb the slab to a slanting heather ledge at 6m. Continue up the slabby wall above on wart-like holds, crossing a small bulge.

CAVALRY CRACK BUTTRESS

This is the largest of the lower buttresses. The left-hand face is split by prominent diagonal cracks, easily recognised by a large Scots pine sprouting high up. The lower right end of the wall faces the road and forms a smooth section identified by two big pines. The best descent is by a steep path down the right side (looking out) of Dundee Buttress. Directly above Cavalry Crack Buttress lie After Crag, slightly down to the left, and Two Pine Crag, slightly up to the right.

Cavalry Crack   25m   Moderate   (1947)
The vegetatious gully delineating the left side of the crag is purely of historical and botanical interest.

1   Versus   40m   E1 5b *   (1976)
Follow a left-trending steepening groove 5 metres right of the gully, passing a horizontal break with a sapling at half-height. Easier ground leads to the top.

1a   The Anniversary   40m   E3 5c *   (1985)
This is effectively a direct finish to Versus. Follow Versus to the sapling, then climb up a dwindling ramp to a further horizontal break, move right to a good hold and climb the wall above *via* thin cracks to tree belay. Abseil off or scramble to the top.

2   Before the Flood   55m   E4 **   (1981)
A slick ramp and a technical groove. Start up the wall a few metres left of the long heather-filled crack of The Long Crack.

1. 35m 6a   The wall leads to the base of a tapering ramp which is followed to a small overlap. Move left from the overlap to the base of a groove. Place runners in the side wall of this, then pull awkwardly back right above the overlap (crux) and go up a short steep groove to a good break. Continue more easily up the groove above to ledges and a belay.
2. 20m 5b   Mantelshelf onto the ledge above and move right to finish up the final wide crack of The Long Crack.

3   After the Fire   E4 6b **   (1987)
An interesting link joining the ramp of Before the Flood with the top wall of The Anniversary, giving well protected climbing past an *in situ* peg runner. Follow Before the Flood to the small overlap and the groove above, then follow the groove direct with difficulty (peg runner) to better holds at the top. On the break, step left past a branch to follow an easy ramp. Gain a large hold above and climb wall above *via* thin cracks to a tree belay. Abseil off or scramble to the top.

4   The Long Crack   60m   HVS *   (1969)
This is the left-hand of the two diagonal crack systems splitting the wall.
1. 40m 5a   Follow the crack to a point level with the large pine on Storm. Avoid the bulge above on the left, and regain the crack above a tree.
2. 20m 4b   Finish up the easy crack/ramp.

5   The Old Wall   40m   VS 4b ***   (1963)
Steady open wall climbing on good holds. Protection is noticeably lacking. Start up The Long Crack for 6m to just past a tree. Move right and up before heading across the wall through Storm to finish on the right edge of the wall, level with the pine on Storm.

6   Centrefold   60m   HVS *   (1983)
This climb takes the wall midway between The Long Crack and Storm.
1. 30m 5a   From the start of The Long Crack, scramble up and right to a ledge. Climb the centre of the narrowing wall to the break level with the pine tree on Storm, then cross the bulge above *via* a wide crack (crux) to reach a belay.
2. 30m 4c   Finish up the twin cracks in the rib to the left of the groove of Storm True Finish.

7   Storm   85m   HVS ***   (1959/62)
A classic route with fine situations and generally good protection. Start a few metres up left from the very toe of the buttress, at the left-hand and lower of two groove/ramp systems.
1. 30m 4b   Climb the groove to belay on a ledge at the foot of a long diagonal crack.
2. 30m 4c   Climb the crack to a belay at the large pine.
3. 25m 5a   Follow the shallow groove on the right side to cross the bulge (crux), then continue more easily trending slightly right up the wall above.

7a   The True Finish   E1 5b **   (1970s)
Move out left from above the crux and follow the shallow corner capped by a block overhang.

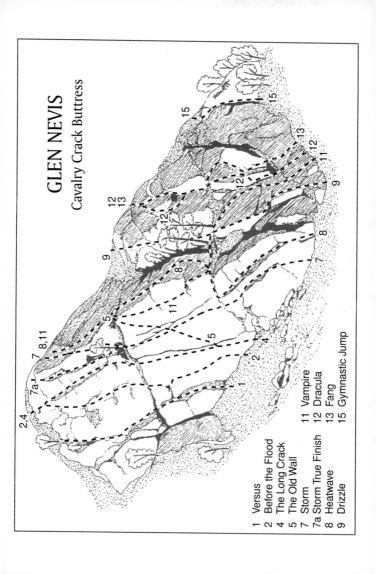

GLEN NEVIS
Cavalry Crack Buttress

1 Versus
2 Before the Flood
4 The Long Crack
5 The Old Wall
7 Storm
7a Storm True Finish
8 Heatwave
9 Drizzle

11 Vampire
12 Dracula
13 Fang
15 Gymnastic Jump

8 Heatwave 90m Mild Severe ** (1959)
Start just left of the toe of the buttress, at a pair of groove/ramps merging at 5m.
1. 25m Follow either of these ramps to belay below the crack of Storm.
2. 10m Traverse right around the buttress and walk up to a holly beside a large pine.
3. 25m Climb the slabby left wall of the gully to a terrace.
4. 30m Finish up slabs above, trending left to a short groove and continue directly above.

9 Drizzle 45m Hard Severe * (1963/59)
1. 25m Start above and behind a holly. Follow the left edge of the Vampire slab to the big pines.
2. 20m Continue up the right wall of the gully *via* an awkward step and a vertical diedre near the top.

10 Vampire Direct 25m E1 5a (1964)
A delicate and poorly protected climb. After the initial slab on Vampire, follow the edge above to gain the large slab below the pine. Step left and follow a vague scoop to the tree.

11 Vampire 80m Hard Severe ** (1959)
A varied and enjoyable route. Start 8 metres right of the buttress edge.
1. 25m 4b Climb a short slab and traverse 3 metres right to a small tree. Gain and follow a left-trending crack, then traverse left to the pine and belay.
2. 30m 4b Walk 5 metres left and climb a groove in the edge. Go up the wall veering left to join the buttress edge near the pine break on Storm.
3. 25m Finish up the left edge of the slabs.
Alternative Finish: 30m VS 4c ** (1978)
From the pine stance, take the obvious drooping flake to the right, and go up right onto the arete proper. Continue up over the bulge to finish at the second stance, as for Heatwave.

A further line, **The Bats, The Bats**, 45m E2 5b (1983) trends rightwards from the initial slab of Vampire Direct heading for the left-slanting diagonal crack line through the bulges to finish up easier ground.

12 Dracula 45m E3 * (1987)
A direct line up the wall left of Fang. Start left of Fang at a prominent deep-cut groove.
1. 20m 5c Climb the groove, pull right onto a slab and step right to gain an obvious triangular niche. Climb directly up the slab to a small sapling, then go straight up the wall above (the original aided line of Fang) to a belay ledge.
2. 25m 5b Climb the first few metres of Fang, then traverse left round the rib and go up obvious line to gain a large sloping ledge. Step right and climb a shallow corner line to finish up the last few easy moves of Fang.

13   Fang   45m   E2 ***   (1963/76)
Bold open wall climbing. Start beneath an open left-facing groove down and
right of the open slab of Vampire.
1. 25m 5b   Go up a steep initial groove past an overlap, then move steeply out
right on good holds. Move up, then pull leftwards along a diagonal crack to belay
on ledge.
2. 20m 5a   Climb the groove above, turning the roof on the right.

14   Lullaby in Black   40m   E4 6a *   (1985)
This route takes the obvious black groove just right of the sharp arete to the right
of Fang. Climb the open corner (as for Gymnastic Jump), then step left into the
groove and move up to the overhang. Undercut this leftwards and swing wildly
round the arete on improving holds. Move up and right and follow a pleasant rib
to the top.

15   Gymnastic Jump   40m   VS 4c   (1970s)
Climb the open corner 5 metres right of Fang and move right at 10m onto the rib
for a short way, then go back left to an oak at 20m. Continue straight up the wall
above on good holds.

16   Sodafarl   10m   Severe   (1970)
Climb the right side of the edge between the corner and the groove.

17   Gymnastic Groove   10m   Hard Severe
This is the groove to the right of the previous climb.

PANDORA'S BUTTRESS

This buttress lies 100 metres to the right of Secretaries Buttress, at about the
same level. Immediately below and to the right is a smaller buttress – Repton
Buttress. Pandora's buttress has a slightly overhanging front face with twin
diagonal left- slanting cracks. Two rock tongues extend down on either side of
the cracks into the trees. The easiest approach is from the path leading past
Pinnacle Buttress towards the 'Alp', the grassy meadow beneath Pine Wall
Crag and Styx Buttress. The best descent is down the left side of the buttress,
looking in. Above Pandora's Buttress, virtually hidden in the trees, lies Tiny
Buttress. Further right is the more substantial Little Buttress.

The Ridge   30m   Very Difficult   (1950s)
This is the leftmost of two ribs midway between Cavalry Crack Buttress and the
top of Pandora's Buttress.

Minipandora   35m   Moderate   (1950s)
The right-hand of the two ribs, almost hidden behind trees, gives pleasant
climbing towards the top.

Dental Groove   25m   Hard Severe   (1959)
Climb the groove (often damp) starting about 20m up left from the left-hand
tongue and which leads up to the corner on the third pitch of Pandora.

Desolation Angel   25m   HVS 5a   (1988)
Climb the wall right of Dental Groove to the large pine *via* the two trees.

1   Phantom Slab   60m   VS 4c ***   (1959)
Excellent sustained slab climbing, well worth the trouble of searching it out.
Start by climbing the first two pitches of Pandora. Descend a few metres to
belay beneath the right side of the slab. Traverse diagonally leftwards and
follow a line up the left edge of the slab, and finish by moving slightly rightwards
at the top. The slab can also be gained direct from below, upping the grade to
HVS 5a.

2   Lucy Lime   25m   E4 5c **   (1981)
Start in the corner to the right of Phantom Slab. Climb the corner until forced out
left, then go up to a recess. Traverse back right and swing wildly right across the
overhang and go up a crack to the top.
Variation: **Juicy Lucy**   E2 5c   (1988)
Climb the corner line direct.

3   Pandora   65m   Severe **   (1959)
Good varied climbing.
1. 25m   Climb the left-hand of two rock tongues below the diagonal cracks to a
large ledge below a corner.
2. 20m   Continue up the rib on the left of the corner to a tree on the right wall of
a larger corner.
3. 20m   Go up the corner to a large ledge, then follow slabs on the left.
Variation: **Pandora Direct**   20m   VS 4c   (1959)
Climb the corner above the first stance.

4   McGonigal's Groove   25m   VS 4c   (1963)
Start at the right side of the wide ledge, 6 metres right of the first stance of
Pandora. Move up broken ground to a short left-facing corner which leads to a
sloping platform. Move up and right round the edge to join Flying Dutchman
below the overhang.

5   Tomag   30m   E3 5c **   (1981)
Strenuous and sustained climbing taking the finely situated parallel cracks
which slant across the overhanging wall. Gain these from the start of
McGonigal's Groove, and follow them round the arete on fist jams (large
Friends useful), then cut back right to the top.

6   Move It or Park It   30m   E5 6c *   (1989)
Hard sustained climbing up the headwall above Tomag, well protected by a pair
of *in situ* pegs. Start as for McGonigal's Groove. Climb the corner to gain the
twin cracks of Tomag. Move along these until it is possible to reach the peg
runners. A hard move past these (long reach) leads to an even harder move to a
small though good crozzly pocket. Small holds on the sloping shelf above and
an awkward exit rightwards lead to an easy slab. Climb directly up this to belay
as for Flying Dutchman.

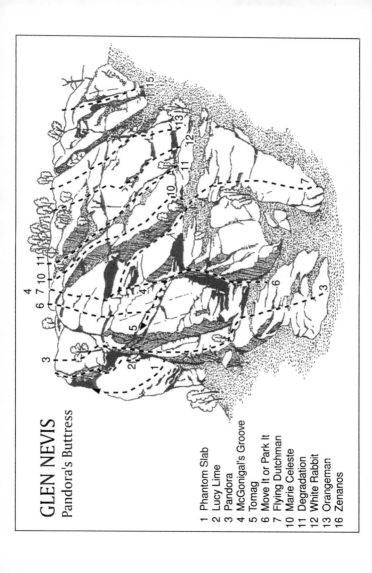

GLEN NEVIS
Pandora's Buttress

1 Phantom Slab
2 Lucy Lime
3 Pandora
4 McGonigal's Groove
5 Tomag
6 Move It or Park It
7 Flying Dutchman
10 Marie Celeste
11 Degradation
12 White Rabbit
13 Orangeman
16 Zenanos

7 Flying Dutchman 60m Severe *** (1959)
A deservedly popular route with an exposed and sustained second pitch. Start
on the lowest rocks to the right of Pandora.
1. 25m Climb the crest, or heathery grooves just to the right, to a terrace.
2. 25m Go up slabs left of a diedre, then traverse diagonally left on good
footholds to a short corner in the left side of a of. Pull over, go up the crack and
around a rib to a tree belay on a capacious ledge and tree belay.
3. 10m Follow the ridge directly, or scramble up easy ledges leading left.
Direct Finish: 10m VS 4c * (1959)
From the tree belay, follow the thin right-slanting crack.

8 Dying Crutchman 25m HVS 5b (1981)
Pull through the left side of the overlap above Flying Dutchman to a small spike,
and finish up the left-trending flakes.

9 Gradation 50m Hard Severe (1970)
1. 20m Start 8m up and right of Flying Dutchman and climb directly up to the
belay of that route.
2. 30m Climb the diedre above, breaking out right at the overhang, to finish up
slabs leftwards or direct.

10 Marie Celeste 30m Mild VS 4b (1971)
Start behind a tree at the top of the first pitch of Flying Dutchman. Pull over the
bulge on the right rib, then go over a further bulge, and climb leftwards to a small
tree. Traverse right and go up slabs to finish.

11 Degradation 30m Mild Severe (1959)
Start behind a small tree 6 metres right of Marie Celeste and climb a left-slanting
vegetatious groove.

12 White Rabbit 20m VS 4c (1984)
Follow the edge of the slab just right of Degradation to a left-facing corner. Move
up this, step right and finish up slabs.

13 Orangeman 15m VS 4c (1984)
Start 5 metres right of White Rabbit below the left-hand trunk of a large dead
tree near the top. Climb straight up over two bulges to the tree.

14 Zenana 30m Hard Severe (1976)
Start to the right of Orangeman, high in the gully between Pandora's and
Repton Buttresses. Climb steep rock until level with a dead tree, then go up a
clean slab which leads to a final steepening.

15 Zenanos 30m Difficult (1976)
This route follows the pillar marked by a nose above Repton Buttress. Start
below and right of a pine 4m up, and climb the pillar, keeping just to the right of
the edge.

REPTON BUTTRESS

This crag is slightly below and immediately to the right of Pandora's Buttress.

Repton Ridge   35m   Difficult   (1947)
The ridge forming the left edge of the buttress.

Tyke's Climb   10m   Very Difficult   (1959)
Climb the left-slanting slab which leads onto the ridge. The left side of the slab can be climbed almost anywhere at a similar grade.

Sprauchle   30m   VS 4c   (1969)
Start midway between Tyke's Climb and Repton Gully. Move over the first bulge just right of a crack, and trend left to a ledge. Go up to an undercut crack below an overhang and follow this leftwards to gain a groove. Surmount the nose above the groove by 'sprauchling', whatever that is!

Repton Front   25m   Hard Severe   (1960s)
Start about a metre left of the gully, climb up to a holly above a short groove, then move left to the ridge.

Repton Gully   25m   Hard Severe   (1950s)
This is the central gully.

Three Pines   30m   Mild Severe *   (1959)
A popular route. Climb the rib immediately right of Repton Gully to the pines. Follow the groove behind the central tree, moving right under the roof to a platform, and continue by a crack.
Variation: 30m   Very Difficult   (1960s)
Start 6 metres right of the original route, traverse left to the rib and follow it to the pines. Escape out left, then go back right.

Bullet   20m   Severe   (1960s)
Climb straight up from the start of the previous route to the pines.

Half Sheet   35m   HVS 5a   (1969/70)
Start at a large flake between Three Pines and Right Wall. From the top of the flake, move left up a diagonal crack to the overhang. Pull over on the right at a large doubtful thread and finish easily up the slab above.

Dirty Sheet   30m   Mild VS 4b   (1964)
Start a short way right of Half Sheet. Climb the slab to an overhang, mantelshelf over it on the left and continue up to a tree. Climb over the cleft and trend right to finish up a crack.

Right Wall   30m   Very Difficult   (1950s)
Start on the right of the crag. Climb up to the right end of the overhang, step left onto it and go up to a tree. Traverse 3m to another tree and go through yet another tree into a cleft. Finish up behind this.

Winter Wall   35m   Difficult   (1950s)
Climb to the left of a wet area, 20 metres right of the main crag, passing some
bushes at 10m. Awful.

PINNACLE RIDGE

This is the lowest of all the buttresses at Polldubh, being immediately above the
lay-by. Consequently it is the most popular and polished of the crags here (but
not indicative of what is on offer). To approach from the lay-by, follow the small
stream that bounds the left side of the crag (known as Pinnacle Burn) by a well
trodden path. Erosion has been a problem here, but Loch Eil Outdoor Centre
have done some remedial work and it would help to reduce future problems if
visitors kept to the path rather than take short cuts. The buttress is composed of
a slabby front face and a two-tier left wall with a large ledge between.

1   Soap Suds   15m   E4 6a *   (1981)
Start at the left side of the wall beneath a curving overlap. Undercut rightwards
and pull over the overlap at a hold on the lip. Step right to gain better holds, and
finish up the left-slanting crack. Bold.

2   The Sugar Puff Kid   15m   E4 6a *   (1985)
Midway between Soap Suds and Chalky Wall is a very shallow groove running
up to the right side of the overlap. Climb this to the overlap, step right to gain a
spike and make a hard move to reach the diagonal crack. Finish direct.

3   Chalky Wall   12m   E4 6a *   (1977)
The inaugural hard Polldubh test-piece. Start 2 metres left of the prominent
vertical crack of Clapham Junction. Climb past a flake with a hard move to gain
holds in the start of a diagonal crack. Pull somewhat blindly onto the rounded
slab above.

4   Clapham Junction   10m   VS 5a *   (1950s/64)
Climb the obvious crack, hand traversing right at the top. Technical and well
protected. The obvious direct finish pushes the grade up to HVS 5a (1964).

5   Severe Crack   10m   VS 4b   (1950)
The crack with a perched block near the top is harder than its name suggests.

A number of eliminates have been recorded on this wall. **The Counter
Reactionary**, E5 6a (1986) moves left from the flake of Chalky Wall and breaks
out leftwards from the Soap Suds roof. Other lines either side of The Sugar Puff
Kid and between Clapham Junction and Severe Crack (all 6a, and unprotected
without side runners) may interest those who climb with their hands tied
together and wear blinkers.

The following routes are on the tier above the Soap Suds wall. The right side
of the blunt rib to the left of Hodad, is taken by **Nomad**, E1 5b (1986) to finish up
the final moves of that route.

GLEN NEVIS
Pinnacle Ridge

1 Soap Suds
2 The Sugar Puff Kid
3 Chalky Wall
4 Clapham Junction
5 Severe Crack
6 Hodad
7 Stage Fright
8 Pinnacle Ridge
9 Diamond
10 Staircase
11 Tip Toe
12 Tip Toe Direct
13 Burma Road
14 People Will Talk

6   Hodad   10m   HVS 5b *   (1967)
Climb the left-slanting diagonal crack, making a long reach right to finish.

7   Stage Fright   10m   E5 6b   (1986)
Climb the scooped wall just right of Hodad, finishing direct. A skyhook in a
pocket and an RP protect the crux.
Variation: **Exit Stage Right**   E4 6a   (1986)
Climb the obvious exit right.

   Orgasmatron, E2 6a (1987) climbs the thin crack further right. Another even
shorter boulder problem climbs up the cracks right again.

8   Pinnacle Ridge   50m   Severe *   (1947)
This extremely popular route is now somewhat polished. Start at the toe of the
buttress. Climb near the left edge of the slab to a tree, then go up an
easy-angled scoop to another tree on the terrace. Move along the top of a large
flake and go up rough slabs to the top.

9   Diamond   10m   VS 5a   (1971)
Climb the thin slab on the front face, 3 metres right of Pinnacle Ridge.

10   Staircase   15m   Severe   (1950)
Start 6 metres right of Pinnacle Ridge. Climb staircase-like holds to the first tree
on that route.

11   Tip Toe   25m   Hard Severe   (1950)
Start immediately right of Staircase. Go up the slab to a small foothold, then tip
toe left to good hand holds at 10m and traverse left. Climb a niche or the crack to
its right to the terrace on Pinnacle Ridge. Poorly protected on the lower slab.

12   Tip Toe Direct   25m   E1 5b *   (1964)
Climb through the break in the overlap right of the niche and go up the slab.

13   Burma Road   40m   VS 4c   (1959)
This route takes the slabby groove on the right, left of the overhang.

14   People Will Talk   25m   E5 6c   (1992)
The overhanging broken groove above a large fallen block, above the start of
Burma Road, is barely protected by some old pegs. A short but very powerful
route on uninspiring rock.

15   Waznusmoles   35m   HVS 5b   (1970/76)
Start 10 metres right of Burma Road. Climb the overhanging wall by a crack,
and pull over onto the slab (often dirty) with difficulty. Continue more easily.

   A number of routes have been made on the more broken rock in the trees
right of here.

Upper Pinnacle   10m   Difficult   (1940s)
The small crag above Pinnacle Ridge can be climbed by a variety of routes.

WALL END CRAG

This crag is situated in the trees 50 metres right of Pinnacle Ridge, above the old wall.

Breathing Like a Drowning Man   20m   HVS 5a   (1990)
Start below large roof by a fallen tree. Climb up to a left-slanting groove and go up this to the left side of the roof. Pass this by cracks on left and follow a flake above the roof to finish up slabs.

Pink 'n' Trees   20m   E3 6a   (1990)
Strenuous and technical climbing up the slab and centre of the roof in the centre of the crag.

ROAD BUTTRESS

This distinctive buttress can be seen clearly from the road 200 metres right of Pinnacle Ridge. The approach starts from the small bridge 100 metres further up the road from the lay-by below Pinnacle Ridge.

1   Sidewalk   25m   Severe
Climb the left edge of the buttress, avoiding the overlaps, either on the left or by the wall just to the right.

2   Trottoir   25m   Severe   (1975)
The mossy wall between Sidewalk and No Entry, starting by a shallow groove and finishing by a rib.

An eliminate, **Lacerations**, E4 6a (1989) takes the blunt bulging rib and slab left of No Entry, pulling through slightly right to thin diagonal holds, then going up an easy flake in the slab.

3   No Entry   30m   VS 5a *   (1976/78)
Start just left of the groove of The Web. Climb up to a curving crack and follow it to a heathery scoop.

4   The Web   20m   E2 5c **   (1969/76)
The open groove with an obvious overhang halfway up provides an enjoyable and technical climb. Layback round the first overhang on good holds, and cross the top crux bulge with interest.

5   Wee One   25m   E3 6a *   (1973/81)
Start just right of The Web. Very hard bouldery moves lead into a shallow, left-facing groove with a peg in it. Climb this and finish by a layback crack leading out right. The upper layback crack of Wee One can be gained by starting up The Web at E1 5b.

6   Cubsville   20m   E5 6b **   (1973/85)
An excellent route which starts in the centre of the crag. Climb the undercut groove to gain the crack above the overlap with difficulty, then continue up this.

7   Withering Crack   20m   E3 5c **   (1972/78)
This is the jam crack splitting two overhangs on the right side of the crag. After a
bouldery start, difficulties soon ease just above the first overhang. The rock is
always vegetated, but the route is climbable all the same.

8   Atree   20m   VS 5a *   (1978)
The groove to the right of Withering Crack contains a tree. Reach this by a tricky
wall and finish by a slab.

Further lines have been recorded: **Jasper's Jumper**, E1 5b (1988) takes a
line 3 metres right of Atree, and an unnamed VS 5a (1988) starts at the foot of
Atree and traverses the crack in the centre of the buttress.

UPPER ROAD BUTTRESS

This lies about 50 metres above Road Buttress. Approach either up the left side
of Road Buttress, or along the path alongside Pinnacle Burn, descending down
the right side (looking down) of the crag, from just below Pine Wall Crag in the
'Alp'.

Mo's Got Her Knickers in a Twist   15m   E4 6a *   (1984)
The obvious crack in the rib left of High Street. Start at the toe of the buttress.
Climb an oblique crack and a slabby groove to the base of a steep thin crack.
Gain the scoop on the left, and swing wildly left around the arete and go up to
the top.

High Street   15m   HVS 5a   (1981)
Climb the scoop and crack above Zephyr Street.

Zephyr Street   15m   VS 4b   (1978)
Start 3 metres right of a fallen birch. Climb a left-slanting crack to the stepped
wall above.

Roundabout   15m   VS 4c   (1975)
Start just right of the lowest rocks on the front face. Climb up to a tiny pine, then
move right to finish by a crack 3m short of a holly.

Lismore Avenue   15m   Difficult   (1972)
Start at a block on the right. Follow the left-slanting ramp to a pine and finish on
the right.

POLLDUBH – THE SECOND TIER BUTTRESSES

This series of buttresses start from the central area of Polldubh above Cavalry
Crack Buttress and extend east (right) into the 'Alp' above Pinnacle Ridge. They
are described in order from left to right. They are referenced to the crags already
described on the lower tier to aid identification and to help in reaching them
through the thick foliage that is normal in summer and which obscures some of
the crags.

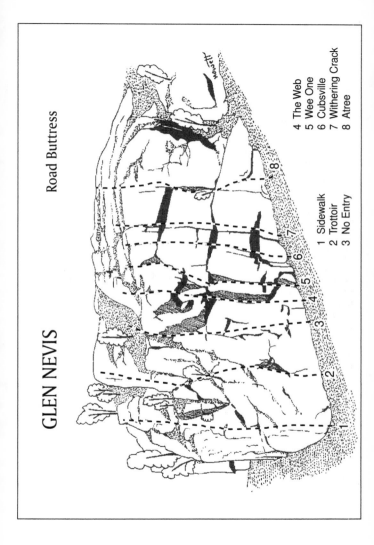

GLEN NEVIS

Road Buttress

1 Sidewalk
2 Trottoir
3 No Entry
4 The Web
5 Wee One
6 Cubsville
7 Withering Crack
8 Atree

AFTER CRAG

This crag is situated about 50 metres above the top of Dundee Buttress, and to the left of the top of Cavalry Crack Buttress. It is most easily approached from the path up the left-hand side of Cavalry Crack Buttress. The features of the crag are those typical of Polldubh – a slabby front face and a steep wall left.

Kraut   20m   E1 5b **   (1969/70)
The prominent left-slanting dyke or fault in the left wall, behind the large tree, is strenuous and well protected with good holds.

Afterthought   20m   Hard Severe   (1960s)
Start on the front wall, 2 metres right of the lowest rocks. Climb over a bulge onto the main slab, then follow a fault which leads into a shallow heathery scoop. Sparsely protected.

Rubberface   20m   E1 5b **   (1968/76)
Start 4 metres right of Afterthought, left of a tree. Climb the bulge (crux), step left onto the slab and continue direct. Quite bold.

Hun   20m   VS 5b   (1982)
Climb the initial bulge as for Rubberface, then move right until it is possible to climb the slab left of the mossy streak. Contrived.

Sauer   20m   VS 4c   (1982)
Start behind a tree just up from Rubberface. Climb direct up the slab just right of the mossy streak.

Right After Wall   20m   Very Difficult   (1960s)
Climb left of and parallel to a slanting overlap, with a choice of finishes.

Ariom   20m   Difficult   (1969)
This is the ridge on the far side of the gully to the right of the buttress.

TWO PINE CRAG

This buttress is situated directly above Cavalry Crack Buttress and to the left of Tiny Buttress. The crag comprises two slabs separated by a tree-filled gully. Two big pine trees grow near the top. Hamlet Buttress and Secretaries' Buttress (on the Upper Tier Buttresses) lie just above.

No Wire   25m   Difficult   (1972)
Climb the ridge left of and slightly below the main crag, hidden amongst the trees.

Wee Wire   25m   Severe   (1970)
Start 12 metres left of the central gully. Trend right, then finish direct or more easily to the left along an obvious fault.

A general view of the Glen Nevis crags above Polldubh. The climber is on The Gutter, Pine Wall Crag, one of the classic early climbs in Glen Nevis

Grope 25m Mild Severe (1974)
This is the shallow heathery groove 4 metres left of the central gully.

Two Pines 35m Severe (1963)
Start at the lowest rocks, midway between the two Pines high up on the face. Go straight up to a tiny tree at 8m, then trend left towards a small oak. Climb a crack on the right to the big Pine. Finish up either of the two cracks above.

Calluna 20m Mild Severe (1969)
Start just right of Two Pines, aiming for the round-topped pine on the right.

Two Pine Gully Edge 30m Difficult (1969)
Climb the edge right of the gully to the crown pine.

TINY BUTTRESS

This crag is above Pandora's Buttress and is distinguished by a 6m diedre topped by a square overhang. Approach as for Pandora's Buttress. Some distance through the trees above Tiny Buttress lies High Crag's Lower Tier.

Left Edge 15m Moderate (1960s)
The ridge on the left.

Layback 12m Mild VS 4b (1960s)
Climb the diedre, exiting right below the overhang. A Direct Finish at the same grade moves back left above the overhang and climbs the centre crack.

Tiny 12m Severe (1960s)
Start at the edge immediately right of Layback. Climb a recess and keep left to an edge. Cross the walk-off ledge of Layback and continue on the right side of the big block to a tree, close to a vegetatious gully.

Wet Slabs 12m Very Difficult (1960s)
The slabs on the right.

LITTLE BUTTRESS

This is above and slightly right of Repton Buttress, between Tiny Buttress and Pine Wall Crag. The front of the crag is a slab almost 60m high, divided at half-height by a ledge with a big pine tree above its left end. The side wall to the left is shorter with a gully leading up to the pine tree. Crack Buttress and Crossbones Crag lie above and to the right and are described with the Upper Tier Buttresses.

Left Wall 15m Severe (1959)
Start near the left edge of the left wall and trend left to the big ledge.

Quartzite Wall 12m Very Difficult (1959)
Start at the same point as Left Wall and climb straight up.

Resurrection on Styx Buttress, Glen Nevis (Climber, Dave Cuthbertson)

Edge Diedre   12m   Hard Severe   (1959)
Climb the groove just left of the buttress edge.

Spike Direct   30m   Severe *   (1960)
Climb a groove just right of the rib for 5m, then move right towards the spike.
Continue straight above the spike, gaining the ridge by a crack on the right to
reach a block.

Spike Wall   55m   Very Difficult **   (1959)
A popular and delightful climb, and good value for the grade. Start right of the
Direct, near some boulders.
1. 30m   Climb the slab leftwards to the spike at 10m. Go over the spike and
traverse left almost to the edge. Climb a recess and the ridge above to the big
ledge with the pine.
2. 25m   Climb the slab above on small quartz holds to finish on the rounded
crest of the ridge.

Blue Monday   30m   HVS 5a   (1988)
Climb the left edge of Spike Direct, keeping right of heather break and
continuing directly to the pine. Poorly protected.

Tutor's Rib   30m   Mild Severe   (1959)
Start at the boulders, move right low down, then climb direct to the big ledge.

Panda   40m   HVS 5a   (1969)
So named because the tree was originally used to reach the slab. Start 5 metres
right of Spike Wall. Boulder up the initial slab, then move up and right (without
using the tree) onto a steep slab. Climb this to a roof, and go over the centre of
this to finish.

Pandy   25   Mild VS 4b   (1981)
Start a short way right of Panda. Go up to the roof, climb over it in the centre and
finish direct up the slab.

Tussi Move   40m   Severe   (1970)
Start 15 metres right of the main crag, just left of a birch. Climb direct to the large
pine, then finish up the slabs above.

THE ALP

To the right of and below Little Buttress, and above Pinnacle Ridge and Road
Buttress, lies a partially hidden grassy meadow. It is relatively sheltered and has
been dubbed The Alp because of its unexpected open aspect. There are
several good quality crags here — Pine Wall and Styx Buttress lying above the
flatter area and SW Buttress lying at the entrance to The Alp. Approach by
following Pinnacle Burn from the lay-by, passing to the left of Pinnacle Ridge to
enter The Alp where the ground flattens out. Crossbones Crag and Cook's
Buttress lie in the trees above SW Buttress and Pine Wall Crag. The Block lies
in a depression about 20m above Styx Buttress.

SW BUTTRESS

A micro-crag which dries very quickly, being much frequented and consequently highly polished. It is just above the origins of Pinnacle burn, before reaching The Alp proper. The crag is a smooth wall characterised by horizontal, vertical and diagonal cracks.

Fred's Delight   12m   Mild Severe   (1963/4)
Climb the left edge of the buttress, passing to the left of the large niche.

Viking's Day Out   12m   E2 5c   (1987)
An eliminate up the baldest part of the left side of the slab.

Tear   12m   Hard Severe *   (1963/4)
The vertical crack just left of centre has good holds and protection.

Scratch   12m   VS 4c   (1963/4)
Climb slightly rightwards up the slab, starting 2 metres right of the crack line of Tear.

SW2   15m   HVS 5b **   (1971)
Climb the short corner just right of Scratch to the diagonal break, step right to a foothold and ascend thin cracks. Thin, poorly protected climbing.

SW Diagonal   18m   HVS 5b *   (1960s)
Climb the diagonal left-slanting crack, with one hard move low down.

Look no Book   12m   E2 5c   (1985)
An eliminate. Go up the wall with a long step to the foothold on Tee, then climb the slab above on small sharp holds.

Tee   12m   VS 5b   (1971)
Follow a direct line just right of the diagonal to join the crack above The Traverse. There is one hard move.

The Traverse   15m   Hard Severe   (1963/4)
Move either way along the horizontal fault at half-height.

Tree Route   10m   Difficult   (1950s)
This is the recess on the right of the buttress.

PINE WALL CRAG

This crag is situated in The Alp a few hundred metres to the right of and above Pinnacle Ridge, above the source of the Pinnacle burn. It is easily identified by a prominent 60m ridge facing the glen, with a large Caledonian pine at two-thirds height. The descent is either down the easy-angled right side of the crag, or the steeper gully separating Pine Wall Crag from Styx Buttress.

Left Pine Ridge   25m   Moderate   (1947)
The ridge separated from the main crag by a tree gully.

Quartz Wall   25m   Difficult   (1960s)
The short quartz wall with mossy slabs above, just right of the tree gully.

Eigerwand   45m   Hard Severe **   (1960s)
Start below a large tree right of Quartz Wall. Climb up to the tree on the terrace
at 8m. Climb a little gully on the left for 3m, then move right and go in a direct line
towards the top. Any deviation on the upper part makes the climbing much
easier.

Slanting Slab   45m   Very Difficult *   (1960s)
Start 6 metres left of the main ridge and follow a wide slabby ramp to a reddish
wall. Climb the steep wall above almost anywhere, then take the broken wall on
the left to finish.

Maintenance   30m   HVS 5a *   (1976)
Climb slabs to the right of the slabby ramp to a steepening at 15m and a
minuscule birch. Continue straight up the bulging wall to the top.

Pine Wall   65m   Hard Severe ***   (1950)
The ridge gives excellent exposed climbing on superb rock, making it one of the
best climbs of its standard at Polldubh. Protection is well-spaced on the first
pitch. Start at the lowest point of the ridge.
1. 35m 4b   Move up to a diedre and climb this to a platform at 12m. Move left
and go over a bulge, then climb the immaculate slabs to the immediate right of
the rounded ridge to a belay on a platform where the angle eases.
2. 15m   Follow the ridge, or grooves left of it, to the prominent pine.
3. 15m   Pass an overlap on either side to reach a small recess just left of the
crest, and continue more easily up this to finish. Much variation is possible,
although the described line gives the best climbing at the grade.

The Gutter   65m   Difficult ***   (1940s/76)
A classic beginner's route, giving pleasant well protected climbing. Follow the
twin cracks 4 metres right of the ridge to a ledge at 12m. Continue in the same
line by a deeper crack to a withering sapling at 30m. Either belay just above, or
continue up the ridge to the big pine. Move up left to a good flake hold on the
wall, then go out right to finish easily up the crest of the ridge.

Dead Pine   55m   Difficult   (1974)
Climb the mossy slabs 10 metres right of The Gutter.

Why   30m   Very Difficult   (1969)
The rib right of the main crag and left of the gully dividing it from Styx Buttress.

STYX BUTTRESS

This lies immediately right of Pine Wall Crag in the 'Alp'. The crag consists of a very steep left wall and a slabby front face. A distinctive tapering ramp lies in the arete between the two faces (Resurrection). The best approach is along the side of the burn past SW Buttress, from where the crag can be seen beyond Pine Wall. The descent follows the steep gully separating the buttress from Pine Wall Crag.

1   Ascension   30m   E2 5b *   (1973/76)
Climb the initial chimney of Doomsday, then the lower of two diagonal cracks to the slanting ledge on Black Friday. Continue over a bulge on the left (often wet) past a tiny sapling and climb the overhung groove.

2   Black Friday   30m   E5 6a**   (1969/81)
The overhanging cleft splitting the centre of the left-hand face provides a well-protected struggle. Climb up rightwards past a sloping ledge to the base of the cleft fault. Climb strenuously up this to easier climbing up the final wider cleft where the angle eases. Low in the grade, but slow to dry.
Right-hand variation: E4 6a   (1982)
This avoids the main challenge (or the wet), by escaping diagonally rightwards on an obvious line of holds from below the main fault to finish up the rib of Resurrection.

3   Doomsday   30m   VS 4c   (1958/68)
Climb the horribly narrow squeeze-chimney (very insecure) in the lower part of the left wall and move right to a platform at 12m. Ascend the wall on the right to finish at the same point as Resurrection.

4   Diagonal Crack   8m   VS 5a   (1960s)
Climb diagonally right from near the foot of the left wall to the tapering ramp of Resurrection.

5   The Amazing Adventures of Smelly MacMoist   30m   E4 6a (1985)
The wall and diagonal crack in the rib left of Resurrection. Start below the crack about 3 metres left of the left edge of the ramp. Make some thin moves to gain the crack and continue up this past a hard section to easier ground. Climb the crack above until eventually forced into Resurrection to finish.

6   Resurrection   35m   VS 4c ***   (1959)
A Polldubh classic, sustained and well-protected with superb climbing up the tapering ramp in the centre of the crag. Climb the slabby ramp, with the crux (and excellent protection) at the narrow middle section to a slightly easier wide fault crack higher up.

7   Broos   30m   HVS 5b   (1976)
Follow the slanting corner crack just right of the ramp until it is possible to break out right across the steep wall to join Curse at its crux. Slow to dry.

8   Curse   30m   VS 5a   (1976)
Start 3 metres right of the ramp of Resurrection. Climb a short gangway to the top of a large flake. Move up rightwards, then traverse left under the overhang, then continue more easily past heather to finish.

9   Damnation   30m   VS 4b **   (1958)
Start on the left side of the wall, 6 metres right of the left buttress edge. Climb a ramp until it is possible to traverse right to a vertical rib which leads to an overhang. Cross this on the left on good holds and continue straight up the fine slab above to a tree. Improbable-looking for the grade.

10   Iche   30m   VS 5a *   (1959)
Start just left of the diagonal heather groove. Climb leftwards up the slab and surmount the overhang 2m from its right end. Traverse left a short way to a thin crack and go up this to a small tree. Finish up slabs.

11   Hades   30m   Very Difficult   (1960s)
From the start of Iche, move right past the overhang to cross a heather groove, then continue by the line of least resistance.

12   Fidelity   30m   VS 5a *   (1959)
Start about 5 metres right of the central diagonal heathery fault. Climb a slab to holly at 6m, or more easily direct. Go past the left side of a protruding pillar to reach the left of a niche. Climb the centre of the large slab, steepening towards the top. Much variation is possible.

13   Right Wall   50m   Very Difficult *   (1960s)
Climb a slab 5 metres right of Fidelity to a small pine and go along an edge past another pine. Keep right of a recess to gain the final slab.

14   Styx Ridge   25m   Very Difficult   (1960s)
This is the ill-defined ridge 8 metres right of Right Wall.

15   Boggle   15m   Very Difficult   (1971)
Climb the slabby ramp some 50 metres to the right.

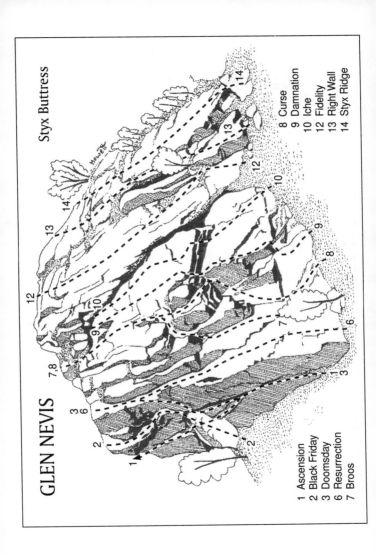

GLEN NEVIS

Styx Buttress

1 Ascension
2 Black Friday
3 Doomsday
6 Resurrection
7 Broos

8 Curse
9 Damnation
10 Iche
12 Fidelity
13 Right Wall
14 Styx Ridge

POLLDUBH – THE UPPER TIER BUTTRESSES

RIDGE BUTTRESS

This is the dog's tooth-shaped crag standing proud high up on the skyline ridge, Leith Aire of Am Nam Buidhe (the yellow ridge) directly above the sheep fank at Achriabach. Reach it by continuing up the hill onto the ridge from West End Crag.

1   Rush   15m   E4 5c *   (1988)
The overhang at the left end. Move up right into a niche in the centre of the overhanging wall, go through this and finish up the ramp above.

2   Nevil   15m   HVS 5a   (1976)
The mossy groove line right of the overhanging section.

3   Pale Face   20m   E2 5b *   (1978)
A wandering and poorly protected climb up the steep wall, following the line of least resistance. Climb up to a small niche at 5m, then trend right across the wall and move up to gain left-slanting grooves which lead to the top.

4   Painted Face   20m   E3 5c *   (1986)
A direct through Pale Face. Start directly beneath a ledge 3 metres right of that route. Gain this and pull right onto the wall and go up this direct to gain some good holds just before the traverse of Pale Face. Follow this, then continue traversing left to a left-slanting groove which leads up the left edge of the pale streak. Finish up this.

5   Canine   20m   Difficult   (1964)
Start halfway along the left wall. Follow holds leading rightwards to a rib just left of heather.

6   Chimney Crack   20m   Severe   (1964)
This route lies just right of Canine.

7   Son of a Bitch   20m   E4 6a *   (1988)
Start at a quartz blotch 5 metres left of South Diagonal. Go up the wall for 6m to reach the diagonal cracks and protection. Reach up and right to good holds, then hand traverse right to a tiny overhung corner. Climb this to exit blindly with difficulty on sloping holds.

8   South Diagonal   20m   HVS 5b *   (1969)
Follow the left-slanting diagonal crack until forced left at a bulge. Continue up and slightly right to the final rib.

9   Bitch   25m   HVS 5a *   (1963)
Start at a groove on the front face. Climb diagonally left to the rib and climb up keeping near to the edge. Reasonable but poorly protected climbing with some friable holds.

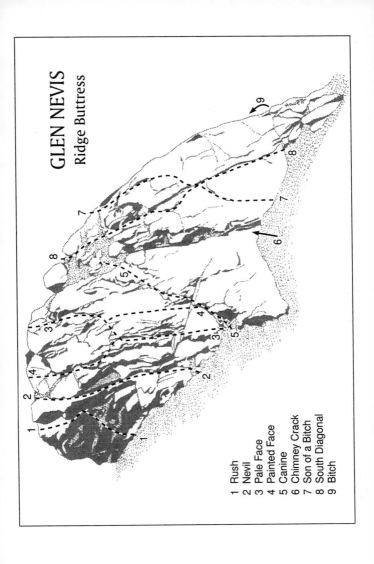

GLEN NEVIS
Ridge Buttress

1 Rush
2 Nevil
3 Pale Face
4 Painted Face
5 Canine
6 Chimney Crack
7 Son of a Bitch
8 South Diagonal
9 Bitch

10   Peg Route   8m   VS 5a   (1960s)
The crack at the steepening can be reached by a crack from the start of South Diagonal.

11   Howl   30m   Mild Severe   (1964)
Continue up the initial groove of Bitch for 8m, then move right and up to finish up the right side of the Bitch slab.
Variation: Severe
Climb the second groove further to the right.

BLAEBERRY BUTTRESS

This is the large slabby buttress about 100 metres left, and at a slightly lower level than Secretaries' Buttress. It is the right-hand section of broken slabs that lies above those containing Tricouni Buttress. It is easiest to approach it by skirting right from Tricouni Right-Hand Slab and ascending a less tree-infested line leading up and slightly right towards Secretaries' Buttress.

Hedge of Insanatree   60m   E2 *   (1988)
Exposed climbing up the undercut left arete, with a large square-cut overlap at half-height. Start at the lowest, leftmost part of the crag.
1. 45m 5c   Initial hard moves up the arete leads to easier ground. Move up to the overlap. Pull over this and rock over on the far left edge (crux) and continue up the edge to tree belay in recess.
2. 15m 5c   The steep crack behind the belay leads to good holds and an easier slab.

Scorpion   55m   E1   (1988)
Start above a large elm 6 metres right of the arete.
1. 35m 4a   Go up a quartz band to a grassy ledge, step right, then climb a black streak up the main slab to a tree belay below the upper wall.
2. 20m 5c   Climb the wall above the belay to a crack. Step onto the upper slab and make some hard moves up the blunt arete to gain the upper slab.

Run to the Hills   55m   VS   (1988)
1. 35m 4a   Start as for Scorpion, and follow it to the main slab, then take a line right of the black streak to a lower tree belay.
2. 20m 4c   Climb the right-slanting ramp to a smaller slab above. Move up this and climb the crack to finish up the slab.

HAMLET CRAG

This crag is situated midway between the top of Cavalry Crack Buttress and the foot of Secretaries' Buttress, and is well hidden in the trees. Approach as for

Cavalry Crack Buttress, then search through the undergrowth to the right of the well worn path that leads to Secretaries' Buttress. The crag comprises slabs on the left of a central gully and a clean buttress with roofs on the right. Secretaries' Buttress lies above the trees about 100m above Hamlet Crag.

Hamlet Edge   30m   Very Difficult   (1950)
Climb close to the left edge before trending left, then go right again below a platform at 10m. Follow slabs right of an ill defined ridge and finish up a steep groove.

Cigar   25m   Severe   (1979)
Climb straight up the cleanest rock 5 metres right of Hamlet Edge.

Shakespeare Wall   30m   Mild Severe   (1969)
This route follows a line left of and parallel to the central gully, starting left of a block and crossing an easy overlap. There are various finishes.

William   30m   Severe   (1976)
Trend left above the overlap and follow the rounded left edge of the gully.

Black Horse   30m   Mild Severe   (1969)
Climb the slab 3 metres right of the central gully to a ramp which leads to the left. Cross the overlap and go up to the right of the gully.

Foil   10m   E3 6a *   (1976/78)
Walk up a grassy slope to the foot of a short shallow groove. Step right across the initial overhang and climb the groove, protected by small wires, to an excellent finishing hold.

Simple Deduction   12m   E3 5c   (1986)
This climb traverses the prominent undercut flange above Cubby's Route and right of Foil. Protection is in Foil. Ascend Foil to gain a standing position beneath the groove. Traverse right to finish at the same point as Cubby's Route.

Cubby's Route   12m   E1 5b   (1983)
Move under the roof, as for Foil, but pull over it sooner and traverse right between the roofs to gain and finish up a shallow groove just left of Jam Crack.

Side Arms   12m   E3 5c   (1987)
Start at a crack beneath the first overhang, left of Jam Crack. Layback through this, continue direct through the second smaller overhang and go on up the delicate slab to finish.

Jam Crack   15m   Hard Severe   (1960s)
This is the prominent crack high on the right, reached by a left-slanting ramp.

SECRETARIES' BUTTRESS

This excellent crag lies high up the slope directly above Hamlet Buttress, and about 100 metres left of High Crag. It is easily recognised from the road as one of the larger crags in the upper area of Polldubh and by a three-tier steep left wall split by two oblique faults, with a slabby frontal face to the right. The best approach is *via* the faint path up the left-hand side of Cavalry Crack Buttress. The routes are described starting from the left-hand end of the steep left-hand face, then working down to the right and onto the slabby front face.

1   Naetitheraba'   25m   HVS 5a   (1992)
Start at a short overhanging groove at the left side of the buttress, just left of the roof of Ring of Fire. Go up this to gain a shallow left-facing groove split by some ledges. Follow this to the top. The upper groove can also be gained by a diagonal traverse in from the left, reducing the grade to VS 4c.

2   Ring of Fire   25m   E5 6b *   (1981)
Start at the foot of a shallow groove at the far left of the buttress. Swing right to a large flat hold above the lip and go up to a ledge. Climb the groove (doubtful RP placements) and the thin crack with a hard move on the arete. Climb the arete and the slab to the top. Serious and technical.

3   Ring of Fire Right-Hand   30m   E3 6a ***   (1984)
Fine open wall climbing, with a gymnastic start. As for the original route to the ledge. Break out right and follow an obvious line up the wall leading to the top crack on Vincent and finish up this.

4   Secretaries' Crack   20m   Difficult *   (1950)
The fault splitting the second and third tiers of the crag gives one of the few deep chimney lines hereabouts. Follow this to a ledge on the front wall. Either walk off rightwards, or continue up the crest of the ridge (Severe) as for Secretaries' Direct.

5   Footnote   20m   HVS 5a   (1986)
Follow a direct line up the wall to the left of Last Word, avoiding the initial bulge by moving in from the left. Other more difficult (5c/6a) boulder problem starts are possible.

6   Last Word   20m   HVS 4c *   (1959)
Follow small left-trending ramps, then head direct for the right end of the diagonal break between the first and second tiers. Spaced protection.

7   Just Passing   25m   E1 5a   (1989)
Start at the lowest rocks, as for Last Word. Climb direct to the break of Vincent and continue up the wall above *via* two thin cracks to reach the Super Direct on the arete.

GLEN NEVIS
Secretaries' Buttress

2 Ring of Fire	6 Last Word	9 Secretaries' Super Direct
3 Ring of Fire Right-Hand	7 Just Passing	11 Secretaries' Direct
4 Secretaries' Crack	8 Vincent	12 Right Wall

8   Vincent   60m   E3 ***   (1981)
A diagonal line across the left wall of all three tiers gives fine open climbing.
Start at the toe of the crag.
1. 20m 5b   Climb the wall to join the first diagonal crack and traverse along this
to a ledge.
2. 10m 5c   Move left round the overhang above and go up the wall
(unprotected) to better holds just below the top. Continue up the slab to a ledge
and belay.
3. 30m 5c   Descend about a metre and pull round onto the wall (hard). Follow
the crack with interest until a leftward traverse can be made to a ledge. Climb
the cracks to the top.

8a   Little Blind Spider   25m   E1 5c   (1997)
Start in the middle of the gully at the base of the crag. Climb the overhanging
arete above on good holds to gain the slab at the traverse on pitch 1 of
Secretaries' Super Direct. Climb a thin overhanging crack in the overlap above
using quartz nubbins to its right. Move slightly left and climb the slab above
direct to the first ledge.

9   Secretaries' Super Direct   50m   HVS ***   (1969/73)
A fine exposed line up the left edge of the slabby face. Start at the left side of the
front face, below the corner of the Direct.
1. 20m 4c   Move left across the steep slab to cross the overlap near the left
edge, then go up this to the first ledge system.
2. 30m 5a   Follow the thin and exposed left edge of the slab to the second
ledge (possible belay). Cross the gap and finish up easier slabs.

10   Twitch   15m   E1 5b *   (1969)
The thin slab midway between the second pitches of the Super Direct and the
Direct. Gain the start from the right along the first ledge, or better, start up Little
Blind Spider. Although unprotected, the difficulties ease as height is gained. An
eliminate line right of this has also been climbed at E2/3 5b (1989).

11   Secretaries' Direct   80m   Severe ***   (1959)
Excellent climbing, giving one of the best lines of its grade in the glen. Start
below the shallow left-facing corner.
1. 15m   Climb the corner to the first ledge system. Move right to belay below a
crack.
2. 20m   Follow the central crack on superb quartz holds to the second fault
system.
3. 45m   Easier climbing up the slab above leads to a horizontal ridge. Continue
rightwards over several short steps.

12   Right Wall   50m   Very Difficult   (1960s)
Climb the slab by the line of least resistance near the right end of the wall,
passing an overlap on its right. Other lines of similar standard can be climbed
almost anywhere on the slab.

NAMELESS CRAG

This crag lies above and right of Secretaries' Buttress, at the same level and immediately to the left of the skull of High Crag (Upper Tier). It is characterised by two steep walls either side of an overhanging nose above a broken rib. The left-hand, west-facing wall is composed of slabby grooves, the right-hand side has a smooth wall facing the skull. The first routes are on the left wall. Approach as for Secretaries' Buttress, then walk up the open slope on its right side.

Anonymous   30m   Very Difficult   (1970)
The shallow diagonal chimney at the left end of the crag.

Les Boys   30m   E3 5c *   (1981)
At the left end of the wall, just right of the chimney, a shallow quartz vein runs up the face, giving the line of the route. Start up the chimney, then step right onto a ledge. Move up a quartz vein past a small overlap with a hard move to gain the broken slab above. Follow a line diagonally rightwards past two small ledges, and finish on the left.
Direct Finish: E3 5c *   (1983)
Ascend the wall directly above the crack on the normal route.

Savage Cabbage   30m   E4 5c *   (1985)
The shallow hanging groove in the centre of the wall, just right of the previous route. Climb the short groove just right of Les Boys to a ledge. Move up then horizontally right to a poor peg runner at the base of the groove. Follow this with a hard move to reach a second peg runner on the rib out right (also poor), then pull onto the slab on the left and finish more easily.

Risque Grapefruit   30m   E4 5c **   (1981)
Thin bold climbing up the slightly slabbier right side of the face, with a run-out crux. Start under a short open groove in the centre of the face. Pull rightwards across the wall and go round the arete onto the slab. Continue direct over a tiny overlap and climb up with some stretchy moves (crux) to reach a shallow scoop. Go up the shallow groove and the left-trending ramp to finish.

Faceless   30m   E2 5b*   (1986)
The deep-cut groove at the right end of the face.

Above the terrace at the top of this face is a short clean wall. A line up the centre has been climbed, **Ladybird Wall**, HVS 5a (1986). The following routes are all on the shorter, slabbier right wall, facing up the glen. It is split into three walls by a pair of vertical lichenous fault lines.

Bitter Days   25m   E3 6a *   (1987)
The bulging arete, slab and roof forming the apex of the crag where the two faces abut. Start directly below the arete, reached by a narrow ledge system from the right. Climb the left side, swing round the arete and go up the slab to good holds and protection under the roof. Pull through this to superb finishing holds.

Overlode   20m   E4 6a   (1987)
The rounded left edge of the wall is hard at the start. Climb the thin hairline cracks with difficulty to a jug (runners). Go straight up the wall above, ignoring the desire to escape left, with a further hard move with no gear to gain the top break. Climb more easily up the edge to finish.

Quadrode   20m   E2 5b *   (1987)
Bold steady climbing up the centre of the wall near the left end of the face. Start at a triangular niche at the base of the wall. Climb easily on good holds to an RP placement in the second break. Step left and follow obvious left-trending holds with interest to finish at a good incut. Peg belay.

Cathode Smiles   20m   E2 5c *   (1987)
The central tower of rock formed by the two vertical fault lines. Move up through a quartz-riddled wall to a good break at half-height. Climb the wall above heading direct for an obvious thin crack, and go up on good holds to finish. Peg belay just above.

Triode   20m   E5 6a **   (1987)
Thin bold climbing up the blankest section of the face. Start beneath a shallow left-facing groove. Climb this for about 6m, then move right to a crack leading to a horizontal break (protection in a slot above). Move left along the horizontal, then go up to a quartz hold. Continue on small holds to a series of stepped undercuts heading out left to finish.

Diode   20m   E2 5c **   (1977)
A thin crack splits the right end of the face. Climb this direct, passing a narrow roof at mid-height.

KING SLAB

This low-angled slab is immediately left of the middle tier of High Crag and to the right of Secretaries' Buttress. It has a short overhanging wall at its base, and a huge boulder on top.

1   Nosbulgia   40m   HVS 5b   (1969/70s)
The easy left edge of the slab can be gained by a thin overhanging crack.

2   Duskscreams   40m   Very Difficult   (1975)
Climb the diagonal fault at the right end of overhanging base to a tree, then continue straight up to the right side of the boulder.

3   King's Slab   30m   Very Difficult   (1960s)
The slab is climbable almost anywhere.

4   High King Hole   25m   Very Difficult   (1964)
Climb the gully between King Slab and the Middle Tier of High Crag, passing behind a large chockstone.

HIGH CRAG

This massive buttress is composed of three tiers of slabs and is nearly 155m high. The lower tier is scrappy, split halfway by a ledge with an overlap above. Most of its height is obscured by trees. The middle tier is more appealing and about 60m high. Its left side forms a red wall facing west. The upper tier, again 60m, lies above a large terrace and is undercut along its length. Its left wall forms a distinctive shape reminiscent of a skull which stares westwards down the glen.

THE LOWER TIER

The following routes start from the lower tier. Some only climb this tier, others climb two or all three.

5   R-T Route   30m   Very Difficult *   (1960s)
Start at the left side of the tier, left of a crack with a twin-trunked tree. Go straight up the slab, cross a bulge above a ledge and finish by a groove.

6   Wutz   85m   Hard Severe   (1971)
1. 30m   Start 5 metres right of R-T Route and climb straight up to a recess leading to the first terrace.
2. 20m   Climb the block slab and easy groove above, then step left and go up a vertical crack to a stance.
3. 35m   Follow steepening slabs, veering slightly right to finish at the second terrace.

7   Central Route   35m   VS 4c *   (1969)
Start midway between Wutz and Autobahnausfahrt. Climb straight up, crossing an overlap on the upper half, to finish close to a small tree on the first grass terrace.

8   Autobahnausfahrt   160m   Mild VS **   (1969)
The longest route in the glen, with pleasant and varied situations. Start near the right side of the base of the crag.
1. 35m 4a   Climb slabs, crossing a ledge and an overhang with a tiny tree, then climb steeper slabs to the first terrace.
2. 15m   Climb a block and the bulge above to a tree ledge.
3. 45m 4b   Surmount the overhang 5m above and head for a small groove. Climb this to the second terrace.
4. 15m 4b   Walk right to climb the steep slabs at the right end of the overhanging base, passing a heather groove at 8m on its left.
5. 30m   Continue straight up over a bulge to easy slabs which are climbable anywhere.

further left. Move right to a small ledge with trees and finish direct. Take belays where necessary.

15 Patdoug 110m Severe (1971)
Start 15 metres right of Thirst. Go up to a slanting ramp, then climb a short wall right of a crack with a pine. Cross the second terrace 12m right of and below the damp break of Thirst. Follow a right-slanting crack behind a tree to easy slabs. Belay where necessary.

16 Cervix 30m VS 4c * (1969)
Start above the gully between High Crag and King Slab, on the left wall of the tier. Climb the initial wall by a left-slanting crack, with a strenuous crux at 10m. Continue along the fine steep slanting chimney above.

17 Chugger 40m HVS (1985)
An exposed line up the right arete of the left face of the middle tier. Start below a short right-slanting corner, best gained by descending from the top of the crag.
1. 10m 4c   Gain and follow the corner to a good ledge.
2. 30m 5a   Climb the shallow left-slanting groove above until forced out right onto the arete. Pull round onto the slab and go up its left edge to the top. Thread belay further back.

THE UPPER TIER

The following routes climb all across the skull and the slabs to the right. The latter routes all start by climbing through the steep lower roofs.

18 Hawk's Nest 30m Hard Severe (1959/60s)
Start at an obvious horizontal crack high on the left wall of the crag, just below the left eye of the skull. Follow the obvious traverse line right to finish below the easy final chimney of The Paunch.

19 Circus 30m E4 6a ** (1987)
An exposed right traverse above the lip of the huge roof forming the right eye of the skull. Belay at a small tree halfway up crag, reached from any of the adjacent routes. Climb up to an obvious break and follow this strenuously to a peg at its end. Pull right onto slab and continue more easily up this to finish up broken ground.

20 The Swing of Things 20m E3 6b * (1987)
A diagonal line swinging through the lower roof forming the nose of the skull. Start down and left of the roof. Climb easily up and rightwards (often wet) to the roof. Go through this and continue up a rising crack line past some small trees to tree belay.

21 Hot Spots 45m E4 * (1965/88)
This line through the bridge of the nose is often dripping and is very slow to dry. Start at the steep wall at the lowest point of the front face, just left of an obvious diagonal hand crack.

1. 25m 6a   Follow the thin crack, mainly on face holds, to reach a wider crack which soon eases. Continue to belay at a small tree level with the eyes.
2. 20m 5b   Follow the wider crack above.

22   The Paunch   55m   VS 5a   (1959)
Defining the right edge of the skull is a prominent wide red granite dyke, slightly overhanging at the start. Climb the wall to a tree at 15m. Head directly for a slanting chimney and finish up this. The rock requires care.

23   Stone Cold   30m   E3 6b *   (1985)
This hard bouldery route follows the series of right-trending grooves at the left end of the overhanging wall. Start on top of an obvious boulder, about 5 metres left of the top pitch of Crag Lough Grooves. Pull onto and climb the left-hand crack and pull right to the next crack. Go up this with difficulty, then move right to finish up the obvious right-trending groove.

The top pitch of Crag Lough Grooves climbs the obvious hanging ramp right of this route.

24   Slatehead Slab   30m   E2 5b **   (1985)
Directly behind the top of Stone Cold, and right of the rightmost eye of the skull, is a fine slab above a tree with a short wall at its foot. Start below this. Traverse left from the tree, then move up the wall to pull left onto the slab at good sidepulls. Follow an obvious line right across the slab to a good pocket at a break. Continue past another break to the top. The route can also be gained from the right.

25   Sky Pilot   30m   E5 6b ***   (1981)
The centre of the overhanging 45 degree wall is breached by a hanging crack, forming a block near the lip. Climb up and out on improving holds (crux at half height) to the lip, and step left to gain easy slabs. No pitch exists in the glen that is more 'out there'. Bouldery. The wall below this route gives good bouldering, and is worth knowing about for a rainy day if you can bear the walk in.

26   Auto Roof   30m   E2 6a   (1969/81)
Climb the break through the steep wall on the right to a niche. Exit rightwards out of this and continue up slabs.

27   Direkt und Links   30m   E2 6b   (1986)
Right of Auto Roof is a short overhanging wall leading to an obvious hold in the short left-rising break. Gain this and the quartz holds on the lip to the right, and continue up the slab above with difficulty.

A further line (**Undergrabbens**, E2 6b) has been climbed through the break further right.
The top pitch of Autobahnausfahrt climbs the slabs at the right end of the overhanging section passing a heather groove. The following routes are on the more broken area of rock right of the middle and upper tiers.

Knees   80m   Difficult   (1975)
Start at a short block crack 40 metres right of and below the Upper Tier. Pass behind a large tree to reach a clean slab.

Malaw   90m   Difficult   (1974)
Start directly above Crack Buttress, at the lowest blocks to the right of the Middle Tier.

Cucumber   70m   Moderate   (1969)
The prominent curved ridge between High Crag and Black's Buttress, and above Cook's Buttress.

UPPER CHOSSHEAP CRAG

An aptly named crag, directly above High Crag and below Crown Buttress.

Fool in the Rain   10m   HVS 5a   (1985)
Climb a series of narrow ledges just right of the crack on the left.

The Compost Heap that Time Forgot   10m   Mild VS 4b   (1989)
Climb the arete of the corner on the right to a ledge and finish direct.

CROWN BUTTRESS

Above High Crag and the tiny Upper Chossheap Crag lies a 25m-high buttress, with a left-facing open groove on the left.

Frenzy   20m   Severe *   (1970)
Climb the leftmost edge, gained by a short crack on the left.

Tom's Arete   25m   HVS 5a *   (1986)
Climb the arete direct.

Crown Groove   25m   Mild Severe   (1970)
The large groove on the left gives a pleasant pitch.

Fibrillation   20m   Severe   (1970)
The wall right of the groove. Reach the terrace at two-thirds height by a short recess near the edge.

Jewels   12m   VS 5a   (1976)
The recess reached from the start of Palpitation.

Palpitation   20m   VS 4c *   (1970)
Start round the edge just right of Fibrillation. Go over initial bulge to cracks further right. Climb these, and traverse right from their top to a recess and easy ground above.

Pal   12m   Very Difficult   (1970)
Climb the crack left of the wide fault on the right.

Palpal   12m   Severe   (1970)
This route follows the fault.

Tom's Other Route   12m   HVS   (1986)
The obvious line at right end of crag.

CROSSBONES CRAG

This crag lies just to the right of the upper part of Little Buttress, immediately below Crack Buttress and below and right of High Crag's Lower Tier. It is a slab with a large birch tree at its base.

Soldier   35m   Very Difficult   (1975)
Climb the left side of the mossy slab, starting below a small pine.

Bite the Dust   35m   Hard Severe   (1983)
Start 6 metres left of Mini Mantel and follow a crack to a small tree on a grassy rake. Continue directly above to the top.

Mini Mantel   35m   Hard Severe   (1983)
Start down and left from the large birch, near the centre of the crag. Climb to the grassy rake, then go up the wall and a slab to a terrace. Continue up the obvious weakness above to the next terrace.

Gibbon   35m   Severe   (1983)
Start just left of a tree to the right of the large birch. Gain the slab above and move up to a steepening. Wander up the slab above to the terrace, then climb the right side of the recess above.

CRACK BUTTRESS

This buttress is situated above and right of Little Buttress, 60 metres right of the High Crag, Lower Tier. It is just above Crossbones Crag. The front wall is split by a wide crack and is topped by a slab ridge. The descent is down the easy gullies on the right.

Boorock   25m   Very Difficult   (1970)
Climb the prominent blocky rib on the left flank, finishing by a wide crack in the final block.

Left-Right   20m   Very Difficult   (1960s)
The slab left of Wide Crack can be climbed almost anywhere.

Wide Crack   40m   Difficult   (1960s)
Follow either of the two wide cracks which unite at 5m, and follow a narrower crack to a terrace. Take the easy rib on the right to finish.

Mani Mintel   40m   Severe   (1980s)
Climb slabby rock to the right of Wide Crack.

COOK'S BUTTRESS

Located to the right of Crack Buttress, and directly above Pine Wall Crag, this buttress has three 12m slabby walls separated by two terraces, with slabby rock extending further right towards Black's Buttress. The best approach is from Pine Wall Crag.

Por Ridge   60m   Very Difficult *   (1970)
Start in the gully to the left of the crag, just left of and slightly below the first terrace. Follow the buttress edge to the second terrace, then move left and go up the crest of the ridge to the top. Pleasant climbing on good rock.

Three Pitch Climb   60m   Severe   (1969)
Start at a small groove in the lowest rocks of the crag and follow three successive steps, keeping close to the left edge of the crag.

Kitchen Rib 85   25m   Very Difficult   (1970)
This is the ill defined rib 40 metres right of Three Pitch Climb.

Liaison Dangereux   25m   Very Difficult   (1971)
The line 8 metres to the right of Kitchen Rib is usually wet.

Goldener Oktober   35m   Very Difficult   (1972)
Start from the first ramp up and right of Kitchen Rib 85, 40 metres left of and below the lower tier of Black's Buttress. Follow a short wall to a recess above a terrace. Climb 4 metres left of the Horsi Slab to exit left onto slab.

Horsi   45m   Hard Severe   (1972)
Start 6 metres to the right of Goldener Oktober. Follow the groove right of a heathery gully to a terrace at 10m. Step left and go up to a crack leading over a steep section to pleasant slabs.

Rhubarb   35m   Severe   (1972)
From the terrace on Horsi, go right and follow a right-trending crack, then finish direct, heading for a small tree.

BLACK'S BUTTRESS

This buttress is situated far to the right and on the same level as the Upper Tier of High Crag, approximately 60m above Pine Wall Crag. The buttress is composed of a vegetatious lower tier marked by a clean left edge. Immediately above, separated by a flat grassy terrace is a smooth 30m slab of immaculate white rock. Approach either by following a small sheep path along the natural terrace from the base of the last tier of High Crag ('The John Muir Sheep Trail') or by continuing above Pine Wall Crag to reach a terrace leading back left.

Zelos   60m   Very Difficult   (1969/70)
This route climbs both tiers. The first pitch is also a useful approach to the main crag. Follow the clean left edge of the lower tier (30m). Continue 2m left of a small tree, again keeping close to the edge.

Knucklebuster   30m   Severe   (1972)
Start to the left of the main crag. Climb up leftwards around an overhang, then move right onto a slab and finish up this on crack holds.

Shergar   30m   HVS 4c **   (1981)
From the foot of Knucklebuster, climb thin right-slanting cracks to gain a shallow left-facing corner. A great route, low in the grade.

Land Ahoy   30m   E3 5b ***   (1981)
Start midway between Shergar and Kaos, at an arrow. Climb the wall direct to the crack in the upper half of the wall, then finish more easily. Brilliant climbing, sustained and unprotected before the crack.

Centrepiece   30m   E6 6b ***   (1987)
Superb fingery climbing directly up the centre of the slab, right of Land Ahoy. Start at some quartz in the centre of the wall. Climb up to a prominent small L-shaped hold at 5m. Hard climbing past this leads to the thin horizontal. Pull direct past this to better holds and a reasonable stopping place. Poor RP placements in the incipient crack system above protect a further tricky move to reach a large flat hold. Easy climbing remains.

Kaos   30m   E2 5c *   (1968/80)
Follow the obvious thin vertical crack, then climb up and left with difficulty to gain a further crack and small ledge at 10m. Continue in the same line to the top. Delicate and fingery, and a bit run-out at the crux.

Desmo   20m   HVS 5b   (1981)
Climb the thin crack just right of Kaos, then step right into another crack and climb this to a recess at the top.

Crybaby   20m   VS 4c   (1970/72)
Start midway between Kaos and the rib on the right side of the crag. Follow the crack rightwards past a small triangular niche to a ledge at 12m, and continue by a crack on the left.

Heulsuse   20m   HVS 5a   (1973)
Start midway between Crybaby and the right rib of the crag. Climb straight up until forced left to join Crybaby before the ledge.

Kyanite   20m   HVS 5a *   (1976)
This route gives delicate and poorly protected climbing directly up the rib at the right side of the crag.

Close to the Wind   35m   E1 5b*   (1981)
A girdle, crossing some impressive ground for the grade. Start at a tree just left of Kyanite. Move up, then go horizontally left to meet Kaos just above its crux. Continue to the left to Land Ahoy, go up this for a couple of moves, then move left again across Shergar to finish up a rib.

A Bridge Too Far 20m Hard Severe (1984)
Climb the centre of the rock nose to a ledge. Continue up the crack on the left.

Nostril 20m Severe (1984)
The ramp to the right of the rock nose leads to a crack. Follow this to a ledge and finish up the chimney on the right.

Cheek 20m Mild Severe (1984)
Start as for Nostril and climb to a steepening in the slab. Climb this *via* a crack, then go straight up to the top.

SCIMITAR BUTTRESS

This is the most easterly of the Polldubh crags, approximately 300 meters right of Road Buttress and slightly higher. It is about 100m above the road, on the rock spur called Mam Beag which runs up the hillside from the road. The crag is essentially made up of a series of barely connected buttresses on the west-facing side of this spur. The routes are described from left to right.

Nutcracker Chimney 25m Hard Severe 4b ** (1958)
Climb the shallow flared chimney at the upper left-hand side of the crag.

The Short Straw 25m E4 6a (1990)
Steep and strenuous climbing over the bulge just right of Nutcracker Chimney.

Rip 25m HVS 5b (1978)
Trend right from near the foot of Nutcracker Chimney to join the arete which trends back left from Break.

Break 25m HVS 5a (1975)
Start 5 metres left of Neck. Traverse right to a thin crack and go up this to the holly, then finish either to the right or the left.

Neck 20m HVS 5a (1975)
Start below a holly near the centre of the face. Climb a right-trending line to a metal spike, then go left and up to a ledge. Enter the groove with the holly, exiting right above this. Poorly protected.

Fingertip Finale 25m E4 5c * (1985)
The central impending wall gives a number of sparsely protected pitches, this one being the original and least daunting. Start midway between two pink streaks. Climb directly up the wall on reasonable holds to a quartz blotch and good holds (poor RP on its side). Traverse hard right to a flange and better holds. Move up then back left to finish up the obvious thin crack. Nut belay far back on the right.

Precious Cargo 20m E5 6a * (1990)
Very serious, although escapable from the direct line where Fingertip Finale escapes right. From the quartz blotch, pull through the bulge slightly leftwards to reach a large sloping hold and go up to a good horizontal break (good gear). Further hard moves leaving this lead to better holds in the short corner to finish.

Evil Eye 20m E5 6a (1990)
Virtually unprotected extended bouldering, following a parallel line up the wall just left of Diagonal. Start about 2 metres left of the diagonal crack. Move up the wall on positive holds, heading for a short vertical finger slot at about 6m (poor HB1 in this, or slightly better, a tied down skyhook on an incut just below). A sharp pull on thin edges leads to better holds and some respite at the end of the traverse of Fingertip Finale. Finish up this, or reverse the traverse and finish as for Precious Cargo.

Diagonal 20m VS 4c * (1958/69)
The left-hand and most obvious of two right-slanting crack lines is well protected and on good holds.

Razor 20m VS 4c ** (1978)
From the start of Wanderlust, climb straight up to join Diagonal Crack. Step left and follow a thin crack to the top.

Wanderlust 35m Very Difficult (1959)
Further right the wall becomes shorter and much more broken. Climb the crack to its end, then traverse left and up to the top.

A veritable profusion of eliminates have been squeezed into every available piece of rock on this crag. Only the above are considered to be independent enough for inclusion in full. The centre of the slab 50 metres right of the main crag has been climbed at VS 4c (**Stretcher Lower**, 1969). There is also a small sheltered and very hidden crag on the ridge above this slab, with a number of routes on a slabby face and a good easy bouldering traverse opposite – **The Traverse of the Bogs**. Midway between Scimitar and Upper Scimitar Buttresses lies **Epileptic in a Bathtub**, 10m E3 5c (1988) following a small groove then a left-slanting diagonal line up a slab.

SCIMITAR UPPER BUTTRESS

This is the steep isolated gritstone-like slab 150 metres up the ridge from the left end of the lower crag. All three routes are unprotected, their difficulty dependent on how high the cruxes are.

Sweet Little Mystery 10m E4 6a * (1984)
From the bottom left end of the crag, ascend diagonally rightwards to a steepening. Make an awkward step up to a good break and finish directly.

Jahu 10m E6 6a *** (1984)
Climb the right-trending scoop in the centre of the slab in its entirety. Very thin and committing.

Where the Mood Takes Me 10m E5 6a * (1984)
Start at a thin crack on the right side of the crag. Climb up to a flat hold, stand awkwardly on this, then move up and slightly right to finish.

A poorer line up the left edge of the buttress, **Jesus Christ Come On Down** (1986) has been climbed, with grades quoted varying from VS to E2 5b.

BISTRO BUTTRESS

Hidden away from sight from the general Polldubh area, this steep slab with a Caledonian pine on top, sits just above a slight col behind the Mam Beag spur. It is actually about 500 metres right of Waterfall Crag (described with those buttresses on the upper tier) and at the same level. The best approach is from Upper Scimitar Buttress across the flat ground heading direct towards the crag.

Gregory's Crack   15m   HVS 5a   (1985)
Climb the crack at the left edge of the buttress.

Self Control   17m   E3 6a *   (1985)
Start in the centre of the slab. Make hard moves over the overhang, then move right to gain a diagonal crack. Move left to a vertical crack and go up this to an easy slab.

Cool Cookie   18m   E1 5a *   (1985)
Climb the curving crack line past the sapling, with some thin moves to a gain ledge, then continue by an easy slab to the top.

Winter Blues   20m   E2 5c *   (1985)
The blunt nose on the right of the slab. Start up a thin crack in the nose, crossing three horizontal breaks. Finish to the right of Cool Cookie and ignore the temptation to step into that route.

UPPER POLLDUBH

The crags of Upper Polldubh are situated on the southern slope of Carn Dearg (South) of Ben Nevis just above Am Mam Buidhe, (that is above Polldubh) at a height of 500 metres. They are mostly south-west facing. The area is best approached *via* the top of Am Mam Buidhe (Map Ref 154 692). From the bridge at the Lower Falls at Achriabhach, follow the ridge left of all the crags, or more interestingly, by linking climbs on Polldubh. The buttresses are described from right to left, in the direction that the crags would be encountered from the triple summits of Am Mam Buidhe.

SADDLE CRAG   (Map Ref 154 693)

This is the buttress nearest to the summit of Am Mam Buidhe, 200 metres north of the top, just across the small saddle. It is formed by a ridge on the left, with a groove cutting an easy-angled slab to the right of its upper part. Further right the crag becomes steeper forming a wall decreasing in height.

Comeback   45m   Mild Severe   (1996)
Follow a direct line up the pillar 5 metres left of Chick.

Gnork   45m   Hard Severe *   (1996)
Climb a direct line on steep ribs and grooves to the left of Chick.

Chick   45m   Difficult   (1972)
Climb the ridge on the left throughout. There are harder variations further right.

Penguin   30m   Moderate   (1970)
The slabby gully on the upper left of the crag leads into a final groove with several harder finishes.

Seal   35m   Very Difficult *   (1970)
Start below a short wall 5 metres right of and below Penguin. Climb to a ledge, then continue by a groove/crack leading to easier ground and a final mantelshelf.

Albatross   25m   Difficult *   (1970)
The groove between Pinguin and Seal leads to a short final wall which is climb on the left.

Pinguin   25m   Difficult   (1970)
Start below a groove 8 metres right of Seal. Climb up to the groove and exit from it at an overhang. Continue directly above.

Fossil Bluff   25m   Difficult   (1970)
Climb the quartz-studded wall on the right face, finishing by a right-slanting crack.

Hoteye   25m   Difficult   (1970s)
Start right of Fossil Bluff and climb direct to a line of holds trending diagonally right, or gain these from the right.

ROUNDED CRAG

This crag is located above and 70 metres north-west of Saddle Crag. The buttress is formed by a half-dome shaped 30m slabby wall flanked by gullies on either side. The rock is particularly rough and solid, providing the best climbing on Upper Polldubh.

Coryza   35m   Difficult   (1976)
Start at the leftmost rocks. Traverse right above a grassy patch at 8m and continue directly above.

Acceber   25m   Severe *   (1976)
Climb steeply by the leftmost crack to a beautiful slabby wall. Finish by a short crack above a ledge.

Singer   35m   Severe *   (1974)
Gain a ledge and follow the second right-trending crack for 4m, then move delicately left and up. Cross a ledge, then finish between two cracks.

Omalegs   35m   Severe *   (1974)
Start below the left end of the bow-shaped overhang. Go up past it on the left, then move right and go up to a ledge. Climb the final steepening 4 metres left of the finishing groove of Blow.

Blue Lace   35m   Mild VS 4b **   (1976)
Start below the bow-shaped bulge and cross it at its centre to reach the slabs above. Climb the final steepening by a crack.

Blow   35m   Difficult   (1970)
Start directly below the groove at the top, just right of the centre of the crag. Trend right past the bow-shaped overhang and finish up the groove, or the crack in its right wall.

Ord   35m   Difficult   (1974)
Go straight up to less steep ground near the right end of the crag, then continue by the leftmost of two left-trending cracks.

GULLY CRAG

This lies midway between Rounded Crag and Boulder Buttress, about 50 metres west of Rounded Crag and slightly higher. It is flanked by gullies and is formed by two steep ribs left of and below an easy-angled slab. Descend to the right across the flanking gully towards Rounded Crag.

Achdalieu   60m   Difficult   (1970s)
Start 15m up and right from the left-hand flanking gully, and follow the stepped ridge throughout.

Pink Plastic Pig   55m   Very Difficult   (1975)
Start at the leftmost of the two ribs. Move up left to a crack which leads over two steepenings. The second, slightly easier crack further left can also be climbed.

Staythere   55m   Mild Severe   (1974)
Follow the left-hand rib to the left of a vegetatious groove throughout. Either walk off right across the slab of Sheslept, or finish up that route.

Hyphen   55m   Difficult   (1973)
Climb the right-hand rib.

Sheslept   80m   Difficult   (1974)
Start below the large upper slab on the right side of the crag. Climb the rib right of a recess with a small tree, then go up an easy slab and move rightwards up a wall to gain the upper slab near the right edge. Climb anywhere above.

Gaers   15m   Difficult   (1970s)
This is the grassy groove between Sheslept and Cracians.

Sky Pilot, High Crag, Glen Nevis   (Climber, Dave Cuthbertson)

Cracians   35m   Very Difficult   (1970s)
Climb the steep rib left of Sheslept, then continue by either of the two cracked grooves to join the slab.

BOULDER BUTTRESS   *(Map Ref 152 695)*

This is situated a further 70 metres slightly down and along to the north-west of Gully Crag, and just beyond a prominent gully. The buttress presents slabby ribs topped by a large boulder and large slabs on the right, together with a copious amount of vegetation. The best way off is towards the left of the crag.

Schnooful   60m   Difficult   (1975)
Climb the rib on the left of the big boulder halfway up *via* grooves for the first pitch, then continue by right-angled diedres and short steps.

Clach   55m   Mild VS **   (1974)
1. 20m 4b   Start up the left-hand of two pillars, then climb to a steepening crack to a ledge.
2. 35m 4b   Climb the centre of the slab, keeping to the right on the upper section to a huge perched block. Finish by either of the adjoining routes.

Schnooks   90m   Very Difficult   (1975)
1. 20m   Start at the right-hand of the two lowest tongues. Go up right, then move left and follow easy slabs rightwards to a ledge.
2. 35m   Continue easily trending left, then go right across a grassy rake to the leftmost lowest rocks of the slab of Airlift.
3. 35m   Climb a 6m vertical rib, then continue more easily by a series of slabs and grooves.

Airlift   90m   Difficult *   (1972)
1. 20m   Follow a slab rib on the right of the crag to a sloping terrace.
2. 35m   Climb the centre of the narrowing slab to a steep step.
3. 35m   Cross the step and climb directly up the large final slab to finish by a small groove.

Windfall   80m   Moderate   (1970s)
Follow a rib 12 metres left of Airlift, then go right to a narrow slab. Climb this and finish leftwards up the final slab.

TWIN BUTTRESS

This is the most westerly and lowest of all the crags at Upper Polldubh. It is the most conspicuous buttress in this area, divided by a prominent central gully. The left-hand and lower sector is interrupted by a mid-height terrace, whilst the right-hand sector is formed by superb slabs above a steep wall. The crags are only 20 minutes above Creag an Fhithich Mor, and can either be approached from that direction, or by the route described on p.81.

Travellin' Man, Gorge Crag, Glen Nevis   (Climber, Ian Sherrington)

Tamoira   60m   Severe   (1976)
A right-leaning line starting at an awkward small groove at the lowest point, left of the central gully.

Dogsway   35m   Moderate   (1976)
The rib to the left of the central gully. The first canine first ascent hereabouts.

Middlelast   70m   Hard Severe **   (1975)
Start 10m up and right from the central gully.
1. 20m   Climb the steep wall leftwards to heather. Move up the clean slab above, keeping left of another heather area, then go right to belay at a small tree.
2. 35m   Go back left onto a slab and climb up for 10m until level with a small tree on the far right of the central slab. Traverse horizontally across to reach a recess just above the tree.
3. 15m   Traverse further right and follow a superb slabby wall 4 metres right of Samantha to easier steps above. Scrambling remains.

Cigol   45m   Severe   (1975)
Continue from the first stance on Middlelast, initially bearing left then right.

Samantha   40m   Severe   (1975)
Start below a fault on the far right. Move up past a heather ledge and a vertical section, then go along the fault. Scramble to finish.

Banns   40m   Mild VS 4b **   (1976)
Start in the gully right of the main crag. Climb the steep wall, moving left to a horizontal crack at the edge. The thin slab immediately left of the rounded edge leads past some short steps to the top.

Rump   35m   Moderate   (1976)
Climb the rib on the far right.

CAR PARK AREA

Between Polldubh and the carpark at the end of the road there are a number of crags which are all, with the exception of the small Barrel Buttress, on the lower slopes of Sgurr a' Mhaim on the south side of the road. Whale Rock is the first to come into view across the river, from the point where the road passes under a pair of distinctive Scots pines. About 100 metres beyond the twin pines, Barrel Buttress can be seen on the left of the road. Further on, opposite the carpark, lies (unsurprisingly) carpark Crag itself. Rising for some 60m, this is the highest, most continuously steep crag in the glen. Below and right of this is Creag Uamh Shomhairle (Samuel's Cave Crag), the name referring to a wide overhung gully affair at its left-hand edge. There are also a number of less obvious buttresses scattered across the hillside, not all of which have been climbed upon to date, and at least some would repay further investigation.

   To get to the crags across the River Nevis without getting wet feet, park at the layby next to a wooden bridge across the river about 1.6km beyond the bridge

GLEN NEVIS
Car Park Area

1 Whale Rock
2 Porpoise Rock
3 Creag Uamh Shomhairle
4 Boot Hill Crag

5 Buccaneer Crag
6 The Bog Wall
7 Phantom Crag
8 Car Park Crag

over the lower falls at Achriabhach (Map Ref 158 164). This is near the base of Mam Beag, a couple of hundred metres before the road passes under the twin Scot's pines. Approximate approach times are 5-10 minutes for Whale Rock, Porpoise Rock and Creag Uamh Shomhairle, 20 minutes for Boot Hill and 25-30 minutes for Phantom Crag, Buccaneer Crag, The Bog Wall and carpark Crag.

BARREL BUTTRESS   (Map Ref 160 687)

Up the slope on the left from where the road passes underneath the Scot's pines, is a small distinctively-shaped south-west facing buttress with an even smaller Scot's pine growing on top. Approach direct, crossing the old drovers' track halfway up the slope.

The Beer Hunter   10m   E4 6b *   (1985)
Gain the thin crack directly below the tree with some hard bouldery initial moves. Continue to a belay and lower-off.

A-Propa-Kiss Now   10m   E2 6a   (1985)
Climb the diagonal fault, starting at the same point as the previous route. A solo.

WHALE ROCK   (Map Ref 163 684)

The main north-west facing frontal wall of this excellent crag is split by the central widening crack of Earthstrip, with a shorter more broken area of rock left of a heather-filled gully. Steepening and sweeping round to the right, it forms a series of discontinuous scoops, with striking twin ragged cracks up the blunt prow. To approach, cross the river at the bridge, then cross the stream (Allt an t-Snaig) low down (near where it joins the river) and follow a diagonal line direct to the crag. Descent is possible by steep ground either side of the crag.

The first three routes are on the shorter more broken slabs left of the heather gully.

1   Dirty Tongue   20m   Very Difficult   (1984)
Start left of a forked birch, follow dark-coloured rock to a ledge, then climb the cracks above.

2   Big Mickey   20m   Hard Severe   (1984)
Follow the line behind the birch to the ledge, then climb a steep crack past a flake to the top.

3   Stretcher Case   20m   VS 4c   (1984)
Start 3 metres left of the heathery gully. Go straight up to a left-trending ramp, then move up and right into a niche. Exit right.

4   The Fascination Trap   25m   E1 5c *   (1984)
This route follows the right-slanting diagonal line across the wall, with a bouldery start. Just right of the heather gully is a thin crack. Climb this to ledges, then follow the obvious slightly rising traverse line, with a further hard move across the slab to reach good holds leading into Earthstrip. Continue in the same line to the top right of the crag. It is possible to start further to the left at 5b.

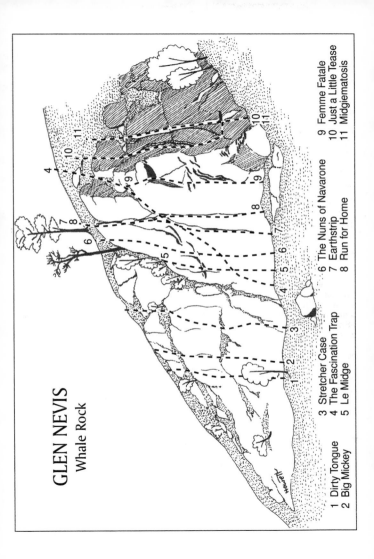

GLEN NEVIS
Whale Rock

1 Dirty Tongue
2 Big Mickey
3 Stretcher Case
4 The Fascination Trap
5 Le Midge

6 The Nuns of Navarone
7 Earthstrip
8 Run for Home

9 Femme Fatale
10 Just a Little Tease
11 Midgiematosis

5   Le Midge   20m   E3 6b *   (1984)
Directly below a dead pine on the top, and just right of the gully, is a thin hanging crack. Start directly below the crack. Climb the slab to broken ledges, then follow the crack above.

6   The Nuns of Navarone   20m   E5 6c *   (1987)
The centre of the slab between the gully and the widening crack of Earthstrip contains a faint bulging crack at about mid-height. Climb direct up the slab to the crack, then climb past a poor peg runner directly and with difficulty. Weave around the lichen to finish.

A wandering line, **Wiggly Worms** (E2 5c, 1986) avoids the main challenge taken by the previous line by wiggling way over right and back left.

7   Earthstrip   20m   E2 5c **   (1983)
The central, widening crack line gives excellent sustained climbing, easing towards the top.

8   Run for Home   20m   E5 6a **   (1985)
This route presents thin sustained climbing on small edges up the diagonal hairline cracks starting 3 metres right of Earthstrip, joining that route at half-height. Many small RPs are required.

9   Femme Fatale   25m   E7/8 6c ***   (1986)
Very serious and technical climbing up the bulging scoops in the steepest section of the crag. Pull directly over the first bulge with difficulty (runners used in opposition to protect this; a peg on the ledge on the left, and small RPs low down in a crack on the right) and reach a no-hands rest and a skyhook placement in the first scoop. Move right and blindly place an HB2 and an HB1 in the thin crack to the right. Move up rightwards into the second scoop to two peg runners, and follow the diagonal crack out left to the top.

10   Just a Little Tease   25m   E5 6b ***   (1984)
Excellent climbing up the scoop and twin cracks at the point where the crag bends around the hillside. Place a high runner on the right, and a second, opposing runner in the boulder at the foot of the previous route. Make difficult moves across the scoop to gain good holds and protection. Attain a standing position on the good hold (rest possible) and climb the cracks to the top.

11   Midgiematosis   25m   E2 5c *   (1985)
The groove and cracks up the right wall of the crag, just right of Just a Little Tease. Start up that route and continue straight up to a ledge below the top. Finish with a mantelshelf just right of the final crack.

12   Strategic Midge Limitation Talks   25m   E3 5c * (1988)
Further up the hillside from the right side of Whale Rock is a short red-coloured wall with a thin crack in the centre, and a Caledonian pine sapling sprouting halfway up this. Follow the crack, climbing through the sapling with interest to pull slightly left onto a slab at the top. Climb easily rightwards up this to finish.

PORPOISE ROCK   (Map Ref 165 685)

This north-west facing crag is situated a couple of hundred metres further up the glen, and at a slightly lower level than Whale Rock. It is distinguished by a prominent notched slab, obvious from the road. To approach, cross the river at the bridge, then follow the path parallel to the river for a couple of hundred metres, before cutting up the hillside.

No Porpoise   35m   VS 5a   (1991)
Climb directly up the notched slab following flared cracks past a small pine to a ledge at 25m. The protection is good after a steep start. Climb up the back wall to a tree belay.

CREAG UAMH SHOMHAIRLE   (Map Ref 170 689)

Better, though incorrectly known as Evening Crag, this is the small buttress low down on the hillside, facing north-west directly opposite the carpark at the end of the road. Approach directly from the carpark, crossing the river at a weir or by boulder hopping if the water level is suitably low. Otherwise, especially after heavy snow-melt in the spring, cross the river by the footbridge about a kilometre further downstream, as for Whale Rock.

Lord of the Midges   20m   E5 5c *   (1985)
An eponymous route – short and mean. Protection is not over-abundant. It follows a slightly left-trending line up the wall left of the central groove line. Start up the first few moves of the central groove of Choc Ice, then pull left to a large flake and a small sapling. Climb the wall above, heading for good holds near the arete, then move right and go straight up the wall to finish past good flake holds and an awkward mantelshelf.

Choc Ice   20m   E1 5c *   (1983)
The centre of the crag is split by a shallow groove line. Pull over the initial overhang (crux) and continue up the groove, exiting left.

Pagan Love Song   20m   HVS 5b   (1984)
Start at a shorter, undercut groove 3 metres right of the more prominent Choc Ice groove. Climb the groove to a holly below a small overhang, then climb the crack through this.

Take Two   20m   HVS 5a *   (1983)
This route takes the short steep crack in the right wall of the crag.

One further line has been added at Very Difficult, following a line across the right side of the wall.

BOOT HILL CRAG   (Map Ref 168 686)

This 50m north-west facing crag is mostly broken and disjointed, and is situated diagonally up and right from Creag Uamh Shomhairle. High up in the centre of the buttress is a steep face with a series of diagonal cracks and a blunt arete. Approach as for Whale Rock, continuing towards Creag Uamh Shomhairle, then head directly up the hillside. Both routes start by scrambling up a small gully into an elevated eyrie below the steepest central section.

Tectonic Man   30m   E4 6a *   (1988)
Layback up a large precarious hanging flake to gain a ledge below the overhanging headwall. Follow a series of cracks out right to gain a left-trending crack with difficulty. Move right along the flake crack, make a long reach to the arete and finish up this.

Vertigo   30m   HVS 5a   (1988)
Climb the same hanging flake, then trend left up slabs and ledges into a short corner on the right.

BUCCANEER CRAG   (Map Ref 168 684)

This is a long north-west facing escarpment-like crag lying near the upper limit of the crags on the hill above and right of carpark Crag and almost directly above Whale Rock. The crag is characterised by an impressive higher section in the centre containing a hanging crack. There is scope for development for those with the energy for the slog up. To approach, park at the layby next to the bridge, as for Whale Rock, and approach up the right bank of the Allt an t-Snaig to reach a small U-shaped valley just beyond a fine stand of mature Scot's pines. Cross the stream and cut up the small chasm with a small rock bluff on its right. This levels out, with the crag coming into view on the right after a couple of hundred metres. The climbs are described left to right.

Hard Station   20m   E5 6a *   (1985)
The clean wall with a hanging crack in the centre of the crag. Climb flakes strenuously rightwards to the base of the hanging crack. Pull over the bulge with hard stretchy moves to reach better holds, then continue more easily up the fine crack to the top.

Pieces of Eight   15m   E1 5b   (1987)
Start beneath cracks 6 metres right of Hard Station. Follow a bulging crack to a ledge and finish by either of two obvious crack lines at a similar standard.

Altitude Sickness   15m   E2 5c   (1988)
Climb the short wide vertical crack at the right-hand side of the face.

THE BOG WALL   (Map Ref 169 694)

About 5 minutes above and left of Buccaneer Crag is a short north-west facing wall above a bog. There are two routes. **Midsummer Nightmare** (E3 6a, 1988) takes the wall starting just right of the prominent crack, and **Bog Crack** (E1 5b, 1988) goes up the crack.

PHANTOM CRAG (Map Ref 168 685)

This is another small north-west facing crag, almost hidden in the jungle somewhere in the centre of the hillside (hence the name?). Approach as for Buccaneer Crag, then continue along the plateau for a couple of hundred metres before descending a good path to the base of the crag.

The First Cut   25m   E6 6b **   (1988)
The crescent-shaped finger-crack splitting the right side of the crag provides a ferocious test-piece. Very well protected, it gives a powerful and sustained exercise in finger jamming despite its meagre length.

CAR PARK CRAG (Map Ref 172 684)

The large north-west facing buttress overlooking the carpark gives the highest vertical face of any of the crags in the glen, though others give longer slabbier routes separated by grassy ledges. Approach directly from the carpark, crossing the river at a weir, or by boulder hopping if the water level is suitably low. If the water level is too high, cross the river by the footbridge about a kilometre further downstream, as for Whale Rock. The crag can also be reached from Steall meadow, by crossing the river at the head of the gorge.

Ex-Lax   20m   E4 6a *   (1988)
This route tackles the obvious blunt arete on the small buttress to the left of the main crag. Start on the right of the arete at a thin crack. Climb up and left to a small ledge and a poor peg. Move up and slightly left, then go right to a hidden hold. Climb direct past a second peg runner to the top.

Mouseface   45m   VS 4c   (1970/76)
Climb the line up the centre of the large mossy slab on the left of the main section of the crag to a steepening. Climb this to the conspicuous break, entered from the right, and continue to the top.

Forestwalk   60m   Very Difficult   (1960s)
A horticultural ramble up the left edge of the slender clean buttress. Aptly named.

1   Restless Natives   90m   E5 **   (1988)
Fine climbing up the deceptive grooves in the clean buttress at the left end of the crag. Start below a small niche about 5m up the wall.
1. 25m 6a   Climb directly into the niche (tied-down skyhook and RP under the overlap). Make hard moves up and right to better holds at the base of the slender bottomless groove. Climb this and the continuation to pull onto a crack on the slab with better holds. Nut belay on a small ledge.
2. 25m 6a   Continue up the crack in the slab to reach an obvious line of holds leading out right into the centre of the prow. Follow this to a ledge (poor nuts above). Pull up the bulging tower above to the lip of the overlap. Move through this slightly leftwards onto the bald slab (crux), and go up this to a grass ledge.
3. 40m 5a   Finish up the right-trending rib. Block belay well back.

2 Diagonal 60m Hard Severe (1960s)
Climb the obvious diagonal line rightwards to a tree belay near the top, then go straight up to finish.

3 The Strip 90m VS (1971)
1. 20m 4c Follow Diagonal to a niche with trees and continue to a holly.
2. 35m 5a Move left and go up into a corner which leads to a ledge on the right. Move right a few metres, then climb a vertical groove, exiting left to a bay with trees.
3. 35m 4a Continue up the rib above, moving left at 15m, with scope for variation above.

4 Gobstopper Groove 60m E2 ** (1981)
Start at the right-hand side of a large tilted roof, 12 metres right of Diagonal.
1. 35m 5b Climb the crack and groove into a large depression. Exit from this on the right and go up a quartz band to a terrace.
2. 25m 5c Move onto the rib on the left and climb it by a shallow groove and thin crack. Steep, well situated climbing.

5 The Mint 60m E2 * (1981)
Steep well protected crack climbing.
1. 35m 5c Climb a right-trending crack 5 metres right of Gobstopper Groove to some small trees. Step left and follow the steep left-slanting crack to the terrace.
2. 25m 5c Finish up the top pitch of Gobstopper Groove.

6 Sunset Boulevard 85m Severe (1960)
Start 6 metres right of The Mint.
1. 35m Climb a crack for 3m, then traverse left into a scoop. Move up and left to a holly, then go rightwards through the top of the scoop to a terrace.
2. 20m Climb the chimney above and traverse right to trees in an overhung bay.
3. 30m Go right to a corner and move round the rib on the right to finish by a vegetated chimney.

7 Quality Street 70m E3 *** (1970/81)
Superb, sustained and well protected climbing up the tramline cracks in the centre of the crag. High in the grade.
1. 40m 6a Start directly beneath the cracks at an inset block. Climb thin cracks on the right side of the block, then move up to gain the twin cracks. Follow the left-hand crack, then transfer to the one on the right and go up this to the base of a ramp leading into a grassy gully. Make a bold step out right into a shallow left-facing groove. Continue up this to easier ground and a small ledge. Nut belay.
2. 30m 5a Finish up the right-facing corner.

8 Bounty Hunters 75m E2 * (1981)
1. 45m 5c Climb the open corner 6 metres right of Quality Street, moving leftwards at its top to the stance on Quality Street.
2. 30m 5a Finish up Quality Street.

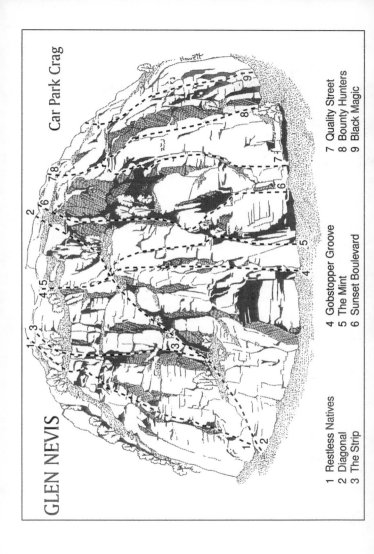

GLEN NEVIS

Car Park Crag

Howett

1 Restless Natives
2 Diagonal
3 The Strip
4 Gobstopper Groove
5 The Mint
6 Sunset Boulevard
7 Quality Street
8 Bounty Hunters
9 Black Magic

9 Black Magic 60m E2 (1981)
1. 35m 5c Climb a shallow left-facing corner 5 metres right of Bounty Hunters, then follow a faint crack line to easier-angled rock leading to a heather ledge and a small tree.
2. 30m 4c Vegetated rock leads to the top.

10 Sundowner 60m Severe (1960)
Start from a tree near the far right side of the crag.
1. 25m Climb leftwards, then go up to a terrace.
2. 23m Climb diagonally rightwards and go up a steep wall. Move left along a ledge and climb a groove to a flake.
3. 12m Continue up the slab on the right and finish up the wall above.

STEALL AREA

This section contains all the crags within the gorge of Eas an Tuill, those scattered on the hillside (Meall Cumhann) above the east side of the gorge, and those in and around the Steall meadows. All are approached from the carpark at the end of the road. Both Gorge Crag (nestling in the trees) and Wave Buttress (on the open hillside directly above, with a prominent quartz patch in the centre) can be clearly seen from the carpark, as can a number of the other crags on this hillside.

The Nevis Gorge, Eas an Tuill, has been described as one of the finest examples of its kind in Britain: 'Taken alone it is without counterpart in this country, its Himalayan character arises from a peculiar combination of cliff and woodland and water, which is not repeated elsewhere in Britain.' (W.H.Murray, *Highland Landscape*, 1962). From the carpark at the road end, an excellent path contours the wooded slopes above the river. The gorge itself extends for about 1½km, the river level falling some 130m in that distance. The rocky side walls are covered in native pine, birch, oak and rowan. Above the gorge the scene changes to one of Arcadian grandeur, the transition to flat meadow land is sudden and truly stunning.

GORGE CRAG   (Map Ref 175 691)

This is the first crag encountered along the path through the gorge, well seen amongst the trees from the carpark. A slabby west-facing left wall sweeps round into a steep and imposing frontal face, with a couple of corner systems bounding the right side. The crag squats in the trees about 50 metres above the path, 10 minutes walk from the carpark. Descend from the routes either by abseil from trees at the top of Plague of Blazes and Travellin' Man, or contour right from the top of the crag and descend a steep slab just before a stream.
The first two routes are located on a steep slab up and left of the main crag.

Acappella 10m E3 6a (1987)
This is the thin crack line near the left edge of the slab.

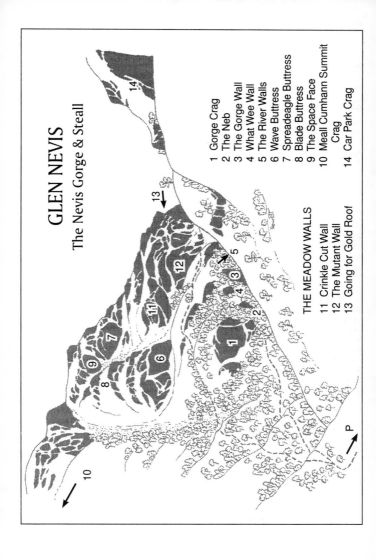

GLEN NEVIS
The Nevis Gorge & Steall

1 Gorge Crag
2 The Neb
3 The Gorge Wall
4 What Wee Wall
5 The River Walls
6 Wave Buttress
7 Spreadeagle Buttress
8 Blade Buttress
9 The Space Face
10 Meall Cumhann Summit Crag
14 Car Park Crag

THE MEADOW WALLS

11 Crinkle Cut Wall
12 The Mutant Wall
13 Going for Gold Roof

Mother's Day   12m   E4 6a *   (1984)
A serious route with delicate and committing climbing. Start 3 metres right of the
lowest rocks. Climb easily for 3m (protection can be arranged in a crack further
up and right). Move up and left and climb a thin incipient crack to reach the
left-hand edge of a grassy ledge. Continue easily up wall above.

The following routes are up the slabby side wall of the crag proper.

1   Pupil Power   35m   Severe *   (1982)
Climb the obvious left-trending stairway at the left side of the slab.

2   Plague of Blazes   30m   E2 5b ***   (1982)
An excellent and popular route with varied, interesting climbing. Start 5m up and
left from the toe of the crag, at the left-hand of two thin crack systems running up
the slab. Follow the zigzag crack for 12m to a flake. Move left, then go up into a
recess. Step right and climb the slab to the final wall. Pull up this on good holds.

A parallel line up the slab to the left has been climbed (**Solstice**, E2 5c,
1988). The next routes climb the grooves in the arete between the two faces.

3   In the Groove   40m   E3 **   (1982/83)
Another good route with an awkward finish.
1. 15m 5b   Climb the diagonal thin cracks in the right side of the slab. The
shorter, right-hand crack in the slab above leads to a ledge.
2. 25m 5c   Climb the groove above, then trend right into a subsidiary
right-hand groove on the frontal face. Exposed moves past an obvious block
lead to a potentially inelegant roll onto the slab above. Easier climbing up the
ramp above leads rightwards to the top.

4   Travellin' Man   35m   E2 ***   (1982)
The groove system splitting the rib between the left-hand and front face
provides an outstanding climb which challenges both technique and the ability
to place protection.
1. 12m 5b   Climb the strenuous cracked groove just right of the toe of the
buttress to a ledge and belay.
2. 24m 5c   Follow the right-slanting groove above until it is possible to step left
(crux) to reach a crack in the slab. Climb this and finish up the easy ramp above.
Variation Finish: **Driving Ambition**   E2 5c   (1987)
Climb the wall where the last two routes diverge to gain a niche. Finish up the ramp.

5   Cosmopolitan   30m   E5 ***   (1982)
The original and best line on the crag gives a fierce, well protected technical
test-piece. Start below and left of a hanging left-facing groove in the centre of
the overhanging wall.
1. 15m 6a   A bouldery start leads to a handrail leading out right to the groove.
Follow this, exiting out rightwards to a spacious ledge and belay.
2. 15m 6b   Gain the thin diagonal crack from the right with a hard initial move,
then go up to good holds just below the top. Brilliant.

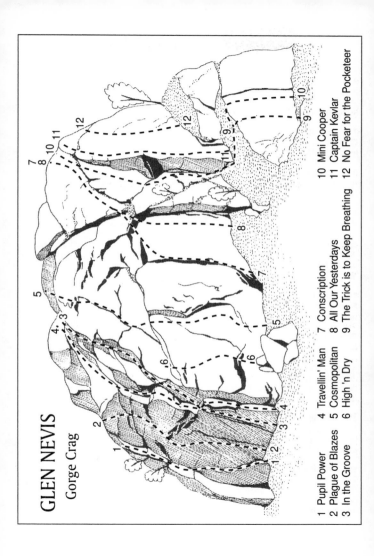

GLEN NEVIS
Gorge Crag

1 Pupil Power   4 Travellin' Man   7 Conscription   10 Mini Cooper
2 Plague of Blazes   5 Cosmopolitan   8 All Our Yesterdays   11 Captain Kevlar
3 In the Groove   6 High 'n Dry   9 The Trick is to Keep Breathing   12 No Fear for the Pocketeer

6   High 'n Dry   15m   E3 6a *   (1982)
An alternative first pitch to Cosmopolitan. Start atop a rounded boulder, just to the left of the normal start. Climb directly up to a short crack. Arrange protection in this, and follow a line of holds leftwards below this to a small niche and better holds leading to the left end of the ledge.

7   Conscription   45m   E1 5b *   (1982)
Climb the obvious wide crack on the left wall of the corner, then exit right onto a ledge and finish up an easy flake.

8   All Our Yesterdays   40m   E1 5b **   (1982)
A good, well protected climb which often stays dry even in the rain. Climb the corner crack, exiting right to finish up the easy flake as for Conscription.

9   The Trick is to Keep Breathing   15m   E5 6a *   (1996)
Very serious climbing up the quartz wall just left of the groove of Mini Cooper. Start 3 metres left of that route, below a short finger crack. Climb easily up the crack to a heather ledge on the left. Step up right onto the wall and ascend directly up the left side of the blunt arete to good holds. Pull out right to finish more easily to a tree belay. Many skyhook placements were used, mainly on quartz.

10   Mini Cooper   40m   HVS *   (1983)
Start at the foot of the groove near the left side of a lower buttress below and right of the main crag.
1. 15m 5a   Gain the groove by some steep moves, then go up to the terrace.
2. 25m 5b   The steepening corner leads to the top of the flake on the previous two routes.

   Two poorer lines have been climbed on the right side of the lower tier, about 20 metres right of Mini Cooper. **The Cubby Hole** (HVS 5b, 1983) goes up to the diagonal fault, then takes the vertical crack. The wall right of the dirty corner, a few metres further right, is taken by the unpleasant **No Name** (Severe, 1983).

11   Captain Kevlar   20m   E4 5c *   (1985)
This route takes the square-cut arete at the right end of the main crag. Bridge up between the wall and the corner for a few metres to gain holds on the wall (RP3 at 5m). Continue up the right side of the arete all the way.

12   No Fear for the Pocketeer   10m   E5 6a *   (1986)
This short but hard route tackles the pocketed wall just before the crag disappears into the hillside. Step left onto a quartz hold and go up to a good pocket at mid-height. Make hard moves above this to pull onto the small ledge on the right. Finish up the easy slab above.

THE NEB   (Map Ref 175 690)

The next obvious neb of rock abuts the path and faces west-south-west below the right end of Gorge Crag, just before reaching The Gorge Wall.

If Looks Could Kill   20m   E5 6b **   (1985)
Bold and technical with sparse protection. Start on the right. Trend left up the wall to the roof, pull over, then go left along a break to a good foot ledge. Go up right on good sidepulls to better holds. Make hard moves slightly right onto the slab and continue to the top.

THE GORGE WALL   (Map Ref 175 690)

This buttress faces west-south-west and has a striking arching crack line above a roof system, and an innocuous looking crack line leading to it. Further right beyond another crack system the crag forms a corner before deteriorating into the hillside. Descent is either by abseil, or down either side of the crag, depending on the route.

Chimera   30m   E4 6a **   (1985)
The overhung left arete. Climb the initial unprotected arete to gain better holds and protection in the upper groove. Follow this strenuously and make a difficult exit leftwards in a fine position.

The Gallery   30m   E4 6a *   (1986)
The striking diagonal crack line across the crag is unfortunately slow to dry. Start up the arete, as for Chimera, to gain the crack and follow it across the wall with increasing difficulty to an exposed final pull round the bulges.

Easy Pickings   30m   E4 6a ***   (1985)
The deceptive looking crack line in the rib a few metres right of the arete. Climb the crack with hard moves to reach a resting place. Move up and left to swing onto a ramp. From the top of this, a hard mantel leads to a thin slab to finish.

Power in the Darkness   20m   E1 5c *   (1984)
This route follows the steep jam crack with a tree in it.

Darkness on the Edge of Town   25m   E1 5b   (1984)
A couple of metres left of the right-hand edge of the crag is a thin crack leading into a V-groove. Follow this to a tree at the base of a deeper groove, then climb the very thin crack in the right wall of the groove to the top.

WHAT WEE WALL

Left of the top of The Gorge Wall is a small rectangular wall, composed of some of the roughest rock in the glen. Approach up the open gully at the left side of Gorge Wall.

Carpe Diem   15m   E5 6a   (1991)
Serious fingery climbing. Start on the right side of the wall at a tiny ramp feature. Climb this to a tiny overlap where an assortment of protection (including

skyhooks) can be arranged. Make a hard move to a slightly better hold, then go up to two peg runners. Descend a short way and move leftwards to a good hold at the top of the left-hand ramp line. Easier climbing leads to the final slab.

THE RIVER WALLS   *(Map Ref 175 689)*

These walls are situated on the other side of the river from the path, beginning almost directly opposite The Gorge Wall and continuing leftwards to the head of the gorge. They are composed of steep slabs and walls rising abruptly above the river. The starts of some, or all, of the routes may not be possible to reach if the river is full. The most obvious feature is a prominent steep rectangular hanging slab split by thin vertical cracks, with a shorter, wider, left-trending one on the left. The climbs are described left to right. Descend either by abseil from trees on top, or down the extreme left or right side of the walls.

Sue's Crack   30m   HVS *   (1984)
Start 30 metres upstream from the hanging slab, at a huge water-worn cauldron.
1. 15m 4b   Climb the wide crack past a giant pocket to a ledge.
2. 15m 5b   Follow the left-slanting crack up the slab above.
Direct Start: E1 6a   (1986)
Thrutch through the bulging scoop with overhead protection.

Liquidator   12m   E1 5b **   (1985)
A logical start to Gawping Grockles. Start from the boulder choke at the bottom left of the buttress rising from the water. Traverse rightwards across a scoop to the foot of the left-trending hand crack. Follow this to a belay on the grass gangway above.

Gawping Grockles   35m   E2 *   (1984)
Cross the river at the boulder choke, and scramble up through vegetation to a wide crack.
1. 25m 5c   Climb the crack to a ledge, then make a rising traverse right (difficult to protect) to a crack which leads to a tree belay.
2. 10m 5b   Continue up the spidery crack line in the headwall.

Aquarian Rebels   25m   E4 6a ***   (1985)
Excellent climbing up the thin cracks in the centre of the slab. Start from the boulder choke, as for Liquidator, and cross the scoop to gain the left-trending crack. Arrange protection a short way up this, then step back down and traverse hard right to follow thin cracks (not easy to protect) to a final steep crack. It is possible to stay higher in the crack of Liquidator before stepping right (E3 5c).

The Amusement Arcade   25m   E5 6b ***   (1985)
The line of thin cracks up the right edge of the slab. Start down at the river bed. Climb a pillar of rock for approximately 5m, then move awkwardly left into a scoop and climb the thin crack (nut runner *in situ*) to gain a line of quartz holds leading to a sloping ledge. Climb the cracks in the wall above with difficulty past a peg runner to the top.

Rats in Paradise 20m E5 6b ** (1985)
This route follows the thin crack and slab about 50 metres downstream from the hanging slab, and more or less opposite The Gorge Wall. Gain the ledge at the foot of the route by jumping across the river (crux!). From the ledge, hand traverse left to pull onto the next ledge. Make a difficult move to gain the crack and go up this to the slab (nut runner *in situ*). Make a series of hard pulls rightwards on quartz holds to a rounded ledge. Move left to a horizontal break and climb a thin crack and blunt arete to the top.

Mice on the Riviera 20m E4 6a * (1989)
The short blunt arete right of Rats in Paradise, climbed on its left side. Traverse diagonally across the wall to a ledge on the arete. (protection in the thin crack round on the right). Make some committing moves to gain a good flake and easier ground, and finish as for Rats in Paradise.

WAVE BUTTRESS (Map Ref 176 690)

This excellent crag is clearly visible from the carpark, on the open hillside of Meall Cumhann above and slightly right of Gorge Crag. A south-westerly aspect and a relatively exposed position ensure a fast drying time, and sometimes a midge-free haven when the gorge is unbearable. The crag is generally slabbier than most of the crags hereabouts, and is split into two buttresses by a heather-filled gully. The left-hand buttress has two obvious crack lines: the left-hand one (the line of On the Beach) fades out at a horizontal crack at mid-height while the other is a continuous right-slanting diagonal crack (taken by Crackattack). The right-hand buttress isn't as extensive but is defined by the clean arete of Edgehog.

The approach follows the main path through the gorge into the Steall meadows, then take a steep zigzagging path up the hillside left of the wide open gully, left of the Meadow Walls. Alternatively, the old drovers track, avoiding the precipitous section of the gorge, affords a slightly more direct approach. This branches off left from the tourist path about 150 metres beyond where the path has been blasted across a stream (before a tiny wooden footbridge), and rises initially before contouring around the hillside above the gorge, to link up with the zigzag path from the meadows below Wave Buttress. Descent is either by abseil, or by an indistinct path along the top, crossing the gully with care (easiest low down) and down the right-hand side.

The routes are described from left to right.

1 First Wave 30m E1 5c ** (1982)
The left edge of the crag has a narrow left-slanting ramp with a series of ledges and short walls above. Start at some quartz blotches. Boulder diagonally rightwards to the foot of the ramp, then climb this and follow a direct line to finish up a steep wall on good flakes.

2 Freddie Across the Mersey 30m E5 6a ** (1984)
This route takes a direct line 2 metres left of the vertical crack of On the Beach. Climb boldly up the initial section, with difficult moves to reach the horizontal break, then continue up and pull rightwards into the base of the big scooped groove. Follow this to the top.

3 On the Beach 30m E5 6a *** (1984)
Bold open wall climbing with spaced protection in the upper half. From the pedestal follow the crack line moving slightly rightwards to the horizontal break. Step left and follow the shallow runnel above to better holds at some quartz. Continue more easily above.

4 Jodicus Grotticus 30m E5 6c ** (1984)
A serious lower section up the black pitted wall, followed by a very technical sequence along a diagonal crack above, protected by a peg. Start midway between the two cracks of On the Beach and Crackattack. Trend slightly leftwards to a tiny scoop, then go slightly right to the centre of the small overlap (HB4 on its side, pulling to the left, in the shallow horizontal above). Move up and right into Ground Zero from the small overlap, then traverse back in higher up to gain the peg in the crack. Desperate moves past the peg lead up and left into a scoop. Finish up an easier groove.

5 The Edwardo Shuffle 30m E6 6b * (1985)
A somewhat hybrid route that nonetheless gives very good climbing. It follows Jodicus Grotticus to the small overlap, then steps left and makes thin and committing moves to the horizontal break and RP protection of On the Beach up which it finishes.

6 Jodicus Direct 30m E6 6c *** (1987)
A direct uncompromising line up the wall in the centre of the buttress. Follow Jodicus Grotticus and The Edwardo Shuffle to the horizontal break and RP protection. Climb the scoop above (RP2 on left) to the peg and make desperate moves past this as for the original route, then finish up this. All ascents to date have employed a long sling *in situ* from the peg.

7 Ground Zero 30m E2 5c ** (1983)
Varied open wall climbing, high in the grade with a bold lower section. Start just left of the diagonal crack. Climb directly up the wall past some thin flared cracks, moving slightly right on good holds to the base of a diagonal crack/ramp. Climb the crack in the groove past an awkward bulge, and finish up the quartz staircase above.

8 Crackattack 30m E3 5c *** (1983)
The diagonal crack is well protected, with the crux at the top.

9 The Dark Crystal 30m E5 6a ** (1986)
The hanging flake and intermittent crack in the slab below Crackattack. Start 2 metres right of that route, beneath a prominent quartz blotch. Bouldery moves up the hairline crack lead to a good quartz hold and protection in the quartz

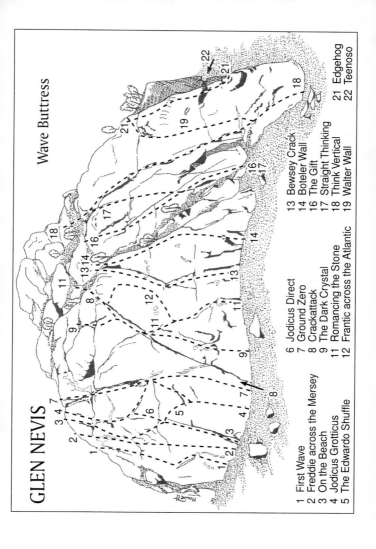

GLEN NEVIS

Wave Buttress

1 First Wave
2 Freddie across the Mersey
3 On the Beach
4 Jodicus Grotticus
5 The Edwardo Shuffle

6 Jodicus Direct
7 Ground Zero
8 Crackattack
9 The Dark Crystal
11 Romancing the Stone
12 Frantic across the Atlantic

13 Bewsey Crack
14 Boteler Wall
16 The Gift
17 Straight Thinking
18 Think Vertical
19 Walter Wall

21 Edgehog
22 Teenoso

crack. Pull right onto a flake and go up to a good flat hold. Attain a standing position on this, and follow the intermittent cracks in the slab above into Crackattack. Gain the scoop to the left of the headwall, from the right, and move up past a rounded break. Pull over onto the easy ramp which leads left to the top of Ground Zero.

10 Psycho Cats 30m E4 6a * (1986)
Start a couple of metres right of the hanging flake of The Dark Crystal at a pink area of rock. Climb steeply on layaway holds to a runner placement in the thin diagonal cracks just to the right. Continue straight up with a hard move to reach good holds which lead to a junction with The Dark Crystal. Continue up this to join Crackattack, and any of the available finishes.

11 Romancing the Stone 30m E5 6a * (1984)
The original line on the slab. Start at a shallow vertical groove midway between two quartz veins, a couple of metres left of the short fading groove of Bewsey Crack. Climb up with the help of the quartz seam. When it disappears, head up and slightly leftwards *via* a blind crack to gain a prominent large flat quartz hold at 10m (dubious protection here). Steady though worrying climbing moving slightly leftwards gains good thin cracks leading to Crackattack.

12 Frantic across the Atlantic 30m E5 6b * (1987)
Good, though escapable climbing. The route follows the first half of Romancing the Stone, before breaking out rightwards and finishing at the same point as Crackattack. From the large quartz hold, a committing series of moves leads rightwards to the lower of two horizontal breaks and an *in situ* nut runner. Technical and fingery climbing directly above leads to a peg. Step left to finish up the last few moves of Crackattack. Bold and technical.

13 Bewsey Crack 30m HVS 5a * (1983)
The shallow fading groove runs into a diagonal crack. Follow this into a sentry box near the top, and exit from this on good holds. ·

14 Boteler Wall 30m E1 5a/b (1983)
Cimb the right-hand of the three short groove lines (poor protection), then take the right edge of the slab to gain the sentry box on Bewsey Crack. Finish up this.

An eliminate has been recorded midway between the last two lines, **A Spaceman Came Travelling** (E2 5b, 1987).

15 Nowhere Near the Sea 45m E5 6a ** (1986)
A girdle of the left-hand section of the crag, going from left to right. Start up First Wave, then move right to gain a horizontal crack. Follow this to good holds and a rest at the vertical crack of On the Beach. Continue with difficulty past a good two-finger pocket (crux) to reach better holds on Ground Zero. Reverse the crux of this and pull out right on good flakes to join Crackattack. Continue traversing at the same level to reach good quartz holds (as for Romancing the Stone), then make a difficult series of moves rightwards to reach the lower of two horizontals and pull into Bewsey Crack. Either finish up this or continue across to the gully.

The following routes are on the right-hand sction of the crag. Two obvious, slightly left-trending crack lines provide the lines of The Gift and Think Vertical respectively, with the even more striking clean cut arete of Edgehog standing out on the right.

16   The Gift   30m   E5 6a *   (1985)
This route takes the line of the diagonal crack just right of the gully. Climb easily at first to a ledge, then with difficulty to a break. Continue up the twin grooves formed by a huge block, then follow the central groove on the right to finish by a tricky mantelshelf. Low in the grade.

17   Straight Thinking   30m   E5 6a **   (1986)
A direct line following a vague crack line running up the steepest part of the buttress, bisecting the crack of The Gift low down. Start just right of the gully. Follow the vertical crack and its continuation, with a hard move to gain a good flat hold. Attain a standing position on this (good break for gear) from where bold climbing up the wall above (crux; crucial Friend round the arete) leads to another break. Teeter up and right to finish at the same point as Think Vertical. Committing climbing on the crux.

18   Think Vertical   30m   E3 6a *   (1983)
A fine natural line, though it also happens to be a natural watercourse, and therefore slow to dry. Start at the lowest point of the buttress, 6 metres right of the gully. Climb cracks leftwards into a right-facing groove. Go up this to a ledge, and climb the steepening groove above (crux) to the top.

19   Walter Wall   30m   E4 6a **   (1984)
Serious though steady wall climbing up the shallow depression in the centre of the wall. Start at the toe of the buttress, as for Think Vertical. Go up this a short way, then move easily right across a scoop to reach good holds above. Climb boldly up the wall with no protection to a good horizontal break and protection. Hard moves past this lead to the 'Walter Wall bellyflop' onto a shelf. Exit rightwards.

20   Washington   35m   E5 6a **   (1985)
Essentially an alternative start and finish to Walter Wall, offering more sustained climbing with well spaced protection; low in the grade. Start just left of the prominent sharp arete of Edgehog. Climb a shallow left-leaning groove to some quartz holds at 6m (runner in the thin crack above). Move left to a shallow groove, then make difficult moves across the wall into the scoop of Walter Wall. Continue up that route, taking in its crux. Instead of traversing right at the top, climb a shallow groove to a bulge, then turn this and go up the slab above moving rightwards to finish.

21   Edgehog   30m   E3 5c ***   (1982)
No prizes for guessing which route this refers to. Gain the arete from the right, and follow it with a hard move past a flange on the left (Friend protection, hard to place) leading to a good resting spot. Continue steadily to a good horizontal

break near the top. Easier climbing leads to a large ledge. It is better protected than first impressions would suggest.

Variation: **The Extended Start** E3 5c (1985)
This lengthens the climbing by a further 8m or so by starting up Washington and swinging right onto the start of the normal route.

22 Teenoso 30m VS 4c * (1983)
The corner crack is a bit grassy, but worth doing all the same.

23 Ziggy 12m Hard Severe (1983)
This route follows the lesser corner in right wall of Teenoso. Climb past an oblong roof to gain slim the ramp/corner.

24 Social Democrack 12m Hard Severe 4b (1983)
Start up the rib 5 metres right of the main corner and follow the crack line past a ledge.

25 Lateral Thinking 45m E3 6a (1986)
A girdle of the right-hand section of the crag, going from left to right. Either abseil down the gully, or climb the diagonal crack of The Gift to the good break. Follow this, with the crux moves to gain Walter Wall. Continue in the same line to the arete, then across the easier crack into the corner. Belay here, or on a ledge on right. Continue along the crack to finish up the ramp/corner of Ziggy.

SPREADEAGLE BUTTRESS (Map Ref 178 689)

This large west-facing buttress is situated a few hundred metres above and right of Wave Buttress on the other side of the open gully. The crag is characterised by a prominent arching stepped roof/corner system on the left, sweeping over a steep, square lower wall, which tilts back to form a steep slab in its upper section. There is a short corner on the right, running out at a wide ledge halfway up. Approach as for Wave Buttress, then take a path crossing the open gully just right of that crag. Descend by an easy gully and the rock shelf down on the left-hand side of the crag (looking outwards).

1 Veinity Fair 30m E3 5b ** (1988)
Start at the left side of the wall, directly below a small tree. Climb directly up to small tree and grassy ledge (to either its left or right end). Traverse 5 metres right, then climb direct up the slab to a vein of quartz. Follow this rightwards to its end. Finish up and right. Poorly protected.

2 The Singing Ringing Tree 30m E5 6a ** (1983)
In the centre of the wall left of the hanging groove of Spreadeagle is a short crack, running out at a bulge. Start beneath this. Climb the crack to a good nut slot near the top, and pull right (there is a good sling on a large spike hold, equalised by RPs in a thin crack down and right) on improving holds to reach an obvious flake crack. Easier but bold climbing leads up the wall above trending leftwards. The difficulties are concentrated on the initial steep start.

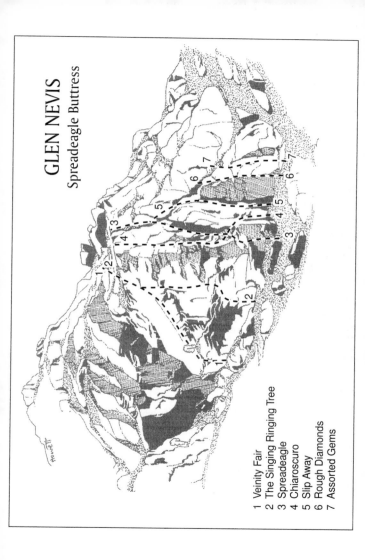

GLEN NEVIS
Spreadeagle Buttress

1 Veinity Fair
2 The Singing Ringing Tree
3 Spreadeagle
4 Chiaroscuro
5 Slip Away
6 Rough Diamonds
7 Assorted Gems

3 Spreadeagle 30m E4 6a ** (1982)

The shallow hanging groove in the centre of the wall. Start left of the groove beneath an obvious scoop/depression. Move up into this and make a hard move rightwards at a horizontal hairline crack to reach better holds at the base of the groove. Finish up this. The upper groove is often wet, though usually avoidable.

4 Chiaroscuro 30m E7 6b ** (1988)

A varied pitch of much contrast; a hard and strenuous lower section leads to a very bold upper half. It follows a fairly direct line up the blunt rib bisecting the groove of Spreadeagle. Start beneath the scoop just left of the prominent corner crack of Slip Away. Climb the scoop, then move up past a series of vertical slots to an obvious projecting nose on the arete. Gain the hanging groove of Spreadeagle and break out left onto an obvious hanging block. Continue up the wall above, keeping just left of the arete. This leads with increasing difficulty to hard moves pulling over onto a sloping ledge at the top.

5 Slip Away 30m E3 ** (1982)

1. 20m 6a Climb the clean-cut corner crack, going past an obvious smooth section with difficulty on the right wall. Continue more easily up the wide crack to a spacious belay ledge.
2. 10m 5b Step left off the ledge and trend leftwards to finish up the final section as for Spreadeagle.

6 Rough Diamonds 20m E4 6a * (1985)

This route takes the short arete right of the corner crack. Climb the arete past a hard move to good holds and protection at 8m. Continue more easily up the arete to the wide ledge, and either take a choice of finishes or scramble off rightwards and down the descent rake.

7 Assorted Gems 20m E3 5c * (1987)

The steep flaky scoop to the right of the arete. Start just right of the arete, at an obvious layback flake. Climb this to small nut placements at a quartz blotch. Make a long reach, then gain the smaller flake above and climb this to enter a shallow groove. Continue more easily to small ledge and finish either up the broken crack in the arete or *via* easy ground on the right.

8 Fool's Gold 35m HVS 5a * (1989)

This pitch lies above the wide ledge at the top of Rough Diamonds, but it can also be reached from the right by scrambling along the grassy ledge. From a nut belay on the ledge, follow the prominent contorted fault past some flakes to gain a slim hanging groove in the easier-angled slab above. Pull onto this, and go up trending slightly rightwards to the edge of the slab, avoiding heather ledges on the right near the top.

BLADE BUTTRESS   (Map Ref 178 690)

This impressive-looking buttress lies above the right side of Wave Buttress, on the opposite side of the gully from Spreadeagle Buttress but slightly higher. The crag gets its name from the prominent hanging blade-like arete forming clean-cut grooves on either side. Round to the right is a narrow clean slab, sometimes referred to as a pillar. Approach as for Wave Buttress, then continue up the hillside, initially by an indistinct path (which veers off rightwards to Spreadeagle Buttress), then crosses back over the open gully to the crag. The descent follows a steep muddy gully on the right, or alternatively head left into the wide open gully.

The first three routes all start in the open bay beneath the blade. Start by scrambling up into this.

The Barn Door   25m   E3 6b   (1986)
Start beneath a crack in the centre of the slab. Easy climbing up the slab leads to an off-balance layback up the short innocuous-looking groove.

Cruisability   20m   E5 6b ***   (1986)
The stupendous overhanging groove up the left side of the blade. Gain and climb the flake crack leading to the roof. Pull through this with difficulty, using a good incut hold over the lip on the left. Continue up the groove, pulling out right to finish. Strenuous and well protected.

Sabre   20m   E3 5c *   (1984/86)
The shorter, overhung groove up the right side of the blade. Start at a short crack directly below the blade, as for the previous route. Climb this into the groove, and continue up this (crux) to exit onto a jug-ridden slab. Climb easily up this to finish. Well protected.

Ugly Duckling   25m   E2 5b *   (1985)
This route provides good climbing with a bold start, following the arete and crack up the left side of the narrow south-east facing slab, round to the right from the previous routes. Start at a flake belay at the base of the wall, directly below the thin crack. Climb to the roof, traverse left to the arete, and go up this (crux) to a good ledge. From the right side of the ledge, climb directly up the crack to the top and a Friend belay next to a large flake well back.

Flight of the Snowgoose   30m   E6 6b **   (1985)
After sharing a common start with the fledgling Ugly Duckling, this route climbs the centre of the narrow pillar with thin, bold climbing in its upper reaches. Flight would not be advisable. From near the top of the crack, traverse right across the wall, then move up to a small ledge (tied-down skyhook runners). Ascend the wall just left of the arete with increasing difficulty to reach better holds just below the top. Belay well back.

THE SPACE FACE   (Map Ref 178 690)

This is an imposing south-west facing crag in a commanding position near the top right side of the gully above Blade and Spreadeagle crags. The distinctive frontal face is seamed with a series of criss-crossing cracks. The shorter, more broken left side of the crag, overlooking the gully, forms a series of short corners. Approach as for Wave Buttress, then continue up the hillside, initially by an indistinct path, then directly up the right side of the open gully. To descend, scramble back a short way, then go rightwards and down the easy gully.

Dancing on the Edge of Existence   35m   E4 5c *   (1986)
Climb up and left along the lip of the small roof at the toe of the crag into the centre of the wall. Traverse right to pinch grip flakes and go along a diagonal fault to a large hold on the arete. Go right again to the obvious vertical crack-line up the centre of the wall above. Follow this to step left and finish on the arete.
Variation: **The True Edge**   E5 6a ***   (1988)
Spectacular climbing up the hanging arete in a stunning position, very well protected after an initial bold start. After the lower wall and from a standing position below the upper arete, use good underclings to gain a good flake and finger locks in the base of the bottomless crack in the arete. Swing round and layback up the overhanging left wall of the arete to gain a good foothold in the crack. Swing back round passing a further tricky section which enables a good horizontal break to be reached. Saunter to the top.

WAVELET BUTTRESS   (Map Ref 178 692)

Further up the hillside above Blade Buttress is a small triangular crag facing south-west, resembling a miniature Wave Buttress. Approach as for Blade Buttress, heading diagonally left from the top of that crag.

Wavelet   12m   E2 5b *   (1984)
Climb the unprotected shallow depression in the centre, with the crux at the top.

MEALL CUMHANN SUMMIT CRAG   (Map Ref 176 695)

This south-west facing crag is easily seen high on the left of Meall Cumhann, well up and left of Wave Buttress. It is characterised by two large overhangs on the cleaner right-hand side, left of a gully cutting up the hillside. Approach by going directly up the hillside from the carpark, finally scrambling up the gully itself to the foot of the route. Descent by abseil is recommended, rather than continuing up or looking for other ways off.

Druim   70m   VS **   (1971)
1. 35m 4c   Climb the obvious deep crack that splits the right-hand side of the buttress, then ascend the overhanging wall above, moving left into a groove at a holly level with the large overhang.
2. 35m 5a   Move left across the slab and go up to the overhang. Turn this on the left, then climb easily to a large ledge and the top.

Croch   60m   VS/A2   (1971)

This is the last line to hold out for a free ascent, perhaps because it also happens to be on the furthest crag from the road! Scramble up the gully on the right until below the two overhangs. There is a crack 10 metres left of the prominent deep crack on Druim, splitting the right side of the buttress. Enter the crack by a hand traverse and a steep wall, and continue to a good ledge (20m). Climb to the 3m roof, surmount this (5 pegs were used on the first ascent) and continue up to join Druim with difficulty halfway up its second pitch (40m).

STEALL MEADOWS AREA

Beyond the gorge, the transition to flat meadow land is truly stunning. This 'scene of Arcadian grandeur' soon gives way to one of grim desolation where the hills open out — a barren rockless wilderness. A number of fine crags lie in these beautiful surroundings "where crenellated crags tower" (W.H.Murray, *The West Highlands of Scotland,* 1968)

THE MEADOW WALLS

Situated on the left on entering the flat meadows from the narrow confines of the gorge are a number of crags, the first a small wall on the left. Above this is a long wall, sculptured by glacial and subsequent water action. This curves round to the right past a pothole feature, eventually to form a long terrace of unbroken rock higher up, with a prominent 3m wide roof in its centre, just left of a steep gully. The first routes are approached directly up the hill from the head of the gorge. For the other routes, see particular instructions at the start of each crag. The best descent goes leftwards along the terrace and into the wide gully by the foot of Wave Buttress.

Stuffed Monkey   10m   E4 5c   (1985)

One for lovers of the esoteric! The route is situated on the small wall on the left on entering the meadow from the gorge. Climb directly up the centre of the wall, exiting slightly leftwards at the top. The protection is spaced and the crux is at the top.

The next three routes are all on the obvious long sculptured wall above Stuffed Monkey. This is a fine wall containing unusual routes on excellent rock.

Mutant   40m   E4 5c **   (1985)

Start in the centre of the wall. Climb the water-worn runnel to a ledge (unprotected). Move left to the start of a diagonal crack, then gain elevated scoops above the crack and follow these to a small ledge. Go right round the prow and follow a thin crack and ramp to finish on an easy slab. Peg belay well back.

Sammy the Seal   40m   E4 5c *   (1985)

Start just left of the last route, just right of the left-bounding corner. Go up the wall directly at first, then trend left into the corner for protection. Move right and climb directly to a ledge, or head rightwards across scoops (harder). Trend leftwards up a quartz wall to reach some flakes at the base of thin cracks. Move right, go back left to enter a scoop, then climb this and continue to the top and a peg belay well back.

A slightly easier route combines Mutant with the upper part of Sammy The Seal.

Reptile   40m   E2 5c **   (1985)
This route follows a left-slanting diagonal line taking in the obvious cracks. Start to the right of the centre of the wall at a scoop containing a thin crack. Climb this to ledge, trend left under a crack line, and continue up a quartz wall to flakes at a junction with the final twin cracks. Follow these with some interest to the top.

The following three routes lie on the west-facing grey wall up and left of the previous routes. It is at a slightly lower level than Wave Buttress, and is characterised by a right-facing groove in the centre. The best approach is to use a convenient terrace leading in from the left and abseil in (two pegs *in situ* at the top). It is also possible to scramble up to the base of the routes.

Tickled Pink   15m   E3 5c *   (1985)
Start beneath the central groove. Climb the wall right of the groove to an escape ledge on the left, then take the thin crack to finish. Protection is better than first impressions would suggest, entirely from small RPs.

Crinkle Cut   15m   E4 5c *   (1985)
Bold climbing up the wall left of the central groove of Tickled Pink, starting 2 metres further left. Make an awkward move to attain a standing position on the obvious ledge and continue to a jug. Trend right onto the rib which leads to the ledge on Tickled Pink. Finish up this.

Comfortably Numb   15m   E4 5c *   (1987)
Bold climbing up the centre of the wall to the right of the groove.

Three Cracks Route   12m   VS 4b   (1990)
At the left end of the terrace leading to the top of the previous routes is a trio of cracks running up a short slabby wall. Follow these by the line of least resistance.

A Cut Above the Rest   12m   E1 5b   (1987)
Further right along the terrace, above the left side of the lower crag (Tickled Pink) is a shallow scooped groove and wall which provides the line of the route. Protection may be sparse.

The following routes are all on the large south-west facing expanse of rock, sweeping round to the right from the sculptured wall, and directly overlooking the greater part of the Meadows. More broken and easy-angled lower walls lead to a terrace and a long band of walls above, split centrally by a deep loose gully. It is dominated by a prominent roof system to the left of the gully.

Sisyphus   45m   E1   (1983)
1. 25m 4c   Well left of the roof system is a shallow right-facing corner above the heathery terrace. Start below a shallow groove in the lower slab, below the upper corner. Climb the slab and gain the main slab by a break in the main slab. Go up the faint groove, then climb the right-sloping crack to the terrace.
2. 20m 5b   Climb the corner above, exiting left onto a ramp and easy ground. Beware the large loose block at the top of the corner (hence the name).

Going for Gold   15m   E4 6a ***   (1983)
A fine exercise in hand-jamming, tackling the prominent crack through the centre of the roof. Approach as for the lower slab of the previous route and walk right along terrace, or start from the right, as for the following routes, and continue at the same level, crossing the gully. Climb the roof past some evil flared jams to a good horizontal flake near the lip, then continue up the wide flake crack to the top. Very well protected; carry some large Friends for the upper crack.

THE TERRACE

The following two pitches are located on the walls above the terrace, at the same level and to the right of the large roof of Going for Gold. Approach from the right by scrambling up the open gully bounding the right edge of the crag.

Resurrection Shuffle   20m   E4 6a*   (1988)
Climb the right-slanting diagonal crack 2 metres left of The Quartzmaster to a small spike at 6m. Continue up the crack to a junction with that route. Move up and left to a small groove and finish up this.

The Quartzmaster   20m   E2 5b *   (1986)
Start just left of the prominent quartz band at the right end of the wall. Pull onto the ledge from the left, then go up the quartz past a series of sloping ledges to reach a right-slanting crack. Finish up this.

GALAXY BUTTRESS   (Map Ref 178 687)

Beyond the Meadow Walls the hillside recedes a little before rearing up again as the craggy spur of Aisridh Mairi Bhan. Near the beginning of this area, facing towards Steall Hut, is a distinctive and isolated clean-cut hanging slab guarded by a long roof, known as Galaxy Buttress. There are broken areas of rock on either side of this buttress. Approach directly up the slope, leaving the path midway between the right end of the Meadow Walls and the wire bridge across the river. The descent goes down the shallow gully/rake midway between the buttress and Steall Slabs, at the left side of the crag.

Steall Slabs   55m   Hard Severe 4a **   (1970)
The narrow clean slab to the left of the main buttress. Climb the centre of a 25m slab, then continue by a blind crack to finish by an easy ridge. Difficult to protect.

Diamond Delight   50m   E3 *   (1985)
A line up the left side of the buttress, with an exposed start. Start at the left edge
of the crag, beneath a flaky crack.
1. 20m 5c   Climb the crack until it is possible to gain an obvious line of holds
leading horizontally right. Move across these and go up to a small foot ledge
and nut belay.
2. 20m 5b   Ascend the crack above, then move into a scoop on right. Follow
this and the continuation to the top.

Short Man's Walkabout   45m   E5 ***   (1983)
Stunning, well protected climbing up a thin crack in the centre of the hanging
slab. Start by scrambling up to beneath a short right-facing corner and thin
crack splitting the centre of the roof.
1. 35m 6b   Move up to a peg runner at the back of the roof and go across this
with difficulty to a good finger-lock over the lip. Climb the crack (a no-hands rest
is possible out right) to a ledge and belay.
2. 10m 5a   Gain the scoop above from the right and continue to the top.

Poor Man's Wimpabout   30m   E2 5c *   (1989)
Start at a small tree on the right-hand side of the roof. From the corner above the
tree, gain a good hold on the left, and swing leftwards into a scoop. Climb up to a
horizontal crack and hand traverse this leftwards to gain and finish up the crack,
as for the previous route.

Galaxy   55m   Mild Severe   (1953)
1. 30m   Start down the slope below the chimney on the right side of the main
slab and climb to a niche at the right end of the main overhang.
2. 25m   Move rightwards up a ramp for 3m, pull onto the next ledge and move
left to finish up the chimney. The chimney can be reached with less deviation to
the right, upping the grade to Hard Severe.

Toadal   60m   VS   (1953)
Start below a tree some way up heathery rock to the right of Galaxy.
1. 30m 4b   Climb broken rock to a shelf, then move left to a slab in a gully.
Climb the slab, then go right below the lower overhang. Turn a rib on the right,
then go up the wall to a tree at the left end of a shelf.
2. 30m 4c   Climb the overhanging chimney at the right end of the shelf, and
finish up the steep heather above.

Pich   25m   VS 4c   (1973)
Start below trees on the left end of a large shelf, approximately 15m up and right
from the start of the previous route. Go up steep ground to below a short
overhanging groove. Move right 3m and climb to a ledge, then go back left on
the next sloping ledge. Step left to a small tree, and climb to the shelf below the
top chimney of Toadal. Finish up this.

Lame Beaver, Steall Hut Crag, Glen Nevis (Climber, Andy deKlerk)

Flapjack Gully   60m   Difficult   (1953)
The gully right of Galaxy Buttress, with a large chockstone at mid-height.

Route II   60m   Difficult   (1953)
The narrow rib near the centre of the craggy area.

Route I   45m   Moderate   (1953)
The right-hand ridge of the semi-circle of crags.

AN STEALL   (Map Ref 180 683)

The rock on the left side of the impressive Steall Waterfall has been climbed, trees on the left providing belays. Gradings quoted vary from Moderate to Severe, depending upon the line taken. The easiest descent is by abseiling from the trees on the left. During prolonged cold spells An Steall provides by far the best low level winter climb of the area, at Grade III or harder, again depending upon the line taken.

TRILLIAN SLABS   (Map Ref 182 683)

This is the area of north-facing rock to the left (east) of the waterfall. To approach, cross the wire bridge at Steall and follow the path underneath the waterfall.

Mostly Harmless   125m   E2/A0   (1997)
Start 100 metres left of An Steall at a ramp below a yellow triangular overhang.
1. 35m 5c   Climb a marble slab to the top left side of an overhanging corner. Move up the short slab and go left along very overhung holds until below a block. Exit the left side of the block with two points of aid.
2. 15m 4b   Climb the corner above and cross vegetation to a vertical wall.
3. 45m 4c   Climb the bulge above and slightly right to a small ramp trending left and up along an obvious line to a belay.
4. 30m 4a   Straight over slabs to the top.

Infinite Improbability Drive   100m   HVS   (1997)
A rising traverse up the far left side of the slabs in fine surroundings. Start at the lowest point of the slabs.
1. 4b   Follow fault lines on a leftward rising traverse to a belay on a grass ledge.
2. 4c   Continue up along the same line and climb a small overlap at about its mid-point. Keep rising left (poorly protected) to a grass ledge. Climb the obvious right-slanting crack to belay under a bulge below the right-hand arete.
3. 5a   Tiptoe across the damp scoop to the left side of the arete, then swing out and climb the arete. Belay in a small cave at the top. A bold pitch.

Ardverikie Wall, Binnein Shuas   (Climber, Catherine Howett)

STEALL HUT CRAG   (Map Ref 176 683)

This impressive north-east facing crag lies, not surprisingly, on the hillside behind Steall Hut, to the right of the waterfall. It is slow to dry, although some of the routes on the frontal face should be climbable during inclement weather. On the left is a slabby wall whilst the main face is very steep. This is dominated by a shallow cave in its centre base with a groove system above and a superb diagonal crack cutting rightwards across the face from the caves lip.

To approach, cross the wire bridge at Steall and head diagonally up the hillside behind the hut.

Steelyard Blues   30m   E2 5b   (1983)
A poorly protected line up the slabby left wall of the crag. Move left towards the corner near the top, climbing the steep wall immediately to its right.

Lame Beaver   25m   E7 6b ***   (1985/87)
A sustained pitch with sparse protection breaching the left side of the extremely overhanging front face. Start at the left end of the wall, about 2m from the left edge. Climb up past a shield of rock, heading for an obvious hold in the apex of the niche above (protection, including a Hex1). Undercling the roof system rightwards with difficulty and move into the niche on the right. Pull over, go slightly left, then up and right using a good hidden pocket to gain the base of a quartz crack. Finish up this with further interest.

Trick of the Tail   30m   E6 6b ***   (1989)
A stunning pitch up the left-slanting diagonal groove dominating the centre of the crag. Climb easily up a short slab leftwards to an old ring peg under the roof. Move up and left into the crack, and follow this to make a hard lunge leftwards (crux) for a good undercling. Using this, reach a superb block hold in the base of the triangular niche, and climb into this (no hands rest possible). Swing wildly out right to better holds, and climb the twin cracks above with further difficulty to a recess and easy ground. Well protected; many Friends are useful.

Two prominent diagonal cracks offer superb sustained climbing. Both share a common start up the prominent left-slanting flake crack in the right side of the central triangular cave.

Arcadia   25m   E7 6b ***   (1993)
The left-slanting diagonal crack right of and parallel to the groove of Trick of the Tail offers sustained climbing with good gear including 3 peg runners. Pull right out of the shallow cave to a PR and good holds, then attack the left-slanting crack, finishing up the final twin cracks as for Trick of the Tail.

Leopold   25m   E7 6c ***   (1992)
The wider, right-hand diagonal crack, with a deviation out right on good undercuts at the obvious shield of rock. It was first climbed with pre-placed gear and has been partially retro-bolted as part of a sport project.

Steall Appeal   15m   F8b ***   (1993)
The line of 6 bolts at the right end of the crag, 3 metres left of the crack of
Watermark, gives the first sport climb completed in the glen and amongst the
hardest of its genre in Scotland. A hard boulder problem start (crux) followed by
a powerful undercut move leads to some slightly easier climbing.

Watermark   25m   E4 6a *   (1989)
The diagonal crack line bounding the right edge of the face. Start just right of the
crack. Gain a flat hold and a hidden incut just to its right, and pull left to good
incuts at the back of the ramp. Continue up the crack using good holds on the
right wall to move left to a prominent undercut flake. Make a hard move to gain
the ledge above, then pull up left to finish up an easy (often wet) corner.

LOCH LINNHE

The following small crags are scattered along the length of Loch Linnhe from
just north of Fort William to south of Oban. They are often climbable when the
weather rules out even the Polldubh crags, so they can save a washed out
weekends' trip. They are described from Fort William southwards, while the
crags around Kinlochleven at the head of Loch Leven are described separately.
The maps for this area are Ordnance Survey 1:50,000 Sheets 41, 49 and 55.

CREAG DUBH NA CAILLICH   (Map Ref 155 764)

This small north-facing granite crag lies above Torlundy, a few kilometres north
of Fort William. It is clearly visible from the main A82 road and can be
approached directly from the forestry road (30 minutes). Many easier routes
have been climbed, all on good rock and following obvious lines, but detailed
descriptions are not provided here.

The Kiss of the Spiderwoman   25m   E3 5b *   (1986)
This climb takes the longest part of the wall on the left side of the crag. Climb a
line just left of a broken arete (serious) to reach eventually good holds and
protection at a good block. Go up a thin finger crack to a ledge and continue
direct to a tree belay on the right.

The Big Tree   HVS 5a 10m   (1986)
A wall and a short crack lead directly to the large tree left of the centre of the
crag.

DUBH-GHLAC   (Map Ref 027 618)

This is the dry melt-water channel clearly visible from the road ½km west of the
Onich Post Office and shop. The south-east facing slabby wall at the start of the
gorge has some good routes, including an excellent Very Difficult (not
described). The nature of the rock means that many of the routes are very

similar, and difficult to protect. The crag is used by some of the local outdoor centres, who have established stakes at the top for anchors.

Animal   30m   HVS 4c *   (1986)
The rippled slab at the far right end of the crag has good rock, if it has not been overgrown again.

Mitchell's Crack   30m   HVS 5a   (1980s)
This is the crack along at the far end of the gorge.

CREAG MHOR   (Map Ref 044 612)

This is a unique south-facing crag composed entirely of quartz, situated about 100m above the bend in the road between the Lodge On The Loch and the Creag Dhu Hotel. It sits above a small quarry on the roadside at the bend. The main features are two roofs slanting across the highest section and a striking crack to the right.

Christie's Crack   40m   HVS   (1978)
At the left edge of the main wall is a left-slanting corner.
1. 10m 4b   Go up the corner (loose) to a small tree belay a few metres below a larger tree.
2. 30m 4c   Move 10 metres right to a dark broken corner and climb this, exiting to the right.

Left-Hand Crack   35m   E1 5b   (1970s)
Climb the crack line which slants left to the right-hand end of the lower roof. Pull over this and follow the crack leftwards to the next roof. Move right to finish.

Tao Mood   35m   E3 5c *   (1990)
Start midway between the cracks at a cleaned line on the lower wall. Climb to a ledge before making a sharp pull onto the lower slab. Follow this direct via a ragged fault before an awkward step up leads to Right-Hand Crack. Climb the left side of this for 4m (useful to place some gear here) before quitting it for a shallow left-facing groove, gained by a difficult move (crux) through a bulge. Belay on trees well back.

Right-Hand Crack   35m   E1 5b   (1970s)
Climb the crack which twists first right then left some 5 metres right of Left-Hand Crack.

STAC AN EICH   (Map Ref 031 593)

This is the collective name for the two good north-west facing granite outcrops in the woods of Leitir Mhor (Lettermore) overlooking Loch Linnhe, about 2km down the A832 Oban road west of the Ballachulish bridge. Turn off left about a kilometre south of the old ruined Ballachulish pier, go up a forestry track (signposted 'The Monument') just before a telephone box, and park here, taking care not to cause an obstruction. Cross the stile and follow the track round a bend to where a smaller track to the monument branches off left. The crag is directly up the slope from here, and is only 5 minutes from the road.

The lower crag is dominated by an imposing wall in the centre, split by three short groove lines. Right of this is the central corner line of Marathon and a further overhanging wall split by a couple of cracks, bounded on the right by an easier-angled area of rock. Descent is by abseil from trees, or a fight through the undergrowth and down the steep descent gully at the right end of the crag.

Historical Note:
The memorial cairn is situated on the particular spot on the old bridleway, where on the 15th of May 1752, Colin Campbell of Glenure, the government appointed factor (the character of the Red Fox in Robert Louis Stevenson's novel Kidnapped) was murdered, which resulted in the wrongful conviction and subsequent hanging of James Stewart, better known locally as James of the Glen.

> *"The mountains look on Marathon, and Marathon looks on the sea."*
> George Gordon, Lord Byron.

THE LOWER CRAG

Heather Rib   25m   Very Difficult   (1960s)
Left of the overhanging central wall is an easier-angled area of rock forming a bay. Climb the heathery rib of the orange groove at the back of the bay.

Autan   25m   E1 5b   (1981)
Follow grooves in the right side of the orange groove to a ledge below a right-slanting zigzag crack. Climb the left side of the rib, left of the crack, to large overhangs which are avoided on the left.

Shuttlecock   35m   HVS   (1981)
Start at the left edge of the overhanging central wall.
1. 20m 4c   Climb a thin crack leftwards and go over a bulge into a left-facing corner. Climb this and move out right at its top to belay on slab at an obvious spike.
2. 15m 5a   Climb the deep chimney-groove above to a pedestal on the left, then traverse left to a tree. The massive keystone block that forms most of this pitch is dangerously loose — beware! A safer alternative is to traverse obliquely rightwards, heading for a tree.

The Leisure Trail   20m   E4 6a *   (1986)
This climb takes the leftmost of the three groove lines on the central wall. Enter and climb the groove past a good nut slot (good RPs up on the right). From here, either gain the flange on the left, or climb straight up to reach two poor peg runners at the most prominent roof. Pull over this from the left to gain a good hold, and climb the easier hand crack and slab to a belay. Finish up Shuttlecock or abseil off.

A diagonal line across the wall, **Hallmark**, E3/4 6a (1986) gains the flange on The Leisure Trail from the left, climbs past the pegs, then traverses right to join and finish up Seal of Approval.

Let Sleeping Dogs Lie   20m   E4 6b **   (1985)
The deceptive central groove line has a perplexing and desperate crux, which is high in its technical grade. Climb the groove to a good flat hold, make a long reach for a sidepull on the right, then regain the groove (crux) which leads to easier ground. Move up onto the slab and belay as for The Leisure Trail.

Seal of Approval   25m   E4 6b **   (1985)
A spectacular line across the centre of the crag. Start beneath twin cracks in the centre of the overhanging wall, just right of the previous route. Climb the twin cracks to gain a scoop (crux). Go up this and the flaky groove to good incut holds and a nut placement in an undercut. Swing right across the blank wall to a shallow groove system and pull leftwards from the top of this to a tree belay. Either scramble up broken ground or abseil off.
Direct Start: **Gold Seal**   E4 6b   (1986)
Follow the right-hand crack to a prominent undercling, then pull into the base of the hanging groove on good holds.

Orifice Party   10m   E3 6a   (1987)
This is a better finish to any of the three main groove lines. Climb the short thin crack in the pillar of rock directly above the centre of the crag.

Bill's Digger   25m   E4 6b ***   (1984)
This excellent route gives well protected climbing, with a very reachy contorted crux, taking the shallow stepped groove in the arete delineating the centre of the crag. Pull over the initial bulge leftwards on improving holds and move up to a thread runner in a recess. Continue up the steepening groove with a powerful reachy move to gain good holds in a horizontal break, step right and continue up an easier crack.

A traverse of the crescent-shaped flake, **From Here to There**, E3 6a (1986) starts up Bill's Digger to finish at the small tree. The route was reversed to retrieve the gear. A top-rope problem (or a route with a very high side-runner), **Bill's Digger's Fucked**, 6b (1985) follows a line up the slab just left of Marathon, heading for a large flat hold, after which the difficulties ease.

Marathon   30m   E1 5b **   (1981)
The central corner line gives an absorbing well protected climb with some weird moves. At the top, traverse left onto the slab to a belay on the rib. Either scramble rightwards to finish, or abseil off.

Gunrunner   10m   E3 5c   (1986)
An alternative start to either Marathon or Gunslinger, useful as the start of Marathon is often wet. Start midway between the two, at a prominent down-pointing flake. Climb this and pull directly into the groove. Move up this to the roof, and pull into either Marathon or Gunslinger.

Gunslinger   25m   E3 5c **   (1981)
Well protected, strenuous climbing on big holds up the deceptively steep cracks in the highest part of the wall right of Marathon. Start at an undercut flake. Climb this and the crack above, passing a small resting ledge at mid-height, to finish on good blocks.

The Monument   15m   E3 5c *   (1982)
The crack line and capping roof at the right end of the frontal face. Enter the ramp and climb the crack to pull over the roof on good holds, then trend easily rightwards to a belay.

The crag continues round right to form a shorter, easier-angled wall.

Original Route   12m   VS 4c   (1960s)
Pull onto a square block just above the start of the previous route and follow an easy gangway to the break at the top.

The Covenant   12m   VS 4c   (1981)
Move left from the foot of the groove and climb direct up the shallow rib to an awkward pull over.

Appin Groove   10m   Hard Severe ***   (1981)
The left-facing layback groove at the highest point of the wall provides an excellent climb.

Red Fox   10m   E1 5a   (1981)
The left edge of the slab is unprotected.

An eliminate between the two previous climbs has been squeezed in at 5c. Again, it is not to be fallen from.

Old Fox   10m   E1 5b *   (1981)
Climb the weakness in the centre of the slab, with a hard unprotected move to gain the overlap. Step right and go up to the top.

Cracks   10m   VS 4c   (1981)
The cracks in the right wall of the gully are dirty and the rock requires care.

THE UPPER CRAG

This rather broken crag lies further up and right of the main crag. It is dominated by a narrow deceptively steep slab on its right edge.

Death's Distance   30m   E3 5b *   (1987)
Bold wall climbing, almost entirely protected by small RPs. Start beneath the centre of the slab. Climb to good holds at 5m, then move right and up past a crack (good RP3 placement at the top end of the undercut flake below the overlap – difficult to place). Move left into a shallow incipient groove, then go directly up on good edges past a long reach to an easing in the angle. Pull onto the rounded slab and step right to a good spike runner. Continue up the easier rounded edge to finish.

KENTALLEN QUARRIES   (Map Ref 022 590)

A small number of loose and poorly protected routes in the E1 to E3 range have been recorded in the small north-west facing quarries on the east side of Kentallen. Due to the uninspiring nature of the setting, and recent development of one of the quarries as a site for travelling people, it has been decided not to describe the routes here.

CREAGAN FAIRE DHAIBHIDH   (Map Ref 013 577)

This is the correct name for the north-west facing crag above Kentallen Bay. The rock is limestone, with reasonable friction, offering climbing very similar to, and often mistaken for sandstone. Kentallen Bay lies 5km down the A828 Ballachulish-Oban road. Do not walk up the hillside directly below the crag (tortuous). Instead, park at the hotel turn-off (Map Ref 007 573) at the south end of the village and approach along the crest of the ridge. This is much easier as it avoids all the steep broken ground below the crag.

The crag is undercut all along its base, and the steep starts provide the technical cruxes on all the routes except the most recent addition.

Barnacle   20m   VS 5a   (1982)
Climb the crack up the left side of the recess for 5m, then go up the left wall of the chimney.

Cop Out   20m   VS 4c   (1982)
Start just right of the previous route. Move up and right to the holly tree, then climb the corner above to the top of the pedestal and finish up slabs.

Fall Out   20m   VS 4c   (1982)
Surmount the broken bulge to reach the crack running to the top of the right side of the pedestal.

The Powerbulge   20m   E4 6b **   (1987)
A fun technical problem attacking the hanging flake through the bulge in the centre. Start on undercuts and move up to a good pocket, then make a long reach for a good break. Move right to a good undercut, from where it is possible to place runners in the flake above (RP4 in a slot to the left, RP2 just to the right). Pull up on half a wrinkle, and using powerful undercutting, gain a pinch at the right end of the flake. A further snatch gains better holds, including a chickenhead. Layback onto the slab above, then trend right more easily to a fixed sling and belay ring around a tree root. Lower off.

Up Periscope   12m   HVS 6a *   (1982)
About 10 metres from the right-hand end of the crag is a right-facing corner with a holly. Start 5 metres left of this. Climb a thin crack through bulges, then step right onto a slab where the crack becomes heathery.

Prawn   12m   VS 5a **   (1982)
Climb the bulges 3 metres right of Up Periscope into a shallow right-facing corner, and go up this to the top.

Cocktail   12m   VS 5b   (1982)
Pull left over the bulge from the foot of Open Corner and climb up the rib.

Open Corner   10m   Mild VS 4b/c   (1982)
Climb the right-facing corner next to the holly.

Creel   8m   Mild VS 4c   (1982)
This is the right-leaning crack in the south-facing wall where the crag ends.

DALLEN'S ROCK   (Map Ref 930 485)

This west-facing broken quartzite crag overlooks the A832 Oban to Ballachulish road at Lettershuna, just south of Portnacroish, Appin. It is about 30km south from the Ballachulish bridge, and is visible from the road. Very limited parking may be possible at the turn-off for Lettershuna farm. Walk up the hill a little, and struggle through dense undergrowth to the base of the crag. The crag is characterised by a large roof at two-thirds height and a steep slabby wall below the roof on the right side of the slab (The Golden Slab). The best descent is by abseil from trees.

As with most quartzite crags, the rock should be treated with care in places. The crag dries quickly and receives the benefit of any late afternoon and evening sun.

Skywalker   30m   E1 5b   (1991)
A wildly exposed route in its upper reaches, which climbs leftwards across the entire crag, before cutting back right above the main roof. Start 3 metres to the right of a tree towards the right-hand side of the crag, at an obvious ramp running leftwards up the lower part of the crag. Climb easily along the ramp past a huge recess (slightly loose) to a ledge on the extreme left of the main face. Climb back up diagonally rightwards onto the hanging ramp above the main roof. Continue to the far right end of the ramp, moving beneath a small nose midway. A final awkward move at the end of the ramp leads to a tree belay.

The Golden Slab   30m   E1 5b *   (1991)
A fine route which utilises the maximum height of the crag, climbing the striking slabby wall mentioned in the introduction. Start just left of the tree, as for Skywalker. Climb the ramp for 2m before pulling out rightwards onto the slabby wall. Climb the centre of the wall in the general line of the obvious brown streak (runners in horizontal breaks). Move out right just below the roof to the right arete and a small ledge. Climb the steep wall above (2PR) for 5m (crux), then pull out left below a bulge. Continue up to a ledge and follow it out right before moving back up left to a tree belay.

Power of the West   30m   E1 5b   (1991)
This route takes the vague corner line directly behind the tree near the right side
of the crag, just right of The Golden Slab. Climb the steep corner for 10m to the
last of the three small rocky beaks which bounds the right edge of the slabby
wall just below the roof. Finish up the final crux wall of The Golden Slab.

THE BISHOP'S MANTLE, EASDALE   (Map Ref 743 184)

The Bishop's Mantle lies about 1km north of the village of Easdale on Seil
Island, in Lorn. It takes the form of a a prominent sharp triangular block of basalt
jutting into the sea, some 50m high. To reach Easdale, follow the A816
Oban-Lochgilphead road south from Oban for 16km, then take the B844 for a
further 11km to reach the village. The easiest approach is to follow the obvious
open glen running north, just before the village is reached.

   A cleaner slabby north face and very vegetated south face form the fin,
abutting a broken ridge. There is a prominent arch through the west end of the
fin. The first route described may be affected by high tide as it starts on the
beach. The cliff immediately to the north, overlooking the fin, may repay further
investigation, for those willing to put in the effort cleaning. The descent is by
abseil, but the equipment may no longer be reliable or *in situ* , so spare gear
should be carried.

North Face of the Sharkstooth   50m   E2/3 5b *   (1987)
Start about 5 metres left of an obvious recess and a roof, at a shallow
depression and vague line of cracks running up the slab. Climb direct past a
large break to a further shallow break. Move past this and continue more or less
directly by the line of least resistance to finish up a strip of rock between the
grass-covered top section. There are nut and Friend belays on the top, and 50m
ropes just reach on the stretch. An abseil sling and karabiner is *in situ* to
facilitate a descent through the triffids on the south side.

North Face   35m   VS 5a   (1982)
A less direct version of the above route. From the large arch, traverse left and
down 15m to a belay, then climb directly to the top.

   The easiest route to the top (Severe, 1982) takes the right-hand rib of the
large arch for 12m, then traverses left and finishes diagonally up left to the
highest point.

South Face   35m   VS   (1980)
Climb up the back of the large arch, then move right into the loose chimney
which leads to the top.

Some 5km north of Oban, down on the shore near Dunstaffnage, is a small
conglomerate crag. It is useful for bouldering, although of purely local interest.

KINLOCHLEVEN

Lying at the head of Loch Leven, this village was effectively by-passed on the opening of the Ballachulish bridge. Recently it has seen some rejuvenation and there are now better facilities to cater for the hoards of walkers passing through on their pilgrimage to get their 'I've done the West Highland Way' badge. Although a bit of a backwater as far as climbing is concerned, with so much more impressive cliffs in nearby Glen Coe, these small crags are worth a visit if you are passing.

TORR GARBH   (Map Ref 198 618)

Locally known as The Boulder, this small crag provides good bouldering and some short routes up to 7m on excellent quartz-studded and pocketed mica-schist. Follow a well-worn footpath parallel to, and a few hundred metres north of the river Leven until the distinctive triangular-shaped boulder comes into view, less than 100 metres from the path. It is about 10 minutes from the centre of the village.

From left to right, the routes are: **Left-Hand Crack** 4b; **Magic Fingers** 5b; **Harry the Bastard's Coming Out Party** 5a; **A Bit Thin** E1 5c; **The Bulge** 6b; **No Brain No Pain** 5b; **Electric City Blues** VS 4c and **Diagonal Crack** VS 4c.

B STATION BUTTRESS   (Map Ref 196 616)

This finely situated north-east facing mica-schist crag overhangs the River Leven and lies directly beneath the B-Station above Kinlochleven. There are 6 routes from VS to HVS of around 30m, mainly following obvious vertical crack lines. It has an atmosphere similar to the River Walls in the Nevis Gorge, with a better selection of routes in the lower grades. Approach as for Torr Garbh, continuing along the path until it starts to descend. Break off right and descend due south to reach the crag. Alternatively, from the footbridge at Map Ref 193 688, follow a well worn path close to the true right bank of the Leven and cross the river by boulders just upstream of the crag. This is 15 minutes from the village.

All the routes start on a large boulder in the river at the left-hand side of the crag.

Route I   25m   VS 4c
Step off the boulder and go up a black scoop straight through the traverse, with an awkward move onto a tapering ramp. Finish up this.

Route II   25m   VS 4c
Traverse right just above the water to a crack with an old peg. Go up the crack to a ledge, then climb the slightly wider crack to the traverse fault. Continue straight up an obvious line of holds to finish at the same point as Route I.

The Big Crack   25m   HVS 5a *
Start as for Route II. Traverse right from below the first ledge to a point below the prominent wide crack. Move through the overlap directly below the crack to reach a traverse fault, then climb the crack itself.

Route IV   HVS 5a
Climb the wall just to the rightof the previous route.

Route V   25m   HVS 5a
Move left 5 metres from pegs and climb straight up an obvious line of good holds to finish on easy ground.

Route VI   30m   HVS 5b
Climb the right-trending diagonal crack, reached from the traverse.

Route VII   30m   HVS 5a
This is the left-slanting diagonal crack. Climb onto a ledge above the peg belay, then finish up the crack with some loose holds.

Twisting by the Pool   25m   HVS 5a
Climb onto the ledge above the pegs and make a rising traverse right under the roof. Finish out right steeply on good holds. This pitch can be gained from the bottom of the scoop at the right-hand end of The Girdle by moving left just above the waterline into a crack which leads to the peg belay.

The Girdle   50m   Hard Severe ***
Atmospheric climbing, taking the obvious fault line at one-third height, usually followed from left to right. Step off the boulder to gain the fault and follow it to belay at a clutch of pegs (30m). Continue round the arete and move down into a scoop to finish on the far right of the crag (20m). Either reverse the route or scramble up a dirty gully on the right.

There is a small outcrop on other side of river which provides good bouldering and four short routes from VS to HVS. There is also good traversing in summer of the entire walls of the River Leven from the footbridge to the B-Station.

On the lower slopes of Garbh Bheinn (at Map Ref 178 616, above the Doctor's House, just before descending into the village) is Wilson's Wall, a 15m slabby north-west facing buttress containing **Into the Sun** (VS 5a, 1988) which follows a groove and cracks just right of a left-facing corner. Further up the hill, **Chris's Climb** (Very Difficult, 1988) takes an obvious groove up a pink area of rock. Earlier ascents may have occurred.

Glenfinnan and Mallaig

To the west of Fort William lies an exceptional area of remote and wild hills whose flanks have been scoured to leave large expanses of naked rock. Between Fort William and the sea port of Mallaig is the area known as Morar. The main A830 road marks the southern boundary of Morar and contains the single track rail line which, with its summer steam locomotive, is regarded as one of the great train journeys of the world. Morar is split into north and south by the deep Loch Morar (home we are told to another secretive beastie related to Nessie). Little climbing has been done in this area as a whole, as the midges and rain are unusually plentiful, but some good cragging has been done where it is more easily accessible.

There are two areas. Firstly, that along the A830 near Glenfinnan village and its famous monument standing at the head of Loch Shiel. Also included here are two crags some distance down the loch into the Moidart area. Secondly, a collection of crags on the knobbly hills of North Morar just east of Mallaig. OS 1:50,000 Sheet 40 covers both areas.

ACCESS AND ACCOMMODATION
A visit to the Mallaig crags is best done with a local overnight stay. The area is essentially remote so wild camping is rarely a problem. The white sands of Morar down by the sea give a delightful setting and an escape from the midges. There are some official campsites, a Youth Hostel near the village of Morar, and a few hotels in the area. Arisaig in particular is a lovely wee spot with a good seafood restaurant. This is also the departure point for the boat to the Isle of Eigg. The train stops at all the small villages and those without a car can access any of these crags in this way. The Glenfinnan crags are easily visited from Fort William for a day trip, but although the train goes past the base of the crags, British Rail overlooked the installation of a platform so a walk from Glenfinnan is required. The only other form of transport feasible for a quick trip is the car.

HISTORY
The first recorded climbing in the area was an ascent of The Rising by an unknown party in 1969 on the somewhat remote Beinn Odhar Mor, followed by Mic on the same buttress in 1970 by Klaus Schwartz and Sam Crymble whilst they were both working at Loch Eil Outdoor Centre. Ian Sykes explored the area in 1972 and 1973 and made ascents of Locomotion, the excellent Calop Junction, Absent Friends and Humfibacket on the Railway Buttresses near Glenfinnan. Sykes also visited Beinn Odhar Mhor with Ian Sutherland (both partners of the local outdoor shop, Nevisport) and under the impression they were discovering it, climbed two routes. This partnership also definitely found Creag Mhor Bhrinicoire and established the first route, Grand Old Master (HVS).

No other interest was shown in the area, although many had passed through on their way to the islands. Ed Grindley had been resident in Fort William (teaching at the High School) since 1976 and had been instrumental in pushing the development of Glen Nevis. By 1984 he had almost finished the manuscript for a new guide to the area and through that summer he and Dave Armstrong from Nottingham made a concerted effort to climb every line on the Railway Buttresses near Glenfinnan for inclusion in the guide. The routes on Dancing Buttress and Roof Buttress in particular gave excellent, though initially lichenous routes; Don't Fear The Reaper, Danceclass and Scaredevil (all E3) from Armstrong and Reaper Direct (E3), Eegy Weegy and Ghost Train (E2) from Grindley. The guide was published in 1985, but new activity it generated was concentrated on the Nevis crags rather than these more remote areas.

In 1985 Graham Little and Dave Saddler went on a trout fishing trip in wet weather and discovered the impressive 100m high Central Pillar of Carn Mhic a'Ghille-chaim near Mallaig. They returned the next year and climbed the stunning arete of The Edge of Perfection (E1). That same year saw more interest in Creag Mhor Bhrinicoire from Nevisport employees, quickly followed by employees of another Fort William outdoor emporium, West Coast Outdoor Leisure. In 1989, Little returned to the crag with the unpronounceable name with Gary Latter, who established Into The Light (E3), and a few years later, with Kevin Howett, he did Smoke Screen.

Little also did the first routes on Sgurr Bhuidhe with Saddler. He returned with Howett to try an impressive overhanging crack, only to find Rick Campbell and Latter had beaten them to it by a few days establishing Going for the Jugular at E5. Locals from Fort William, Craig Smith and Jason Williamson polished off remaining lines on Creag Mhor Bhrinicoire in 1989; A Reflection (E3) being of particular note. The only other activity in this area has come from George Szuca with Falling Like a Stone on the Railway Buttresses in 1993, although there is undoubtedly much still to do.

MALLAIG CRAGS

The hills to the east of Mallaig, Morar and Arisaig, flanking Loch Morar, although not very high are very rocky in character and hold a wealth of small crags. Many of these are as yet without recorded routes. The area can be conveniently visited en route to or from Rhum and Eigg, although it is worth a visit in its own right. Access to the crags is generally much easier than the pronunciation of their names!

CARN MHIC A' GHILLE-CHAIM   (Map Ref 715 955)

The north face of this hill, overlooking the outfall of Loch Eireagoraidh, comprises an extensive series of ribs and buttresses. The hill name has been adopted as the crag name although for those who find the Gaelic too much of a challenge, the name Crooked Crag is suggested. The central, highest and dominating feature of the crag is Central Pillar. The rock is schist, liberally studded with quartz, providing good quality climbing. The crag, despite being north-facing, dries fairly quickly. In late summer and autumn, swarms of midges and particularly voracious cleggs can act as a major deterrent. Although the plums of the Central Pillar have been picked, development of the crag is still in its infancy, with considerable potential remaining.

The crag is accessible *via* Loch an Nostaire in about one hour from the A830. Cars can be parked on the east side of the road about 1.5km south of Mallaig (just south of the bridge over the railway) at Map Ref 675 956. Walk under the railway underpass, then follow the path round the north side of Loch an Nostaire to head east by the line of least resistance to gain the crag.

A grassy gully, 60m right of Central Pillar provides an easy descent route.

The trilogy of fine routes on Central Pillar converge to share a common upper section and final belay. The first and second pitches of Into the Light and Smoke Screen have been interchanged to create more direct and sustained lines.

Edge of Perfection   95m   E1 **   (1986)
A high quality if pretentiously named route taking a fairly direct line up the edge of the Central Pillar. Start at a point where the overhanging base of the pillar meets the slabby wall on the left.
1. 20m 5b   Climb a crack past a large spike to a flake edge. Descend 3m to the right, then pull right around the bulge into a corner. Climb this, surmount the block overhang, then continue up a crack to a niche.
2. 20m 5b   Hand traverse 2 metres left, then go up the slabby wall until it steepens. Make a short delicate traverse right to a rock ledge. Climb a slight corner to another rock ledge, then climb close to the edge to belay on a small ledge on the edge of the pillar (shared by Into The Light). A fine, intriguing pitch.
3. 40m 4b   Continue up the pillar, just left of the edge, to reach a commodious ledge. Climb two short easy slabs to a heather ledge below the final vertical wall.
4. 15m 5a   Climb a flake crack splitting the wall to reach a thread belay well back on the right.

Into the Light   100m   E3 **   (1989/91)
A very good route with sustained and contrasting main pitches. Start below the undercut base of the Central Pillar just left of a large pinnacle-like flake.
1. 20m 5c   Climb left-trending overhanging cracks to a good rest. Pull right and move up strenuous bulging cracks to a ledge. Climb up and right to belay below a large flake.
2. 25m 5c   From the top left end of the flake a series of small quartz holds allow an otherwise featureless slabby wall to be climbed. Move slightly right, then go up an open groove to the belay on the edge of the pillar shared with Edge of Perfection. A fine pitch.
3. and 4. 55m 5a   Finish up Edge of Perfection.

Smoke Screen   90m   HVS *   (1989/91)
Start a short distance up a grassy groove immediately right of the overhung base of Central Pillar.
1. 25m 4c   Climb an open slabby groove leading out left, then go up easier rock to belay on top of a large flake on the right, overlooking the grassy groove.
2. 30m 5a   Move up, then follow a left-trending flake crack to a niche. Climb the cracks above and a short slabby wall to a commodious ledge. An excellent sustained pitch.
3. 35m 5a   Climb two short easy slabs (in common with Edge of Perfection), then follow the flake crack splitting the final, vertical wall. Thread belay well back on the right.

Carpet Bagger   40m   VS 4b *   (1986)
Start just left of the toe of the broad buttress lying to the right of the descent gully. Climb cracks trending right to gain the arete. Climb this directly, passing a short heather section, to reach the top. Belay well back.

CREAG MHOR BHRINICOIRE   (Map Ref 743 922)

Creag Mhor Bhrinicoire is a large south-facing crag situated on the north shore of Loch Morar. It is easily reached by taking the small single track road off the A830 Fort William – Mallaig road at Morar just south of Mallaig. There is limited parking at the road head at Bracorina at Map Ref 722 928. Walk along a good track, then take a path which follows the north shore of the loch and passes under the crag after 2km. The Main Wall is the lowest cliff and is characterised by clean red-coloured rock. The rock here is a horizontally bedded schist offering steep and juggy climbing, but some of it requires care. High up and left of the Main Wall is a huge foreboding wall of less attractive rock which appears to be composed virtually entirely of loose-looking quartz. There are no routes on this.

On approaching the Main Wall from the path one arrives at the lowest point of the cliff on the frontal face. A subsidiary left wall cuts up the hillside on the left. This side wall contains the prominent flake crack of Pump and Dump. The frontal face has several main features. Firstly, right of the lowest point, is a continuous shallow groove and fault line which gives Grand Old Master. Further right again is the most prominent feature, a left-curving corner line taken by Nobs up North and Morar Magic. The routes are described from left to right.

Invasion   25m   Severe   (1989)
Start at the far left end of the crag under an obvious roof. Climb the left wall to a belay. Traverse left to descend by abseil from a tree.

Far West   60m   HVS   (1990)
This climb takes a line about two-thirds of the way up the left-hand side wall of the crag in three pitches (4a, 5a, 4a). Climb easy ground above a jumble of boulders, then follow cleaner rock to a sentry box. Exit out right from this and continue to the top.

Callanish   30m   E2 5b   (1989)
Starting some 30 metres left of the foot of the crag, take a stance directly below
a small tree about 30m above. Climb directly to the tree, with poor protection on
the crux.

LJ   30m   E1 5a   (1989)
Start as for Callanish and climb stepped holds diagonally rightwards for 12m,
then move left and go up to finish at the tree.

Pump and Dump   30m   E1 5b   (1990)
Climb the blatantly obvious overhanging flake crack on the steep left side-wall
of the main wall.

West Coast Boys   55m   E1   (1987)
Climb the chimney and crack at the very corner of the crag in two pitches (4b,
5b).

Grand Old Master   135m   HVS *   (1984)
The climb takes the obvious open groove/fault which splits the steeper left-hand
side of the frontal face. Start below the groove.
1. 35m 5a   Climb the overhanging groove to a ledge. Go up the steep flake and
bulging wall to a grass ledge.
2. 30m 4c   Scramble along the ledge for 15m until an overhanging crack can
be climbed onto a slab. Traverse left under an overhanging wall to a stance at
an eyrie.
3. 35m 4b   Move awkwardly left and climb a crack to a ledge.
4. 35m 5a   Climb over a bulge and go up the slab above into a deep corner.
Step delicately left (crux) and finish up a crack.

Nobs up North   100m   E1   (1986)
This route climbs the obvious central left-curving corner line in the middle of the
frontal face. Start directly below an overhang that bars entry to it, 5 metres left of
an undercut slab at the base of the crag.
1. 25m 5c   Step up left into a groove, then climb diagonally left and go up the
wall to pull onto a ledge under the main overhang just left of some undergrowth.
Traverse right to a quartz crack which goes through the roof. Climb this (crux) to
belay at the foot of the main corner.
2. 25m 5a   Climb the corner onto a heather ledge and a possible escape to the
right.
3. 25m 5a   Move 8 metres left along the ledge and climb a corner to another
ledge. Move right and go up a short wall to a belay ledge.
4. 25m 5a   Climb the rib above until under a large overhang. Traverse right
and go up to finish.

Morar Magic   60m   E1   (1993)
This route again climbs a line based around the obvious corner line. Start 50
metres right of the toe of the buttress at a square undercut slab with oak trees at
the top and bottom.

1. 20m 5a   Climb through the roof at the notch and get onto the lip of the slab. Step left and climb the slab by obvious flakes to a tree belay.
2. 15m 5b   Go up behind the trees for 5m, then traverse left (protection under the edge of the roof above). Step down, then make a hard move up to gain a belay in the groove.
3. 25m 5a   Climb the excellent groove. Walk off to the right.

Penguin Monster   55m   HVS   (1986)
This route takes an easier entry into the main corner line of Nobs up North from away on the right.
1. 15m   Scramble up to an oak tree about 15 metres right of the obvious corner.
2. 15m 5a   Move up a few metres from the tree and traverse delicately left across the slab above the roof to the corner.
3. 25m 5a   Climb the groove direct over a bulge to a heather ledge. Walk off to the right.

Election Mania   55m   E1   (1987)
A groove to the right of the one taken by the last three routes provides the line of this climb.
1. 20m 5b   Climb the centre of the smooth slab below and to the right of the groove line of Penguin Monster (delicate) to gain the oak tree belay.
2. 10m 4a   Climb the easy corner behind the tree to a belay on a sloping ledge on the right.
3. 25m 5b   Climb the continuing corner until a step left can be made under the overhang. Move left up a crack and move strenuously over the overhang onto a slab. Climb up to a roof, then either continue directly by bridging up the steep hanging corner, or more delicately by moving left and climbing a slab and a wall. Finish up the slab above. Belay well back.

A Reflection   20m   E3 5c *   (1989)
Right of Election Mania, approximately 75 metres right of the toe of the face, is an overhanging lip in the rock at head-height. Climb over the lip and head up left until halfway up the wall. Move gently right to good protection. Move back left and climb to a tree belay. There are some bold moves on the lower section.

SGURR BHUIDHE   (Map Ref 723 946)

A small but interesting south-facing crag sits just below the summit of the hill and is accessible from a road bridge between Bracora and Bracorina via a pleasant 30 minute walk up the east side of the burn. The crag's main features are a slabby wall on the right and a very steep rock mass bounding the left flank. The rock is rough quartz-studded schist which dries quickly. The fine views over Loch Morar and out to the Small Isles in the west are an added bonus; the perfect crag for a summer evening.

Going for the Jugular   25m   E5 6b ***   (1991)
A strenuous well-protected pitch up the left side of the severely overhanging buttress bounding the left side of the crag. Start directly beneath the widest part of the large roof. Climb the short black wall past ledges to a deep groove. Follow a slim overhung groove with difficulty to good holds on the lip of roof. Make further hard moves left into a crack and follow this on improving holds to finish by moving slightly left at the top.

After the Dance   30m   Severe   (1986)
Climb the left-hand side of the slab wall, finishing up a short corner.

Dawn Patrol   30m   Severe   (1990)
This route climbs the diagonal rib near the centre of the face, just left of a sapling at half-height. Climb the rib with a move left to flakes at half-height. Finish by a steep left-trending groove.

Before the Rain   20m   VS 4c *   (1986)
Start left of centre at a grassy bay at the right side of the overhanging buttress. Ascend cracks on the left-hand side of the bay and climb an obvious slim corner to the top.

CHARLIE'S CRAG   (Map Ref 715 859)

About 6km beyond Lochailort on the A830 Fort William – Mallaig road is Loch nan Uamh on the left. Park about 500 metres past the railway viaduct at the head of the loch opposite Prince Charlie's cairn. Head up the hillside towards its highest point. A steep red south-facing slab is reached after about 20 minutes. The view from the crag is delightful.

Chockstone Arete   60m   Severe
There is a large detached block forming a chimney with a chockstone, about 50 metres left of the red slab.
1. 30m   Climb the chimney to behind the chockstone, then traverse right to the arete which leads to a belay.
2. 30m   Follow the rib to the top.

Red Wall   60m   Mild VS 4b
1. 30m   Immediately to the right of the chimney is a steep red wall. Climb this direct to a small bay on the left.
1. 30m   Traverse back right and continue straight to the top.

Sunset Slab and Rib   55m   Mild VS 4b
Climb the red slab direct to a large heather ledge. Continue directly up the rib above.

CHOCAHOLIC'S BUTTRESS   (Map Ref 714 844)

This is a small buttress on the north side of the A830, just east of a cutting where the road bends northwards. Park opposite the crag. The approach takes at least 20 seconds. New road building will bypass this after 1998.

Cadbury Flake   12m   E1 5b   (1997)
Start at the toe of the buttress and climb a stepped groove to a hollow flake, move right into a square-cut overhung groove, then move right again and go up the wall to a tree belay.

THE GLENFINNAN AREA

Glenfinnan is 25km from Fort William on the A830 road to Mallaig road. The railway buttresses offer a fair variety of climbs, which are especially pleasant when the sun catches them in the evening. The whole area between Glenfinnan and Lochailort offers lots of scope for further development of roadside crags.

THE RAILWAY BUTTRESSES   (Map Ref 873 813)

These buttresses lie 4km west of the Visitor Centre at Glenfinnan. There is a good parking place on the road above the railway, and it is also possible to park about a 500 metres further on to get a good view of the buttresses. The crags are about 15 minutes from the road. Seen from the road, the crags comprise of a series of buttresses divided by trees and slanting away from the road.

CAVE BUTTRESS

When seen from the parking space, this small buttress lies about 400 metres to the left of Dancing Buttress at the same height across a belt of trees. It has a dark recess on its right with a sharp arete to the right again.

A Simple Twist of Fate   15m   HVS 5c   (1984)
Start at the bottom left side of the arete. Climb the arete, then follow a V-groove to the top.

DANCING BUTTRESS

This is the lowest of the main buttresses, on the left. It is characterised by several bands of overhangs running across the lowest third of the buttress. Towards the right side is a conspicuous vertical recess containing a tree and capped by a triangular overhang. There is a sharp rib forming the left side of the recess. To the right the rock is vegetated in its lower half.

Don't Fear the Reaper   25m   E3 5c *   (1984)
Some 10 metres left of the recess, the initial band of roofs form a large oval
overhang with a slight break to the right. Climb the break and traverse left to
gain a standing position on top of the oval overhang. Step left and climb a
shallow unprotected groove to the next overhang. Step left again and go up into
the wide groove for a short way. Move left around the rib, then climb slightly
rightwards to the top.

Reaper Direct   25m   E3 5c **   (1984)
Continue up the wide groove to the next roof, step right and climb the groove
above. More sustained quality and difficulty than the original.

Scaredevil   25m   E3 5c   (1984)
Between Reaper Direct and Danceclass is a prominent rib starting from a
triangular overhang about 10m up. Gain it from the foot of the open corner on
Danceclass and follow it with a move up and left, almost into Reaper Direct,
before heading back right to the top. A fine line, though rather contrived and not
well protected.

Danceclass   25m   E3 5c **   (1984)
Start 4 metres right of Reaper Direct and climb a slight break through several
bands of overhangs into an open right-facing corner. Climb this trending right.
Sustained and interesting climbing, but not well protected.

Pas de Deux   25m   E1 5b *   (1984)
Start below the sharp rib forming the left edge of the recess. Move up to the
triangular overhang at the foot of the rib, then traverse left below a small band of
overhangs for 3m. Pull over the overhang and climb the slab slightly leftwards.
The overhang move is rather strange.

Eegy Weegy   25m   E2 5b   (1984)
Start as for Pas de Deux and gain a standing position on the triangular
overhang. Climb the sharp flake above, then go up just left of the rib. There are
some very friable holds.

MACDONALD BUTTRESS

MacDonald Buttress is situated immediately left of Roof Buttress, separated
from it by a tree-filled gully. To the left and below the buttress is a slanting
grassy ramp which narrows and becomes rocky as it gains height. An obvious
crack is the main feature of the buttress.

Free Style   35m   Mild VS 4b   (1984)
Climb the obvious but rather dirty crack starting from a chimney.

ROOF BUTTRESS

This is the right-most of the buttresses. Its most obvious feature is a large horizontal roof band cutting across the central part of the buttress about 20m up. Immediately right of the buttress is a steep stream gully. The best decent is to come down well to the right of this gully. Note: A huge rockfall in 1997 has obliterated the lower left section of the crag, and much unstable rock remains.

1   Absent Friends   45m   VS *   (1973)
Start just right of the chimney, just right of the tree-filled gully at the left side of the buttress.
1. 30m 4c   Climb up, then move rightwards before heading up left to the right end of a large terrace.
2. 15m 4a   Climb the easy-angled rib above the right side of the terrace.

2   Even the Camels are Weird   25m   E3 5c *   (1984)
A steep route which is not over protected in the lower part. From just above the start of Ghost Train, traverse 3 metres left along a heather ledge. Climb straight up the wall passing just left of Ghost Train to the right end of the terrace.

3   Ghost Train   45m   E2 *   (1984)
1. 30m 5c   Climb the open groove to the left end of the roof. Traverse left a short way (crux) until clear of the roof. Follow a couple of scoops and step right to a small stance above and 5 metres right of the terrace.
2. 15m 5b   Step left and climb a right-slanting crack in the rib.

4   Callop Junction   55m   HVS **   (1973)
This route should be avoided during the nesting season. Start 3 metres right of Ghost Train, immediately right of a grass ledge 3m up.
1. 35m 5a   Climb to a rock ledge at 8m, then go slightly right to the roof. Traverse right to Hunchback and follow this through the roof to the stance. Care is needed to avoid rope drag.
2. 20m 4b   Step left and climb to the top *via* a chimney.

5   Cat People   25m   HVS 5a   (1984)
About 3 metres right of Ghost Train is a shallow yellow groove with a couple of flakes. Climb the groove slightly rightwards to the roof. Move right to a peg and either abseil off or continue as for Callop Junction.

6   Hunchback   55m   E1   (1984)
This route is well worth doing, but it should be avoided in the nesting season. Start below the break in the right side of the roof, just right of a grass ledge at head-height.
1. 30m 5b   Climb straight up to the break, the final 6m being the hardest. Go through the break, then climb up for a few metres before traversing left to a small grass stance.
2. 25m 5b   Traverse up rightwards and pull up a short buttress to easier ground.

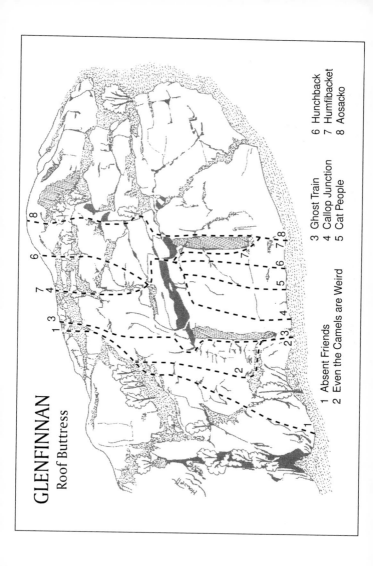

GLENFINNAN
Roof Buttress

1 Absent Friends
2 Even the Camels are Weird
3 Ghost Train
4 Callop Junction
5 Cat People
6 Hunchback
7 Humfibacket
8 Aosacko

7 Humfibacket 55m HVS * (1973)
Another route to be avoided during the nesting season. Start just right of
Hunchback.
1. 35m 5a Climb past a grass ledge to another grass ledge at the foot of a
groove leading to the roof and an old peg runner. Climb the groove and go over
the break, as for Hunchback to its stance.
2. 20m 4b Finish by the second pitch of Callop Junction.

8 Aosacko 55m E2 * (1984)
This climb is quite sustained above the peg on the first pitch.
1. 30m 5b Follow Humfibacket to the old peg runner, then climb slightly
rightwards to the right end of the roof. Continue in the same line for 5m before
stepping right into a corner with a tree belay.
2. 25m 5a Step back left and go up the left rib of the corner.

9 Corner and Slab 30m VS 4c (1984)
Start two-thirds of the way along the terrace which leads right into the gully from
the top of Hunchback. Climb a right-facing corner and the slab above.

DOME BUTTRESS

Dome Buttress lies about 1km further down the Mallaig road from the normal
parking place for the Railway Buttresses and on the same side of the road. It is
just across the railway and is unsurprisingly a dome-shaped buttress, undercut
on the right-hand side, with slabs to the left.

Silicon 12m Mild Severe (1984)
Climb the centre of the oval-shaped quartz slab 30m down and left of the main
buttress.

Wrigley Slab 25m Difficult (1984)
This route takes the rib about 10m down and left of the main buttress.

Spearmint Slab 25m Moderate (1984)
Amble up the slab between Wrigley Rib and the main buttress.

Ramp and Crack 25m E2 5b/c (1984)
Climb the left-trending ramp, just left of the foot of the buttress to its top.
Continue up a thin crack to a terrace. Quite serious for its size.

Manic Laughter 25m E1 5b (1984)
The prominent central groove starting just right of the foot of the buttress
provides the line of this route. Go up a corner, then take a right-slanting groove,
using holds on the left rib near the top.

Night Games   30m   HVS 5a   (1984)
Start about 3 metres left of the highest point of the slanting roof which undercuts the right side of the buttress. Pull over the roof and climb the corner and cracks to a rib near the top. Finish up this.

Overhang and Groove   30m   HVS 5b *   (1984)
Pull over the roof at its right end, then follow the quartz groove slightly rightwards to the final rib on Night Games.

Finally, 500 metres after Dome Buttress there are three small buttresses on a small ridge on the north side of the road. One route has been done on the clean upper buttress, lying above an oak tree.

Falling Like a Stone   15m   E3 5c   (1993)
Follow the wide crack to a ledge, gain the crack up and right and follow it to good holds above. Finish left past a small tree. The belay lies 15m back to the right.

BOATHOUSE CRAG   (Map Ref 801 831)

A red slab can be seen from the north shore of Loch Eilt. Park at a boat house and small graveyard, then walk direct to the crag in 5 minutes.

Very Gneiss Wall   15m   HVS 5a **   (1997)
Climb the obvious line up the centre of the slabby wall. The rock and the climbing are immaculate — it's a pity it's so short.

BEINN ODHAR MHOR

Beinn Odhar Mhor is situated on the north side of Loch Shiel, about 5 kilometres from Glenfinnan village, and the climbing lies on the south-east facing Shiel Buttress (Map Ref 860 781). Access is difficult. From opposite the hotel, about 1km west of the Monument, cross the Abhainn Shlatach and head due south-west, starting by either flank of the Allt na h-Aird, or walk along the lochside from the Glenfinnan Hotel. Thick bracken and much boggy land make for a 2 hour or more approach, probably longer in summer. A much more viable alternative would be to canoe or row along the loch and head directly up to the cliff, reducing the approach time by half. If the gate on the bridge over the Callop River 2km east of the Monument at Map Ref 924 793 is negotiable (unlocked), it is possible to drive down the forestry track and row or paddle directly across the loch. A further alternative approach would be to cross over the mountain from the pass between Lochs Shiel and Eilt.
    The buttress is on the lower slopes of the mountain overlooking Loch Shiel, and forms part of the narrow ridge sweeping down in a south-easterly direction from Sgurr an Iubhair *(peak of the yew tree)*. The buttress is about 130m high, and is well seen from the road just east of Glenfinnan.

The Rising   110m   Severe   (1969)
The front of the buttress is divided by a dark overhung recess high up. Start at the lowest rocks of the left-hand section.
1. 45m   Climb to a wide ledge where the buttress steepens.
2. 20m   Climb up right, then go back left and climb a steep shelf to a small stance below overhangs.
3. 45m   Climb by grooves and cracks to the top.

Mic   90m   VS   (1970)
1. 35m 4a   Climb the obvious groove near the left end of the front face, and continue up to a large perched block on ledge.
2. 15m 4c   Go up and left to the peg stance of The Rising below small overhangs.
3. 40m 4b   Move right and up to the overhang vertically above the perched block. Use a sling on the chockstone in the overhang to gain the wall above, then climb this trending slightly left. Scramble to the top.

Egret   110m   Hard Severe   (1973)
This route shares much ground with the previous two routes, and is included for completeness. A huge boulder stands on a ledge approximately 30m up the centre of the left side of the crag. Climb easily rightwards to the boulder and take a stance just to the left. Step onto the wall and either climb directly to the overhang and move left to a small perch below the roof, or step onto the wall, move left and go up a crack to the perch. Climb the overhang on huge holds, then follow a slabby crack to a stance. Continue up the crack and slabs to the top.

Eyrie   130m   HVS 5a **   (1973)
Start at a prominent vertical crack in the centre of the lowest part of the buttress, just left of a distinct deep V-gully.
1. 15m   Climb the crack to a small stance.
2. 15m   Move right a short way and go up the wall to a precarious grass ledge. Move up diagonally right to the eyrie on the left of a large roof. Climb the chimney past the overhang to a small stance.
3. etc. 100m   Traverse delicately left and climb slabs for two or three pitches to the top.

MEALL DOIRE NA MNATHA   *(Map Ref 895 768)*

On the upper western slopes of Sgorr Craobh a' Chaorainn and Sgorr nan Cearc on the south side of Loch Shiel are several buttresses, with the cleanest rock just west of and below the top of Meall Doire na Mnatha. The crag is about 400 metres long and up to 90m high. Its southern end is characterised by two obvious chimneys, the centre being formed by a steep slab wall with easier-angled rock on the far north. Belays are generally poor. Only brief descriptions are included here. The crag is best approached from

Guesachan (Map Ref 885 779) about 3km along the forestry track on the south side of Loch Shiel. Gain the start of the forestry track by the bridge over the Callop River at Map Ref 924 793. Allow about an hour and a half for the approach.

1901   60m   Difficult   (1973)
This climb is on the easy-angled northern part of the crag. Climb a short wall 7 metres left of McAlpine, and just right of a groove. Cross a ledge and follow grooves, then leave these where they turn right to continue on steeper rock further left.

McAlpine   65m   Very Difficult   (1973)
Start up a short groove (Severe) below the obvious clean rib on the northern part of the crag, and climb to a ledge at 10m. Take the rib above directly to a wide ledge (40m). Climb the wall above, 4 metres right of a right-angled groove (15m).

Concrete Bob   70m   Difficult   (1973)
Start on a slab below and right of the recess halfway up the northern part of the crag, just right of the McAlpine rib. Climb up left towards the recess, then move up to the barring overhang above. Climb over this on the left and go along cracks to the right-angled groove which leads to top.

Mallaig Extension   80m   Difficult   (1973)
Start on the lowest slab below the northern part of the crag. Climb the rib just right of the Concrete Bob recess, finishing on right-trending cracks.

Black Five   70m   Very Difficult   (1973)
Start on the lowest rock to the left of the large, steep central slab. Follow the rib for 20m and move left to a chimney. Climb this for 20m, then move left and go up to a grass ledge. Easier rock above leads to the top.

West Highland Line   85m   Very Difficult   (1973)
Follow the obvious light-coloured grooves to the left of the southern-most chimney to ledge (35m). Continue trending left (35m). The last pitch is on easier-angled ground ending in scrambling.

The Whistle of a Train   80m   Moderate   (1973)
The southern-most chimney provides the line of this easy climb. A rib and the right branch of the chimney lead to a tree, then continue directly above.

Six-Five Special   75m   Very Difficult   (1973)
Start at the bottom of the right-hand edge of the crag. Climb straight up for 40m and belay in corner 4m to the left. Go up the corner or turn it on the left and continue straight up to finish on a grass terrace.

Strathnairn and Strathspey

The following crags are scattered in two distinct areas. The first lies in or around the upper reaches of Strathnairn just south of Inverness. The area is very scenic with small lochs nestling amongst small perfectly formed wooded hills, blessed with an abundance of outcropping rock. They are all accessed easily along the B851 from Daviot, a small village off the main A9 road. The second area includes the upper and middle reaches of the mighty river Spey. This section of the Spey valley provides part of the route for the A9 and the crags are spread along it's flanks, making for easy access to them all. The weather is generally a lot milder and drier than the crags described in this guide that are on the west of Scotland and one can climb all year round, often without recourse to thermal underwear and duvets.

Until recently, the outcrops in the Strathnairn and Aviemore areas were the preserve of locals and information was only available from a variety of disparate sources including a small home-grown volume produced by the staff of Glenmore Lodge National Outdoor Training Centre; indeed many of the crags were developed by the instructors at the Lodge. This is the first time that all this information has been brought together, and as such many of the crags will be a surprise to those resident south of the Highland boundary fault. Of course, the wealth of climbing at Creag Dubh, which is described in the next chapter, is already well known and adds to the attraction of the area.

STRATHNAIRN

The maps that cover this area are Ordnance Survey 1:50,000 Sheets 35 and 36. Local amenities for those that do not wish to travel to Inverness are limited. There is a shop and petrol station at Inverarnie on the B861 on the way to Duntelchaig. The only good pub, which although rather smart seems to tolerate climbers, is The Grouse and Trout Hotel on the B851 Daviot to Fort Augustus road, immediately west of Brin Rock. Accommodation in the area is principally geared to tourists but there are two Independent Hostels within reasonable driving distance; Foyers House in the village of that name, on the south shores of Loch Ness and only a few miles south-west of Inverfarigaig (Tel. 01456 486 405) and further south, The Fort Augustus Abbey Backpackers Lodge (Tel. 01320 366 703).

DUNTELCHAIG   (Map Ref 643 316)

This group of west-facing rocks lies above the eastern end of Loch Duntelchaig just a few minutes walk from the carpark. From a distance they merge somewhat into the hillside and do not look worthwhile, but closer inspection reveals several buttresses of good quality gneiss which provide a wide variety of interesting technical climbing on well defined lines. In particular there are many crack and groove lines, generally with excellent protection. The slabs and aretes also offer some good climbing despite a tendency to smoothness and scant protection. The rock becomes very slippery in the wet. It is best visited on a sunny afternoon or evening; and is exposed to the prevailing westerly wind which can keep the midges at bay. Original exploration removed large amounts of vegetation, moss and lichen and there is little loose rock. A tendency to re-growth, hopefully discouraged by increased popularity, has given this crag a bad reputation. There is, however, some excellent climbing and as a result, opinions of the crag's quality are invariably polarised.

HISTORY

Duntelchaig was first visited by Richard Frere and friends from their Highland Mountaineering Club in 1936. It was then named The Mica Ridge and the gully formed by the pinnacle at its top right end, The Mica Chasm. In 1937, they climbed Mica Slab, Mica Arete and the "inaccessible" Mica Chimneys, left and right. The latter "is seldom followed as it is smooth and holdless, and is infested with a peculiar species of red spider". The quote is from Rock Climbs: A Guide to the crags in the neighborhood of Inverness, by Richard Frere (1938), written when aged 16. His other claim to fame was the first ascent of Savage Slit in the Cairngorms in 1945. But the most compulsive feature was Monolith Crack, first tried in 1936 and during retreat, Inaccessible Crack was spotted along a ledge and attempted also. Inaccessible Crack was climbed in 1937 by this line, not the more direct current version, and hence its name. In June 1937, Frere and Ian M.G. climbed Drum (named after the noise made by a rocking boulder), then descended Monolith Crack, a devious plan of attack for an off-width chimney. The first ascent was never noted. Little was recorded until the early sixties when many routes on Dracula Buttress and Seventy Foot Wall were pegged by members of the RAF Kinloss Mountain Rescue Team (Sullivan, Sykes, etc.). Local climbers were also active in the sixties, climbing Top Corner (R.P.Bell, R.Todd, 1964) and many of the VSs (often Ken Anderson). In autumn 1969, Robert Brown freed Dracula, one of the most strenuous routes in Scotland at the time.

There followed a lull in development, although Razor Flake and Seventy Foot Wall became established routes. The crag's popularity increased again in the late seventies and early eighties. Local climbers (particularly Duncan McCallum and John Mackenzie) were active simultaneously with Glenmore Lodge folk, (particularly Allen Fyffe and Ado Liddell). There was little contact between the two groups, so first ascent details have been hard to sort out. In general the old aided names have been retained, continuing the Dracula theme. The lower E grade routes date from this period and are among Duntelchaig's best, including Slings, Monolith Recess, Misty Crack, Timpani Rib, Garlic and Vampire.

In 1983, Duncan McCallum climbed Cyclops, the hardest on the crag until Chris Forrest succeeded on the desperate hanging groove of Wolfman to give the only E5. Interest has waned since, although the recent additions from Ian Taylor, the technical Sare and Gearr, may indicate a resurgence.

ACCESS

From the A9, turn off at Daviot on the Fort Augustus road (B851). After about 5km turn right at Inverarnie on the B861, then take the first left and follow signs to and then through Dunlichity. After another 1km the road takes the shore of a small loch, and 1km futher on, an unmetalled road leads down left to a parking place and the main loch (hidden in the trees).

From Inverness follow the B862 Dores Road for approximately 2km, then turn left on an unclassified road through Lochardil and continue along this past Loch Ashie. At a crossroads turn left and continue to find the parking place at the end of Loch Duntelchaig.

CRAG LAYOUT

There are three sections of crag, which face west on the slopes above the east end of Loch Duntelchaig. A fourth section, the Pinnacle Crag, is approached from the same parking place but away from the loch and is described later. From the parking place, an unmetalled and locked road runs below the crags on the south-east shore of the loch. The crags are not visible from the parking place. About 250 metres along the unmetalled road is a prominent short arete. Another 80 metres beyond this is access to the clearly visible nearest section, the prominently roofed Dracula Buttress. The somewhat rambling Main Crag is immediately beyond and slopes up from left to right. Below its further and higher end is a steep clean wall, Seventy Foot Wall, best seen from its obvious access point, further along and uphill on the unmetalled road. Access to the climbs (except Seventy Foot Wall) involves irritating jungle bashing. The base of the Main Crag is particularly bad and it is easiest to return to the road when going from Dracula Buttress to Seventy Foot Wall.

Saville Row   20m   Mild Severe   (1987)
This is the cleaned groove seen up on the left before reaching Dracula Buttress and from a point 200 metres beyond the locked gate.

ROADSIDE ARETE

The arete 250 metres along the access road gives three short problems. The arete climbed direct is 5a. The wall immediately to its right, finishing by a flake on the right, is also 5a. The cracks on the right, finishing by the same flake, is 4b.

DRACULA BUTTRESS

This is the first large buttress to be reached when approaching the crag from the carpark (approximately 350 metres) and it offers excellent climbs on good rock. The big roof crack of Dracula is an unmistakable feature. All the routes on Dracula Buttress were previous aid climbs; the dates recorded are those for the first free ascents. Descent is on the right by a grassy ramp which slopes up under the buttress. The climbs are described from left to right.

DUNTELCHAIG
Dracula Buttress

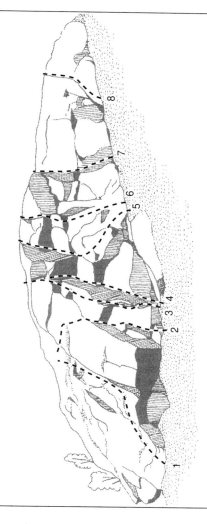

1 Soul Horror
2 Cyclops
3 Wolfman
4 Dracula

5 Vampire
6 Garlic
7 Frankenstein
8 Balrog

1   Soul Horror   25m   Severe   (1970s)
Low on the left of the buttress is a long overhang. Start left of it and traverse rightwards above it until it is possible to go up. Three trees mark the line, and although it is unpleasantly vegetated it has some good positions.

2   Cyclops   30m   E4 6a/6b   (1983)
Just to the right of the lowest point of the buttress is an overhanging right-facing corner. Climb the corner to the lip of the roof (excellent protection but very strenuous to place). Either continue up the corner (6b, overhead protection) or gain the arete on the left (poor rest) and climb it to the ledge above the corner (6a). Continue up the next corner to a belay. Finish up the easy slabs above, or escape left.

3   Wolfman   30m   E5 6b   (1991)
The hanging groove in the arete between Cyclops and Dracula. Start close to Dracula at a large block. Go out left to the arete (2 peg runners) and pull over a bulge to the base of the groove. Climb the groove with difficulty (hidden hold on left, 2 peg runners) and pull right to a resting place. Traverse right to join Dracula in the middle of its roof pitch. Finish up Dracula.

4   Dracula   30m   E3 ***   (1969)
A magnificent and strenuous climb taking the obvious corner leading to the largest roof.
1. 15m 4c   Climb the corner to a belay below the roof.
2. 15m 5c   Take the roof crack on the left to gain the front face and an easy finish.

5   Vampire   30m   E3 6a **   (1980)
The next roofed corner above and right of Dracula.
1. 20m 5a   Start 15 metres right of Dracula and take a left-slanting line of flakes to the base of the corner (serious). Climb the corner to a sloping stance under the roof.
2. 10m 6a   Precarious moves gain excellent holds on the lip and in the overhanging groove above. It is easier for the tall, both for the move and in placing the gear.

6   Garlic   20m   E3 6a   (1970s)
The corner system at the right end of the Vampire roof. Climb a green groove and move left to a fern ledge. Regain the groove, surmount blocks and move immediately left using the arete and a hidden foothold on the lip of the roof. Finish up the groove. The grade will vary with reach.

7   Frankenstein   10m   E2 5c   (1990)
Some 30 metres right of Dracula is a prominent right-facing groove, starting above the end of the last overhanging wall.

Dracula, Duntelchaig   (Climbers, Roger Webb and A.N.Other)

8   Balrog   10m   HVS 5b *   (1980)
Another 10 metres right of Frankenstein is a right-slanting crack sprouting a tree. Climb straight up the wall to reach the tree, then finish up the crack.

THE MAIN CRAG

This part of the crag, rising above a jumble of huge boulders, starts immediately right of Dracula Buttress. It starts first as steep vegetated slabs terminated in the upper half by the right-facing corner taken by Inaccessible Crack. Right of this is a halfway terrace with several big trees (Monolith Crack and Monolith Recess being behind the trees) and below them is a distinctive block at the cliff base, the Monolith. Right of the Monolith, the cliff base turns uphill to a bay with a large cluster of Rowan trees on a ledge 6m up. From these trees Great Eastern Traverse goes off left and Upper Traverse diagonally left. Above the trees is Mica Groove and right of this is the big groove of Top Corner. Right of Top Corner the crag becomes more broken and ends at an enormous detached block which appears as a pinnacle on the skyline when seen from the track. The gap between the block and the hillside is the Chasm. The routes are described from left to right.

1   Excavator   15m   Severe 4b   (1982)
The left end of the slab sports a cleaned crack leading into a left-facing corner. After a tricky start, climb these to the terrace. Abseil off a tree or a peg at the finish of Babylon (or make a descending traverse left – yuk!).

1a   Bongo   7m   HVS 4b   (1997)
On the steep headwall above the finish to Excavator is a green area of rock with a crack bordering its right side. This route starts just right of the crack and follows a line a jugs to a ledge. Finish by the wide crack on the right.

2   Long Slab   25m   Hard Severe 4b   (1964)
This route follows an obvious cleaned line in the centre of the slab, gained from the left. The start is poorly protected and the upper half is common to Babylon.

2a   Dragonfly   30m   VS 5a   (1997)
This route takes the right-hand crack line in the slab. Start 2 metres right of and below Long Slab. From a ledge, climb the bulging wall on the right (good holds), then continue easily from a sapling to a left-facing corner at the top. Step right to finish near Long Slab.

3   Misty Crack   30m   E1 5b *   (1970s)
The roofed corners and upper crack which bound the right side of the main slab provide the line of this good route. Climb the first corner and exit right, then follow the second corner and exit left onto slabs. Traverse right just above the lip, then go up a few metres to a possible belay shared with Babylon. Climb the fine crack in the steep upper wall to a tree belay. Abseil descent.

Bo-Po Crack (centre) and Double Overhang (right), Huntly's Cave
(Climber on Bo-Po Crack, Neil Morrison)

4   Babylon   40m   Severe
Start 20m up to the right from the lowest point of the crag.
1. 20m   Climb a thin crack diagonally left to reach the prominent ramp. Follow this to the skyline and belay just beyond.
2. 20m   Traverse a crack horizontally left and finish up a cleaned crack to a belay peg. Abseil off or continue up and descend to the left, cutting under Dracula Buttress.

5   Inaccessible Crack   30m   Mild VS   (1937)
1. 20m 4b   Climb the initial crack of Babylon for 10m, then take the crack above leading to a large right-facing corner. Follow this to a huge flake belay, or a better belay at the right end of the flakes.
2. 10m 4c   From the top of the flake, finish up left with a strenuous start.
Direct Start: HVS 5b
Climb the obvious overhanging crack starting 5 metres left of Drum.

6   Monolith Slab   10m   E1 5a   (1984)
This route takes the unprotected right side of the mossy slab right of Babylon start with the crux at the top. A good brushing would reveal pleasant climbing. Climb the slab trending slightly left (or start more directly), then go up to a small recess. Good holds on the wall right of the recess lead to a thin finish (avoidable on the right). The route can be used as an alternative start to either Monolith Crack or Monolith Recess.

The cliff base now drops down to the Monolith, a 5m detached pillar. Above this is a terrace with several big tress. Behind the left-most and largest tree is the quickest descent by Great Eastern Traverse or Upper Traverse.

7   Monolith Crack   30m   VS 4b   (1937)
Some 8 metres left of the monolith is a rowan tree growing out of the cliff with a crack above it. Climb the crack, then go up vegetated slabs to the largest tree at the left and scramble to the tree. Climb the offwidth chimney-crack in the huge corner (serious and harder for the short).

8   Monolith Recess   30m   E2 *   (1970s)
A strenuous route but low in the grade; splendid for lovers of jamming.
1. 20m 5a   Climb the left edge of the Monolith. Step into the groove on the left, then go up this and vegetation to belay below the obvious crack in the steep green headwall.
2. 10m 5b   Climb the crack; a fine pitch with a strenuous finish on good jams.

9   Drum   60m   Very Difficult *   (1937)
Right of the Monolith the cliff base rises again. From the first bay uphill, start left by a short chimney with a capping chockstone. Climb the right-facing corner above, or go left through a slot and back right, to reach a tree. Go out left and move onto the front face. Climb this and easy ground to a final chimney. It is often split into 4 short pitches.

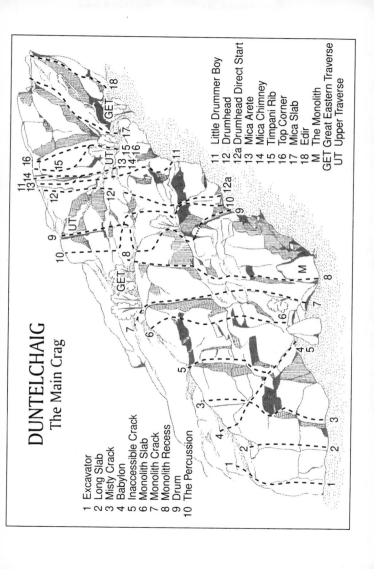

DUNTELCHAIG
The Main Crag

1 Excavator
2 Long Slab
3 Misty Crack
4 Babylon
5 Inaccessible Crack
6 Monolith Slab
7 Monolith Crack
8 Monolith Recess
9 Drum
10 The Percussion

11 Little Drummer Boy
12 Drumhead
12a Drumhead Direct Start
13 Mica Arete
14 Mica Chimney
15 Timpani Rib
16 Top Corner
17 Mica Slab
18 Edir
M The Monolith
GET Great Eastern Traverse
UT Upper Traverse

10   The Percussion   65m   E4   (1994)
A fine series of linked pitches; the crux may not have been led properly! The line
climbs walls right of Drum, crosses it in its easy middle section, then finishes by
three slabs on the left. Start at the same point as Drum.
1. 25m 5b   Climb a shallow corner into a V-notch; junction with Drumhead
Direct. Move left to the base of a crack (just before a tree) which leads to a
horizontal crack. Traverse this to the right for a couple of moves and ascend the
right edge of the slab on easy ground to belay on easy ground.
2. 10m 5c   Walk across Drum to climb a wall and a slab.
3. 15m 5c   Climb the unprotected slab above.
4. 15m 6a   The third slab is thin and also unprotected.

11   Little Drummer Boy   45m   HVS 5a *   (1970s)
A scrappy climb despite a good start and finish. Start in the next bay uphill from
Drum. On the left wall is a shallow cave.
1. 30m 5a   Climb into the cave, then exit to the right by a hand traverse leading
into a short hanging groove. Climb this to a tree on the left, then go up heather
ledges to a belay on the Upper Traverse below the final wall.
2. 15m 4c   Step onto the wall above, move right to the arete (the lower
continuation of Mica Arete) and finish up this (unprotected).
Variation: **Drumstick**   E1 5b   (1992)
If the hand traverse is overgrown, an option is the short crack above the right
end of the cave.

   Above and to the right is a large cluster of trees on a ledge at about 5m. **Great
Eastern Traverse** (45m Moderate 1930s) starts from the cluster of trees, then
traverses left including a short descent to cross Drum. **Upper Traverse** (60m
Moderate 1930s) also starts from the cluster of trees and goes diagonally left by
a series of grooves and blocks to the top of the crag.

12   Drumhead   25m   Mild VS 4b   (1962)
The second and best pitch is an obvious stepped flake crack left of Mica Arete. It
can be climbed alone by starting up Upper Traverse. The true start is from Great
Eastern Traverse, climbing up a corner and onto a block perched under a short
overhanging wall.
12a   *Direct Start:*   25m   HVS 5a
Start 5 metres right of Drum and directly below a V-notch splitting the overhang.
Climb through it (often wet) to join Drumhead.

   From here rightwards, the easiest descent back to the base of the routes is to
follow a path rightwards along the cliff top. When the top of the Chasm block
appears close to the path, cut down right just beyond it. The main path
continues beyond Seventy Foot Wall. Return right (looking down) under The
Chasm and the Main Crag.

13   Mica Arete   20m   Mild Severe *   (1937)
Start as for Upper Traverse. Climb the first easy groove, then move up the right-facing groove above. Climb the V-groove on the left to a short crack leading left to the arete. Climb the groove and a slab to finish.

14   Mica Chimney   20m   Very Difficult   (1937)
Climb as for Mica Arete to the V-groove. Continue up the groove to the top, finishing by a deep slot.

14a   Mica Chimney Right-Hand   20m   Severe   (1937)
From the right-facing groove of Mica Arete continue up right to a ledge. Climb the groove above, finishing in the deep slot (rather dirty).

15   Timpani Rib   20m   E3 5b   (1970s)
The arete left of Top Corner gives a fine climb, unfortunately with groundfall potential. From the foot of Top Corner climb a steep crack leading out left to a ledge at the foot of the arete proper. Climb this to the top.

16   Top Corner   20m   Hard Severe 4b *   (1964)
From the cluster of trees, scramble up and right over blocks to a tree belay at the foot of the obvious corner. Climb this direct to an exit left at the top. From below its final and crux section a ledge leads out left and finishes much more easily.
Variation: **Banker's Doom**   Mild VS 4b
From the second tree, traverse rightwards along a flake crack. Move up and continue traversing into a heathery corner. Harder and inferior.

17   Mica Slab   30m   Difficult   (1937)
Right of Top Corner is a mossy slab. Start in a bay below and just right of Top Corner. Climb the slab, moving up then left to below a large undercut wall. Move up and right under the overhang and continue up the corner and the slabs above.

18   Edir   20m   Mild VS 4c   (1967)
Some 30 metres right of Mica Slab, beyond an overhanging nose, is a bay. Start at the top of this. Climb an easy vegetated groove, then take the steepening on the left to gain a right-slanting layback corner. Descend by scrambling down to the right.

19   Triple Overhang   20m   HVS 5a   (1968)
Midway between Edir and The Chasm is a long low roof. Start towards its left side, just left of a wider slot which leads to vegetation. Take a crack through the roof using an obscure jug, then climb a shallow groove with a bulge. Finish up a slab on the left (invisible from below). A very high step or a squirm is required to gain the slab.

20   The Mica Chasm   12m   Difficult
Needs no description. If you can't find this one — go home!

21   Outside Route   5m   VS   (1970s)
Climb the Chasm slot on the outside by wide bridging and a pull over the chockstone. Ungradeable.

22   Chasm Crack   5m   Very Difficult   (1937)
Climb the crack in the right wall of The Chasm finishing on top of the block.

23   Chasm Roof   10m   E3 6b   (1983)
The obvious roof crack is desperate, safe and painful.

SEVENTY FOOT WALL

This is the clean steep wall below the right end of the Main Crag, below The Chasm. It is recommended for first time visitors to Duntelchaig, being easy of access from a small path from where the wall becomes visible, and the descent to the right of the wall is also straightforward. It has some excellent climbs at the HVS/E1 level, but it is too steep for the lower grades. The left-hand end of the wall is marked by a large pillar reaching to two-thirds height. A corner crack on the left of the pillar gives a poor climb, usually wet. The front face of the pillar has a thin crack, the start of Bent Peg.

1   Bent Peg   15m   HVS 5c   (1970s)
Climb the thin crack, then follow the wider crack on the right. Pull over the bulge into a groove and finish up this. Using an *in situ* peg for aid, the route becomes Hard Severe.

2   Sweeney's Crack   15m   Severe   (1958)
Climb the blocky crack to the right of the pillar, then traverse left along the top of the pillar and step awkwardly onto ledges. It is better to finish up Bent Peg.

3   Slings   15m   E1 5b **   (1970s)
Start 5 metres right of Sweeney's Crack at a thin crack. Climb it into a right-facing groove, then follow this to the roof and pull out right to finish. A sustained climb with a perplexing finish.

4   Save the Trees   15m   E3 6b   (1996)
Climb the hanging scoop in the nose right of Slings, finishing by a thin crack. Place side runners in Slings.

5   Razor Flake   15m   HVS 5a *   (1970s)
The wall right of Slings has a huge sharp-edged flake as its base. Gain the right edge of the flake and hand traverse it leftwards. Climb a crack to the halfway ledge, then finish by thin cracks above, moving left near the top. The finish is unfortunately often muddy.
5a   Direct Start: 5b
Start very directly if you are tall enough, otherwise by a short traverse from the right. The thin crack a few metres further left gives a 6a start.

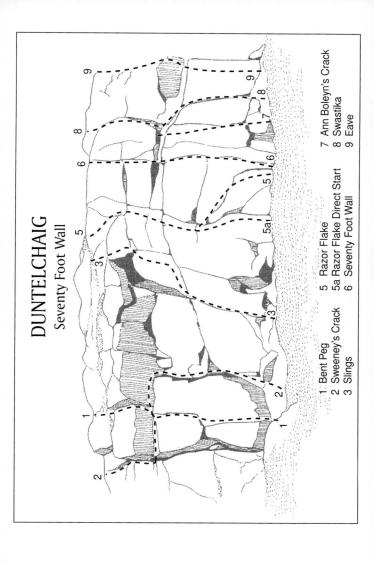

DUNTELCHAIG
Seventy Foot Wall

1: Bent Peg
2 Sweeney's Crack
3 Slings

5   Razor Flake
5a Razor Flake Direct Start
6   Seventy Foot Wall

7 Ann Boleyn's Crack
8 Swastika
9 Eave

6   Seventy Foot Wall   15m   HVS 5b *   (1970s)
The next crack line to the right has a serious start up a wide flake crack, which leads to an obvious break in the overhanging wall above.

7   Anne Boleyn's Crack   7m   E1 5c   (1979)
On the wall just left of Swastika is a shallow corner and thin crack (not to be confused with a thin crack just right of Seventy Foot Wall). The route ends at the halfway ledge; finish up Swastika.

8   Swastika   15m   Severe   (1963)
The two-tiered right-facing corner on the right. The first tier is strenuous, slightly polished, and has ground fall possibilities from the last move. The second tier is easier and finishes by a traverse off left.

9   Eave   5m   E1 5b   (1988)
About 10 metres right of Swastika is an overhanging crack leading to a small roof. Step off a block and climb the crack, pulling through the roof on the right.

10   Outside Lane   5m   HVS 5a   (1988)
At the right hand end of the wall, just before the descent path, is a clean corner chimney. This route follows the arete on the left, using the thin crack for protection and occasional holds.

Further to the right is the obvious Twenty Foot Chimney and to its left is a wall with a small ledge at two-thirds height and a tree on the rightmost of three cracks.

Eeny   5m   VS 5b   (1979)
Climb the leftmost crack, which has a broken peg, then gain the ledge and step left to finish up flakes.

Meeny   5m   Hard Severe 4c   (1979)
Climb the sharp edged layback crack to the right.

Miney   5m   Hard Severe 4c   (1979)
Climb the crack with the tree.

Mo   5m   Severe 4b   (1979)
Climb a left-slanting crack right of Twenty Foot Chimney.

Twenty Foot Chimney   5m   Severe
Descriptively named.

Girdle Traverse   25m   E1 5b   (1988)
Start up Sweeney's Crack, then take the rising crack on the right, passing a peg runner (crux). Continue along the main fault to finish up Swastika.

PINNACLE CRAG

On the opposite side of the tarmac road to Duntelchaig is a clean compact buttress of rock about 10m high. It is visible from the approach road up the hill on the right. It is more exposed to wind and therefore quicker to dry. For access, park as for the main crag but return to the tarmac road. From the junction a footpath leads up to the crag; its start is not obvious due to thick birch trees. The climbs are described from left to right.

Pinnacle Chimney   10m   Very Difficult *
Climb the obvious chimney-crack on the left, formed by the pinnacle. At the top of the fault, climb the back wall opposite the pinnacle, then step over the gap to the top.

Pinnacle Face   10m   Severe
From the foot of Easy Chimney, traverse out left onto the pinnacle and climb the face to reach its summit.

Easy Chimney   10m   Difficult
Climb the chimney on the right of the pinnacle, then finish as for Pinnacle Chimney (crux).

Confidence Wall   10m   Very Difficult
Climb the wall right of Easy Chimney on good holds.

Right Angle   10m   Very Difficult
The obvious slabby corner on the right is technically easy but poorly protected.

Tapered Groove   10m   Very Difficult *
Climb the right-facing groove starting by the foot of the previous route. It widens and eases with height.

The Wall   10m   E1 5b
Between Tapered Groove and Stepped Corner is a smooth wall. Climb it direct, hardest at the start and unprotected apart from the easier ground at the top.

Stepped Corner   10m   Severe *
A shallow right-facing corner is followed by a short crack which leads to the fine top corner. The broken ramp further right leads more easily into the final corner (Mild Severe).

Jam Crack   5m   VS 5a
Climb the right-hand of the V-shaped cracks. It is easiest to descend to the left.

Left Bay Groove   8m   Severe 4b *
The deep groove at the left of the bay has an awkward overhanging start.

Broken Groove   8m   Moderate
The easy broken groove in the back of the bay.

Gearr   8m   E3 6b *   (1995)
The steep hanging corner in the arete right of Broken Groove. Start on boulders below Broken Groove and follow a thin crack rightwards to gain the corner. Climb this using holds on the right arete to reach a jug at the top. Protection can be found in the crack on the right before an awkward move to finish.
Direct Start: E3 6b
This is the obvious direct entry.

Overhanging Chimney   8m   VS 4c
From the top of the flake, climb the obvious overhanging chimney crack. This route is slower to dry then its neighbours.

Push Off   8m   E1 5c
Climb the left-facing corner, then follow the steep V-groove at the top (well protected). The foot of the crux groove can also be reached viaa slabby ramp running up from right to left.

Sare   8m   E4 6b *   (1995)
Climb the very steep wall at the far right side of the crag past 2 peg runners.

DUNLICHITY CRAG   *(Map Ref 657 333)*

This south-facing crag lies above the village of Dunlichity (see access notes for Duntelchaig). It is easily seen when approaching Dunlichity from the east or south. The most obvious feature is an overhanging prow. This is unclimbed and far more impressive than the rather broken and somewhat vegetated crag either side. The routes were climbed in the early eighties by Steve Travers, most commonly with H. Travers. At the extreme right and higher end of the crag is a short steep wall with two thin 6m cracks. The right-hand one is Mild Severe, while the one on the left is Very Difficult.

Four Finger Flake   30m   Difficult
To the left of the wall is a detached flake below a tree. Climb the right edge of the flake, then go behind perched blocks to a ledge. Follow a shallow chimney to its top, then move 3 metres left and follow easy-angled slabs to the top of the crag.

Garnish   25m   VS 5a
The central section of the crag has a fine overhanging buttress. Left of this is a slab with a vertical wall above. Climb directly up the left side of the slab to a recess (old peg). Move diagonally left, then go back right to finish.

Ivy's Slab and Chimney   15m   Severe
On the left is an ivy choked gully. Climb the centre of the short slab under the left-facing corner to gain the foot of a right-facing corner under a small overhang. Climb up to the overhang, then traverse right into an ivy-filled corner and continue up the central rib. A steep wet exit follows.

Minder   30m   Very Difficult
About 10 metres left of Ivy's Chimney is a green scoop with a slanting crack on its left. Trend left up the crack from the scoop, then climb over thin flakes under a shallow overhang. Move left and go up smooth steps to a grass ledge and belay. Climb a crack to a right-facing chimney with a finish just left of a pine tree.

Zigzag   25m   Very Difficult
At the left end of the crag is a large detached block with a long pine tree 10m above and to the left. Climb the left-hand face of the detached block. Follow a right-trending flake crack to a wall, then go left up a ramp to a corner and blocks. Step over the blocks onto the face and climb slabs to a boulder belay. Move 3 metres left and follow a wet shallow scoop to the top.
Direct Start:
Climb the centre of the outside face of the detached block, then climb directly up the slab to join the normal route at the corner.

The Vice   6m   Severe
Start 5 metres left of the detached block. Climb an easy-angled slab to a corner, then continue up a shallow V-chimney to the pine tree.

CONGLOMERATE CRAGS

There are a number of conglomerate crags in the vicinity of Loch Duntelchaig. Some have been investigated and left alone, but they remain a possibility for the adventurous or foolhardy. A large conglomerate crag lies close to the Loch Ruthven road and overlooks the south end of Loch Duntelchaig. It has a number of impressive unclimbed faces to entice the braveheart. A huge rounded rib is a dominant feature, for death or glory. One crag, however, has been climbed on.

ASHIE FORT   *(Map Ref 601 316)*

This south-east facing crag lies on the east side of a knoll which is about 250 metres east of a T-junction on the B862 on Ashie Moor, some 1.3km north of Achnabat and 1.5km north of the road junction with Loch Ruthven near the south end of Loch Duntelchaig. The pebbles in the conglomerate seem well cemented, but don't count on it. The routes follow crack lines, so the protection is reasonable, with large hexes useful. The belays at the top are from small trees or boulders far back. Apparently the crag is not for arachnophobes as "the webs can practically stop you in your tracks". The routes are described from left to right.

Website   8m   Very Difficult   (1996)
Climb a slow-drying stepped crack which leads into a shallow left-facing corner near the left end of the crag.

Flutterbye to China   8m   E3 6a   (1996)
This route takes the left-hand of two obvious cracks just right of Website. Juggettes lead to a technical but well protected crack (take a Hex 8).

Throw Lichen to the Wind   10m   E2 5c   (1996)
Climb the guano-marked crack on the right-hand part of the overhanging section, just left of an obvious bounding chimney.

Web Astair   10m   VS 5a   (1996)
This route takes the X-shaped cracks just right of the chimney, climbed from bottom right to top left.

BRIN ROCK   *(Map Ref 659 292)*

These buttresses lie on the south flank of Creag Dhubh overlooking the B851 Daviot to Fort Augustus road. They consist of four main buttresses composed of the same rock as Duntelchaig (gneiss), but with a sunnier aspect and the stratum provides overhanging rock with incut holds. Crag One is marked on OS sheet 35 as Brin Rock. The described routes have been cleaned on abseil and are generally of high quality. The disadvantage is an awkward approach through scree or deep bracken.

HISTORY
Richard Frere first visited the crag at Christmas, 1937 and named Crag One, The Needle being an older name for the sharp buttress on its right. With Kenneth Robertson and James Walker, he climbed three routes described in his guidebook of 1938, as well as some scrambles. The location of these routes has proved elusive, despite long descriptions and even a photograph. They are probably to the right of The Needle. The rocks were visited subsequently leaving rotting pegs in The Gangplank, but the next recorded route was by Richard McHardy who climbed Treasure Island in 1975. Brin was rediscovered in 1984 by Allen Fyffe and Ado Liddell (Making Movies and The Block), but the full potential was only realised in 1985 when Fyffe returned with Andy Nisbet, repeated Treasure Island and walked The Gangplank. Nisbet climbed more routes that summer, importing Dougie Dinwoodie to lead Gold Digger. The following year, Andy Cunningham led Skytrain and Andy Nisbet climbed The Wild Man.

ACCESS
The crags are obvious from the road but the river has to be crossed. For Crag One, start to the south-west and cross the bridge to Achneim (a more direct route has a shallow wade). For The Needle and the other crags, park just over the bridge on the minor road near Brin House and head westwards through fields. Choose the least unpleasant route to the crags through scree and bracken (periscope useful). Allow 20 minutes.

CRAG ONE
This is the largest buttress high on the left. Near the left edge of its base is a pink overhung recess. Rising left is more broken crag with ribs and ramps, then a shorter steep wall containing Catweazle.

Catweazle 20m E1 5b * (1986/1987)
Left of the Pink Rib area is an overhanging wall split by a right-slanting slabby ramp leading into a deceptively steep corner. Climb a flake crack up the wall to gain the top of the ramp, then climb the corner above (crux, close to 5c). An easier start is *via* the ramp, but the lower crack is good (5a).

Pink Rib 35m Severe (1985)
Left of the huge pink recess is a large right-slanting black ramp. The route takes the rib left of this. Climb it to a tree, move right and finish up the obvious gap.

The Gangplank 40m HVS 5a ** (1985)
This route takes the right-slanting ramp on the left wall of the huge recess. Start at some blocks about 5 metres left of the recess. Climb cracks to below a shallow corner, or traverse in from the corner at the foot of the recess. Climb the left-facing corner to gain the ramp, follow this over the bulge at its top and traverse right to another corner system which leads to the top.

Treasure Island 40m E2 5b ** (1975)
A sensational route although still a little dirty. Towards the right end of the cliff, above a bulging lower wall, is a left-facing corner system bounding the right edge of a huge hanging slab. Start directly below the corner. Work diagonally left to gain a narrow hanging ramp which leads back right to the hanging slab. Climb the slab just left of the corner (or the corner itself), then continue up a ramp angling out right to finish near the fence.

THE NEEDLE

This is the next largest buttress, to the right of Crag One but closer to Block and Zed Buttresses. It has a prominent jutting nose which gives the following two routes.

The Prow 30m E1 5b * (1985)
Start at a ledge above the lowest bank of rocks and just right of the crest line. Go up between two overhanging flake cracks (old peg), then climb straight up to a ramp leading left to the crest. Climb the crest to the last ledge and make a long and scary reach up left for a flake crack and a very sensational finish.

Gold Digger 25m E3 6a *** (1985)
This route takes an overhanging groove just left of the crest line. Scramble up left from the start of The Prow to a large ledge. The groove is now on the right. Climb the groove to a point where one can move right to join The Prow. Continue upwards by an apparently loose flake to climb the finishing flake crack of The Prow from its base.
Variation: E2 5c
Move right from the groove and finish up The Prow.

Turkish Cracks   40m   HVS 5a   (1985)
Right of The Prow is an obvious recess with parallel cracks forming its corners.
Climb the left-hand crack until it becomes vegetated, traverse right and climb
the right-hand crack to the top.

Skytrain   20m   E2 5c **   (1985/1986)
Right of the recess with Turkish Cracks is an overhanging wall. The route takes
an overhanging flake crack leading to a left-slanting ramp which breaks through
the wall to the top. The original start avoided the overhanging crack by going up
right, then traversing back left (slightly easier).

ZED BUTTRESS

Right of The Needle are two buttresses one above the other. The lower buttress
is characterised by a Z-shaped fault near its left edge.

Making Movies   30m   HVS 5a *   (1984)
Left of centre is an obvious smooth right-sloping ramp which provides the climb.
Climb the ramp to its top, move left along a sharp flake, step right and up, then
work leftwards to finish left of the obvious roof.

The Wild Man   20m   E2 5b **   (1986)
A fine, sustained and well protected route. Right of the ramp of Making Movies
is an obvious flake crack. Climb it to the top, surmount the bulge immediately
above and follow a short groove into a niche with small trees. Finish
sensationally out right.

Giant Flake   20m   HVS 5a   (1986)
Climb the obvious dirty flake chimney near the left edge of the buttress, then go
up the wall above on good holds.

BLOCK BUTTRESS

This lies above Zed Buttress and shows a spectacular leaning block on the
skyline. It is cut at mid-height by a terrace.

Screen Test   35m   HVS   (1984)
Start at an obvious clean groove/ramp at about the centre of the cliff.
1. 15m 4b   Climb the ramp up leftwards to the terrace.
2. 20m 4c   Go up and slightly right to a flake crack, climb this and go left to a
hanging ramp. Follow this left past a small tree, move left round the nose, then
continue up to finish. After the nose, one can go down to a ledge and take in the
top crack, which is the best part of The Block.

The Block   20m   HVS 4c *   (1984)
The skyline block is cut by an obvious overhanging crack, the line of the climb.
Start on the midway terrace at a short corner below the crack. Climb the corner
to a terrace, then climb the crack on flakes to the top.

TYNRICH SLABS   *(Map Ref 635 273)*

Low down on the south-east slopes of Stac Gorm (Craig Ruthven) is a two-tiered slabby buttress, well seen from the Daviot to Fort Augustus road. The routes are short but with a good view and a sunny outlook. The rock is gneiss, similar to Duntelchaig, but as the crag faces south it is less lichenous and quicker to dry. The climbing is on knobbly slabs, about 60-70 degrees, and the easier routes follow shallow crack lines. Protection is often poor.

HISTORY
The slabs were named around 1937 after the farm to the south when Richard Frere and Kenneth Robertson climbed an easy vegetated line just right of the listed routes. The slabs were revisited by Inverness Mountaineering Club in May/June 1982 with the easier routes climbed by Fin Adams, Neil Lawford and Paul Saville. Brian Davison, Helen Geddes and Andy Nisbet paid two visits in 1988 and climbed all the routes, unaware of previous exploration. Puff Ball was cleaned and led, previously only top-roped ascents having been noted.

ACCESS
The best approach is from the north-east. When heading towards Fort Augustus, go about 2km past Brin Rocks and take a minor road on the right at East Croachy, signposted to Loch Ruthven Nature Reserve; follow this for about 1km. Just before Loch Ruthven comes into view, the upper tier of the crag can be seen silhouetted as the lowest crag on the left skyline. Allow 10-15 minutes for the approach; a disused track on the left is useful.

LOWER TIER

Puff Ball   15m   VS 5a *   (1988)
Climb the obvious steepening crack which splits the lower tier centrally.

Just right of Puff Ball is a sloping vegetated ramp. Right of the vegetated ramp three lines have been climbed at Difficult. From left to right these are **The Good**, **The Bad** and **The Ugly**. In practice all are ugly.

UPPER TIER

Between the two tiers is a grass terrace which ends on the left by an easy short chimney descending behind a flake. Wrinkle and Crack climbs the slab above this. There are a number of vegetated lines to the left of here, at least one has been climbed and named **Warm-Up** (Difficult). Another obvious feature is a group of large blocks sitting in the middle of the terrace below a short groove leading into a left-slanting crack (Scorpion). At the far right end of the crag a horizontal crack cuts across the bottom of the face and gives a scrappy severe route. The routes are described from left to right.

ACCESS
The nearest village is Errogie, which lies midway between Fort Augustus and Inverness on the B862 on the east side of Loch Ness. It can be reached from the south-west from the shores of Loch Ness on a minor road *via* the Pass of Inverfarigaig. Approaching from the east from the A9, take the B851 from Daviot, continue past Brin Rock and Tynrich Slabs and continue to Errogie after about 7km. From Errogie go south on the B862 to a small road which turns off to the east and goes over Loch Mhor to Wester Aberchalder. Turn left, then right to Easter Aberchalder and skirt the big house to continue on a track leading into Conagleann. Climbers are made unwelcome during the stalking season. Another approach from Dunmaglass to the north-east is difficult due to hostile natives.

LAYOUT
Although the whole hillside is rocky, the climbing is located on three buttresses of more continuous rock on the lower half of the face. These are, from left to right, Hailstorm Buttress, Raven's Roost and Scarlet Wall. Hailstorm Buttress and Raven's Roost are close together, separated by a big gully, and extend down nearly to the base of the glen. Scarlet Wall is smaller and forms the right boundary of rocky ground apart from a smaller but similar buttress well to the right. The best climbing is on Raven's Roost, which is characterised by a scoop of red overhanging rock right of its base.

HAILSTORM BUTTRESS

This is the large buttress left of the dividing gully which extends slabby rocks (whose routes are not described) well up the upper hillside. The buttress is divided into two sections by a big groove leading into a recess with twin steep grooves and many small trees above. The right-hand section has a large rowan at its base next to the gully (the start of Dropout). The left-hand section is bigger and is capped by a roof system. Gonzo and Foe finish to the left and right of these overhangs while Umbrella forces a way through the middle. Fanone lies on a steep fan-shaped slab about 100 metres left of Hailstorm Buttress and lower down. The routes are described from left to right.

Fanone   25m   Hard Severe   (1966)
Start in the centre of the fan-shaped slab to the left of the main buttress. Climb direct to a small ledge, then traverse left for 4m below the ledge. Go up a small corner and surmount the overhang. Finish by a V-notch.

Hushpuppy   70m   Very Difficult   (1966)
This route follows the left edge of the buttress. Climb the intermittent arete over several steps, then trend right over steep ground passing left of the big overhangs to finish at the same place as Gonzo.

Umbrella   70m   E2 *

(1986)

A direct line through the overhangs. Low down in the centre of the buttress is a big rock fall scar where a corner forms the stem of a big L-shaped overhang.
1. 25m 5b   Climb the corner and move out right below the overhang.
2. 20m   Go up the slab to a ledge beneath the big roof.
3. 25m 5c   Climb out right through the roof *via* a break at the right-hand end of its horizontal section and just left of the trees. Finish up a slab.

The following two routes have similar lower sections, then avoid the challenge of the upper overhangs in opposite directions.

Foe   60m   VS

(1966)

Follow the right edge of the main face (the left arete of the big V-groove) until forced onto the right wall. Climb up to a grass ledge, then climb direct to a tree below the big overhang (crux). Traverse right and exit by a waterfall!

Gonzo   80m   HVS

(1981)

Start just right of the huge V-groove at the base of the buttress.
1. 45m 5a   Climb the slab on its right side, then go over a step and move left into the groove below its very steep section. Go up the wall on the left and exit onto the slab at a big grass patch. Climb the fine crack to a tree belay.
2. 35m 4c   Traverse left under the overhangs, climb a short wall, then go back right to finish up a crack.

Dropout   6m   Severe

(1965)

This is the diagonal vegetated corner on the right section of the buttress.
1. 40m   Start by the big rowan tree and climb the clean rib on the left of the corner to a tree belay.
2. 20m   Cross the corner and climb the rib on the right on big holds.

RAVEN'S ROOST

This crag lies right of the big gully which separates it from Hailstorm Buttress. The main buttress is the most impressive piece of rock in the glen with its scoop of red overhanging rock. Above the scoop is an extensive heather terrace with a small forest. The main buttress is bounded on the right by a big roofed corner, right of which is slabby ground called The Eastern Slabs. One particular feature (at least from close up) is a small pinnacle on the buttress's left edge just right of the gully. Right of the pinnacle is a steep face containing the rather vegetated corner of Molar which leads up the left side of an overhang. Between this face and the overhanging scoop on the right is a vague arete, the line of Toad's Arete. Right of the scoop is an inset right-slanting slab containing Grande and forming a sharp arete on its right side overlooking the big roofed corner.

The most popular descent is by abseil from the terrace as the climbing deteriorates higher up. To descend on foot, continue up another tier above the forest and traverse right to a slope which leads from above Scarlet Wall back towards the base.

Tipussip   55m   Severe   (1966)
Start at the bottom left corner of the buttress.
1. 40m   Climb up the edge until it is possible to move left towards the pinnacle.
Climb a corner on the right which leads back to the buttress edge and follow this
to an overhang.
2. 15m   Traverse left and go round the arete to a pine tree, then continue to the
top.
Variation: **Pinnacle Start**
Climb the crack formed by the left side of the pinnacle.

Tip Slab   55m   VS   (1982)
Start as for Tipussip.
1. 40m 4c   Climb the edge, but soon trend right to a snaking crack. Go up this
and heathery ground to a slit cave.
2. 15m   Go up the steep wall on the right of the cave, then go back left to finish
up pleasant slabs.

The first pitches of the next three routes are much better than their upper
pitches.

Molar   90m   VS   (1981)
The big open groove is vegetated but still worthwhile.
1. 15m 4c   Climb the groove, move left, then go back right to belay under the
overhang.
2. 25m 4c   Climb the overhang by the large block and the crack above. Move
diagonally left to a huge block belay.
3. 20m   Climb the easy groove and slab to gain the left end of a heather
terrace.
4. 30m   Continue directly up the clean slab above.

The Raven   30m   VS 4c   (1981)
A sensational start leads to less clean slabs. On the face right of Molar is a
right-slanting face crack. Climb this and exit onto slabs. Trend right, then go
back left on the slabs to belay to the left on a small tree.

Toad's Arete   40m   VS 4b *   (1981)
This route follows the flakes and cracks just right of the arete which forms the
left edge of the overhanging scoop; it has big holds and is well protected. Exit
onto the arete and go up a slab to the left end of a small grass ledge. It is
possible to traverse left and abseil off the small tree of The Raven.

Grande   45m   Mild VS   (1981)
The slabby corner to the right of Toad's Arete is better than it looks, keeping to
clean rock beside the corner.
1. 15m 4b   Climb a slabby crack and a steep chimney to a stance.
2. 30m 4b   Traverse right and go up to a grass ledge. Follow the right-slanting
corner to the top.

THE EASTERN SLABS

These feature a very clean water-washed upper slab. Down the left edge of this is a black streak that peters out before reaching the ground.

Black Slab   50m   Very Difficult **   (1981)
1. 15m   Climb a slabby corner or the rib on its left.
2. 35m   Climb directly up the black streak, which is unfortunately slow to dry.

Ash Slab   50m   Hard Severe *   (1981)
A fine finish up the top slab. Start 10 metres right of Black Slab.
1. 30m   Climb a slabby depression and the steep wall right of its overhanging section. Traverse left along a big turfy ledge, then climb a blocky groove and rib just to the left of a tree to reach a ledge.
2. 20m   Climb the rib above.

Hoody Climb   50m   Very Difficult   (1981)
There is a shallow gully 10 metres right of Ash Slab with a hanging tree at 30m.
1. 35m   Climb the clean rib on the left of the shallow gully, occasionally being forced into the gully. Above the tree move left on the edge of the upper slab.
2. 15m   Climb the rib above.

Right of Hoody Climb is a rib with a large roof at its base. There are two routes on the rib, neither is well protected.

The Streak   40m   VS 4b *   (1985)
Scramble leftwards up vegetation, then climb the water streak in a vague scoop to the top.

The Grey Arete   50m   VS 4b   (1985)
Start just left of the roof. Trend right above the roof and follow the grey arete to a more broken section. Go straight up cracks to a turfy ledge, then move left and finish up pleasant slabs close to the streak.

SCARLET WALL

Low down at the northern end of the glen is the Scarlet Wall. It has a triangular bay in the centre at the base. Left of the bay are two distinct ribs separated by a groove with a small rowan tree at the top (Advisor and 7-Up). Left again is a V-groove capped by a roof (Crack and Corner), then a squat rib with a low roof. Above the bay is a large ledge with two ash trees and above them a fine slab with three water-washed streaks. Right of the bay are three ribs, the nearest having a tall finger flake (Finger Arete). The central rib has a lage rowan tree at its base. The rock on this buttress is quartzite, so the holds tend to be incut but protection can be poor.

Crack and Corner   50m   Severe   (1982)
Left of the left rib is a V-groove topped by an overhang and a crack line which leads to the top. A belay can be taken at the top of the groove.

Advisor   25m   VS   (1982)
The left-hand rib has a small overhang at 3m. Start right of Crack and Corner and turn the overhang on the left. Go diagonally right to the right edge of the rib, then climb the edge and continue to broken ground.

7-Up   60m   Severe   (1982)
The right-hand rib has a defined left arete.
1. 30m   Climb the arete to reach the left end of the big ledge with the ash trees.
2. 30m   Climb the left edge of the upper slab by the left-hand pink water-washed streak.

Little and Large   60m   Mild VS   (1982)
This route has good rock but it is close to vegetation and poorly protected. On the left side of the triangular bay is a crack with a small tree at 10m.
1. 25m 4a   Start on the left and climb to the tree. Take the narrow rib on its left, then go right over broken ground to the big ledge with the ash trees.
2. 35m 4a   Climb the upper slab up the central watermark, starting just left of the left tree.

Plumb   55m   Mild VS *   (1982)
This is the best climb on the Scarlet Wall, particularly if started up the rib of 7-Up or Little and Large, followed by a traverse to the wall. Start at the top left of the bay.
1. 20m 4b   Trend left into a right-facing corner crack. Follow this until a step left gains an arete which leads to the base of a wall. Step right to follow a crack and belay on the two ash trees.
2. 35m 4b   Starting behind the tress climb the right-hand watermark, then go right up easier slabs.

Finger Arete   90m   Severe   (1982)
A very escapable climb.
1. 25m   Step right and climb to a tree in the winding crack of the finger. Climb the arete to a ledge.
2. 25m   An awkward start on a loose spike followed by a delicate slab leads to easier ground and jammed blocks at the head of the gully which rises from the initial bay.
3. 30m   Step over to the left wall of the gully, then climb to a shallow V-groove which is followed by easy slabs.
4. 10m   Finish up a steep delicate wall.

Streaker   35m   Very Difficult   (1982)
Climb the scrappy central rib.

STRATHSPEY

Most of the crags described in this section are located close to the A9 road between Newtonmore and Aviemore. The exception is Huntly's Cave which lies north of Grantown on Spey.

AMENITIES

The Spey Valley is geared up for tourists and has a wide selection of accommodation, cafes and restaurants. There are several Independent Hostels covering the area. If wishing to be based around Aviemore there is Glen Feshie Hostel, Kincraig (Tel. 01540 651 323) and Ardenbeg Bunkhouse in Grantown on Spey (Tel. 01479 872 824). If based around Newtonmore there is Newtonmore Independent Hostel (Tel. 01540 673 360) and slightly further afield but handy for Binnein Shuas are Aite Cruinnichidh on the A86 just 5km north of Roy Bridge (Tel. 01397 712 315), and The Grey Corrie Lodge in Roy Bridge itself (Tel. 01397 712 236). Glenmore Lodge National Outdoor Training Centre, although a little off the beaten track at the end of the Glenmore road near the Cairngorm Ski slopes, offers good accommodation and a bar and is well suited for climbers. It has a good indoor climbing wall offering leading as well as bouldering (Tel. 01479 861 256). There is also a large Forestry Commission campsite at Glenmore. The Skye of Curr Hotel at Dulnain Bridge, Grantown on Spey welcomes climbers and does excellent home-made curries. It also offers bunkhouse accommodation (Tel. 01479 851 345). Aviemore has the only late-opening petrol station in the area.

There are mountaineering club huts in the area available to MCofS and BMC members. The most useful of these are Mill Cottage at Feshiebridge, Jock's Spot at Creag Dubh and the Raeburn Hut near Dalwhinnie. Details can be obtained from the MCofS.

HUNTLY'S CAVE   *(Map Ref 024 328)*

Although not strictly within the boundaries of Strathspey, this crag is most easily considered with the other crags in the Aviemore area. Huntly's Cave lies just 3 minutes walk from the main road between Grantown and Nairn. Situated in a sheltered gorge it is impressively steep and is composed of a blocky schist. It is compact, 40m long and varying in height between 6m and 25m. It is seldom less than vertical, and is characterised by vertical crack and groove lines and large blocky overhangs. Despite its steepness, most routes are easier than they appear as the rock strata dips slightly downwards giving large and numerous holds; many of the crux sections are over roofs. In general, the protection is very good and the rock excellent. The north-facing aspect and overhanging nature give shelter from wind and rain (but not midges). There are other small cliffs in the area, such as the two-tiered buttress to the left of the descent path and crags on the other side of the burn. These give some short routes. Huntly's Cave itself lies in a jumble of boulders at the downstream end of the main crag.

HISTORY
The crag was developed by instructors from RAF Grantown who climbed many of the obvious lines in the early seventies. Glenmore Lodge staff, particularly John Cunningham and Bill March, soon joined in. As with many crags in the Strathspey area, the routes have dull names because they were known by their position or feature until recent popularity required their appearance in a guidebook. Pete's Wall may have been due to Pete Boardman while Lime Street was the work of Pete Livesey. Martin Lawrence succeeded on Bo-Po Crack after several attempts and was the first to detail the routes in the Northeast Outcrops guide of 1984.

ACCESS
The crag lies just off the A939 Grantown on Spey to Nairn road, about 5km north of Grantown and 24km from Aviemore. It is named on the 1:50,000 map. Where the road runs through a cutting, there is a lay-by formed by the old road. Park at the south (Grantown) end of this cutting. From here, a stile leads to a path down across a disused railway line, over another stile and so down to the top of the cliff. A muddy path on the left (facing out) leads to the foot of the climbs.

The routes are described from the right side of the crag downwards.

1   Block Chimney   8m   Very Difficult
Climb the obvious cave-like chimney at the right end of the crag to finish at a large birch tree.

2   Jam Crack   8m   Hard Severe 4b
Start just left of Block Chimney and climb the strenuous prominent crack which splits a roof at half-height.

3   Hanging Groove   10m   E1 5c *
A short technical pitch. Start just left of Block Chimney and climb the wall to the roof at a small jammed block. Cross this to gain a short crack and a hanging groove.

4   Huntly's Jam   10m   E2 5b *
Climb the right arete of Pete's Wall, with the initial roof providing the crux. Continue directly up the arete to finish on its left side.

5   Pete's Wall   12m   E2 5c **
The climbing is sustained, strenuous and a little reachy, but very well protected, with small Friends useful. Climb the wall right of Right-hand Groove to the smallest point of the long roof. Cross this with difficulty and continue up the wall above. An easier variation trends left above the roof.

6   Right-Hand Groove   10m   Very Difficult *
Climb the obvious groove over a jutting block to finish by a horizontal tree.

7   The Curver   10m   Severe
Start at a groove 2 metres left of Right-hand Groove. Go up the groove to a roof and exit rightwards.

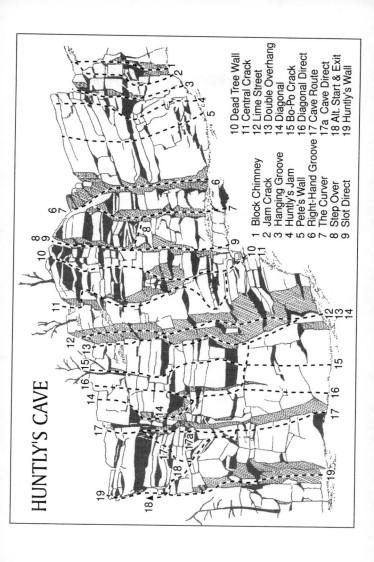

HUNTLY'S CAVE

10 Dead Tree Wall
11 Central Crack
12 Lime Street
13 Double Overhang
14 Diagonal
15 Bo-Po Crack
16 Diagonal Direct
17 Cave Route
17a Cave Direct
18 Alt. Start & Exit
19 Huntly's Wall

1 Block Chimney
2 Jam Crack
3 Hanging Groove
4 Huntly's Jam
5 Pete's Wall
6 Right-Hand Groove
7 The Curver
8 Step Over
9 Slot Direct

8 Step Over 15m Very Difficult
Start as for Curver, step left across the groove and finish up the slot above.

9 Slot Direct 10m Severe **
A steep and enjoyable route which goes directly up the third and leftmost of the grooves.

Left Rib 10m Very Difficult *
From a subsidiary groove at the foot of Slot Direct, move left to a triangular recess, step onto a pedestal, then go left round the edge. Continue up cracks to finish up the slot.

10 Dead Tree Wall 15m VS 4c *
The top overhang is now harder since the demise of the dead tree. Start below the obvious roof which is level with the start of the previous climb. Go up a crack through the right end of the roof, hand traverse left a move, then surmount the roof and go up a wall just right of a groove. Go more easily up to finish by a spectacular move through the split roof left of the more obvious Slot Direct.

11 Central Crack 20m Hard Severe 4b *
Start at the same point as the previous route. Traverse left under the roof to the edge, move up then go back right (alternatively, reach this point as for Dead Tree Wall). Work up slightly left to gain the deep crack which is followed to an exit leftwards below the final roof.
Variation Finish: 4c
Go straight over the roof to the right.

Lime-Ade 20m E2 5c *
Climb the initial overhang of Lime Street (crux), move right to the arete and follow its right side keeping left of Central Crack. This requires some willpower, but a runner might be allowed. Surmount the final roof at a small 'swallow's nest' block.

12 Lime Street 20m E4 5c **
The overhanging right wall of Double Overhang gives a fine, strenuous and well protected route which loses a star for escapability. Start off blocks at the foot of Double Overhang. Move right and pull through at a flake. Return left (subtract a grade for continuing to Double Overhang for a rest) and climb the central crack line which curves left to join Double Overhang above its second roof. Just before Double Overhang, make a long reach up right and climb walls to the top

13 Double Overhang 20m HVS 5a ***
The classic of the crag. Climb the obvious corner which is blocked by two roofs.

14 Diagonal 25m VS 4c ***
A good climb up the bottomless corners left of the Bo-Po roof. Climb Double Overhang to the first roof, traverse left and gain the left-facing corner either by a low line (strenuous) or a high line (technical). Go up the corner and move up to the next corner (possible belay). Traverse right under the final roof to finish.

15   Bo-Po Crack   20m   E3 6b *

The focal point of this route is the brief but hard roof crack which splits the hanging block left of Double Overhang. Start just left of that route and climb the scooped wall directly below the block. Climb the thin crack to gain ledges, then go up a crack in the wall above to finish beside a rowan tree.

16   Diagonal Direct   25m   E1 5c *

Start right of Cave Route on the frontal face. Climb a scooped green wall to gain the first corner of Diagonal. Go up this and exit right to an optional belay under a roof. Climb over the roof (crux) and go up the wall above.

Slabby Groove   25m   HVS 5a **

A fine route, daringly named but less strenuous than many here. Start as for Diagonal Direct but trend leftwards to the arete. Step left round the arete and pull awkwardly into a shallow groove. Continue up the stepped rock behind to finish up the bottomless crack of Cave Route.

17   Cave Route   25m   Hard Severe ***

The other classic of the crag, often split into 3 pitches. The final section is unusual and very exposed. Start at a recess near the left end of the cliff. Climb the slabby corner on the right to gain a ledge. Go up the corner at the back of the ledge for 2m, then traverse the banded wall leftwards to the prow. Move up and right to the cave below the huge final roof, then go right and finish up the bottomless crack. From the cave, thin people can escape through the squeeze chimney running leftwards or the one at the foot of the bottomless crack.

17a   Cave Direct   VS 4b

Climb the corner direct from the right end of the first ledge to the cave.

18   Alternative Start and Left Exit   25m   HVS 5a

Climb the shallow crack line on the slab 5 metres left of the normal start to the first ledge of the normal route. Continue out left to the prow, then follow a fault out leftwards to a ledge. Finish up the short steep wall to a dead tree.

The Ramp   10m   Difficult

Climb the obvious slabby ramp at the left end of the cliff.

19   Huntly's Wall   25m   E3 6a **

Start at the base of the ramp. Climb the yellow wall on the right to a crack in the first roof. Surmount the two roofs, then make fingery moves to a big ledge. Continue easily up to the left edge of the main roof, hand jam out to the front and using a flange and a hold just above, stretch for good holds high up and swing out to the lip to gain the top.

Rentokil   12m   HVS 5a

Start just below the top of the ramp. Climb a crack in the yellow wall until forced rightwards along a break to a ledge on Left Exit. Step back left and climb a steep wall to the final ledge of Left Exit. Finish at the dead tree, as for Left Exit.

Chockstone Chimney   5m   Hard Severe 4b
This short problem lies on the broken left face of the crag above the top of The Ramp, near the exit of the left squeeze chimney of Cave Route. Climb the awkward corner to the easy wide chimney.

Girdle Traverse   40m   HVS 5a *
Start from a ledge above the top of The Ramp. Traverse right to the prow, then go up into the cave. Go down and right under the roofs into Double Overhang. Cross the wall by the horizontal crack, then continue easily to Right-hand Groove. Cross Pete's Wall by a horizontal crack and finish at Hanging Groove.

BURNSIDE CRAG   *(Map Ref 884 134)*

This north-facing crag is situated just to the west of Aviemore on the north slope of the distinctive craggy hillside of Creag nan Gabhar, right next to the A9 Aviemore bypass. It provides the nearest rock climbing to the village. The crags seen from the road are broken and bird infested. As it is the smallest crag in this guidebook, and the routes are packed together, it is best considered as a locals' crag. Many of the routes are poorly protected, but as there are positive holds, just enough good runners and good landings, calculated leading is the name of the game. Grading has been difficult and opinions will vary. The forest setting means midges are in abundance.

ACCESS
Take the road north out of Aviemore. Some 120m beyond the end of speed limit signs, take the track leading left under the A9 to Burnside caravan site. Continue past the main entrance for 50m to a locked gate and a parking space. Continue along the track to another locked gate, cross it and follow a track leading left alongside the fence. Cross over a ford easily and continue to a track T-junction. Go right uphill for 500 metres to the end of the track, then turn sharp left just below a birch tree (a more obvious animal track goes diagonally left). After 200 metres the small track meets a fence, crossed by a crude stile. Continue on the track and the crag is very soon visible. In all, this takes about 20 minutes.

   Some 200 metres east of the main crag is an area of slabs which provide pleasant easy routes and good bouldering.

Wing Commander   10m   Difficult   (1986)
Climb the stepped rib on the left of the crag, just right of the descent gully.

Sideburn Corner   10m   VS 4c   (1986)
The obvious corner to the right of Wing Commander.

Grendel   10m   E3 6a   (1986)
The wall immediately right of Sideburn Corner (which is used for protection).

King Prawn   10m   HVS 5a   (1986)
Start about 3 metres right of Sideburn Corner and climb the thin crack to the small overlap and continue to the top.

Tricky Dick   10m   VS 4c   (1986)
Start at the same place, climb to the *in situ* thread and continue to the top.

Quick Flee McGee   10m   VS 4c   (1986)
Start at the same place, go up for 3m to a good runner, traverse right to a smooth overhung niche and go straight up to finish.

Inverted Schuss   10m   E1 5b   (1986)
Start 6 metres right of Sideburn Corner below a roof. Surmount the roof and climb straight up, finishing between Quick Flee McGee and the buttress edge.

Ram Hawk   15m   HVS 5a   (1986)
Start as for Inverted Schuss. Take a right-rising traverse between overlaps to the nose of the buttress. Go delicately round this and finish up the left edge

Clear for Landing   10m   E2 5b   (1986)
Start to the left of the nose of the buttress. Go straight up to cross the traverse line of Ram Hawk and instead of going right round the nose, climb straight up. Fingery and serious.

Petal   10m   E2 5b   (1986)
Start directly below the nose. Climb overhangs and move directly over the nose. Easier climbing leads to the top.

Conservancy Crack   8m   HVS 5a   (1986)
Take the obvious groove and flake corner just right of the nose of the buttress, starting with an awkward move right, then going left into the groove.

Flight Deck   8m   E3 5c   (1986)
Start just right of Conservancy Crack and climb a short groove to a ledge on the left. Climb the wall above to cracks and go over a boulder to the top. Sparsely protected, but small wires are useful.

CREAG A' MHUILINN   *(Map Ref 843 094)*

This crag is on The Alvie Estate and is very prominent on the hillside on the north west flank of Strathspey, 2 miles north of Kincraig. The rock is sound clean granite and being angled at 70-80 degrees, it has climbs of a generally delicate nature often with spaced protection, which is unique as far as Strathspey is concerned. It is in the sun most of the day and dries quickly. The estate is accessible from the A9 and permission to use the estate roads can be gained from the estate office (Map Ref 840 077). The best access takes about 15 minutes from the quarry near Easter Delfour. Cross the burn and walk uphill rightwards from the quarry. Once through the trees the crag is clearly visible. The crag is about 30 metres long and 25m in height. It is characterised by a mitre-shaped buttress on the left and a scree slope on the right, which provides the descent path. There is a ledge across the crag just past halfway and from this an overhanging wall before the final slab. There is a peg belay well back and above the right centre of the wall (sometimes hidden by vegetation).

Brian 25m E1 5a (1990)
Start on the cleaned strip on the mitre-shaped buttress. Climb straight up to the ledge (minimal protection), then go up the right-slanting corner onto the face and continue straight up to the top.

No Worries 25m E2 5b * (1990)
Take the obvious corner crack to the big ledge. Pull up the bulging wall about 2 metres right of the arete, then climb straight up. Drop a grade by climbing closer to the arete.

Blissful Thinking 25m E1 5c (1990)
Start as for No Worries, climb up to the small ledge, then take the right-trending crack to the ledge. Continue up the groove and crack to the top. The grade assumes no bridging into the corner of No Worries.

The Pinch Panther 25m E4 6a * (1990)
Start just right of Blissful Thinking. Go up easy ground before following vague cracks and a short rightward traverse to the ledge. Climb over the overhang into a small niche, then go boldly straight up to the top, trending slightly right.

Jug Addict 25m E3 5c (1990)
Start right of The Pinch Panther beneath a vague niche. Climb through this easily, then go straight up on horizontal shallow faults to the ledge (peg runner on the left). Climb over the overhang on jugs, then delicately follow the shallow finger groove on the left to the top. Poorly protected.

Myopic Bogey 25m E3 5b (1990)
Start in the rightmost niche, 2 metres right of Jug Addict. Climb the steep wall, step delicately up to the ramp trending slightly right to gain the ledge, then continue straight up the broken ground to the top. Poorly protected.

Sarcoptic Mange Mite 20m VS 4c (1990)
Start to the right of the ramp of Myopic Bogey beneath two distinct parallel cracks. Climb the cracks to the ledge. The ground above is loose and dirty — it is best to traverse off right.

FARLETTER CRAG *(Map Ref 826 032)*

The rock on this north-facing crag is schist and very similar to Creag Dubh (particularly to the upper tier of Bedtime Buttress), offering bold strenuous climbing. The crag has a high concentration of hard routes (E4-E6) tightly packed into a small area but worthwhile because they are so sustained. It is gently overhanging and dries very quickly, but because of the proximity of the trees it sometimes acquires an unusual condensation when everywhere else is dry. There have been few repeats by climbers unfamiliar with the crag, so key runners have been described. The grades assume their placement, which may not be obvious. Again it can be very heavily infested with midges.

HISTORY

Despite rumours that George Shields climbed the line of Farr One around 1970, the first known route was Strike One by John Lyall in 1983. Blyth Wright and Keith Geddes from Glenmore Lodge re-discovered the crag in the spring of 1985 and repeated these two routes but failed on a line later to become Too Farr for the Bear. They passed on the knowledge of the crag to Andy Cunningham and Andy Nisbet. The pair of Andys cleaned and climbed many of the lines at E4 and below, including Too Far for the Bear by Cunningham and The Art of Coarse Climbing (heavily pre-practised, and with a long sling on the peg) by Nisbet. In 1986 the crag became popular for top-roping. Also Farrletter South was discovered by Andy Nisbet and Keith Geddes.

In 1988, Alasdair Ross climbed the Master Farrter by a line which breached the smoother right-hand walls. In 1990 Martin Burrows-Smith adopted the crag and soon proved that the smooth walls were vulnerable anywhere at a determined 6b. He also conquered the overhanging central wall of Farlletter South which its pioneers had declined to try.

ACCESS

From Kincraig take the road to Loch Insh. Go past the loch and turn right at a junction towards Insh. About 2km beyond this junction (and 1km beyond a minor left turn for Glen Feshie) the forest clears on the right at a white cottage (Farrletter). Some 50 metres past the cottage the crag can be seen through the trees on the left, 30 metres from the road. There is parking at a forest track entrance 200 metres to the north.

The main crag has two tiers separated by a narrow ledge. This middle ledge has an assortment of pegs and trees for the convenience of top-roping. As a result the crag is popular for training and only continuous rain will prevent this. Please use slings on the trees (some are in place) to prevent damage to the trunks and roots. The upper tier has poorer rock; only KG Crack is described on both tiers. The ground below the crag is broken by an obvious step.

The routes are described first leftwards, then rightwards from the step.

Farr One   20m   E1 5b   (1985)
Start left of the step at a ledge 2m up. From the left end of the ledge, follow a right-slanting break to finish at a small rowan tree. There is some loose rock.

Private Farr   15m   E1 5b   (1985)
Climb the wall just left of the ledge to hanging blocks, then continue straight up the wall above.

Ceasefarr   15m   E2 5c *   (1985)
A good sustained route. About 3 metres left of the step is a tiny ledge 3m up. Climb up to this, then go up the wall above (peg) until moves right (peg) give a semi-rest on a good foothold. Traverse left with hands in a break just above the bulge, then finish up the left edge of the wall, passing the right end of a small slab. A right-hand finish linking with the top of Private Farr is a popular and easier alternative.

Farrplay   15m   E1 5c   (1987)
This route takes the left edge of the steep wall. Climb leftwards to a peg, move right and back left to another peg, then go diagonally leftwards to a block on the crest. Finish easily up Farrlake.

Einfahrt   25m   E2 5c   (1990)
From the far left of the crag a natural right-slanting diagonal line can be seen finishing to the right of the Ausfahrt Yew Tree. This climb attempts to follow this line. Traverse across to the first peg on Farrleft, then go up to clip the next peg and move right to join Ceasefarr. Continue up and right under the Yew Tree to finish as for Ausfahrt.

Farrlake   15m   Severe   (1985)
This route follows an obvious corner formed by a huge flake. Gain the corner from the left, or more directly from below (5b).

Ausfahrt   15m   E1 5b   (1990)
Start below a right-facing groove and roof just right of Farr One. Climb the groove and go over the roof to join Farr One. Step left and go up to finish at the Yew Tree.

Farrout   15m   E3 5c *   (1985)
Start just left of Too Farr for the Bear and go diagonally left to a small protruding block. Move up to quartz (Rock 5 and 6 in a small slot 10cm up and right from the quartz), make fingery moves up and right to a good hold, then reach left to a small niche (runners). Make a huge reach for a jug over the bulge, then forge boldly up the wall to the small tree at the end of Farr One.

Too Farr for the Bear   15m   E4 5c ***   (1985)
A remorselessly strenuous route, perhaps the best here. A vertical crack line with a porthole near its base and finishing at a chain lies 3 metres right of the step. Climb the crack past a peg runner with a move right and back left near the top. A safe route!

The Farrter   15m   E5 6a **   (1990)
Start below a peg runner high on the wall right of Too Farr for the Bear. Step up left onto a shelf and reach a long way up right for a hold in the rusty wall. Go straight up to a thin crack above the left end of a small overlap (Rock 1 and RP runners). Step up right to clip the peg and take the small overlap on the left. Finish by either stepping right and going straight up, or with a move left and up to the top.

The Master Farrter   15m   E5 6c   (1988)
The original line on this section of the wall. The move to leave The Farrter is exceptionally hard. Climb The Farrter for 4m, then move up right to a rounded hold. Continue to a jug under a small niche below and right of the peg. Go up to the peg and finish as for The Farrter.

Liquid Quartz   15m   E5 6b   (1990)
An artificial line which provides a direct start and alternative finish to Yet so Farr.
Start just left of Yet so Farr. An extended boulder problem leads to the peg on
Yet so Farr. Move up to the niche, step up right to another niche and finish direct
just left of the tree.

Yet so Farr   15m   E3 6a **   (1985)
The well chalked initial section of this route usually has a flat stone underneath
it. The difficulty depends on reach, or use of the stone. A boulder problem start
goes up to the main left-slanting crack. Follow this (peg runner) to the large
niche (good runners). Finish straight up the wall above.

Yet so Farther   15m   E5 6b   (1990)
Climb Yet so Farr to the left-slanting break (poor Friend 2 and Friend 1). It's
probably worth clipping the peg further left. Move slightly right, then go straight
up to the next horizontal break (Friend ½). Finish direct to the tree.

The Art of Coarse Climbing   10m   E5 6a **   (1985)
A very sustained route, arguably 6b. On the wall to the right is a tied-off but good
peg runner. Climb the unprotected wall slightly leftwards to the peg, step up left
then back right to a good slot. A long reach gains the top.

Links Fahren   30m   E5 6b   (1990)
A devious but reasonably logical traverse of the right section of crag giving
excellent sustained climbing. Start as for The Art of Coarse Climbing and follow
it to the slot above the peg. Traverse left along the thin break (Friend ½) to a
small niche. Step down to the larger niche on Yet so Farr, then move up left to
clip the peg on The Farrter and step down to traverse left to the peg on Too Farr
for the Bear. Climb this for 4m, then go across left to a jug on Farr Out. Finish up
this. A variation to the initial section is to traverse the break left from the peg on
Art of Course Climbing to join Yet so Farr and hence gain the niche. This is
easier (6a) and not as good as the upper traverse.

Strike One   30m   E1 5b   (1983)
Just left of the big tree is a right-curving crack line; climb it with a hard start. The
crack line continues in the same line up the next tier, becoming a shallow
groove. Finish by a short wall.

Farrt   10m   Very Difficult   (1983)
Just right of the tree is a blocky left-facing corner which provides the route.

FARLETTER SOUTH

Traverse 100 metres right from Farrletter Crag, then go up 50m to find Farrletter
South (rough going, it seems further). The routes are described from left to right.

Farralaff   10m   E1 5a   (1991)
Climb the groove 6m left of Backwoodsman and at the very left end of the crag,
finishing up the overhang on large holds.

Backwoodsman   12m   E2 5b   (1986)
Start at another shallow groove leading up to the centre of the roof. Climb the
groove to the overhang (excellent runners on the right). Pull out left through the
roof and go straight up to finish. Low in its grade.

Holiday Tricks   15m   E3 5c *   (1986/1990)
Start just left of the juniper tree at the top of the crag and climb up to the
bottomless corner at the right end of the roof. Strenuous but protected (take
three Rock 1 nuts).

Leeper Madness   15m   E3 6a/b *   (1990)
To the right of Bushwacker is a smooth bulging rusty wall low down with a
shallow groove and pine sapling in the central section. Climb to a peg at 5m and
lunge up to the right for an edge (variable grade for reach). Pull into the groove,
clip the prominent Leeper and move up to a slot (Friend 2). Finish slightly
leftwards.

Farrouche   12m   E4 6b   (1991)
The hardest line on the wall, going direct between Leeper Madness and Mighty
Mouse, using the first and second peg runners on the latter as side runners. Go
directly up to the large flat hold beside the second peg, then move slightly left to
finish.

Mighty Mouse   12m   E3 6a *   (1990)
The smooth overhanging white wall on the right looks improbable but has 3
useful pegs and some surprising holds. Start on the right, climb diagonally left
and finish direct. The crux is between the second and third pegs.

Farrthest South   10m   E2 5c   (1991)
This route takes the blocky overhang, small roof and tiny groove right of Mighty
Mouse (Friend 2½s are essential). It is easier moving right below the roof (as for
Farr Too High), which gains an extra runner high on the right.

Farr Too High   20m   E3 6a   (1991)
Start as for Farthest South. Enter the tiny groove from the right and just below
the top of the crag traverse left to the third peg on Mighty Mouse. Descend
diagonally left to below the Friend 2 slot on Leeper Madness and finish up this. If
feeling inspired, continue left to finish up Backwoodsman.

THE BADAN   *(Map Ref 827 001)*

This north-facing mica-schist crag is situated near the top of Creag Dubh, to the
south-east of Insh village. It is reported that further new routes will require
substantial cleaning. About 1½km south-west from Farrletter, just before Insh
village, there is an electricity pylon close on the left. A forestry road leaves from
here, with a left and then a right fork, which leads in about 35 minutes to the
crag.

The crag is in two sections. A northerly and higher section is seen on the left from the forestry road. There are several buttresses of maximum height about 20m. The two routes described are on the first buttress encountered from the road, characterised by a shallow cave. The southerly crag is gained by leaving the forestry road at the last left-hand bend before the exit for the northerly crag. After about 200 metres the crag becomes apparent. There is scope for extensive gardening to produce about 25 easier routes here, but as yet no-one has bothered.

NORTHERLY CRAG

The Bad Uns   20m   HVS 4c   (1987)
This route starts on the left-hand corner of the northerly crag, left of the cave, and is poorly protected for 10m when moves right lead to a deep crack with a tree.

Vrotan   20m   E4 5c   (1991)
Climb the right-hand side of the crag, starting up brittle ledges, with further strenuous climbing leading to a spectacular finish left in an overhung groove. Poorly protected on the lower (crux) section.

KINGUSSIE CRAG   *(Map Ref 748 017)*

This group of rocks lies on the eastern flanks of Creag Bheag overlooking Glen Gynack and Kingussie golf course. There are two tiers of crag, each composed of a slabby east face (Front Faces) and a vertical south face (Side Walls). The Upper Tier is compact, the Lower Tier more rambling. The Front Faces offer good easy climbs suitable for novices, but many are unsuitable for them to lead as protection is often poor and the rock slightly polished. There are stakes for belays above the Upper Tier. The Side Walls are short and vertical, often on incut holds. Protection is sometimes good and the walls are recommended for an evening visit by those leading HVS or above. The rock is a smooth mica-schist and it is very slippery in wet conditions (similar to Creag Dubh).

HISTORY
The crag was discovered by Bill March in the early seventies as an alternative to the Chalamain Gap for Glenmore Lodge National Outdoor Training Centre parties. The routes required extensive cleaning close to excavation on the Lower Tier Front Face and were equipped with bolt belays. The popularity of the crag and the controversy over bolts were both unforeseen and the belay bolts were recently replaced by stakes, but many of these have been removed recently too. The Lower Tier Side Wall was originally used for aid climbing practice. Hanging Crack and Slanting Crack have been widened by pegging and two practice bolt ladders are in place at the time of writing.

ACCESS
Near the west end of Kingussie take the road to the caravan site and golf course. The turn-off is by the Duke of Gordon Hotel and the road runs north along the side of the Gynack. From the caravan site and golf course parking area go north along the golf course on a path close to the forest fence. Where the fence turns west follow the path which leads under the side wall of the lower tier and so to the upper tier (10-15 minutes walk).

The routes without an adjectival grade are unprotected and have been soloed. The routes are described from right to left.

LOWER TIER, FRONT FACE

Classic Crack   20m   Difficult **
At the top right side of the face, often approached from above, is an obvious well protected crack.

Tennis Shoe   20m   Very Difficult **
Start 5 metres left of Classic Crack. Zigzag up on small quartz holds to a recess at 10m. Move left, then continue more easily to the top. Poor protection.

Albatross   25m   Mild Severe
Below Classic Crack, a terrace runs onto the face. This climb starts from its far end. Climb up right in a shallow groove, then go up the slab above by the thin crack.

Corrugated Slab   25m   Very Difficult
Start at the same point as Albatross. Go up a left-facing corner which soon disappears. Trend left, then finish straight up.

Freeway   45m   Very Difficult
The obvious roof at the foot of the face is split by a crack which has been climbed on aid. Start on the sharp rib below and right of the roof. Climb the rib, then go straight up to a terrace. Alternatively, trend left above the roof to gain an obvious crack which leads to the top.

Spare Rib   20m   Mild Severe
At the top left side of the face are two left-facing corners. Start 5 metres right of the bigger corner (Yellow Groove), generally following the rib overlooking the corners. Climb to a grassy bay below an overhang. Step right onto the edge and climb this directly to the top.

Groove Above   20m   Mild Severe
This route takes the bottomless corner above Yellow Groove. Climb that route for 5m, then move right into the groove above.

Yellow Groove   20m   Mild Severe
In the top left side of the face is a left-facing corner rising above the highest grass slope. Climb the corner.

Green Rib   60m   Difficult
Start on the left of the face at its lowest point. Climb the rounded edge direct to the first big ledge (belay). Continue up the ridge above trending right to gain grassy slopes leading into a left-facing bay (belay). Move out left and climb a corner crack and a rib to the top.

SIDE WALL

This wall lies below and left of the start of Green Rib. The first routes here finish on ledges. It is normal to finish by walking off rightwards although the rock above can be climbed to join Green Rib. For the routes starting further on it is normal to scramble off to the left.

The Bolts   5m   VS 5b
This route is on the first steep wall left of Green Rib. Climb the wall by the bolts finishing on the right.

Checker   5m   Very Difficult
Climb the broken left wall of the groove on the left of the bolts, then pull out left to finish.

Hole in the Wall   5m   5c
Climb the peg-scarred crescent wall to the left, moving right to finish on Checker (serious landing). Possibly it could be protected with small Friends, but it is usually soloed.

Green Wall   8m   5c
Climb the wall 3 metres left of the Hole on the Wall.

Hanging Crack   5m   HVS 5b
This is the obvious thin peg crack starting 3m up the wall.

Direct Route   6m   HVS 5b
Climb Slanting Crack to ledge at 4m, then move right and up to finish.

Slanting Crack   10m   HVS 5a *
Follow the obvious slanting crack for 6m, then move up and right to finish.

Left of Slanting Crack is a mossy scoop and left again steep walls above a slanting ramp (Devil's Staircase).

The Nose   6m   5b
Start 6 metres right of Devil's Staircase and climb the steep undercut wall keeping just left of the arete. Descend from the tree on the right.

Devil's Staircase   35m   Moderate
The obvious ramp leading up to the left.

Block Buttress   12m   E2 5c *
The blocky overhanging buttress right of the Flake. Start about 5m up Devil's Staircase and from a subsidiary ramp on the right. Move up and left to the bottom end of the flake. Pull through the bulge into a short hanging groove on the left, then move right to stand on a nose. Trend left to the top.

The Flake   12m   HVS 5a **
Start up Devil's Staircase until level with the foot of the flake. Climb to the obvious flake crack which leads to an exit to the right. Finish up easier slabs.

Bolt Revolt   10m   E4 5c   (1992)
A bold route with limited RP protection which takes the wall between the bolt ladder and The Flake. Start just right of the bolts. Move onto the wall *via* a small rock step and climb straight up, finishing to the right. Clipping the bolts reduces the grade to E2.

Bolt Ladder of the Flake   10m   E3 5c   (1980)
A bolted wall lies 6 metres left of The Flake. Follow the bolt line and belay well back. Sustained and strenuous, but safe.

Hole in One   10m   E4 6a   (1988)
Left of the bolt ladder is a shiny diamond-shaped wall bounded on the left by a capping roof. Start below the centre of the wall and move diagonally right to a flange. Go up the overhanging wall above, then reach back left to jugs at the top of the shiny wall (poor Rock 1 out on the left). Climb the shallow overhanging groove above to good finishing holds. Bold.

UPPER TIER, FRONT FACE

First Pull   6m   VS 4c
Climb the short thin crack just left of the corner.

Pullover   10m   Severe
Start 3 metres left of the corner bounding the right end of the crag. Climb left-trending ledges to the overhang, pull over and finish up Little Wall.

Little Wall   12m   Difficult *
Traverse left into a left-facing corner, then climb the corner and the continuing crack to the top.

Little Wall Direct   10m   Very Difficult
Start by a triangular niche at head-height. Climb into the niche, then move up into the hanging corner.

Little Crack   10m   Difficult
Climb the short thin crack at the left edge of the wall to a block. Continue up the scrappy groove and the crack above.

Mango Rib   8m   Very Difficult
Climb the clean rib above and 5 metres left of Little Crack, finishing by some overhangs.

Capped Corner   12m   Mild Severe *
Ascend the left-facing groove right of the obvious slab, pull out right at the roof and finish up a rib; poor protection.

The Slab   12m   Difficult **
From the foot of Capped Corner climb the slab diagonally leftwards to The Edge.

The Edge   15m   Very Difficult *
Start from a rock ledge below a steep wall. Climb the steep wall and finish up the easier arete. Poor protection.

Quartz Wall   15m   VS 4c
Climbs the wall to the right of the groove without using the easier routes either side.

The Groove   15m   Hard Severe **
Climb the fine open corner.

Grooved Arete   15m   VS 4c
Start in a recess and climb the steep 3m wall on the right, pull right onto a rib, climb a short corner and continue direct.
Direct Start: 5b
Climb tthe rib directly into the short corner.

The Block   10m   Very Difficult
From the recess, move out left and climb up to obvious blocks. Finish straight up.
Direct Start: Severe
Climb direct up the rib to the blocks.

Far Right Crack   6m   5c
Climb the thin crack immediately left of the edge.

Right-Hand Crack   10m   HVS 5a **
This is the obvious steep crack on the right of the wall. It is also possible to hand traverse to the right-hand rib at about half-height.

Central Wall   10m   E2 5b
Start 3 metres left of the previous route. Climb the green wall direct to the start of a left-slanting crack high up (good runners here). Follow this crack leftwards to the obvious crack leading back right (Deputy Dawg).

Left-Hand Crack   10m   E1 5b *
Climb the crack to a small roof. Reach right and move back left to finish up the thin crack above the lower crack (or finish up Deputy Dawg to reduce the grade to HVS overall).

Leftover   10m   E2 5c *
A direct line up the wall and stepped roofs close to the left edge of the wall. Two peg runners indicate the line.

Deputy Dawg   10m   HVS 5a
Follow the crack which rises diagonally to the right.

Finale   8m   Very Difficult
Climb the left bounding corner of the wall.

DYKE SLAB

This small outcrop lies below and left of the Upper Tier. The best route lies up the clean rounded rib at its centre (10m, Very Difficult). Other short routes and variations are possible.

ORDAN SHIOS   *(Map Ref 715 969)*

This is a small but conspicuous north-facing outcrop south of the A9 road just past the turn to Newtonmore. About a dozen 20m routes have been done, varying from about Very Difficult to Severe.

Creag Dubh and Laggan

CREAG DUBH   (Map Ref 672 959)

Creag Dubh is one of Scotland's largest roadside crags with over 100 routes of up to 100m in length. In fact, it can justifiably claim to be the finest roadside crag in Scotland. The rock is mica schist with horizontal strata providing big flat holds on steep exposed rock, sometimes with spaced protection, giving the crag a reputation for exhilarating, occasionally scary climbing. Facing south, the crag dries quickly on the whole. There is, however, some drainage and the smooth rock is lethal in the wet. Similarly, hot sweaty weather is a disadvantage however big a chalk bag is carried. The rock is generally good but occasionally blocky; rock failure has led to some spectacular consequences in the past.

Creag Dubh is not a good choice for beginners; the protection requires too much calculation and there is little below Severe. From VS upwards the climbing is good and the choice increases with one's ability. Many of the routes have unpleasant grassy finishes and long descents so it is common to abseil from trees. Specific details are included in the text to help. Many old slings are *in situ* but none of them should be regarded as totally reliable.

The whole crag is inhabited by a small but hardy herd of feral goats which provide interest for the bored belayer, but they also dislodge rocks, particularly from above the Central Wall area. Although helmets might provide some protection from stone fall they would be no help in the event of falling goats (and sheep). This occurs surprisingly often and the carcasses at the base of the crags are smelly on a hot day.

AMENITIES
See page 171 for information

HISTORY
The first proper recorded route in this area was Rib Direct. However, an article in an early edition of the SMC Journal by Raeburn and Walker shows how climbers had taken an interest in these cliffs as far back as 1903. Indeed, these earlier writings clearly describe the lines now taken by Fred and the big vegetated gully bounding the left side of Great Wall. In the late fifties and early sixties development really got under way. In 1959, Sullivan and Parkin climbed the obvious line of Nutcracker Chimney. That same year Sullivan returned with Collingham to climb the steeper and more impressive Brute. In October 1964, Dougal Haston climbed Inbred, up the steepest part of the most impressive wall on the crag. The route soon gained a reputation as one of Scotland's most intimidating free climbs.

In May the following year, Haston and the Edinburgh Squirrels added no less than 18 new routes, including the three star classics, Tree Hee (Severe) and King Bee (VS). Also included and subsequently dismissed were some lower grade earthy horrors. The total was 36 by the end of 1965 and the refusal of the SMC to publish outcrop routes infuriated the Squirrels so they published a guide themselves (*Creag Dubh and the Eastern Outcrops*, 1967 by Graham Tiso) and gave the routes obscene names to break another SMC rule.

In 1967 the Kenny Spence and Porteous partnership emerged from Edinburgh as one of the strongest teams to appear on the Scottish scene since the days of Smith and Marshall. Spence made his debut with The Hill, a bold and serious lead which still commands respect today.

In 1971, the Great Wall received more attention with the steep and serious Outspan (Barley and Griffiths) and Organ Grinder (Ken Crocket and Colin Stead). Later that year saw the start of interest by staff from Glenmore Lodge, with Bill March and Fred Harper contributing LMF, while Allen Fyffe opened up Lower Waterfall Wall with two routes. These cliffs also witnessed some impressive solo performances, notably Ian Nicolson's ascents of Inbred and King Bee, the former while George Shields was engrossed in the second ascent of The Hill. Living in Aviemore, Shields adopted Creag Dubh as his local crag which resulted in several fine routes. Niagara is probably his best route, but he also freed Minge and Jump so High and soloed Slanting Groove.

After 1972, many of the best lines below E2 had been climbed, and renewed interest awaited a rise in standards. This happened in 1976 when a group of young Edinburgh climbers adopted a more sophisticated style of climbing with training, chalk, and Friends. The group consisted of Dave (Cubby) Cuthbertson, Rab Anderson, Alan Taylor, Dave Brown and Derek Jamieson. Although regarded as 'the new breed', they had a sense of tradition and would hitch hike up to Newtonmore on Friday nights and go straight to the pub. They would then stagger along the road to camp under the crag.

Cuthbertson was the driving force with ascents of Run Free (E4) in 1976 and opening up the Upper Tier of Bedtime Buttress in 1977 with Ruff Licks (E3) and the popular Muffin the Mule (E1). From then on, Cuthbertson climbed a few routes each year, working his way through the big steep walls, like The Fuhrer in 1979 with Ian Duckworth and Instant Lemon in 1980 with Derek Jamieson. In 1981, in preparation for a new guide, 21 routes were climbed, again mostly by Cuthbertson frequently seconded by Rab Anderson. These routes included six of the best strenuous modern routes, producing development of the steepest section of Waterfall Wall with Acapulco (E4), Independence (E2) and Wet Dreams (E2) and filling three hard gaps on Bedtime Buttress Upper Tier with Ayatollah (E4), Cadillac (E4) and Galaxy (E4).

During the Eighties, many of the remaining gaps were plugged. Mal Duff and Tony Brindle climbed a number of eliminates including some scary E4s. Gary Latter added Heather Wall (E4), girdled Upper Bedtime Buttress and repeated Silicosis (E5). Two hard additions from Graeme Livingston were Apathizer (E5) and Bratach Uaine (E4). The Great Wall came under close scrutiny with every last potential line succumbing. Cuthbertson produced the unprotected Colder than a Hooker's Heart (E5); Whilst Steve Monks nabbed the central line with The Final Solution (E5). Grant Farquhar made the second ascent of this latter route thinking it was the first ascent, then returned to squeeze in Harder Than

Your Husband (E5). The Final Solution has been the only one to prove popular (and has seen some long, near ground falls) whilst the others saw second ascents from Kevin Howett. Farquhar repeated Apathizer and Bratach Uaine before adding a serious direct start to the latter with Snot Rag (E6).

It is hard to imagine any extensive development in future as the walls are climbable anywhere and frequently have been. Recent activity has been to fill in some gaps, Jim Kerr and Richard Mansfield being keen, whilst Paul Thorburn produced This One (E4), and Chris Forrest climbed Cross Leaved Heath (E5).

WINTER

Creag Dubh can be used as a valley option for winter climbing in times of bad weather or deep powder in the mountains. The slabby lower half of Oui-Oui is by far the best route. After a few hard frosty nights and cold days at valley level, it provides a popular two-pitch Grade III on continuous ice. About once every five years the weather is cold enough for the top half to be converted into a huge icicle. It tends to form a lattice of smaller icicles which do not take ice protection. It has been led using rock protection on the left to within 6m of the top when a potential ground fall persuaded a top rope escape (1986). It remains a last great climatic problem for Scottish ice climbing. Partially formed icicles are a big threat to climbers on the normal route. Several of the other faults have been climbed, usually with a mixture of ice, semi-frozen turf and tree belays. The turf takes much longer to freeze than Oui-Oui. The lines of Romp and Fred (easy Grade IV) are natural. Some more esoteric lines have been climbed, such as Turf at the Top (III/IV) which starts left of Hornet and finishes up Raven's Squawk and Lethal Affair (V,5) up the fault between Great Wall and Lower Central Wall.

ACCESS

Leave the A9 Perth to Inverness road to go to Newtonmore (15 miles south of Aviemore), then take the A86 towards Spean Bridge for 3 miles. There is a lay-by opposite a small gate leading to a large field at the west end of the western of two lochs. The crag is clearly visible on the right. Travelling from the west (Fort William and Spean Bridge), the crag is even more obvious.

GENERAL LAYOUT

To get a good view of the crag on a first visit, go just through the small gate on the opposite side of the road from the parking space onto to a grassy knoll. High on the right is Sprawl Wall slanting diagonally down the hillside with the black-streaked wall of Instant Lemon at its lower right end. The nearest wall to the road is Central Wall. This is a continuous long wall defined on the right by the Lower Central Wall, with its distinctive growths of ivy, and on the left end by an impressive waterfall (obvious in all but a drought). The tall, smooth and light-coloured wall in the centre is Great Wall. The usual approach path starts from the lay-by and wanders up the hillside to below this wall. Lower and further left, only seen by evading the trees, is Bedtime Buttress with a big roof at its upper right and its Upper Tier is just visible in profile behind it.

BEDTIME BUTTRESS

This is the furthest left (west) and lowest buttress. The routes are shorter than at other sections of Creag Dubh, but they are of excellent quality and on perfect rock. The walls are not visible from the Central Wall area but the large roof at the top right of the buttress is often seen in profile.

Approaching from the Central Wall area, go to the base of the waterfall (Waterfall Wall), then pick a line diagonally leftwards and descend almost to the base of the slope to pass immediately under the Lower Right Wall of Bedtime Buttress. A direct approach starts at a gate opposite and just east of the gatehouse to the Creag Dubh Lodge (400 metres west of the lay-by). Cross the gate and follow a stalking track through the trees, then ascend beside a stream until the trees thin and a good frontal view of Bedtime Buttress is seen.

The buttress is split into four sections by a horizontal terrace and a vertical corner-gully with many trees. The two lower sections are similar-shaped walls, the Lower Right Wall is the most inspiring giving a continuous 50m slab, whilst The Lower Left Wall contains more vegetation. The upper left is a long low buttress of steep clean rock (The Upper Tier) with many excellent strenuous routes. The upper right is the huge protruding roof.

LOWER LEFT WALL

The main feature is an alcove at the base formed by a roof. The routes are described left to right. To descend, traverse right and go down the unpleasant gully which is the approach to the Upper Tier (or make a short abseil).

1 Negligee 40m VS 5a (1965)
A good route with an awkward start at the left end of the low roof. Climb a short wall to the roof, turn this on the left and continue by a groove and a corner to finish.

2 Quickie 30m HVS 5a * (1977)
A sustained and balancy climb which provides a useful approach to the Upper Tier. Start as for Negligee. After the roof, move right and climb the wall going diagonally leftwards to finish up a short crack.

3 Downtown Lunch 80m HVS ** (1965)
A good technical first pitch, after which it is common to escape to the left, although the last pitch is also good. Start at the right end of the low roof 5 metres right of Negligee.
1. 25m 5b Step up right to a ledge and a small roof on its left. Traverse back left and gain the main slab above with difficulty. Take an obvious line slightly leftwards to belay at blocks.
2. 25m Ascend scrappily to the right end of the terrace below the Upper Tier.
3. 30m 5a Climb the gully round the right end of the Upper Tier to a ledge on the left (Muffin the Mule stands at its left end). Climb a groove, then step left onto the front face and finish more easily.

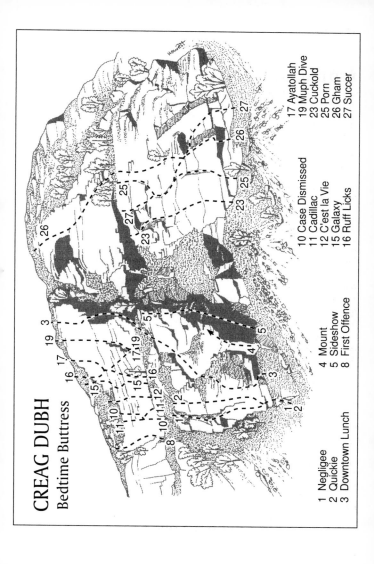

CREAG DUBH
Bedtime Buttress

1 Negligee
2 Quickie
3 Downtown Lunch

4 Mount
5 Sideshow
8 First Offence

10 Case Dismissed
11 Cadillac
12 C'est la Vie
15 Galaxy
16 Ruff Licks

17 Ayatollah
19 Muph Dive
23 Cuckold
25 Porn
26 Gham
27 Succer

4 Mount 30m Very Difficult
This is the scruffy arete right of Downtime Lunch.

5 Sideshow 30m HVS 4c (1976)
A loose and serious pitch. Right of Mount is a sidewall sloping up to a corner crack. Ascend the wall diagonally from left to right and climb a loose overhang to finish.

THE UPPER TIER

This immaculate smooth wall is split by horizontal breaks; most are good, but some are not so good. It is reached by a short wet fault left of the Lower Left Wall, followed by a diagonal scramble to the right to reach the terrace under the wall. It is essentially divided into two sections, left and right, as defined either side of this access route. The routes are described from left to right.

Descent is either by abseil (but abseil points are awkward unless returning to the top) or by traversing the cliff top westwards and descending just beyond a single big pine amongst birch to gain the upper west end of the terrace (or go further and lower for an easier approach).

The left-hand section consists of a small, but very steep compact buttress up and left of the diagonal gully-fault reached on the approach to the crag.

6 Unlawful Behaviour 15m E2 5b (1991)
This route takes the left-hand wall finishing just left of a dead bush. Climb up and left of a damp section and continue direct to a small niche and so to the top.

7 Jailbreak 15m E3 5c (1991)
Very good climbing taking the wall direct. Start as for Unlawful Behaviour, then move slightly right to a good hold. Climb direct to finish right of the dead bush.

8 First Offence 30m E4 5c ** (1981)
A fine climb up the left-hand edge of the right-hand section just above the approach. Start at the base of the left-slanting gully-fault. Ascend to a sapling (often wet), then swing out right and go up the wall rightwards to a pocket (protection). Climb leftwards to the obvious flake, go up this, then move left over the bulge to finish.

9 The Art of Relaxation 25m E4 6a *** (1981)
A sustained pitch. Start just left of the obvious overhanging crack of Case Dismissed. Climb the wall to a good break on the left. Move slightly right and continue up a crack line to a ledge and tree belay.

10 Case Dismissed 25m E3 6a *** (1978)
A fine pitch up the obvious overhanging crack left of the large boulder on the ledge. Climb direct to gain the crack. At its top, step up and right onto a foot ledge. Traverse right along this to its end and climb the quartz crack on the left to a block overhang before moving left to a ledge and tree belay. It is possible to continue directly to the tree at E4 6a.

11   Cadillac   20m   E4 6a *   (1981)
Start on top of the boulder right of Case Dismissed. Step onto the wall and
traverse left to join Case Dismissed at the top of the crack. Continue up in a
direct line to the tree belay.

12   C'est la Vie   15m   E3 5c   (1981)
A poorly protected pitch. Start just right of the boulder. Ascend a thin crack to a
niche, then exit leftwards to finish.

13   Hands Off   20m   E2 5c   (1981)
Start 5 metres right of C'est la Vie and gain thin cracks which lead to the right
side of the niche of that route. Finish direct up the wall.

14   Legover   15m   E2 5c   (1986)
This route climbs the wall directly above the start of Hands Off. Ascend the wall
to a good break. Move up and left to gain a good layaway, then finish up to the
right.

15   Galaxy   25m   E4 6a **   (1981)
This tenuous route climbs the wall left of the crack of Ruff Licks. Climb directly
up indefinite hairline cracks to a good break line. Continue first left then right up
the difficult wall above to finish at two short finger cracks.

16   Ruff Licks   25m   E3 5c ***   (1977)
Sustained and enjoyable climbing after a bold start. Start below the obvious
quartz crack and gain it via the thin crack on the left. Climb this to a sapling in a
horizontal break at two-thirds height. Step left and climb the thin crack to the top.
A good introduction to the harder routes on this wall.

17   Ayatollah   25m   E4 6a ***   (1981)
Excellent sustained climbing with improving protection taking a left-slanting
diagonal line up the wall right of Ruff Licks. Start in the corner of Muph Dive.
Follow this for 4m to a roof. Pull left round the arete to a quartz pocket
(protection). Move left and up to a horizontal break, then continue left and up to
a small circular quartz recess. Climb past this to the top break and move left to a
junction with Ruff Licks at the sapling. Move out right up the wall and slab to
finish.

18   Apathizer   25m   E5 6b **   (1986)
A more direct version of Ayatollah; strenuous and fingery. Start just left of the
arete of the corner. Climb direct to the quartz pocket of Ayatollah. Follow this up
and left to the break. Step up, traverse back right, then continue up and slightly
leftwards with difficulty to gain the top break. Step right and finish directly up the
slab.

19   Muph Dive   25m   E2 5c **   (1965)
A superb technical pitch climbing the stepped overhanging corner near
the right-hand end of the wall. It is quite serious and at the top of its grade.

20   Muffin the Mule   25m   E1 5c *   (1977)
Good, well protected climbing up the wall right of the corner. Start up a thin
awkward crack to gain a horizontal break. Follow this rightwards to a ledge
before climbing the slabby wall above.
Direct Start: E2 6a *
Gain the ledge on the normal route by the shallow overhanging groove.
Indirect Start: HVS 5b
Start as for Muph Dive, then traverse the horizontal break throughout to join the
parent route. Popular.

21   Nobodies Fault but Mine   60m   E4 *   (1985)
A left to right girdle of the Upper Tier. Start from just below the tree in the
gully-fault above First Offence (abseil to here recommended).
1. 20m 5c   Pull round onto the wall 2m below a projecting triangular block.
Follow a fault until it fades at some quartz and descend for about 3m to follow a
break into Case Dismissed. Go up this to a spike runner, then move across to
the foot ledge. Continue along the break to belay in the niche of C'est la Vie (tree
useful above).
2. 40m 6a   Follow the lower of the two most obvious breaks until it becomes
blind, where a difficult move up gains the lowest point of the top of the wall.
Hand traverse this to gain a good break and follow this to a good rest on Ruff
Licks. Continue in the same line (strenuous and sustained) to reach easier
ground on Muph Dive. Follow the obvious line through Muffin the Mule and
finish up the more broken slab to the right.

22   Downtown after Lunch   HVS 5a **
Taken as a separate route in its own right, this is the last pitch of Downtown
Lunch just beyond the right end of The Terrace. Start as for Muffin the Mule.
Climb the thin crack and traverse of that route to the ledge. From the right end of
this ledge climb a groove, then step left onto the front face and finish up more
easily. This is the easiest pitch on the Upper Tier.

LOWER RIGHT WALL

This excellent quartz-streaked slab gives two pitch routes on good rock. Most
finish on a terrace below the Roof of the Upper Right Wall. The routes are
described from left to right. Descent is by abseil from trees on the terrace, or
from the top descend on foot well to the right.

23   Cuckold   50m   E1 **   (1965/74)
An excellent route up the left side of the slab with fine contrasting pitches. Start
below a thin diagonal crack near the left edge.
1. 35m 4c   Gain and climb the crack. Where it fades make a delicate left
traverse into a corner and climb this to a cramped stance and belay on the left.
2. 15m 5b   Climb the quartz groove above to the overhang. Turn it awkwardly
on the left, then go up to a ledge and tree belay.

24   Most Girls Do   30m   E1 5a *   (1985)
A direct line up the middle of the wall between Cuckold and Porn. Start just left of a small corner. Climb the wall taking a direct line towards a prominent quartz intrusion high up. Cross this moving up and right (crux) to reach the top. Continue up Porn or abseil off.

25   Porn   45m   HVS *   (1970)
Good open climbing up the left-trending line to the right of Cuckold. Start left of Gham beside a fallen tree.
1. 35m 5a   Climb a short steep wall and thin crack to gain a corner on the right. Follow this and a left-trending line until bold moves up and right can be made to a small cave belay.
2. 10m 4c   Climb a thin crack in the steep wall on the right to a big tree. Abseil descent.

26   Gham   90m   VS   (1965)
Start beneath a pink quartz jutting shelf near the right end of the crag. It is common to abseil off after the first pitch, which is by far the best and hardest.
1. 20m 4c   Mantleshelf onto a ledge and traverse right into a corner. Climb this, avoiding the roof on the left and continue to a tree belay.
2. 30m 4a   Move left onto the wall and climb up to gain a crack which leads to a ledge and tree belay.
3. 40m   Climb the slab and the right side of the roof to finish.

27   Succer   60m   E1   (1980)
This route follows the left-slanting diagonal quartz band. Start at an overhanging groove near the right end of the crag.
1. 40m 5a   Climb the groove and quartz to the corner of Gham. Continue round the corner to the left following the band of quartz to gain a belay on Porn.
2. 20m 5a   Go left up the wall to a cracked depression, then climb this over a bulge to finish at a tree belay on the left.

The loose and dangerous corner right of Succer, followed by vegetated slabs right of Gham, is **Prak** (Severe).

LITTLE ROCK

There is a scrappy long wall below and left of Waterfall Lower Wall. The tier below this, but situated well to the left, is Little Rock, a clean yellow overhanging wall with a huge two stepped ramp line below it and near the cliff base (Hungarian Hamstring). The rock is good and clean. The routes are described from right to left.

Mistaken Identity   45m   Mild VS 4b   (1983)
This route takes the obvious arete to the right of Hungarian Hamstring. It is very artificial, close to silly if it weren't so sensational.

5   Zygote   25m   E2 5c   (1990)
Follow Brazen to the bush on the grassy ledge. Continue straight up to the roof and boldly pull through its right end to finish up the wall above.

6   Brazen   25m   VS 5a   (1972)
Start below and left of a perched block on a ledge. Climb a left-slanting crack to the small bushy rowan near the left end of the grassy ledge. Go right, then trend right up the wall above.

7   Warmer than a Badger's Bum   10m   E1 5b   (1986)
Right of Brazen is a wedged block at two-thirds height. This route takes a devious line to this from the left. Start at the foot of a left-slanting crack (Brazen) and climb the wall direct until it is possible to traverse right along a horizontal crack to the block. Climb over this and further blocks to finish.

The Bum Direct   10m   HVS 5a
Avoid the right traverse by going straight up to a messy finish.

The Badger Direct   10m   E2 5c
A more satisfying line going directly to the block. Climb the wall below and slightly right of the block past a small ledge (good runner in a niche on the right), then pull left onto the block. Climb over the blocks to finish.

8   Pattern of Violence   10m   E1 5b *   (1983)
On the wall above the large lower birch is an alcove like a sentry box. Some 3 metres left of this is a left-slanting crack which provides this route.

9   On Guard   12m   E1 5c   (1991)
Start immediately behind the birch and climb the wall (crux) below the right end of the sentry box alcove. Pull into the alcove and out of its top.

10   Take Three   12m   E2 5b   (1991)
Three metres below the large birch a narrow ledge leads out onto the wall to finish at Cockquack. Foot traverse the ledge, until a line can be taken leftwards past three small niches. Serious.

11   Cockquack   15m   HVS 4c   (1991)
Near the right edge of the vertical section of the wall is a left-slanting crack. Climb the crack throughout, passing a small tree.

12   Cockadoodlemoobahquack   40m   Very Difficult   (1966)
Start up the left-slanting crack, but soon go diagonally right on big flat holds until an easier-angled ramp leads back left. Abseil off or finish leftwards.

WATERFALL MAIN WALL

This is the impressive wall containing the waterfall itself, the main section being just right of the fall and the continuing wall steadily decreasing in height as it runs rightwards towards the Central Wall area. The routes are described from left to right.

CREAG DUBH
Waterfall Wall

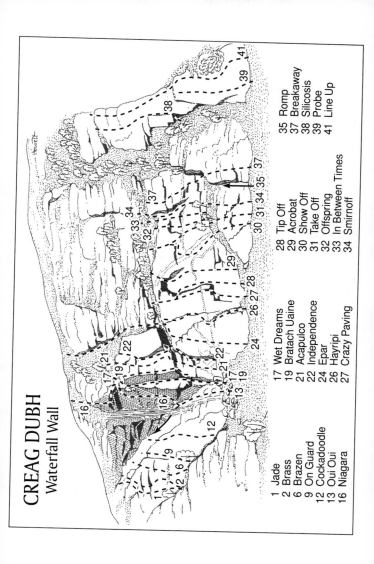

1	Jade	17	Wet Dreams
2	Brass	19	Bratach Uaine
6	Brazen	21	Acapulco
9	On Guard	22	Independence
12	Cockadoodle	24	Epar
13	Oui Oui	26	Hayripi
16	Niagara	27	Crazy Paving

28	Tip Off	35	Romp
29	Acrobat	37	Breakaway
30	Show Off	38	Silicosis
31	Take Off	39	Probe
32	Offspring	41	Line Up
33	In Between Times		
34	Smirnoff		

Abseil descents from various trees or threads are the most convenient. Otherwise, from the top of the cliff, follow a small path going right (west) to descend a gully underneath Lower Waterfall Wall.

13   Oui Oui   90m   Difficult   (1965)
Snorkels and flippers are needed on this unusual climb under the waterfall. The rock is clean and sound, but invariably wet. Climb the slabby corner, then pass behind the fall and exit left in 2 or 3 pitches up the obvious huge ramp.

The next two routes climb the grooves left of the waterfall, starting up Oui Oui.

14   Orinoco   30m   VS 4b   (1984)
This route takes the most obvious large groove left of the vertical section of the waterfall. Start at a left-facing corner which leads into a deep black groove. Climb the corner, then go up the groove into the huge groove and climb this on its left wall.

15   Zambezi   40m   HVS   (1972)
A route up the line of the waterfall. Start as for Orinoco.
1. 20m 4c   Climb up into the short deep V-groove, break right into the next groove, then go right again to belay in the main corner.
2. 20m 5a   Go left below the roof and climb steeply into the corner above. Climb this to below a square roof and exit right.

The impressive wall to the right of the waterfall contains the following routes:

16   Niagara   65m   E1 5b **   (1972/1991)
A fine climb with great exposure following a line through the slabs and roofs right of the waterfall. Omitting the first pitch by scrambling up the waterfall slab to the vertical section of the fall, then traversing right to the belay at the top of pitch 1, reduces the grade to HVS. Start 10m up the waterfall slab where there are two parallel flakes on the right.
1. 25m 5a   Traverse across the flakes and pull up to a ledge beside quartz. Move left to another flake, climb it, then return right to the top of the quartz (following the quartz direct has less protection). Go up a short green groove, then head left to ledges with trees.
2. 10m 4c   Pull out left onto a recessed slab at the right end of a smooth overhanging wall. Go up the slab to trees, then traverse right through the trees and move up to a ledge.
3. 30m 4c   Hand traverse spectacularly left to avoid a roof and climb the arete above, progressively less steep.

The following routes terminate on a grassy terrace with a small bundle of trees which provides a good abseil point for descent.

17   Wet Dreams   35m   E2 5c **   (1981)
A brilliant pitch up the open corner bounding the left edge of the steep wall right of the waterfall. Start from the ledge below the corner, gained by scrambling from the left. Climb the corner to the roof, then surmount this rightwards with trouble and continue up the corner passing a small clump of trees to a belay common with Niagara. The abseil tree can be gained by traversing right under a roof, or continue up the upper pitch of Niagara.

18   Not Before Time   55m   E2 *   (1988)
A spectacular high-level traverse above the roof of the Acapulco wall. Start as for Wet Dreams.
1. 25m 5c   Follow Wet Dreams over the roof and go up the corner to belay on a small ledge above the level of the roof.
2. 20m 5b   Traverse right along the obvious weakness above the roof passing Acapulco, and continue to a belay in a small niche.
3. 15m 4b   Scramble up and back left to the tree.

19   Bratach Uaine   35m   E4 6a **   (1987)
The right arete of Wet Dreams gives an entertaining outing. Start from the belay ledge of that route. Follow Wet Dreams to the roof. Traverse right under this to a good jug on the arete. Pull through the roof just to the right (crux) and continue up the right side of the arete to the top. Tree belay.

20   Snotrag   35m   E6 6b *   (1989)
An eliminate direct start to Bratach Uaine following the arete all the way. Start directly below the arete. The first 5m are desperate and unprotected to reach a conspicuous big sloping hold (runner). Thrutch upwards in an a-cheval position to join Bratach Uaine at the jug under the roof. Finish up that route.
Variation: E5 6b
The initial death arete can be avoided by climbing a shallow groove immediately to its left and reaching out right to grab the sloping hold on the arete.

21   Acapulco   45m   E4 6a ***   (1981)
A brilliant bold outing through the roof right of Wet Dreams. Start just right of Oui Oui at the foot of the wall.
1. 10m 5c   Climb the left-slanting quartz seam to the ledge of Wet Dreams. A serious pitch and the scene of several bad accidents, but it can be avoided by climbing to the right or left to gain the ledge.
2. 35m 6a   Move right to a groove. Climb this and step right onto the wall. Climb the wall veering left to reach for a 'schisty flange' on the lip of the roof. Hand traverse right to gain the obvious block, then pull over and get onto a ledge. Climb diagonally leftwards into the middle of the wall to finish direct up a tongue of quartz. It is also possible to gain the block from directly below at same grade.

22   Independence   45m   E2 5c *   (1981)
Another bold trip up the big wall. Start at a shallow groove 5 metres right of Acapulco. Climb the right-trending grooves to beneath the roof. Traverse right around a rib to a small ledge (possible stance). Pull through the break in the roof (peg runner) and continue diagonally left to a good foot ledge (a recent rock fall has left unstable blocks here). Move up and right into a left-trending line and follow this before moving right near the top to finish up quartz.

23   Face Value   45m   E3 5c **   (1981)
Sustained jug hauling up the wall right of Independence. Start up Epar and follow its second pitch to the ledge above the flake crack. Pull over the roof immediately above (5 metres left of its right end), move leftwards to a foot ledge and continue up the gently overhanging wall on superb holds to the tree belay.

The following routes are on a lower section of Waterfall Wall which extends rightwards towards Central Wall. They finish on a tree-filled terrace below steep, vegetated and broken rock.

24   Epar   50m   Mild VS   (1965)
Start at a shallow groove beneath an obvious flake crack in a middle tier.
1. 10m 4a   Climb a groove to a ledge and belay below the crack.
2. 10m 4c   Climb the flake crack with a strenuous start.
3. 10m   Walk to the right end of the roof above and abseil off the tree on the terrace, or:
4. 20m 4a   Climb the left-slanting hanging groove above. A good pitch with a messy finish. Either traverse right and abseil or continue upwards.

25   Pare   25m   HVS   (1978)
Start at the bottom right of the steep wall between Epar and Hayripi.
1. 15m 4c   Climb a blocky groove and wall, passing a niche at the top right of the wall. A serious start with a strenuous but safe finish.
2. 10m 4c   The wall behind belay is still serious. Abseil, or finish up Epar.

26   Hayripi   50m   Hard Severe   (1965)
This climb takes the obvious shallow right-facing grassy corner on the right side of the buttress taken by Pare.
1. 20m   Climb leftwards up a ramp and corner to belay as for Pare.
2. 10m 4b   Traverse right to a small overhang, then go up a ramp and a groove to a ledge and belay.
3. 20m 4a   Finish as for Epar.

Descent from the following routes is easiest by abseiling from the many trees that grow on the steep hillside above the crag.

27   Crazy Paving   30m   E3 5b   (1983)
The centre of the orange wall right of Hayripi gives an impressive wall climb, but it is artificial and serious. Climb directly to a tiny overlap and pass this on the right. Continue to a V-slot in the roof and exit right (as for Tip Off).

28   Tip Off   40m   VS 4c *   (1965)
This route takes an obvious groove up the left side of an overhung recess.
Scramble up a corner to belay below the groove. Go up the groove until an
obvious step left gains a shallower groove which leads to the top and the tree
belay (abseil descent).
Variation: VS 4c
Avoid the step left and continue up the groove to the roof. Exit left to finish.

29   Acrobat   40m   HVS 5a   (1980)
Climb the groove up the right side of the overhung recess to a roof, then swing
right over dubious blocks to the top.

   The main pitches of the following five routes start from a horizontal ledge 10m
up and with many trees. Either start up a lower wall (as described) or scramble
up to the main pitches from the left. Descend by abseil from a tree above and left
of the finish of Smirnoff.

30   Show Off   45m   E1   (1965)
A committing and strenuous climb with some suspect rock. Start at the left end
of the lower wall.
1. 10m 4a   Climb the wall to a ledge and tree belay.
2. 35m 5a   Pull leftwards onto the overhanging wall and follow a line of holds
into a small groove (peg runner). Go up this and a slab to a roof. Step right onto
a block and finish up a groove.

31   Take Off   45m   VS   (1965)
The stepped overhanging corner to the right of Show Off is in a good position,
but it has some loose rock.
1. 10m 4a   Climb the wall just right of Show Off to a ledge and tree belay.
2. 35m 4b   Move up the left-trending corner to a recess on the right side of a
large block. Pull onto this and finish as for Show Off.

32   Offspring   35m   E1 5b *   (1978)
Start just right of Take Off on the tree-lined ledge. Climb up and make a
technical move through a break in the small roof. Continue up the wall, soon
trending left towards a roofed corner, then finish past the right end of the roof.
The grade can be reduced to E1 5a by starting up Take Off and moving right
above the small roof.

33   In Between Times   35m   E3 5c **   (1978)
Good intricate climbing with scant protection, but slightly artificial as one can
escape left into Offspring below the hard finish. Start midway between Offspring
and Smirnoff. Climb the wall, crossing two overlaps at their obvious weak
points, then continue up the wall and thin crack before finishing direct.

34 Smirnoff 50m HVS * (1965)

A good technical route which climbs the obvious tapering stepped corner. Start beneath some quartz to the right of Show Off.

1. 15m 4c Climb to the left end of a long overhang and cross it just left of quartz. Trend right to a tree belay below a corner.

2. 35m 5a Bridge up between the wall and the tree (or climb the wall itself, harder) until it is possible to pull over the roof on the right. Continue up the corner (peg runner) to finish.

35 Romp 50m Very Difficult (1965)

Climb the big left-facing corner, with much scrambling to finish.

36 Trampoline 25m VS 5a (1967)

Start just right of Romp and climb the obvious tree-filled corner to a ledge.

Moving right from Romp along the cliff base are two similar 25m walls, each with a cap of ivy on their top right. The left-hand wall holds the start of Breakaway; the right has Probe, Straight Line and Line Up. Between here and Great Wall are two slender buttresses separated by a huge roofed alcove and defined on the right by another alcove before King Bee. The left buttress has the right ivy-capped wall at its base and the right buttress is close to Great Wall.

37 Breakaway 60m HVS ** (1977)

A varied and interesting climb, crossing Romp to a fine second pitch. Start beneath the left-hand of two grooves 1m apart on the steep wall right of Romp.

1. 30m 4c Climb either groove (more commonly the left) to a belay on Romp.

2. 30m 5a Cross Romp and follow a left-slanting quartz crack to a roof. Turn this by a bulge on the left and continue up left to the slab overlooking the final groove of Smirnoff.

38 Silicosis 40m E5 * (1981)

An interesting struggle with the crack up the conspicuous quartz wall forming the upper left side of the left-hand buttress. Scramble to a start from trees below the large niche guarding the entrance to the crack.

1. 20m 6a Gain the crack from the niche and follow it (strenuous with hard won protection) and the wall above to a ledge.

2. 20m 4c Continue up the mossy slab to finish *via* a short finger *crack.*

39 Probe 25m E1 5b (1981)

From the toe of the right ivy-capped wall climb near the thin crack 2m from the left edge of the wall, left of the first pitch of Line Up. Climb a tiny ramp leading left until forced right by smooth rock. Move up and follow another tiny ramp leading left to a short groove finishing at the top left of the wall.

40 Straight Line 25m HVS 5a (1991)

Start 2 metres right of Probe at a thin crack. Climb straight up to finish at the left end of the ivy.

41 Line Up 100m VS (1970)
Pleasant climbing up the edge of the buttress. Start beneath the crop of ivy.
1. 25m 5a Either climb a short overhanging groove or the wall on its left. Go diagonally left under the ivy to pull through its left edge (a strenuous finish, but with good runners).
2. 25m 4b Ascend the rib leftwards to turn an overhang on the left. Belay below a roof on the right edge.
3. 25m 4a Turn the roof on the right, then climb the corner above to a tree. Continue to a belay below a slab.
4. 25m Climb the slab and scramble to finish.

42 Route Toot Toot 140m VS (1970)
A very scrappy route with mixed rock and vegetation up the right-hand slender buttress.

43 Easy Going 70m HVS (1978)
A girdle traverse starting from Pare and finishing up Breakaway, with some good climbing.
1. 35m 4c Start as for Pare, then traverse right across the buttress to reach Hayripi. Continue across the wall to gain Tip Off at the step left. Descend for a few metres, then traverse right to join Show Off at the short slab beneath the roof.
2. 35m 4c Traverse right to join Take Off, then descend this until it is possible to traverse the wall into the corner of Smirnoff. Exit right and cross Breakaway to finish.

GREAT WALL

The Great Wall is the big steep wall for which Creag Dubh is famous. Its left edge is defined by the rib of King Bee. Left of this rib is a tree-filled groove with a big triangular roof right of its top. This rib is interrupted by a roof at one-third height and this roof runs intermittently rightwards across the rest of the left section. Run Free climbs through the left-hand roof, Erse takes a direct line through the middle roof whilst Brute climbs up to and traverses rightwards under the right-hand roof. A further roof lies in the wall above these. To the right of the roofs lies the obvious corner of the original finish of Brute. Directly below this corner at ground level is a large birch tree.

The right-hand half of Great Wall is a smooth vertical wall of lighter-coloured rock which dominates this area. The base of the wall sits on a flat grass ledge, accessed from the large birch tree on the left, with broken ground below. The most obvious feature is a triangular niche in the centre of the wall. Several routes go to this niche, the most famous being Inbred which starts from directly below. The wall left of the niche is covered in fine hard, serious routes.

Great Wall is bounded on the right by a narrow right-slanting fault which leads into a huge tree-filled corner with a sharp right arete (Rib Direct). The routes are described from left to right.

DESCENT
On foot, it is best to descend eastwards (left) down the broad wooded shelf below Sprawl Wall, then return under Lower Central Wall. One must go lower and further left than appearance suggests to gain the base of Lower Central Wall (a not very prominent cairn marks the line).

Abseil descent is possible from most of the routes, thus avoiding the acres of steep grass and broken ground at the top. From the King Bee area, from the level of the ledge system after pitch 3 of King Bee, two abseils are required. It is probably easiest to abseil close to the line of Nutcracker Chimney. It is also possible to abseil down to the left of King Bee (looking up) past the right side of the big triangular roof. For routes to the right, abseil down near Organ Grinder using the bolt belay. This is an uncomplicated abseil and the bolt belay is on a good ledge. It can also be used from King Bee, but this involves a 5m descent to the right from the right-hand tree to reach the abseil. From Brute to Inbred, one long abseil from the tree at the top of The Fuhrer reaches the ground. From Strapadicktaemi and Migraine, traverse awkwardly right to a tree near Rib Direct or traverse grass ledges up and left (looking in), then descend to the tree of Fuhrer.

| **1** | **Men Only** | 70m | E2 ** | (1976) |

Highly spectacular climbing with only adequate protection on the hardest section. Scramble up the gully left of King Bee to a small ledge on the left of a green-coloured wall.
1. 40m 5b   Traverse right into a groove on the green wall. Climb this and the overhang above to a ledge with a small tree. Move right and climb a shallow groove to a roof. Pull over and traverse left to a ledge and flake belay.
2. 30m 4c   Ascend the flake and the wall to an overhang. Turn this on the right and continue to a junction with King Bee (peg runner). Step left and go up a corner and over an overhang to finish.

| **2** | **Run Free** | 100m | E4 * | (1976) |

Devious climbing with a hard and serious crux pitch. Start left of King Bee at the foot of an open corner.
1. 25m 4c   Climb the corner and traverse left to a small ledge and belay below a roof.
2. 25m 5c   Traverse right and go up a short steep wall to the roof. Surmount this and continue to belay where Nutcracker Chimney splits.
3. 50m 4c   Ascend the crack in the rib above until a left traverse leads to a black groove. Climb this to a small roof, avoid this on the right and continue to a ledge and easy ground.

| **3** | **King Bee** | 110m | VS *** | (1965) |

A classic, and the best climb of its grade on the crag. Protection is adequate and good on the technical crux. Start at the foot of Nutcracker Chimney.
1. 25m 4c   Climb a rib to a small tree, then move left and up to a roof. Move left again and climb to a tree under the bigger roof of Run Free. Traverse right between the roofs and go up to a ledge.

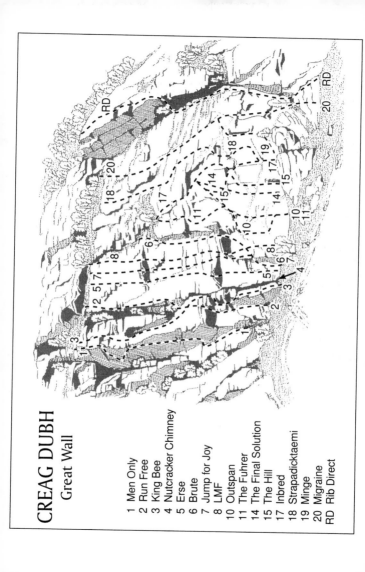

CREAG DUBH
Great Wall

1 Men Only
2 Run Free
3 King Bee
4 Nutcracker Chimney
5 Erse
6 Brute
7 Jump for Joy
8 LMF
10 Outspan
11 The Fuhrer
14 The Final Solution
15 The Hill
17 Inbred
18 Strapadicktaemi
19 Minge
20 Migraine
RD Rib Direct

2. 35m 5a Step left and climb the wall trending slightly left (passing an optional belay in Nutcracker Chimney) to a small bulge out left. Pull through this (technical crux), then climb a vague arete leftwards to an exposed belay.

3. 20m 4c Pull up right to the roof above the belay. Pass it strenuously on the right to reach easier ground. From here, trend either left or right depending on the choice of abseil tree (as described above).

4. 30m 4b For those who choose to continue, pull up the wall above the right-hand tree, then slant left on good rock to reach the upper grass slopes.

Direct Start: HVS 5a

An exciting option on big holds. Where the normal route moves left at the first small tree, continue straight up the slight arete, pulling strenuously through the roof to join the parent route at the belay. A Friend 3 is useful.

4   Nutcracker Chimney   140m   VS 4b   (1959)
Climb the tree-filled narrow chimney.

5   Erse   70m   E3 **   (1965)
An excellent but unprotected first pitch, the epitome of Creag Dubh boldness. Start beneath a small shattered groove immediately right of Nutcracker Chimney and left of the more obvious open groove of Brute.

1. 30m 5b Climb the groove, going over small overlaps, then continue direct up a steep wall to a V-notch in the big roof above. Climb through this and move up to a long ledge.

2. 40m 4c Climb the wall and crack above to a ledge below a further roof. Turn the roof by a bulge on the left and continue up a groove to a ledge. Abseil descent from the tree on the right.

6   Brute   45m   VS *   (1959)
A route typical of Creag Dubh; steep, strenuous and somewhat intimidating at the start, but it deteriorates higher up. Only the good lower section is normally climbed. Start at an open groove 3 metres right of Nutcracker Chimney, just left of the birch tree.

1. 15m 4c Climb the groove, then step right and go up to a ledge.

2. 30m 5a Go diagonally right under the roof until possible to climb it using a crack at its smallest point (peg runner). Continue up until it is possible to move left to the bolt abseil point of Organ Grinder.

Original Finish: 60m   4b

Climb the big corner on the right, then the slabby wall on the left, taking a belay on a tree between the two.

7   Jump for Joy   70m   E2 **   (1981)
An enjoyable route taking a direct line between the roofs of Erse and Brute. Start as for Brute.

1. 30m 5b Climb the corner of Brute to the ledge. Move out left and go up the wall to the right end of the Erse roof (old peg runner). Pull rightwards over the bulge, then go up and left into a groove leading to the long ledge.

2. 40m 5b Ascend the easy wall, then the steepening groove to the roof. Pull direct over this and continue to tree belays.

8   L.M.F   70m   E1 **   (1971)

Another good route taking a parallel line to the right of Jump for Joy and crossing Brute. Start immediately left of the birch tree.

1. 35m 5b   Ascend the steep wall direct to the belay ledge of Brute. Climb up and left around the left side of the roof above to a shattered crack peg runner), then follow this to the ledge.

2. 35m 5b   Climb up for a little, then pull right into a quartz groove. Climb this (peg runner) to a roof. Move right then left before heading straight for the tree.

The next ten routes all start from the raised grass ledge right of the birch tree.

9   Organ Grinder   80m   E1 *   (1971)

A devious line wandering from right to left, crossing Brute and finishing up the top pitch of Erse. Start at a thin crack about 8 metres right of the birch tree and left of the base of a quartz streak.

1. 20m 5b   A tricky start gains a loose block at 4m, then another block just above. Follow the handrail left for 8m to a large open niche above the birch tree. Exit direct to a ledge and belay on Brute.

2. 35m 5b   Climb up right under the roof, then pull over and traverse back left to follow a slab to a ledge and bolt belay.

3. 35m 4c   Climb the wall and crack above to a ledge below a roof. Turn the roof on the left and follow the groove on the left in a fine position to the top. Abseil descent from the tree on the right.

10   Outspan   45m   E1 5b **   (1971)

A hard boulder problem start is followed by sustained and serious 5a climbing snaking its way up the left side of the impressive main section of the wall. Take the tricky start of Organ Grinder at the thin crack 8 metres right of the birch tree. Pass the loose block and gain the handrail. Follow it leftwards for 4m, then ascend directly up the steep black wall on good holds (serious) to gain a horizontal break. Follow this back rightwards to a bulge (peg runner). Step over this, go up right to a large flake, then ascend diagonally rightwards across the centre of the wall to a junction with Inbred on a long ledge. Follow the easy line diagonally leftwards to the tree abseil as for Inbred, or belay here and finish up the top pitch of The Hill.

An eliminate (**King Tubby and the Fat Boy's Rap**, E2 5b) has been recorded starting up Outspan and finishing up the cracked headwall as for Colder than a Hooker's Heart, the meat of which is in the middle. Another eliminate (E3) starts up Outspan to reach the break, takes a slanting weakness right to the big flake on Fuhrer and finishes across the quartz wall as for that route.

11   The Fuhrer   45m   E4 5c **   (1979)

A serious outing even by Creag Dubh standards, although technically not too testing. Start as for Outspan at the thin crack. Climb past a loose block at 4m to reach another block. Thin moves leftwards up the quartz gain a plaque-like block above. Stand on this and move right to the peg runner on Outspan. Follow

Outspan over the bulge and go up right to a large flake. Climb the quartz wall diagonally left to a grotty ledge. The steep shallow groove in the headwall leads to the tree. Abseil off.

12   Colder than a Hooker's Heart   45m   E5 5c ***   (1985)
A brilliant direct version of The Fuhrer, more sustained and even more serious. Start as for the Fuhrer and climb to the block at 5m. Step right to a small overhang (poor protection), pull over and continue direct up the steep wall on barely adequate holds to the peg runner and junction with Fuhrer. Move up and left on jugs to a sidepull at the base of the quartz wall. Climb this direct to the ledge and go left to finish *via* the crack in the left arete, passing a rocking block.

13   Harder than your Husband   45m   E5 6a **   (1988)
Bold climbing up the central quartz streak. Climb directly up the quartz streak right of The Fuhrer until forced right onto a small ledge immediately left of The Hill. Follow The Final Solution up the bulging wall above on the left for 3m to a good hold where that route goes right. Step left and climb the quartz streak past a short crack and quartz bulges to a slanting niche. Easier ground leads to a long ledge on Inbred. Traverse left and finish up the headwall of The Fuhrer.

14   The Final Solution   45m   E5 6a ***   (1987)
A superbly serious outing up the middle of the wall. Start left of the boulder at the foot of The Hill. Climb the wall just right of the vertical quartz streak by bouldery moves to gain the small ledge. Step up left and climb directly up the bulging wall on improving holds to gain a handrail running out right into a small niche and protection (phew!) Continue directly above, passing through the second niche of The Hill to the long ledge on Inbred, then follow this to the tree.

15   The Hill   60m   E2 ***   (1967)
A magnificent and intimidating climb, serious on the first pitch and very exposed on the second. Start at a boulder below some rust-coloured rock, left of the crack of Inbred.
1. 20m 5b   Ascend to a ledge (tape runner), then continue direct up the bulging wall past a poor peg runner (good RP4) to enter a small groove. Climb this until it is possible to traverse right into the triangular niche of Inbred.
2. 20m 5a   Traverse from the lip of the niche leftwards to a smaller niche. Continue by a slightly descending weakness into another niche. Move out left, then follow good holds back right to a long ledge.
3. 20m 4c   From the right end of the ledge climb the bulge and mossy slab to finish. Belay well back.
Variation: 45m   E2 5b ***
A single pitch version is possible by missing out the traverse into the triangular niche to belay. Climb direct from above the peg runner into the first small niche of the second pitch, then follow the normal route left into the second niche. Move left, then go up to the long ledge of Inbred. Follow the line leftwards to the tree and descend by abseil.

Brute, Great Wall, Creag Dubh   (Climber, Di Gilbert)

16   Over the Hill   45m   E3 5c ***   (1980)

A direct version of The Hill giving a superb pitch. Follow The Hill Variation past the peg runner and into the small niche. Move up and right to a small spike. Step back left and ascend the wall direct with difficulty to the belay ledge of Inbred. Climb the bulge at the left end onto the long ledge and continue left to the tree.

17   Inbred   105m   HVS ***   (1964)

A tremendous route, steep and intimidating but on big holds. In the right side of Great Wall, just right of The Hill a thin crack leads to an obvious triangular niche.

1. 25m 5a   Climb the crack to a peg runner, then move left and go up to the triangular niche. Move out right, then go up to a ledge.

2. 35m 4b   Climb over the bulge at the left end of the ledge to gain a long ledge, then continue diagonally left to a tree belay. Abseil from this tree, or:

3. 45m 4a   Climb the slabby wall on the left to finish.

Direct Finish: 30m   E1 5b

Belay in the triangular niche of pitch 1. Climb a thin crack out of the top of the niche to cross the normal route. Continue up a weakness above, passing the left end of a quartz patch and finish up a crack just left of Strapadicktaemi.

The Force (50m, E2 5b), starts as for Strapadicktaemi, then forges up the wall between it and Inbred, joining Inbred Direct Finish above the ledge.

18   Strapadicktaemi   50m   E1 *   (1976)

Juggy and exciting climbing, pitch 1 being slightly more serious than Inbred.

1. 25m 5a   Ascend the initial bulge on Inbred, then follow a obvious right-slanting crack to a junction with Minge. Go up a short crack to a long narrow ledge, then continue over the bulge above to a belay on Inbred.

2. 25m 5a   Move right to gain a left-slanting crack. Follow this to a small overhang, then traverse left to another crack which leads to the top.

19   Minge   35m   E2 *   (1967/70s)

The meat of the route is the short hanging groove in the wall right of Strapadicktaemi. Start on the ledge beside Inbred.

1. 10m   Traverse right to a ledge.

2. 25m 5c   Climb the short crack above to a long narrow ledge. Go up the groove and struggle with the exit right. Continue rightwards to the stance on Migraine, then finish up its second pitch 2.

The next routes start to the right of the raised ledge and are gained from lower down to the right.

20   Migraine   45m   HVS   5a   (1965)

Good strenuous climbing up the crack bounding the right side of The Great Wall, but with some hollow flakes. Start by a scramble to a ledge and tree belay beneath the crack. Climb the crack over two bulges to easier-angled turfy ground. Follow a clean ribbon of slab above until it is possible to traverse right to a tree and abseil descent, or continue up the slab.

Inbred, Great Wall, Creag Dubh   (Climber, Dave Cuthbertson)

21 Bulger 75m E2 (1980)

A sustained and technically interesting outing, wandering around the right-hand side of the wall looking for unclimbed sections. Start above the first pitch of Rib Direct at the foot of a steep rib.

1. 25m 5b Climb the crack in the rib, move left to a slab, then go up the overhanging wall on huge holds to a small niche. Ascend the wall above past a tiny tree and continue to a ledge shared belay with Migraine.

2. 25m 5b Step down and traverse left to the top of the groove of Minge. Bridge across this and continue left on quartz holds to the Inbred belay ledge.

3. 25m 5c Pull directly into the scoop above and continue rightwards to finish up the crack of Strapadicktaemi.

22 Rising Damp 105m E1 ** (1977)

A magnificent low-level, left to right girdle of Great Wall. Start as for Run Free.

1. 40m 4c Climb the corner until it is possible to traverse right onto the arete of King Bee. Continue right across Nutcracker Chimney and Erse, then follow a line of holds to belay on the lower ledge of Brute.

2. 40m 5a Step up and traverse right along the obvious break. Continue past a peg runner and go over a bulge to a large flake. Go right across quartz to a slanting niche, then continue to another niche before moving across to belay in the triangular niche of Inbred.

3. 25m 5a Traverse right and reverse the bulge on Strapadicktaemi to gain the narrow ledge. Continue right around the corner to join Migraine and finish up this.

23 Great Wall Girdle 125m HVS (1965)

A fine natural line.

1. 45m 4c Start as for King Bee, then make a long right traverse to belay at the foot of the Brute corner.

2. 35m 4b Follow the break which cuts across the wall to join Inbred, then reverse this to its ledge and belay.

3. 20m 5a Pull onto a narrow ledge and continue right to a stance at the foot of the Migraine slabs.

4. 25m 4a Finish up Migraine.

LOWER CENTRAL WALL

The lower wall comprises two sections divided by the narrow gully of Fred. The area of rock between Rib Direct and Fred consists of an excellent steep black wall on which Mighty Piston and Ticket to Ride take lines. Right of this lies the chimney of Cunnulinctus and right again lies another steep wall climbed by Phellatio. This is bounded on the right by a thick growth of ivy. The wall right of Fred is much shorter. The routes are described from left to right.

Descent by abseil is recommended since there are convenient trees near all the routes on the left-hand section, although it is possible to scramble to the broad wooded shelf.

1   Rib Direct   110m   Very Difficult *
A reasonable route with a good final pitch. Start at a left-slanting crack.
1. 10m 4a   Climb the crack with a tricky start to a tree belay.
2. 25m   The obvious groove leads to a ledge and tree under an overhang.
3. 45m   Turn it by a crack on the left and continue to a ledge and tree belay.
4. 30m   Traverse right onto the rib which leads to the top.

2   Sense of Urgency   30m   E3 6b   (1983)
A contrived line up the left retaining wall at the top of Rib Direct. Scramble up this to belay at the top of its third pitch. Climb the thin crack to the overlap. Move directly left into the continuation crack (crux) which leads to the top.

3   Snoopy   90m   HVS   (1971/88)
A scrappy line up the mossy slab left of Rib Direct. Start below a black niche right of Rib Direct.
1. 40m 4c   Climb to the niche, then continue to a ledge with a tree belay at the top of pitch 2 of Rib Direct.
2. 50m 5a   Step left and climb to the foot of a mossy slab, ascend this directly and move left to a tree belay.
3. 25m 4b   Climb up to the overhang using the tree, then hand traverse right to step onto the nose. Continue to the top.

4   Mighty Piston   55m   E1   (1971)
A sustained and serious climb up the black wall left of the vertical quartz streak. Start just left of the quartz.
1. 45m 5a   Climb diagonally leftwards to a horizontal band of quartz. Cross this, then continue left until moves up gain a ledge.
2. 10m 4c   Finish up the right side of the quartz above.

5   Arch Enemy   35m   E4 5c *   (1981)
A very serious pitch with no worthwhile protection and some suspect holds which climbs the obvious quartz arch in the middle of the wall. Climb directly up the black wall until level with the lower left side of the arch. Step right to its base and gibber to its right end. Pull over and enjoy easier climbing direct to the top. An eliminate line, **The Snake** (E4 5c), continues directly above the left end of the arch before moving right above it to join the parent route (not quite as nasty).

6   Ticket to Ride   35m   E3 5b ***   (1976)
An excellent sustained pitch with barely adequate protection up the black streaked wall right of the quartz. Start below the quartz streak and ascend up and right across it to a good spike. Go direct to a small niche, move left through the horizontal quartz streak and climb the steep wall to the grass ledge.

Another eliminate line, **Ninja** (E3 5b), climbs the wall immediately right of Ticket to Ride, passing through a circular area of quartz.

7   Sweetness   30m   HVS 4c   (1970)
Climb the wall direct just left of Cunnulinctus to a tree belay.

8   Cunnulinctus   65m   VS   (1965)
Start just right of an obvious narrow chimney with two holly trees at 10m, below
which water usually seeps.
1. 30m 4b   Ascend leftwards to join the chimney at the holly, then climb the
chimney to a ledge with a tree belay.
2. 35m 4b   Go up the continuation chimney and move out right to reach a
ledge and tree belay.
Sheath Variation   HVS 5a
Instead of making the left traverse to the holly bush, climb the wall directly to join
the normal route at the pitch 1 belay.

9   Phellatio   40m   HVS 5a **   (1965/1972)
A sustained and fairly serious pitch. Start at a left-slanting groove 10 metres
right of the wet seeps from Cunnulinctus chimney. Ascend the groove to a bulge
and a ledge (possible belay). Continue up the wall to a ledge and belay.

10   Centrespread   40m   E1 5b *   (1976)
Start as for Phellatio. Climb the right-slanting crack to a flake, then follow the
slimy overhanging groove and wall above the ivy to a ledge and tree belay on
the right.

11   Tongue Twister   40m   E1 5a *   (1970)
Devious but good climbing, not over-endowed with protection. Start
immediately left of the ivy crop. Climb the groove to a roof, then pull over this
and ascend leftwards to a large block. Traverse back right and go up to a ledge,
then continue right to a better ledge and belay.

12   Fiorella   35m   HVS 4c *   (1965)
A very serious but good quality pitch. Start immediately right of the ivy crop
below a left-slanting groove. Climb the groove to a bulge. Traverse right, then
pull through the bulge and traverse back left beyond the initial groove. Climb the
wall above (possible ground fall), then work rightwards to a tree belay.

13   Oddli   30m   HVS 5a   (1976)
Start just left of Mirador. Climb the wall to a scoop. Ascend to the right, then go
back left to finish directly through some bulges on large flat holds.

14   Mirador   30m   Severe *   (1965)
Start at the foot of a short groove on the left-bounding arete of Fred. Climb the
groove, then move right onto the arete and follow it to the ledge and tree belay.
Abseil off.

15   Fred   100m   Very Difficult   (1965)
The obvious gully gives a scrappy climb.

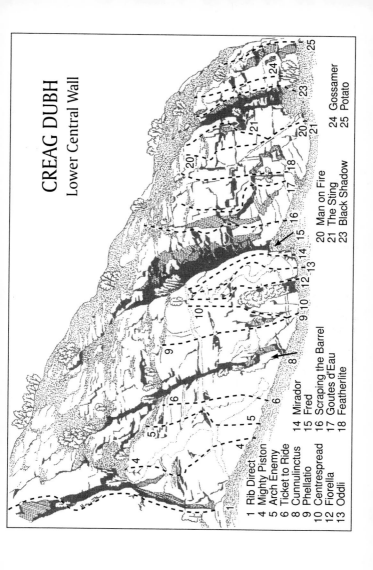

CREAG DUBH
Lower Central Wall

1 Rib Direct
4 Mighty Piston
5 Arch Enemy
6 Ticket to Ride
8 Cunnulinctus
9 Phellatio
10 Centrespread
12 Fiorella
13 Oddli

14 Mirador
15 Fred
16 Scraping the Barrel
17 Goutes d'Eau
18 Featherlite

20 Man on Fire
21 The Sting
23 Black Shadow

24 Gossamer
25 Potato

THE RIGHT-HAND SECTION

Right of the gully of Fred the wall continues unbroken to a black overhanging fault of broken rock. A pine tree sits on an elevated ledge in the centre of the wall. Right of the fault is a smaller buttress ending in a stepped rib of jumbled blocks. Temporary belays can be taken at the end of most of the routes on this section, from where the best abseil descent is from the lowest of a variety of silver birch trees 20m up the steep grass slope.

16   Scraping the Barrel   50m   VS   (1972)
A horrible and aptly-named climb. Start at the foot of a corner crack on the right wall of Fred.
1. 15m 4c   Climb the crack and bulge to a ledge and belay by a small tree.
2. 35m 4c   Climb the right wall to gain a slab, then go up and left before continuing directly over ledges to belay.

17   Goutes d' Eau   25m   E2 5b **   (1981)
A fine pitch requiring some faith. Scramble up from the right to a ledge with a pine tree below a steep wall. Start 3 metres left of the big pine. Climb the wall and pull over a bulge to a spike on the right. Traverse left across the slab to a small groove in the arete. Climb the arete, then go up the easy wall above to a grass ledge. Finish diagonally up rightwards on grass to reach the abseil tree.

18   Featherlight   25m   E1 5c   (1981)
Scramble up and start behind the pine tree. Climb the wall and overhang, then go up a groove to a roof. Pull over this, technical but very well protected, then ascend rightwards to vegetation.

19   Thyme   25m   VS 4c   (1991)
A pleasant juggy route. Start just right of the big pine. Climb a small arete, then trend slightly right.

20   Man on Fire   20m   E1 5b *   (1983)
A well protected direct line. Start below the steep wall behind the tree left of Pshaw. Climb leftwards up the quartz vein to gain a thin crack line which becomes more defined in its upper half. Climb it, moving left at the top to gain grass ledges. An abseil tree lies 20m directly above.

21   The Sting   25m   HVS 5b   (1983)
This route starts as for Man on Fire and ascends the wall slightly right to a short corner bounding the blocky roofs. Enter the corner, then exit out right above the blocky roofs and finish direct to a belay in an outcrop above.

22   Pshaw   25m   Hard Severe   (1972)
Steep climbing on doubtful rock. Start to the left of a black overhanging fault to the left of Potato. Climb straight up the wall to the blocky roofs, turn these on the right by a loose corner and climb the even looser wall to finish.

23   Black Shadow   20m   HVS 4c   (1983)
Right of Pshaw is a black overhanging fault; this route takes its right arete. Start up the first two moves of Gossamer, then launch up the arete.

24   Gossamer   15m   HVS 4c   (1981)
Climb the steep little groove in the buttress between the black fault and Potato.

25   Potato   45m   Difficult   (1965)
Climb the stepped rib at the right extremity of the crag by several possible lines, none worthwhile.

26   The Frustrations   110m   E1 *   (1976)
This left to right girdle of the lower wall is harder but not as good as Rising Damp. Start as for Snoopy below a black niche right of Rib Direct.
1. 40m 4c   Follow Snoopy pitch 1 through the niche and go up to a ledge with a tree belay.
2. 25m 5b   From the right-hand end of the ledge, step down and traverse right across quartz. Continue above the niche on Ticket to Ride to belay on Cunnilinctus.
3. 45m 4c   Step down and follow a quartz band to reach the ledge on Phellatio. Step up and across to the ivy crop. Ascend the wall above, then traverse right finish up Mirador.

SPRAWL WALL

This is the distinctive black-streaked wall at the far right-hand end of Creag Dubh. To approach from the lay-by, walk rightwards up grass to a small flat area (2 minutes), from where there is a good view of Sprawl Wall. The black-streaked smooth wall on the lower right contains Jump so High and Instant Lemon with the slabs of Tree Hee round its right edge. Bounding this wall on the left is the obvious Slanting Groove. The pale wall left of this has several routes including Raven's Squawk while higher up on the left, partially hidden by trees, is the wall of Gang Bang and Hot to Trot. To reach Sprawl Wall from the flat area, continue rightwards beyond the worst of the boulders and fight a way up to its right-hand end (near Tree Hee). To reach Sprawl Wall from Central Wall, traverse rightwards along the base of the cliff with a slight descent before one can go up through trees to the wall. A steep bouldering wall lies below and right of the crag for those so inclined. The routes are described from right to left.

   The best descent for routes on the right-hand section is by way of a long traverse to the left and a faint path which eventually leads back to the foot of the crag. For the Jump so High wall, a single long abseil is possible back to the start. For routes on the other two walls, follow a small path to the right which leads down to the broad wooded shelf at the top of Central Wall.

1   Slabsville   50m   VS 4b   (1967)
A poorly protected climb with pleasant slabs, but it is very artificial to keep off the vegetation. Start 5 metres right of Tree Hee.
1. 20m 4b   Climb close to the right arete of a corner, then move left to a tree belay at the top of the corner.
2. 30m 4b   Return right to the slab and pick as clean a line as possible to the Terrace.

2   Tree Hee   70m   Severe *   (1965)**
A delightful climb on excellent rock. There is some vegetation, but it is easily avoided. The lowest point of the buttress is an overhanging wall. Start at the right end of this.
1. 30m   Make a left-rising traverse above the overhanging wall, then follow a shallow groove to a ledge and belay on the left edge.
2. 40m   Move up and right past a holly tree. Ascend a slab to an overlap, then move up left to belay on a terrace.
Direct Variation: 50m   Mild VS 4b
From halfway along the initial rising traverse, climb directly up near some quartz. Join the normal route just right of the holly, then climb directly up the slab and through the upper overlap by a steep V-groove.

3   Jump so High   70m   E1 **   (1965/78)
Tremendous climbing up the right side of the black-streaked overhanging wall. Start at the foot of the buttress.
1. 20m 4a   Climb the deep vegetated corner left of the lowest point of the buttress to a ledge and belay on the right edge of a slab.
2. 35m 5b   Follow the slab leftwards under a large roof to a small ledge at the foot of an overhanging crack. Climb the crack with difficulty to a very comfortable belay ledge.
3. 15m 5a   Climb the thin overhanging crack above and trend right to finish.

4   Separation   40m   E2 5b *   (1981)
This route takes a line crossing Jump so High to finish up Tree Hee. Start by traversing right to belay at two small trees under the slab of Jump so High. Pull over the break in the roof and climb up to join Jump so High on the slab. Move right to climb the overhanging corner, then exit right to finish up Tree Hee.

5   Jump so High Direct   50m   E1 **   (1967)
Start at the foot of a rib, left of Separation.
1. 30m 5b   Climb the crack on the left side of the rib (avoiding the temptation to step off left onto the grass rib) to reach the foot of the overhanging crack of the normal route. Move out right and climb the wall to the big ledge.
2. 20m 5a   Climb the crack on the right of the thin crack of the normal route.

6   Jump so High Combination   45m   E1 *
The best line on this section of the wall gives a sustained and enjoyable climb, combining the first pitch of the Direct with the second pitch of the normal route.

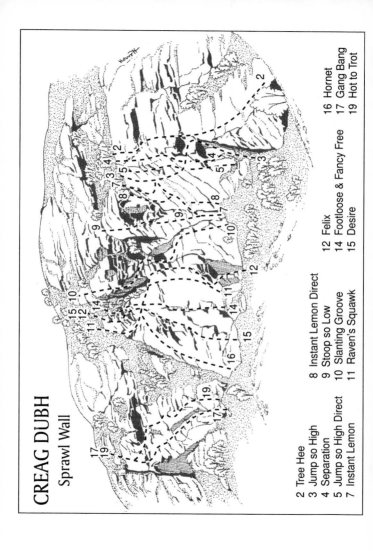

CREAG DUBH
Sprawl Wall

2 Tree Hee
3 Jump so High
4 Separation
5 Jump so High Direct
7 Instant Lemon

8 Instant Lemon Direct
9 Stoop so Low
10 Slanting Groove
11 Raven's Squawk

12 Felix
14 Footloose & Fancy Free
15 Desire

16 Hornet
17 Gang Bang
19 Hot to Trot

7   Instant Lemon   45m   E3 **   (1980)

A serious route winding its way up the impressive overhanging black-streaked wall. Start at the left end of the flat ledge below the wall.

1. 20m 5b   Climb easily up a broken quartz flake on the left side of the wall. Step onto the wall and follow an obvious hand traverse rail rightwards, moving up at its end to gain the large ledge. Belay over on the right as for Jump so High.

2. 25m 5c   Traverse back left from the belay on huge flat holds for 5m. Move up to a line of small holds in a pale streak which lead leftwards to the base of a groove. Follow this to the right, then finish up the left side of a corrugated roof. Tree belay.

8   Instant Lemon Direct   35m   E4 6a **   (1980)

A harder, more direct version of the parent route offering committing strenuous climbing. Start just right of Instant Lemon. Climb directly up the wall (peg runner) to gain the hand traverse rail. Follow it to the right, then move up to the ledge. Immediately traverse left to gain and climb a stepped ramp. Finish diagonally right up the wall and a slab.

9   Stoop so Low   60m   HVS   (1967)

A steep and impressive wall with many ledges, but the rock between them is good. The best line is hard to find, so expect trouble from the quoted description. Start as for Instant Lemon.

1. 40m 4b   Climb a small groove on the left and follow a system of ledges and walls to a shallow scoop below a broken corner. Climb the corner to a ledge and belay.

2. 10m 4c   Climb the small slab on the left, traverse right a few metres and surmount an overhang at an obvious break. Continue to a ledge and belay.

3. 10m   Climb the walls above to finish.

Direct Finish: VS

Instead of following the last pitch, move left and climb the steep loose wall past a peg runner.

Concealed Entrance (E2 4c, 5c) is a somewhat obscure route recorded between Slanting Groove and Stoop so Low.

10   Slanting Groove   100m   HVS   (1962)

A fine natural line, and despite the vegetation and some loose rock, it is worthwhile with the highlight of an overhanging and sensationally exposed section on pitch 3. Scramble up right to belay on the left of the main fault.

1. 30m 4b   Climb a ramp and traverse left to a ledge and tree belay.

2. 30m 4b   Climb the wall behind the tree. From the top of a small grassy slope, traverse left across a black wall and move up to a ledge with tree belays.

3. 30m 4c   Gain and climb the obvious groove, pull over an overhang and climb a short wall to a ledge.

4. 10m   Easier rock leads to the top.

11   Raven's Squawk   90m   Hard Severe *   (1965)
This grand route in impressive surroundings climbs the obvious left-trending line below and left of Slanting Groove. Start near the right end of a raised long grass ledge.
1. 30m   Traverse up to the right following the natural line of the rock, then climb to a steep wall, ledge and belay.
2. 45m   Traverse left onto a steep ramp and climb to its apex. Climb through trees and go up a short wall to a block belay.
3. 15m   Easier climbing leads to the top.

12   Felix   75m   E2 **   (1972/88)
An entertaining route starting up the roof-capped wall between Raven's Squawk and Slanting Groove and finishing up Desire. Start below the lower roof-capped wall.
1. 20m 5b   Ascend to the roof, traverse left under it, then climb to a grass ledge.
2. 30m 4c   Climb straight up left of Raven's Squawk (peg runner) to a ledge and belay on the traverse of pitch 2 of that route.
3. 25m 5c   Finish up the top pitch of Desire.

13   Jack the Lad   70m   E2 *   (1981)
Start to the left of Felix at a thin crack.
1. 20m 5b   Climb the crack to a ledge.
2. 25m 4c   Go up the wall above to a ledge. Avoid the overhang on the right and continue to a ledge and belay on Raven's Squawk.
3. 25m 5c   Finish up the top pitch of Desire.

14   Footloose and Fancy Free   60m   E4 **   (1981)
The open corner right of Desire gives precarious and poorly protected climbing on pitch 1. Start on the long grass ledge left of Raven's Squawk.
1. 40m 5c   Move left, then go right into a corner right of a black groove. Follow this to a ledge. Continue up the steepening groove to where it fades out. Traverse rightwards across quartz, then go up to a ledge and belay on the traverse of pitch 2 of Raven's Squawk.
2. 20m 5c   Traverse right on the slab above to get into the corner. Move back left and go up to an overhang. Pull over this and continue up the overhanging wall on large flat holds to an obvious traverse which leads right to a ledge and tree belay.

15   Desire   75m   E2 **   (1979)
Good but serious climbing with a spectacular finale. Start on the right side of the projecting buttress taken by Hornet.
1. 25m 4c   Climb directly up the right side of the buttress to a ledge.
2. 25m 5a   From the right end of the ledge climb an open slabby corner and steepening rock rightwards to a ledge on Raven's Squawk.
3. 25m 5c   Traverse up and back left to an old peg beneath an overlap. Move back right and surmount it to gain a small ledge beneath a roof. Turn it on the right, then move back left along an exposed shelf to finish directly up the wall above.

16 Hornet 100m HVS (1970)
Left of the raised grass ledge is a projecting buttress. Start at the left corner of the base of the buttress.
1. 25m 5a Pull over a loose bulge to gain and climb a groove which leads to a ledge and belay.
2. 35m 4c Climb over the overlap above, then go up and right to a short groove with an overhang. Pull over this and continue to a belay on Raven's Squawk.
3. 40m Finish up Raven's Squawk.

17 Gang Bang 55m HVS * (1965)
This excellent route follows the obvious left-trending groove line in the centre of the quartz patchworked end face.
1. 45m 5a From the lowest point of the crag, move up right and go back left to a bulge (peg). Surmount this and continue to a ledge (possible belay). Ascend left to an A-shaped niche forming a roof. Pass this direct and continue left to a ledge and belay.
2. 10m Easier rock leads to the top.
Direct Start: 5a
Climb the first 10m direct to join the normal route at the peg runner.

18 Cream Dream 50m E2 5b * (1994)
A direct line up the Gang Bang wall. Start from big boulders below the A-shaped niche of Gang Bang. Climb the steep white quartz groove into the niche. Pass this and climb direct passing through Hot to Trot. Head for the overhang at the top of the wall and take it on the left up a shallow V-shaped groove. An easier wall leads to a tree belay. Abseil descent.

19 Hot to Trot 50m E1 * (1981)
This route takes the obvious line above and parallel to Gang Bang. Start as for that route.
1. 25m 5b Climb to a short corner crack, traverse left and ascend a groove to a small ledge beneath a quartz block. Step right and go over a bulge, then continue to a ledge under an overhang.
2. 25m 5b Pull over the overhang, then go up to another which is avoided on the left. Continue to easy slabs beneath a huge roof. Traverse left under this and continue to join Gang Bang at a ledge. Continue to the top or abseil from trees to the right.

A final route has been recorded 100m up and left of Gang Bang. **Free and Easy** (VS 4c) climbs a left-slanting corner.

Girdle Traverse 170m E1 5b (1967/8)
A right to left wandering line up the entirety of Sprawl Wall for lovers of the obscure. Start as for Tree Hee.
1. 35m Tree Hee, pitch 1.
2. 35m Jump so High, pitch 2.

3. 15m   Follow Jump so High Direct (pitch 2) to belay on a small grass ledge on the left.

4. 25m   Make a descending traverse for 10m on the grass ledge, then climb up and left to a ledge. Descend the ledge a few metres, then climb a groove and step left to a belay.

5. 30m   Traverse up and left to join and follow pitch 2 of Stoop so Low for 5m. Traverse hard left on a steep wall for 5m, then follow a groove to a tree.

6 40m   Climb through the jungle for 12m to join and finish up Slanting Groove.

CREAGAN SOILLEIR   *(Map Ref 618 959)*

These south-facing crags provide short steep routes on sound rock, which dries extremely quickly. They are probably too small to merit a long distance visit, but the climbs are useful if you're in the area. The crags are clearly visible from Laggan village and can be approached by a 20 minute walk.

PINE TREE CRAG

Approaching from the west, by the stream, the first crag is a short green wall below a pine tree.

Ring of Truth   8m   E1 6a   (1989)
The wall to the left of Magical Ring has a very hard start. Finish up the ledged arete.

Magical Ring   8m   HVS 5b *   (1989)
On the right side of the green wall are short twisting cracks. Climb these to gain a short groove and finish out left on good flakes.

   Further right the crag gets higher and has an obvious traverse line just above half-height.

Laggan Behind   12m   Hard Severe   (1989)
Climb the left side of the steep wall. Go up rightwards to a left-slanting corner above the traverse (to the left of some suspended flakes) and climb the corner to the top.

Caledonian Crack   15m   E1 5b **   (1989)
Further right is a thin crack running up a shallow left-facing corner. Climb this and the steep continuation flake crack to the top.

Badenoch Beckons   15m   Mild VS 4c   (1989)
Start 5 metres right of Caledonian Crack and mantelshelf onto a nose. Climb the broken crack above and the left corner of the upper recess.
Variation Start: Severe
Start 2 metres right of Caledonian Crack. Climb up to a line going diagonally right to the top of the broken crack.

Thistle Crack   15m   VS 4c   (1989)
Right of the bulging nose is a thin crack slanting left. Climb this and the right side of the upper recess.

Skylarking   15m   Severe   (1989)
Start where the base of the crag begins to slant up right. Climb up onto a short right-sloping ramp. Leave this leftwards to gain and climb a slab to some trees. Go through these and up the walls behind.

Flypast   40m   VS 4c   (1989)
A girdle of this section of crag. Take the obvious break across the green wall, then move more easily up to the hand traverse across the main wall. Continue right to finish up Skylarking.

RIGHT-HAND CRAG, MIDDLE TIER

The furthest right crag forms three tiers; the middle one contains the best climbing. Approach by passing the right end of the lower tier (past a pinnacle-block), then go up left on a grass ramp to a grassy platform below a corner and steep wall. Belays are well back for all routes. The best descent is to go right, then down a sheep path which gives access to a sloping ledge leading back under the middle tier. This is narrow and not fun in the rain.

The Coroner   10m   HVS 5b *   (1989)
Climb the steep corner line with some wide bridging.

Cracking   10m   HVS 5a **   (1989)
This is the first main crack line right of the corner.

Culture Vulture   10m   E1 5b *   (1989)
The next crack line to the right.

Eternal Optimist   10m   E1 5b   (1990)
The next crack right again, with an overhanging start.

Sanction Busters   20m   HVS 5a   (1990)
At the bottom of the approach ramp is a steep wall. Climb this by a faint crack line, then finish by easier slabs to the terrace.

BINNEIN SHUAS *(Map Ref 468 827)*

On the southern slopes of Binnein Shuas lies one of the most unusual crags included in this guide. The rock type (micro granite) is so different to the schists predominant in the area that it gives a refreshing change in the style of climbing. The hill of Binnein Shuas actually lies in Glen Spean whose waters run west from the Ben Alder area, eventually reaching Loch Linnhe at Fort William, but it is more conveniently considered in this section with the Speyside crags as it is close to Creag Dubh. The crag is in a superb mountain setting overlooking the beautiful Lochan na h-Earba, deep within the Ardverikie deer forest.

ACCESS

Access is from the A86 Newtonmore to Spean Bridge road. At the south-west end of Loch Laggan, just west of Moy Lodge, a concrete road bridge crosses the River Spean giving access to Luiblea. There is parking in a lay-by formed from the old road. A good estate track branches off left before the house (locked gate) and joins an older track which leads to the sandy shores of Lochan na h-Earba. From here a faint path takes a rising traverse line up the hillside on the north side of the loch to the cliff. Allow 1hr 30mins from the road.

HISTORY

Tom Patey was the first to pay the crag a visit with an eye to climbing, but he left having climbed only one route, the upper part of The Fortress in 1964. He later commented that Ardverikie Wall, the classic route of the crag pioneered by Dougie Lang and Graham Hunter in 1967, was the finest route he walked past and didn't climb. 1967 proved to be the heyday at Binnein Shuas with Lang and Hunter bagging the majority of the best lines all through that year. Excited at their find of such a superb virgin cliff and fearful that someone might find out what they were up to and cash in, Lang convinced the estate keeper to park his car, a very conspicuous white Volvo, out of sight behind the keeper's cottage. Subterfuge paid off and the resulting Ardverikie Wall is undoubtedly one of Scotland's best routes at any grade and this pair's other routes here (Kubla Khan, The Keep and Blaeberry Grooves) are also excellent. By 1969 however, they were not alone as another party, J. McDowell and D. Todd were developing the Eastern Sector.

The cliff was made famous by the inclusion of Ardverikie Wall in Classic Rock in 1978, but no further routes were produced for some time except for a visit in winter by John Jeffrey, Steve Kennedy, Charlie Macleod and Malcolm Sclater who climbed the icefalls that form on the lower tier. In the 1980s, Bill Birkett was making regular forays north from his home in the Lake District and he had spotted a plum line on Binnein Shuas. In 1983 he made the long trip and climbed the fine crack line on the Fortress side wall. He named the route Tom's Crack, a significant jump in standards for the crag at E3, only to find that Geoff Goddard had nipped in before him for the first ascent, the name being Delayed

Attack. The route was written up in the new routes book in Nevisport in Fort William and it galvanized a group of North-East England climbers who were resident in the area to pay the crag a visit, where they discovered the remaining potential of The Fortress. Alan Moist and Mark Charlton attacked the obscene off-width chimney cutting through the left side of the roofs of the Fortress. Climbed on sight, it was a superb effort requiring a sling for aid on the lip of the 5m roof to produce Storming the Bastille (E3). Charlton returned some years later to free it. Meanwhile, John Griffiths was persevering with grass-choked, rounded cracks further right with several changes of belayers throughout the day. Griffiths and Moist returned later with Charlton, who found a way through to produce the spectacular and brilliantly named Ardanfreaky (E3).

Development since then has been sporadic with various different people involved. Most notably, Kevin Howett and Andy Nelson climbed Wallachian Prince at E5 in 1988, then the pair failed on a neighbouring line, later done by Rick Campbell (Turning a Blind Eye, E6). Ian Taylor and Andy Tibbs each added some E2s, whilst Grant Farquhar visited in 1992 and made an attempt to climb the impressive wall right of Delayed Attack which resulted in Use of Weapons, again E5, but the challenge of a direct entry to this line remains. Dougie Lang returned after 23 years to add two routes to the Eastern Sector with Nick Kempe, a working day for the presidents of the SMC and MCofS! In 1995 Campbell returned to do the off-width crack of Bog Myrtle Trip (E4), whilst Neil Craig sight led the excellent short diagonal crack next to it to give Wild Mountain Thyme (E4).

CRAG LAYOUT
The crag is divided into two sections, east and west. The dividing point is the deep cleft of Hidden Gully which demarcates the right side of the impressive area of roofs known as The Fortress. From the easy descent on the left, the cliff gains height rightwards being split by the deep slit of the usually wet Western Chimney and a further more obvious Broken Gully. Right of this gully is the start of The Fortress, first as a white-streaked slab (the line of Kubla Khan), then as an impressive roofed section where The Keep, Ardanfreaky and The Fortress routes find their way. The right-hand side wall of The Fortress gives Delayed Attack before disappearing into Hidden Gully (which is hidden from view!).

The Eastern Section, although of greater height, tends to be more scrappy. The exception is the initial slabs just right of Hidden Gully which offer the exquisite Ardverikie Wall. The further right one goes the less appealing the crag (and usually the wetter). The most obvious feature in this area is Eastern Chimney. The climbs are described from left to right.

THE WEST SECTION

The following routes are on the short but steep wall between Western Chimney and Broken Gully. The wall is split by distinctive deep vertical crack lines.

Comraich   60m   E2   (1993)
This route takes a pale streak up the wall to the left of the crack lines. Start below the streak, 5 metres left of Blaeberry Grooves.
1. 30m 5b   Climb the streak to a hollow at 10m. Step left and finish up the cracks above to the terrace.
2. 30m   Finish up easy rocks to the top.

Cowberry Wall   30m   VS 4b
This undistinguished route climbs the quartz-veined rib left of Bearberry Groove, moves right to a crack line going out right to an awful finish *via* a heather ledge.

Bearberry Groove   30m   E1 5b
A route based on the left-hand crack line 3 metres left of the line of Blaeberry Grooves. Follow the crack, moving slightly right after 3m, then finish direct.

Blaeberry Grooves   75m   VS   (1967)
The original line on this wall climbs the most obvious crack line in the centre of the face.
1. 30m 4c   Climb the central and deepest crack with a peg runner at half-height and a thread above to gain a ledge.
2. 45m 4a   Gain the slab above and follow the easy central crack to the top.

Gorgon   75m   HVS
This route ascends the wider tapering crack line to the right of Blaeberry Grooves.

The Perils of Perseus   70m   E1   (1990)
The arete to the right of Gorgon. Start at the foot of Gorgon.
1. 30m 5b   Climb diagonally rightwards to gain a crack which is just left of the arete. Climb the crack to a ledge, then go up and left to the grassy terrace.
2. 45m   Climb the slab above, keeping left of Blaeberry Grooves.

   Broken Gully is often wet and unpleasant, but it is of some use as a descent route (with care) from the terrace below the final pitches of the routes on The Fortress.

THE FORTRESS

This splendid crag, presents a fine steep buttress of roofs and slabs. The slab on the left-hand side has a prominent vertical dyke with a striking pale white slab to its right. The central roofed area sits above a large grassy ledge, The Garden, with a roof and steep vegetated slabs below. Access to The Garden is by a scramble up a grassy ramp and corner containing a rowan tree to gain its left end. The right arete of this buttress gives the line of The Fortress itself, before turning into a steep side wall. An un-named 60m route (Hard Severe, 1980s) follows a line up the edge left of Cube Wall to finish on the first terrace.

1   Cube Wall   120m   Severe   (1967)
A line up the left side of the slab to the left of the dyke. Start at an obvious thin corner a few metres right of a rock scar.
1. 30m   Bridge and layback the corner crack to a ledge on the left. Move left from the obvious quartz cube (peg runner) and continue up to a diagonal fault which runs up right. The fault leads to a larger corner and a grass ledge.
2. 25m   Climb the wall above to the terrace.
3. 40m   From the big boulder on the right, climb a short layback crack and an easy groove to a dodgy belay on a quartz knob.
4. 25m   Finish directly up the slab.

**2   Kubla Khan   110m   Hard Severe **   (1967)
A fine climb up the pale slab right of the dyke. Start just right of the dyke.
1. 20m   Climb a steep vertically grooved wall on rounded holds to a large grass ledge.
2. 40m   Climb the pale grooved slab above until forced to move left onto a small ledge in a recess.
3. 10m   Go straight up to the terrace.
4. 40m Climb the overhang and easy lichenous slabs to finish.

3   The Rubaiyat   70m   E2   (1996)
A direct line up the right edge of the dome-shaped buttress. Start down and right of Kubla Khan, beneath parallel cracks.
1. 20m 4c   Climb direct, passing a tiny rowan sapling near the top, and pull onto a heather terrace.
2. 50m 5a   Climb an easy niche which leads to a flared crack in the slab. Follow this past a thin section low down (poorly protected, crux) and continue in the same line to a prominent right-slanting break. Shuffle right along this and continue in the same line to finish up a wider crack. Move out left to belay as for Kubla Khan. Either finish up this or abseil off.

**4   The Keep   130m   HVS **   (1967)
This route follows the immediate left edge of the steep central section of The Fortress. Scramble up the grassy ramp to the rowan tree.
1. 10m 4b   Climb the crack in the left wall above the tree to reach a block belay on the slab.
2. 45m 5a   Continue by grooves on the edge of the buttress until confronted by twin cracks splitting the vertical wall above. Using both of these gain the flake above and continue up the fault line, passing a loose block and an easy slab to a belay on a grass patch.
3. 30m 4a   The slab above leads to the terrace.
4. 45m   Follow the hog's back ridge to the top.
Alternative Start: 25m   E1 5b   (1996)
This starts at the toe of the buttress, on the front face, to the left of the grassy ramp that leads to the Garden. Follow twin parallel cracks up the front face to finish on good holds on the arete. Scramble up heather to the block belay at the base of pitch 2 of the parent route.

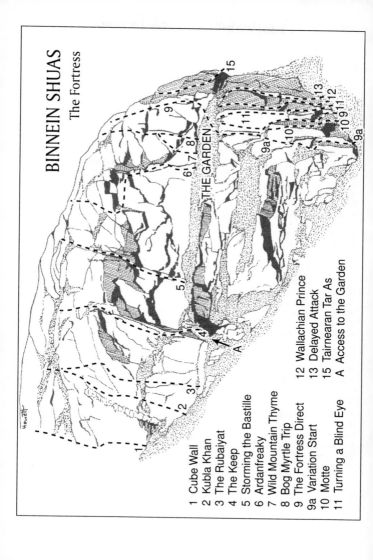

BINNEIN SHUAS
The Fortress

1 Cube Wall
2 Kubla Khan
3 The Rubaiyat
4 The Keep
5 Storming the Bastille
6 Ardanfreaky
7 Wild Mountain Thyme
8 Bog Myrtle Trip
9 The Fortress Direct
9a Variation Start
10 Motte
11 Turning a Blind Eye
12 Wallachian Prince
13 Delayed Attack
15 Tairnearan Tar As
A Access to the Garden

THE GARDEN

5   Storming the Bastille   80m   E3 **   (1984)
This fine route takes the spectacular line of the off-width crack cutting the roof above the left-hand side of The Garden.
1. 40m 5c   Make a hard entry into the bomb-bay crack and follow it to the roof. Back and foot the chimney through the roof to a steep slab. Climb this to good finishing holds.
2. 15m   Climb the easy corner to a ledge and tree belay.
3. 25m 5a   Follow the diagonal crack to reach a slab and the top.

6   Ardanfreaky   105m   E3 **   (1984)
A stunning climb through the centre of the roofs. Start below cracks in the slab below the corner extending down from the right-hand side of the main roofs.
1. 20m 5c   Climb the steepening right-hand crack until it is possible to move right into the corner. Layback up this to a ledge.
2. 20m 6a   Pull over the juggy roof above into a corner. Traverse left under the bigger roof to a strange down-pointing spike. Step up to the roof and traverse across the wall in a wild position into a short hanging corner, which succumbs after a struggle. Exit left onto a ledge.
3. 40m 5b   Follow the diagonal crack above rightwards, then climb a slab to a tree belay.
4. 25m   Climb the corner crack above to the top.

7   Wild Mountain Thyme   45m   E4 6b **   (1995)
The short hanging diagonal crack line in the steep wall right of the cracks of Ardanfreaky gives a hard struggle. Start at a shallow groove leading to the lower bulge. Climb to the bulge, then undercling left to a good runner. Gain the diagonal crack and follow it with one desperate span to join Bog Myrtle Trip above its initial bulge. Finish up this.

8   Bog Myrtle Trip   40m   E4 6b *   (1995)
The vertical crack right of Wild Mountain Time forms a rounded off-width as it cuts through the lower bulge. Strenuous moves laybacking through the bulge lead to good finger locks, then a hard move right gains the upper crack and painful jams. Follow this to easier ground, then climb directly through the roof at the top on jugs and rub some bog myrtle into your skin to repel the midges.

9   The Fortress Direct   125m   HVS **   (1964/1970)
A fine route with sustained climbing up the right edge of The Fortress, starting from round on the right wall at a jumble of huge boulders next to a large roof.
1. 20m 5a   Climb the hanging groove to another roof and pass it on the left to get into another groove with a small sapling over the lip. Continue up the groove until it is possible to traverse right onto a large grass ledge.
2. 30m 4c   To the left of a short right-facing corner are twin cracks. Climb these to a diagonal crack leading right to The Garden. Belay at the right end.
3. 30m 5a   Gain a triangular niche up and right and exit *via* a fine crack issuing from its lip. Step right at the top and go direct to a ledge.
4. 45m   Climb the edge to the top.

9a *Variation Start*
The original first pitch started at the lowest rocks below the jumble of boulders at a mossy groove near the edge. Enter the groove from the right and follow it to a roof. Turn this on the left and continue to the heather ledge. Not as good although a little easier than the line described.

10 Motte 50m E1 * (1985)
A bold, delicate start leads to strenuous cracks on the second pitch. Start 5m down and left of the direct start to The Fortress, just to the right of a small slanting corner.
1. 25m 5b Climb directly up the wall to a break at 7m. Pass this and move delicately left (small spike runner) to another break. Continue up the slabby wall above trending right to the stance of The Fortress.
2. 25m 5b To the right of The Fortress twin cracks is a short corner with a smooth right wall. Climb the corner and the continuation crack to reach The Garden. Either descend from The Garden or continue up The Fortress.

11 Turning a Blind Eye 50m E6 6b * (1994)
This bold and serious climb takes a line up the hanging arete to the right of the second pitch of Motte. Start round to the right of Fortress Direct, below an easy-looking corner ramp that leads to the arete. Follow this to a bulge below the arete. Pull up, swing round left to incipient cracks (*in situ* RP1), then move up and span back right to a flake and follow this to easier ground leading to The Garden.

12 Wallachian Prince 45m E5 6b ** (1988)
The line between the arete of Turning a Blind Eye and the crack and corner line of Delayed Attack gives a necky outing. Start at the crack of the latter route. Climb the crack to a large flake, break out left diagonally to an arete, then move up to a roof. Climb up right of the roof, then step left along the lip to a small ledge. Struggle with the thin crack in the bulge above, then climb blindly onwards past a small flake into a hanging groove to finish. A little horror.

13 Delayed Attack 40m E3 6a *** (1984)
The impressive corner and deep diagonal crack in the side wall gives an outstanding climb. Start at a vertical crack leading up to the hanging corner in the centre of the wall. Climb the crack and pull over the small roof (crux) into the corner. Exit from the corner *via* the diagonal crack with painful jamming to reach the right end of The Garden.

14 Use of Weapons 40m E5 6a * (1992)
This route attempts to climb the impressive wall to the right of Delayed Attack. Follow Delayed Attack into the corner and a good rest on the right arete. Traverse the horizontal break down and right into the middle of the wall (peg runner). Move up and left to gain a thin diagonal seam (peg runner), then follow this up and right. Where it peters out, continue to an isolated overlap. Move up to jugs in the break which lead left to The Garden.

To the right of Ardverikie Wall the cliff becomes smaller and more vegetated, however there are some good sections of rock for the enthusiast.

Whipped Cream   80m   Hard Severe   (1976)
This route takes a line just left of Soft Shoe Shuffle. Start just left of a flat block.
1. 40m   Climb the left-trending fault to a blaeberry ledge. Follow the corner crack above to a small ledge on the right.
2. 40m   From the right end of the ledge go across a white slab diagonally rightwards to below a small bay. Gain the bay and pull through the roofs above on the left. About 100m of scrambling remains.

Soft Shoe Shuffle   85m   VS *   (1968)
A fine climb on steep clean rock approximately 100 metres right of Ardverikie Wall. Start on a flat rock ledge below an overhang.
1. 15m   Climb the overhang by moving in from the right above it. Gain a flake crack which leads to a ledge and flake belay.
2. 10m   Move left below the next overhang to a break in the roof which is climbed on loose blocks. Move right to a ledge and a peg belay.
3. 20m   Take the corner on the right, then go diagonally right by a line of flakes to a small stance on a flake at the left side of a slab.
4. 40m   Go up left to climb a steep quartz band directly, then go over several bulges to a block belay. Scramble 100m to finish.
Variation: 30m   HVS 5a
After the normal first pitch, continue up the crack directly above. At its end, trend up and right to belay at the end of the normal pitch 3.

The cliff continues more broken until the next main features are two chimney lines. The left-hand one is **Second Prize** (Hard Severe) both in name and quality.

Eastern Chimney   75m   Severe   (1969)
The right-hand of the two chimneys gives an interesting excursion with back and footing between two diverging chimneys. There is much grot to finish.

The next two routes have a common start about 75 metres right of Eastern Chimney from below a huge block some 10m off the ground. The block is bounded on the left by a prominent black lichenous corner whilst a turf choked groove leads up to it from the ground.

Differential   75m   VS   (1969)
1. 45m   From the turfy groove climb diagonally left past a grass pocket at 20m until a slab leads to a left traverse to an obvious groove. Climb the groove, then go diagonally right past a shelf overhang to a belay.
2. 30m   Go left into an easy chimney which leads to the top.

Tip Top   80m   VS   (1969)
Start as for Differential.
1. 25m   Climb the turfy groove to the black corner. Move up and right onto the
face of the block and make a nasty move onto a grass ledge on its top. Belay in
the corner on the right.
2. 25m   Climb the corner, traverse the right wall after 15m to reach an arete
which leads to a belay.
3. 30m   Continue directly to the top.

Far Eastern Chimney   110m   HVS   (1994)
About 50 metres right of Tip Top is a prominent chimney.
1. 35m 4c   Climb the mossy chimney.
2. 25m 5b   Gain a platform below the steep corner and crack above. Climb
these direct, exiting right at the top to belay beside large blocks.
3. 50m 4c   Climb the chimney above directly (very airy) to a belay well back.
Finish up easy rocks as for Native Stones.

Native Stones   75m   VS   (1993)
Start about 10 metres right of Far Eastern Chimney, to the right of a vegetated
ledge system and before the final arete of the crag, at the bottom of a
left-slanting corner.
1. 25m 5a   Follow the corner, pass over a projecting block, then move onto the
right wall and go up to a ledge on the right with a block.
2. 25m 4b   From the block, step right onto the face of the buttress, then work
up rightwards and back left to a large belay ledge on the edge of the buttress.
3. 25m 4b   Follow the mossy crack above, then continue up, keeping a corner
system to the left. Join this where it steepens to a vertical corner and follow it up
and left to a belay. Easy ground leads to the top.

Left Foot First   345m   VS   (1972)
This is a girdle of the Eastern Section, giving mostly Severe climbing. Only the
second last pitch warrants VS and this can be avoided. Start up the chimney of
Second Prize.
1. 20m   Climb the chimney to a block belay.
2. 45m   Traverse left along ledges and slabs passing the belay on Soft Shoe
Shuffle. Go up a short corner and a mantle to reach a peg belay.
3. 45m   Traverse left across a quartz band and go up slabs on good holds to a
grass ledge. Belay on the left.
4. 45m   Go left, crossing the top of small square-cut overhang and belay in an
open groove.
5. 45m   Go round the edge to join Ardverikie Wall. Follow it for about 10m, then
leave it to belay in a niche above a grassy terrace.
6. 45m   Move up left to a bulge. Cross this and follow slabs to a narrow terrace.
7. 30m   Cross the slabby wall above from the right edge of a flake.
8. 45m   Go left again for a few metres then continue to a peg belay.
9. 25m   Scramble to the top.

THE LOWER TIER

Below the main crag are two separate short slabby walls. They are generally broken and poor but there are a few routes. Starting with the wall below the main section of the crag:

Criss   75m   Severe   (1967)
Climb the obvious right-trending crack in two pitches.

Cross   70m   VS   (1967)
Start at the first fault to the right of Criss. Climb straight up on small holds before trending left to cross Criss and follow a corner until it overlaps. Break through the overlap and finish direct. Belay where appropriate.

Crisscross Edge   70m   Very Difficult   (1971)
The prominent edge right of Cross. Start just right of a tree, climb steep ramp to a platform and follow the edge above.

The following route lies on the right-hand buttress below the extreme right-hand end of the Eastern Section.

Whiplash   45m   VS   (1968)
This climb takes the imposing chimney. There is some loose rock.
1. 30m   Climb a groove until forced onto a platform on the left. Ascend a recess to reach a large spike, then swing right to footholds. Move into the chimney past an overhanging nose (peg runner) and go up to a ledge.
2. 15m   Climb the wall on the left, then take a line up to the right to a thread belay in boulders.

FAR EAST SECTOR   (Map Ref 469 832)

This is a 90m buttress about 1km east of the Eastern Section and facing Binnein Shuas. To get to it, continue round right from the main cliff, crossing a shallow valley where the crag rears up about 200 metres beyond. There is only one route to date.

Near Miss   75m   Hard Severe   (1971)
Left of centre is a small groove. Start at a small rib just right of this.
1. 40m   Climb 8m up the rib, then go left into the groove and climb it to near its end. Traverse up left to a crack in the overhang. Climb this, then follow slabs to a steepening. Go right to a small niche and climb the vertical crack to steep grass and a belay near a tree.
2. 35m   Go up right to a block, then move left to the edge and finish by a wall on the right.

DIRC MHOR   *(Map Ref 591 861)*

This impressive ravine cuts a slice through the hills to the north-west of Dalwhinnie. It is a giant meltwater channel formed by the draining waters of a receding glacier during the last ice age. The ravine is nearly 1½km long, angled north-east to south-west with the east side being a virtually continuous line of cliffs. The west side is slabby and broken. Guarding the entrance to the north end of the defile is the most impressive buttress, the 90m Sentinel Rock. The rock is a fine grained micro-granite with pegmatite intrusions similar to, but more compact and better than Binnein Shuas, and it is generally sound and clean.

HISTORY

The first route recorded was in 1966 when A.McKeith and party climbed Holy Smoke up the edge of the most impressive buttress, Sentinel Rock. In 1980 Allen Fyffe visited first with Keith Geddes to produce Slow Hand, then the pair were accompanied by Addo Liddell to bag the fine hanging corner of Working Class Hero. Fyffe returned in 1981 with Martin Burrows-Smith to climb Positive Earth. This seemed to be an attempt to breach the impressive front face of Sentinel Rock but they were forced onto the right-hand side. Given the obvious potential for excellent climbing it is strange that they never returned. Dirc Mhor attracted no new suitors until in 1994 Kevin Howett made a checking trip for this guide and, realizing the potential, started a concerted effort to climb the remaining lines in the company of Graham Little and others. The resulting three E5s on Sentinel Rock are amongst the best routes in the guide, indeed all the routes are of excellent quality. George Ridge and Janet Horrocks produced Dry Roasted and Scorched Earth during the height of the 1995 heatwave and Grahame Nicoll led Bournville on sight. A final route was nabbed by Gary Latter in 1996 and named Close to the Wind (E5).

ACCESS

Follow the A889 north out of Dalwhinnie for about 2km, where the road ascends a steep hill. Parking is possible at the top of the hill opposite a locked forestry gate. Follow the bulldozed track through the gate, pass below a new house, and once past the grounds of the house strike uphill to regain a good track which starts in its courtyard. Follow the track until it drops down towards the Allt an t-Sluic, then follow the banks of the burn up the glen until the deep gash of Dirc Mhor opens up on the left. From here it is best to take a rising line on the left of the Dirc to contour into the base of Sentinel Rock, as the base of the defile is full of deep heather and boulders. Allow 1hr 30 minutes.

THE SILVER SLABS

About halfway along the walk-in towards the Dirc itself, where the small glen opens out, there are some clean slabs up to the right (on the north flank of the glen). There are five routes from Difficult to Severe which follow the most obvious lines on the largest slab and the smaller one to its right.

SENTINEL ROCK

The pride of the Dirc. This barrel-shaped 90m-high buttress presents a fine front face split into thirds by two ledges. The left wall is overhanging and split by the excellent line of Working Class Hero. The arete is the line of the stunning The Man with the Child in his Eyes, whilst Fanfare for the Common Man and The Scent of a Woman take lines up the front face. The right side of the buttress is defined by a huge corner in the upper half, capped by a roof where Positive Earth and Holy Smoke find a way. The routes finish on a terrace strewn with boulders at the very crest of the wall. The best way off is to ascend more broken ground above before the crag can be safely quitted over the top of the hillock, followed by a walk back round the northern end of the Dirc to the base.

1   Working Class Hero   85m   E1 **   (1980)
This route takes the fine ramp and corner up the left wall. Start at the toe of the buttress at the base of a big slanting slab.
1. 15m 4b   Climb the big slab to a belay at its top.
2. 30m 5b   Gain and climb the small right-facing corner in the overhanging wall above, which leads to the clean-cut ramp/corner line. Follow this spectacularly to a niche and exit to the right onto a large ledge cutting the front of the buttress.
3. 40m 4c   Step up to the large ledge which leads diagonally right across the face to a corner. Climb this to the top of a pinnacle, then traverse diagonally right using a thin crack and from its end traverse back hard left. Easier rock leads to the top.

2   The Man with the Child in his Eyes   85m   E5 ***   (1995)
A stunning route climbing the left arete of the front face of Sentinel Rock. Start as for Working Class Hero at the big slab.
1. 15m 4b   Climb the big slab to a belay.
2. 30m 6b   Climb a small groove in the wall just right of the corner of Working Class Hero for 4m until it is possible to span out right around the arete to gain a big flat-topped flake. Move up to join Fanfare for the Common Man at the left end of its first belay ledge. Climb the arete past a quartz fin where hard moves gain an obvious hold in the arete. Follow the thin crack on the left side of the arete with sustained difficulty until an exit left near the top gains a belay at the left end of the large ledge above.
3. 15m 6a   Follow slabby rock up and left to gain the thin crack near the arete. Continue up this to a belay.
4. 25m 4c   Trend leftwards to the base of a left-slanting ramp, then follow the crack directly above to broken ground. Scramble rightwards to reach a boulder-strewn terrace.

3   Fanfare for the Common Man   90m   E5 ***   (1994)
A stunning line on the left-hand side of the front face of Sentinel Rock. Start at the lowest point of the crag, as for Working Class Hero.
1. 25m 5a   Climb the easy-angled slab (as for Working Class Hero) for 10m to the point where an obvious flake crack breaks the right wall. Ascend this, then

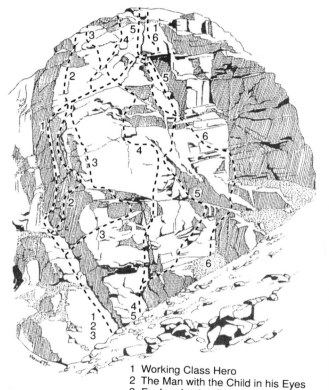

DIRC MHOR

Sentinel Rock

1 Working Class Hero
2 The Man with the Child in his Eyes
3 Fanfare for the Common Man
4 The Scent of a Woman
5 Positive Earth
6 Holy Smoke

traverse right along a fault to step up onto the right-hand of two sloping rock ledges. Move left to an awkward belay at the junction of the two ledges. The direct climb from the fault to the ledges *via* a short steep diagonal crack is 6a.

2. 25m 6b   Step up onto the higher ledge, then move left to the base of a slight groove. Climb this to a thin horizontal crack. Pull up bulging rock with increasing difficulty to a hairline horizontal crack, then make committing moves left and up to gain better holds. A sequence of good holds lead to the large ledge. A brilliant pitch.

3. 20m 5c   Climb easy rock just right of the belay to gain a right-trending ramp shared with Working Class Hero. Follow this to the start of a less distinct left-trending ramp. Ascend this to a deep incut hold below bulging rock. Go straight over the bulge to a thin flake, then move left to gain a flange. Move left and go up to a ledge.

4. 20m 4a   Climb a left-trending stepped groove, then scramble back right and go up to gain the wide block-strewn terrace.

4   The Scent of a Woman   95m   E5 ***   (1994)
A magnificent fairly central line on the front face of Sentinel Rock. The most serious of the trio. Start at the lowest point of the crag below the overhanging Corner.

1. 25m 6a   Climb the flake as for Positive Earth. Carry on up the continuation overhanging corner cutting through the roof (strenuous) to a rest above the lip. Move right, then go up the pod on the right side of a big block to a rock pedestal.

2. 30m 6b   Step right and up into a short shallow-right facing groove. Pull out left to gain a thin crack which leads up to join the left-trending diagonal crack of Positive Earth. Follow the continuation of the diagonal line up left on good holds, then traverse diagonally left to a point under an obvious isolated roof in the centre of the face. Climb straight up the two-stepped overhanging wall above, with hard moves over the final lip, then move up right to a rock ramp which leads to a belay at the right end of the large ledge.

3. 20m 6b   Move left up a short slabby wall to a right-trending ramp. From this follow a less distinct left-trending rock ramp to a deep incut hold below bulging rock (as for Fanfare for the Common Man). Move right and go up to a diagonal crack in the bulging wall, then move up and right again to gain a sharp edge. Make difficult contorted moves up to reach an undercling (Friend 0). Undercling rightwards to gain a poor crack in the bulge. Strenuous moves, on scarcely adequate holds, lead up to a belay ledge.

4. 20m 4a   Climb a short slabby corner then broken ground leading to a block strewn terrace.

5   Positive Earth   85m   E2 **   (1981)
This climb traces a line up the right side of the front face, finishing up the big corner. Start at the toe of the buttress as for Scent of a Woman.

1. 20m 4c   Climb the corner until it steepens and escape up the right wall onto a large slab. Follow a line diagonally up the wall above to belay at the obvious large blocks.

2. 20m 5b   Move slightly left into a niche. Climb the thin diagonal crack which leads leftwards with a hard move to reach a good small triangular ledge (junction with Scent of a Woman). Go up the wall above on good holds leading into the base of the big corner.

3. 15m 4a   Climb the corner and exit left under the roof to belay on the large ledge on the front of the buttress.

4. 30m 4c   Climb the fine vertical crack above to finish.

6   Holy Smoke   90m   VS *   (1966)

Start above and right of the lowest rocks at the lowest of three grassy slabs.

1. 30m 4c   Climb a short wall, then move rightwards to the large blocks of the first belay of Positive Earth. Climb the wall above by a crack on the right to the third grassy slab.

2. 25m 4c   Ascend the corner on the left, then go left onto the wall of the buttress. Continue up to belay on small ledges on a slab below the big corner.

3. 35m 4c   Climb the left arete of the corner (the edge of the front face) to the roof, then go left to the large ledge. From the top of the pinnacle above hand traverse up and rightwards until a narrow ledge leads right. Go straight up, then move left to a slab. Follow the crest to the top.

7   Slowhand   65m   VS   (1980)

This route roughly follows the projecting rib to the right of Sentinel Rock. Start on the right of the rib.

1. 30m 4c   Climb the groove in the rib to the roof, then move up and left round the crest of the rib to a small corner. Climb this to a slabby ramp from the top of which go left to a heather patch.

2. 35m   Continue up the crest *via* a wide crack and short groove. Trend left to finish.

8   Dry Roasted   25m   E3 6a   (1995)

The thin crack that diagonally splits the steep right wall of the projecting rib of Slowhand provides the line of this climb. Go up the initial corner, then step right and up to enter the crack. Climb this very steeply, then ascend the juggy but poorly protected wall above to gain a grass ledge. Belay on blocks above. Abseil off.

The line of cliffs continues beyond Sentinel Rock on a smaller scale, forming two large open bays. At the projecting buttress after the second bay is a very smooth and clean-cut open corner, sitting about 10m above a vegetated lower groove which is flanked by two small rowan trees. This is the line of After Many a Summer. To the right of this corner the cliff continues in its upper half as a series of corners between smooth slabby walls. A lower tier of less attractive rock guards any entry. This section of cliff culminates in an area of smooth, white slabby corners. To the right of here is the expanse of The Sea of Slabs; more mossy and less well defined. There is only one feasible descent from the entire length of this side of the Dirc. Steep broken ground above the crags has to be negotiated before heading south (leftwards) eventually leading to the top of a descent gully about halfway along.

After Many a Summer   50m   E2 5c *   (1994)

Start below the corner between two small rowan trees. Climb the easy groove to the start of the corner. Excellent climbing up the corner leads to hollow flakes on the slabby right wall. Climb slightly above these to an incipient diagonal crack cutting the right wall. Move right with difficulty to a resting position at the base of a short rock ramp. Move up the ramp and make bold moves to surmount bulging rock (crux) and gain a short corner on the left. Go up to climb the wide finishing crack. About 12m of steep heather must be ascended to reach the belay (included in the overall height of the climb).

Scorched Earth   50m   E1 **   (1995)

The clean-cut slab sandwiched between two corners right of After Many a Summer. Start as for that route.

1. 20m 4c   From the start of the big corner scramble horizontally along the grass ledge rightwards, then climb the slabby wall leading up and right to an easy slab. Traverse right and go up to beneath the open chimney on the right of the sandwiched slab. Chockstone belay.

2. 30m 5b   Climb the centre of the slabby wall *via* a vertical crack line and large knobbles to the easier central slab. Go up this slightly left to near its left arete just below the top of the crag. Step right into a short ramp and pull out with trouble. Belay 15m back at a small outcrop of rock.

Working on the Hoof   50m   HVS   (1996)

The easiest line through the area of smooth, white slabby corners. Start at the lowest right-hand side of the buttress.

1. 30m 4a   Climb diagonally up and left on easy-angled rock to reach a weakness in a steeper band. Climb through the weakness onto the easy-angled slab above. Climb up and left to belay on a subsidiary slab below the left retaining wall at a large quartz blotch.

2. 20m 5a   Move up a crack in the side wall onto another easy slab, then climb the steep cracked arete above to the final slab below the steep headwall. Pass a large projecting block on the right and finish up a corner.

Gullible's Travels   85m   VS   (1996)

A line up the centre of The Sea of Slabs. Start at the lowest point of the slabs.

1. 25m   Follow the cleanest rock, then a low-angled vague clean rib to a tree belay in a grassy recess on the right.

2. 30m 4a   Gain the blocky corner above from a slab and climb this on the right to a heather terrace below a wall. Move right round a corner, then go up onto a slab trending left to a belay on a detached flake.

3. 25m 4c   Traverse 4 metres right, then make a long reach to a weakness in the headwall. Climb this moving left at the top. Turn the final headwall above on the right.

Fanfare for the Common Man, Dirc Mhor   (Climbers, Paul Thorburn and Rick Campbell)

SHIP ROCK

Beyond the buttress of the last route the cliffs lie back to form The Sea of Slabs. From the southern end of these slabs is a fine buttress. Its two overhanging walls (Port and Starboard Walls) jut proud from the surrounding cliff line like the front of a huge ship. Although they are only 15m high, sitting above a more scrappy section of grass and slabs, the rock is immaculate and the climbing much harder than it looks. The best approach to the small ledge at the base of the walls is to scramble up easy ground on the left and climb a short corner and arete leading to the left end of the wall (Severe). Belays are scarce at the top. The best bet is to belay at a large block some 10m back from the edge (Friends and nuts). The only way off on foot is to ascend the steep heather slope above until it is possible to walk safely south to the top of the descent gully.

PORT WALL

Spurlash   15m   E4 6b ***   (1994)
This climb follows the deep central crack. Start off the left end of the ledge and move left under a small roof to gain a flake. Pull over the roof rightwards to reach the crack, then difficult climbing leads to a shelf and a big flake. Pull up the wall above and climb the fine deep crack in the pale coloured rib to finish.

A Deep Green Peace   15m   E4 6a **   (1994)
The thin crack immediately right of the deep crack of Spurlash. From the left end of the ledge follow a very thin crack diagonally right into a short corner. Move up this, then make strenuous moves out right to gain and climb the thin crack to the shelf. Stand on the shelf and step left to the big flake of Spurlash and finish up it.

Murderous Pursuit   15m   E3 6a **   (1994)
This route takes the line of a shallow scoop in the right side of the wall just right of A Deep Green Peace and just left of the arete. Climb up to a vertical quartz-studded bore hole. Gain a thin flake crack above and follow it to a jug at its top. Pull up and right to a small flake, then step right to pull onto the shelf. Finish up the cracks above.

Breaking the Wind   15m   E4 6b **   (1995)
Another good climb, following the arete formed by the two walls, which is very steep and harder than it looks. Start up Murderous Pursuit to a point just past the quartz-studded bore hole. Reach out right around the arete to gain a crack. Climb this into the short hanging groove above, then exit onto the easier wall.

STARBOARD WALL

Close to the Wind   15m   E5 6b **   (1996)
Excellent well protected climbing up the obvious crack in the wall right of the arete. Start from the end of the ledge and climb the crack on good holds to an undercut flake. Continue with difficulty up the thin crack above to slabby ground.

The Republic of Scotland, Weem Crags   (Climber, Gary Latter)

No Way Out   30m   VS 5a   (1994)
To the right of Ship Rock there is a deep corner, right of the corner containing the block roof. Start at the lowest rocks on the right side. Climb the slabs near the edge until it is possible to move left onto a grass ledge beneath the corner. Continue up this with interest. An escape route!

Beyond Ship Rock is a further projecting buttress of clean white rock which forms the left side of the only descent gully on the entire east side of the Dirc. The following route climbs the fine white arete of the buttress.

Carry on up the Khyber   45m   E1 5b *   (1994)
Start below the arete where the wall bends round to eventually form the high retaining wall of a deep gully running diagonally behind the cliff. Climb a slim corner, then go up to a ledge. Move up the wall on the left to flakes. Pull round the edge of the arete in a very exposed position, then climb the left side to gain easier-angled rock (alternatively, stay on the right of the arete and climb straight up). Climb cracks close to the edge to reach easy slabby rock. Finish by a steep little corner holding a worrying jammed block.

Bournville   30m   E1 5b *   (1995)
At the back of the descent gully is a beautifully clean brown wall. Start from a good ledge and climb the centre of the wall until it is possible to move right and go up to a ledge. Move left and up to finish.

WORLD'S END WALL

At the very southern end of Dirc Mhor lies one last impressive buttress. It faces due south and overlooks the wasteland of empty moor and bog that leads to Ben Alder. The belay at the top is a long block well back from the edge.

Galileo's Gambol   20m   E5 6a *   (1994)
A serious little excursion virtually up the centre of the wall. Start below the centre of the wall on the raised heather ledge. Gain a small ledge up on the left. Step right and go direct up the wall with thin moves past a tiny white overlap to gain a small block (imaginary runner). Step up left to a large flat hold, then move up and right through the bulging wall via a hidden pocket until it is possible to step right onto the ledge above the overlap. Finish direct.

Crowberry Crank   20m   E3 5c *   (1994)
Start at the right edge of the wall and climb easily up ledges. Continue direct to a right-facing flake which leads to a roof. Pass this on the left to gain good holds and go up to a long ledge. Climb the final tricky wall to finish.

WEST FLANK

The west flank of Dirc Mhor is much more broken than the east. However, there are a number of relatively clean areas of slabby rock bursting through the steep and heavily vegetated terrain. The best and most prominent, Whitecap Wall, lies nearly opposite Sentinel Rock and is characterised by a central roofed bay and a white-streaked cap. The descent is well to the right of the buttress, down a narrow tree-filled gully.

Dust Devil   55m   HVS   (1996)
A direct line on the right side of the buttress, passing just right of the central overhangs, gives good climbing that will improve with traffic. Start from an obvious square-cut block near the right side.
1. 25m 5a   Step off the block onto the wall and climb a thin crack to small ledges. Gain the layback crack above and follow this strenuously through the bulges onto the slab above. Climb up and left for 5m to a devious belay level with a grass caterpillar.
2. 30m 4a   Direct up the slab to the top.

Whitecap Direct   55m   HVS   (1994)
Start to the left of a big ash tree at the base of the crag where a block has dropped from a low roof (just right of a slim corner).
1. 25m 5a   Move up past the low roof to a higher one and pull left onto a steep slab. Climb this to a tree. Scramble through heather past a couple of trees, to a steep slab left of a shallow groove. Ascend the slab to below a thin overlap. Pull over this and go up into a slot. Pull out of this onto a short slabby wall and belay by a perched block.
2. 30m 4c   Move left and pull over the diminishing roof above. Climb the slabby wall to reach a thin heather ledge, then follow the incipient crack and grey slab above to gain the white streaks, finishing just left of a poised block.

About halfway along the Dirc, opposite Ship Rock, there is one piece of very steep rock. It looks almost like a boulder sitting halfway up the side of the ravine. Its left (south) side presents a steep little route.

Schist Hot   5m   E4 6b   (1994)
Climb the overhanging crack in the steep face with a hard pull out onto the top of the boulder.

CREAG CHATHALAIN   *(Map Ref 492 947)*

This promising-looking crag in the upper Spey valley is up to 100m in height, but it is actually very broken and vegetated. One route of Severe standard has been unearthed up the left-hand side, but it is best left to the plants.

CREAG DOIRE NA H-ACHLAISE   *(Map Ref 609 891)*

There is a large-looking crag sitting above the beautiful Loch Caoldair, 5km north of Dalwhinnie. It is however vegetated and where it is steep, it is horribly loose. It is suspected that lots of climbers who were unable to read a map have mistaken this crag for Dirc Mhor in the past as it is clearly visible from the Dalwhinnie to Laggan road and is fairly close to the Dirc. This may account for the apparent neglect of the Dirc.

The crag is best approached from the vicinity of the Raeburn Hut, between Dalwhinnie and Laggan. The east-facing crags visible on the approach are not as big or as extensive as they appear. The best rock lies just around the corner beyond a steep section of loose rock (the Leaning Wall).

THE MAIN WALL

To the left of the Leaning Wall the crag gains in height with roofs at mid-height. A gully/ramp slants up right above the Leaning Wall, whilst the slope below the Main Wall slants up left into a gully on the left. Descent is over the top to come down underneath the Aside Wall, described later.

Quartz Boss   65m   E3 *   (1997)
A good climb which will become better when more ascents remove more of the lichen. Start in the recess in the base of the gully/ramp.
1. 55m 5c   Gain a quartz boss from the right. Climb a short steep section and continue to a fine quartzy wall, just left of a shallow groove. Step left into the middle of the wall and climb this up and right to a smoother section. Pull up right onto the edge, then stretch up left to a protruding hold at the base of a short groove. Move up, step right and climb beneath a steepening where moves up and right lead *via* a groove onto a slab. Climb the slab to a belay just below a notch at the top of the crag.
2. 10m   Easy climbing leads to the top.

Centenary Wall   60m   Severe   (1989)
This climb is on good rock, further up the slope, well to the left of the gully/ramp, shortly below the entrance to the gully at the left end of the crag.
1. 45m   Climb the steep wall, generously endowed with holds, then traverse to a rib. Climb directly to a heathery shelf where a delicate traverse right for 15m is required to gain a good belay.
2. 15m   Climb direct to the top.

THE ASIDE WALL

This lies some 100 metres across to the left of the base of the Leaning Wall. There are some short walls at the start and the crag becomes bigger as the slope rises beneath it to the left. The descent from Main Wall passes beneath this wall.

Zagaboot   40m   E1 5b   (1997)
Towards the left end is a leaning quartz arete above a roof. A wide fault lies on the left. Climb a groove just left of the arete to reach the fault. Move up, then go out right onto the arete. A shelf leading right and a higher one going left enable the final dome to be reached. Move up and right past some blocks, then climb the dome to the top. Belay well back.

CREAG RUADH   (Map Ref 565 912)

This south-east facing crag lies on the hillside above the Black Wood, between Laggan Village and Loch Laggan. It is best approached up the side of the wood, through a steep field just east of Inverpattack Lodge. The crag is fairly broken and relatively mossy.

Pattack View   60m   Very Difficult   (1995)
Start at a cairn at the right-hand side of the western rock mass, at some flat rocks to the right of a wild rose bush. Ascend the wall for 5m to a terrace, then climb a rock cone to a steep wall with a conspicuous large flake on the left. Climb the wall beside a smaller flake, then move left up the rib to finish.

Rowan and Alder Arete   70m   Difficult   (1995)
From the top of Pattack View, descend a sheep track and cross over to an obvious large rowan tree at the base of an arete bounding an open gully. Climb the sharp arete past a rowan tree. After a scrappy section, climb easy rock past an alder tree to the top.

Between Two Rooms   50m   Very Difficult   (1995)
This lies to the left of Pattack View. Scramble up to a terrace below a conspicuous left-facing corner. Climb the rib to the right of the corner and continue through a small break, passing a recent rock scar.

Strathtay and Strathtummel

In the heart of the Central Highlands, the great salmon rivers of the Tay and the Tummel have their beginnings. Waters from Rannoch Moor in Lochaber flow east to form Loch Rannoch and Loch Tummel (The Road to The Isles in reverse) whilst the hills north of Loch Lomond drain eastwards into Loch Tay before flowing east as the Tay. The Tay and the Tummel join and strike a way through the hills south-east to Perth and the Firth of Tay. This is the softer side of Scotland's scenery, of green hills, heather moors and silver birch woods of international importance in an area designated as a National Scenic Area. The main arterial road through the centre of Scotland, the A9, follows this natural avenue northwards before nipping over Drumochter Pass to Speyside.

There are several crags spread out along the route of these glens from Kinloch Rannoch in Strathtummel and Aberfeldy near Loch Tay, to a particularly excellent concentration around the historic village (or rather, city) of Dunkeld, only 27km up the A9 from Perth.

ACCESS
The Dunkeld crags are all easily gained using public transport, being on the main bus and rail routes. Regular services of Stagecoach run from Perth whilst there are a few trains each day. As long as a walk isn't shunned, these can be used to access Bonskeid Crag from Pitlochry. Getting to Kinloch Rannoch is probably too protracted by public means and a car is best.

ACCOMMODATION
Camping at official sites is possible at Inver (Map Ref 016 421), 1km west of Dunkeld. Rough camping is more problematical here as the area is mainly farmed or afforested, although it is possible to bivouac in several caves. Lady Charlotte's Cave beside Lower Cave Crag gives some shelter where water is also on tap as the stream runs through the cave – not always a bonus! There is also a good cave 50 metres left (north) of Myopic's Buttress at Polney Crag which sleeps several people. B&Bs and hotels are abundant in the area for those with more disposable income. The only private hostel in the area is Dunolly House in Aberfeldy which is open all year round (Tel. 01887 820 298).

Similar comments regards wild camping apply for Kinloch Rannoch and Bonskeid Crag, although there are official campsites at both Kinloch Rannoch and Tummel Bridge.

AMENITIES
Perth is the biggest town located centrally to most of the climbing in this chapter. It has all the usual amenities including several outdoor shops. Of these, Mountain Man Supplies in South Street caters best for climbers and houses a

new routes book. The Tiso shop in Dundee also contains a new routes book which often has information about new venues in Perthshire.

Dunkeld has all the usual cafés, shops and bars. In Birnam there is a particularly good café in the Post Office specialising in home-made scones and jams at great value, whilst lounging in the evening sun in front of the Birnam House Hotel with a coffee, a beer and a cucumber sandwich is not a poor second to any Mediterranean ambience. For those with other interests there is much to do in the area, from watching ospreys at the Loch of the Lowes, excellent walking and cycling, visits to Dunkeld square, The Cathedral and The Birnam Oaks. All in all – a good venue for keeping the whole family happy.

Kinloch Rannoch has a good hotel which offers an air of Victorian elegance to a visit. Alternatively, there is a bar with pool tables in the Caravan Park at Tummel Bridge. It is also worth travelling the extra half hour down Loch Rannoch to the superb little café on the platform of Rannoch Station, with its frontier-like position on the edge of the wilderness of lochan and bog that is Rannoch Moor.

Aberfeldy has several cafés and excellent home baking is available at the tearoom inside Menzies Castle itself. Further afield, the Ballinluig trucker's café gives cheap basic food, the Moulin Hotel in Pitlochry supplies excellent bar food and the Grandtully Hotel is also worth a visit (good canoeing and rafting!). Munro's outdoor shops in Aberfeldy and Pitlochry sell climbing gear and chalk.

STRATHTUMMEL

The crags in this region can be found on Ordnance Survey 1:50,000 Landranger Series sheets 42, 43, 51 and 52.

CRAIG VARR   *(Map Ref 669 590)*

This south-facing crag lies at the eastern end of Loch Rannoch. The hillside of Cean Caol na Creige forms a narrow spur running steeply down to the road (the B8019) about 400 metres east of the village of Kinloch Rannoch. The spurs' flanks are covered in outcrops, but only the lowest are worthy of attention. They have been used extensively by the nearby Tayside Outdoor Centre for instruction and have bolt belays at some positions. Although quite a drive to get to from anywhere, they give a fast-drying afternoon or evening alternative when other venues have been exhausted.

Park at a large riverside layby directly below the spur. A gate and style 100 metres east along the road allows access to the hill where a track can be followed back left through the trees. The crag lies above (10 minutes) as two tiers. The first and lowest extends rightwards from a huge electricity pylon and is broken into 3 buttresses. The upper tier is a more continuous wall directly above. A final buttress lies slightly down and right of the upper tier, Mother's Buttress.

LOWER TIER

Immediately right of the pylon is a small slabby rib which gives one pleasant route at Very Difficult. Right again is another larger rib whose left wall is steep and split by a corner and a roof. To the right of the slab of this rib is a large grassy central bay capped by a big black roof and the wall continues rightwards forming the highest part of the crag. A large rowan tree sits at its base and the right side of the wall is defined by a long low roof. Belays above the black roof are numerous bolts in an outcrop.

The following three routes are on the first rib and are described from right to left up the retaining wall.

Mutton   30m   Very Difficult   (1983)
Climb the slab, groove and cracks just right of the rib.

Pork   30m   Severe   (1983)
Climb the arete directly starting at a cracked groove in the arete.

Grouse Wall   20m   VS 4c   (1983)
High up on the left side of the rib is a large detached flake. Climb the crack formed by its left side, then go up the wall above to the top.

Venison   30m   Very Difficult
This route is on the second rib. Climb the slabby front of the rib to a block belay. Either continue up the upper section or walk down the grass from the central bay.

A line of bolts goes directly through the roof on the left wall of the rib, probably placed by outdoor groups for aid practice. The line offers a high solo, about 5c, with a nasty landing and there is no known ascent without the use of the bolts.

The following routes are on the main section, by the black roof.

The Black Hat   30m   VS
Start at the toe of the wall just left of the rowan tree. Follow the shallow corner (grassy) to below the right edge of the roofs. Move up left into the bay below the black roof. From right under the roof traverse right (peg runner) to exit at a small tree.

The Bobble   30m   Severe
Follow The Black Hat for 10m, then trend up rightwards up the wall passing the final overhang by the right.

Dialectic   35m   Hard Severe 4a **
Although a bit mossy, this is an excellent climb. Start on an elevated grass ledge behind the rowan tree. Climb the slab directly above until it steepens. Move up using a hollow flake to a small ledge (a large grass ledge lies down to right). Take a thin crack above, then follow an excellent series of small flake holds up and left to finish on a slab.

The Great Sod   30m   Severe
Start at the long low roof at the right end of the crag. Follow the slab leftwards under the roof, then go up past a small rowan into a slim left-facing corner which leads to the block overhang at the top. Pass this on the left.

UPPER TIER

This is essentially one long wall, with the right-hand section being slightly elevated and set back. The junction between the two is an area of more broken grassy slabs. The first features as one approaches from the left are two left-facing corners, with an orange wall to their right whose base is guarded by three huge detached blocks. A few large boulders lie at the base. The right-hand section is an immaculate wrinkled wall split from right to left by a diagonal crack springing from a large pointed block. There is a sharply defined arete on the right before the crag turns to form a short mossy wall. The routes are described from left to right.

Avenue   20m   Severe   (1983)
Climb the steep slab just left of Boulevard to finish by a left-slanting crack.

Boulevard   25m   Severe
Climb the right-hand, most continuous, corner starting up a crack just left of the detached blocks.

Curved Slab   25m   Severe
Climb the line of an inset slab that forms the left side of the orange wall above and right of the blocks, then exit out right above.

Woggle   25m   Severe
This route take the chossy-looking crack line just right of the previous route, starting off the blocks.

The next routes are on the right-hand section.

Macman   30m   E1 5b *   (1994)
Climb the diagonal crack starting from the pointed block. Where it peters out climb direct avoiding a loose flake, then go slightly left to finish. Steep and surprisingly difficult.

Stratafear   30m   E2 5b **   (1994)
A good climb up the centre of the wrinkled wall above the diagonal crack. Start off the pointed block and climb a thin crack to reach better holds out left at mid-height. Climb directly up the centre of the wrinkles above to the top.

Shakin' not Stirred   25m   E1 5b *   (1994)
There is a smaller diagonal crack starting halfway up the right arete of the crag. Start just right of the pointed block. Climb direct past two ledges to gain the base of the crack. Follow it leftwards and go up to a ledge to finish.

Black Rod (HVS 5a, 1983) finds a way directly up the wall below the obvious small niche just left of Black Handle.

The Black Handle   25m   HVS 5a **
An excellent little route up the arete. Start directly below a small hanging corner in the arete. Gain the corner using the black handle, then follow the right side of the blunt upper arete to finish.

MOTHER'S BUTTRESS

A bigger but scrappier crag than the other two, lying 100 metres to their right and at mid-height between them.

Sprog   30m   Severe
Follow the left-bounding edge of the buttress starting from a grassy bay.

The Womb   30m   Severe
Climb the obvious crack line into and through a small cave on the right-hand section of the buttress.

Tubes   45m   Severe
Follow the right-hand arete of the crag, traverse left across Womb and finish up behind a detached flake.

DRUMGLAS   *(Map Ref 695 592)*

A series of small south-facing buttresses lie just above the B846 between Kinloch Rannoch and Tummel Bridge. The crags marked on the map higher on the slopes of Creag Bhuidhe are very poor. The lower ones are composed of clean solid rock up to 10m high. Reach them through a gate beside the west entrance to Drumglas Farm. They are used by outdoor centres and the buttresses are numbered. There is also some good bouldering.

BONSKEID CRAG   *(Map Ref 908 614)*

An impressively steep little south-east facing wall in the trees above Bonskeid Farm on the B8019 Strath Tummel road, only 2km from the junction with the A9 at the Pass of Killiecrankie. It can be clearly seen from the A9 when heading north. The rock is similar to that at Craig-a-Barns although it has not become popular as it is very disappointing — the lower half has a beard of grass and the rock tends to have loose holds. It is easiest to reach from the houses east of Bonskeid Farm itself and to go up through a field to a gate where a path leads to a clearing in the trees. From Scots pine trees on the left, head up direct to the base of the crag.

The main features of the crag are a steep wall on its left side split by a grass ledge, with a big tree, which runs leftwards onto the left arete (The Arete). Right of this, the lower part of the wall is more slabby, riddled with clumps of grass and undercut. It is capped by an impressively steep series of walls and grooves. Scramble down the right-hand side of the crag to descend.

The Arete   50m   Very Difficult
Start from the lowest point of the crag and climb the left edge all the way in two pitches.

Johnny Apollo   50m   VS   (1972)
A corner line 8 metres right of the arete.
1. 35m   Climb the corner at the right end of the lower wall onto the ledge. Ascend the corner above, moving left at mid-height and back right below an overhang. Step right to a ledge and tree belay.
2. 15m   From the left end of the ledge climb the wall above.

The Wall   50m   VS
Start 5 metres right of the previous route at the foot of a right-slanting groove.
1. 30m   Climb the groove and continue to a recess with a small bush. Go left to a small ledge (peg runner), then climb a right-trending groove to a ledge and tree belay shared with Johnny Apollo.
2. 20m   Finish up the wall above the left end of the ledge.

Lumbar   50m   VS
In the centre of the wall right of The Wall is a cave. Below it is a black slab. Start 8 metres right of The Wall.
1. 30m   Gain a ledge with a black slab on the right. Climb rightwards up the slab, then move up left to a ledge on The Wall. Belay below the cave above.
2. 20m   Climb the right wall of the cave and step left below the roof. Finish up a steep groove.

Diagonal   45m   VS
This route follows the obvious right-trending line of the slabs below the capping overhanging walls. Finish up a steep groove at the right end of the slabs.

Bonskeid Groove   50m   E1 5b *
The best route on the crag takes a line through the lower roof at the right end to cross Diagonal and finish up a steep groove in the headwall. Climb the left wall of the cave-like lower roof, then continue to a ledge. The obvious groove above provides the meat of the route.

STRATHTAY

The Strathtay crags are on Ordnance Survey 1:50,000 Landranger Series Sheets 52 and 53.

WEEM CRAGS   *(Map Ref 840 500)*

Just north of Aberfeldy lies the small village of Weem. The hillside above the village is clothed in ancient woodlands, owned and managed by the Forestry Commission. The Weem forest walks weave around the steep hillside to St David's Well. Also hidden in the thick undergrowth are several clean

WEEM ROCK   *(Map Ref 845 503)*

From the Forestry Commission carpark follow the path (taking the right branch at the marker post) past St David's Well. The path drops steeply down beyond the well where a small carved table and chairs sits next to the path. Take a small trail up the hillside to the crag starting just west of the table and chairs. These carvings can also be gained from the church in Weem village. Follow the small road up through the houses. A track branches off right before the final (gated) house. Follow it just beyond a shack where a path heads up the hillside to join the Forest Walk. Follow this rightwards past a hairpin to the carved chairs. The front wall is a 25m high steep black slab. To the left, the side wall is extremely steep. The routes are described from left to right, starting on the side wall.

High Pitched Scream   15m   7a+ ***   (1997)
A line up the left side starting from a raised ledge accessed from the tree on the left. Climb direct to the roof, then go diagonally right to the top. Easy for the grade.

The Screaming Weem   18m   7b ***   (1997)
A parallel line to High Pitched Scream. Strenuous moves lead to a semi-detached block (handle with care). Use the block to gain a flake, then follow pockets to better holds. A hard move gains the roof above, then jugs lead to the top.

The Last Temptation   20m   E2 5c *   (1997)
The steep crack and the open book corner lead to the roof. Pull out left and step right to follow a crack behind a small tree to the top.

The End of Silence   15m   7b **   (1997)
Steep fingery climbing up the wall right of the corner.

The following routes are on the front face with the main wall containing three excellent bolt lines. The first is a project up the right side of the arete.

The Long Good Friday   25m   6b+ **   (1997)
Start from a ledge 5m right of the arete. Climb the lower slab, then thin balance moves lead through the main overlap.

Confession of Faith   25m   6c **   (1997)
Climb directly up the centre of the wall with thin moves to gain a very welcome side hold under the larger overlap. Blind and difficult moves above lead to easier ground.

Mannpower   25m   6a *   (1997)
Climb the wall just left of a small corner to gain the line of a faint and intermittent crack line. Passing the main overlap proves to be the crux.

On the Tick List   25m   E2 5b   (1997)
Starting on the ledge to the right, follow a faint crack to the top.

THE BOULDERING WALL AND HANGING ROCK

From the carved chairs, take the forest walk down the hillside to the hairpin bend. A vague path continues eastwards from the bend to the Bouldering Wall and a rope swing! From the Bouldering Wall follow a path from the swing, going up the hillside to a clearing in the conifers and a giant old oak tree. Just above lies the crag, a 10m high wall that is very steep. The routes are described from left to right. The first is a very thin and bouldery project at the left end. Next comes:

Drop Dead Gorgeous   10m   E4 6a *   (1997)
The wide crack.

Crushed by the Wheels of Industry   10m   7a+   (1997)
Start just right of the crack. Hard moves lead to a thinner crack.

The Chemical Generation   10m   7b   (1997)
Thug direct up from a layback flake to join a crack, then finish direct passing a thin section. There are lots of bolts to prevent bouncing off the rock behind.

Alien Artifact   10m   7b   (1997)
Thin and bouldery climbing with long reaches linking pockets and edges.

The Glass Ceiling   10m   6c   (1997)
Climb the crack at the right side of the wall to traverse left to a large pocket on Alien Artifact and finish up that route.

AERIAL CRAG

High up to the right of the other crags that have been developed as sport venues, there is another crag with the same peculiar topography of a frontal face and a very steep side wall on the left. To approach Aerial Crag, it is easiest to walk directly up the hill side above Hanging Rock. There is a lower, much smaller tier beneath the crag which is best skirted to the left to arrive below the steep left wall. There is a palatial grass terrace below the front face to the right of a jumble of boulders at the arete between the two faces.

THE SIDE WALL

The wall has a very prominent vertical crack in the centre and a more shattered crack to its left.

Communication Breakdown   20m   E4 6a **   (1997)
The left-hand crack. Start 3m up the slab on the left at ledges and pull into the crack system. Follow it on jugs (very strenuous) to two big holes. The final moves up to and through the notch in the overhang above are the crux.

Pawn Channel   10m   E1 5c   (1997)
Climb the short crack in the extreme right side of the wall which joins the arete, then continue up the less steep upper crack to finish.

THE FRONT FACE

The front wall immediately around the arete to the right has a small bulge at mid-height and a less steep wall above. To the right the most obvious feature is a flake crack, then further right a shallow groove. A small tree sits at the base of the crag to the right again, then beyond this is an open disjointed corner line.

Kissing the Witch   10m   6b   (1997)
Climb a line of bolts just right of the edge of the arete, over a bulge and up the centre of the wall above to a ledge.
Variation: **The Choice of a New Generation**   10m   E3 5c   (1997)
Start from the boulder below the arete. Climb boldly directly up the right side of the arete to the bulge (protection). Pull over slightly on the left onto a sloping glacis and climb the crack of Pawn Channel to the top. A bolt-free version.

Static in the Air   10m   E4 6a **   (1997)
A thin crack snakes up the right side of the bulge. Climb up the start of the large flake crack and gain the base of the thin crack to the left. Climb it directly pulling up and right when it peters out to gain a quartz hold. Climb up to a block and a small sapling at the top.

Cracking Good Reception   15m   E1 5b *   (1997)
Immediately to the right is a large crack. Climb it direct.

Strong Signal   15m   HVS 5a *   (1997)
There is a slight pillar to the right of the crack and just left of a small tree. Climb a thin crack into a shallow groove in the pillar, then climb this direct to a small finishing crack onto a ledge.

Moving the Aerial   15m   E1 5b   (1997)
Climb a slight groove immediately right of the thin crack of the last route to a small overlap. Pull right onto the rib and climb direct, then go right into a small niche. Exit left and finish just right of the last route.

The Detector Van   20m   HVS 5a   (1997)
To the right of the small tree is a disjointed corner line. Climb the corners and the black bulge above the second into a glacis. Pull left round the overhanging arete and go up the wall back right to finish.

Wired for Sound   20m   HVS 5a   (1997)
Climb the wall just right of the corners on sloping holds to enter a small left-facing groove, then move into the glacis. Exit out right and go through the block roof above to finish.

CLUNY ROCK   (*Map Ref 868 513*)

There are a couple of south-facing buttresses hidden amongst the trees on the steep hill behind Tombuie Farm, 2.5km north-east of Aberfeldy. The following routes are on the biggest crag and are on steep clean rock. They are worth checking out if you're in the area. The climbs are described from left to right.

Tartan   30m   VS 4c   (1987)
Climb the left-hand corner, moving left before the top past a bush.

Shortbread   25m   VS 4c   (1987)
Take the wide crack left of the right-hand corner.

Tae the Oaks   25m   VS 4c   (1987)
Climb the right-hand corner which contains a tree, moving left at the top to finish up the arete.

Domino   25m   Severe   (1987)
Climb the corner to the right, gained from the start of the last route.

CREAG NA H-EIGHE   *(Map Ref 009 497)*

This small but steep west-facing crag is a few minutes walk from the road. Take the single track road off the A9 signposted to Tulliemet 9km beyond Dunkeld. Just beyond Guay House the road makes a tight turn left. Limited parking is available on the verge on the bend. Go up the track directly ahead, then continue up the open hillside to the crag. Below the crag is a large boulder, the Tully Stane, which gives some pleasant bouldering.

HISTORY
There are rumours that Phil Gribbon had done some routes here in the 1960s, but the first recorded ascents came from Doug Rennie and other members of the Loch Ericht Mountaineering Club. Doug produced a small guidebook in 1990 detailing most of the easier routes, but the crag's whereabouts was essentially kept quiet. Stewart Downie and Dave Cassidy made an ascent of the fine central crack/groove in 1989 to give the best route of the crag. In 1992 two separate groups re-discovered the crag and it has been difficult to separate out who did what. Willy Jeffrey, Geoff Cohen, I.Hyslop and N.Holmes recorded ascents, including top roped ascents of some of the harder lines. At the same time Bruce Kerr and friends from Edinburgh climbed most of the harder lines including that done by Downie. More recently Rick Campbell and Paul Thorburn climbed the hard Sleeping Sickness.

LAYOUT
The crag is essentially one continuous face, but it is split at regular intervals by deep features to give well defined buttresses. The most prominent one is the roofed buttress just left of centre of the crag (a large rowan tree sits at the base). On the extreme left is a short slab, a vegetated fault defining its right side. To the right is a short but steep wall split by a ledge at half-height. Its right side abuts a slabby side wall (the left side of the roofed buttress) to form a corner with a tree in it (Woodworm). To the right of the roofed buttress lies an overhanging wall set above an easy black slab. A deep recess follows with a roofed overhanging

chimney line (Raptor's Chimney). The crag diminishes in height right of this in a series of slender buttresses ending at a deep chimney. Belays at the top are difficult to locate and arrange. The routes are described from left to right.

Heather Wall   12m   Severe 4a   (1989)
Climb a thin crack in the smooth wall at the left end, 5m down and left of the grassy fault.

Cohen's Climb   12m   Severe 4a   (1992)
Climb a line up the slab just right of Heather Wall.

Wee Arete   8m   VS 4c   (1990)
Climb the steep arete and wall forming the left side of the next buttress to the right of the grassy fault.

Wee Brahmer   8m   Very Difficult *   (1989)
Climb the wall and steep cracks to the right of Wee Arete, finishing at a conspicuous tree at the left end of the steep buttress.

The steep buttress split by a large ledge has no routes up its front face.

Woodworm   10m   Very Difficult   (1989)
The right-hand end of the steep buttress right of Wee Brahmer abuts the slabby side wall of the main roofed buttress to form a corner containing a small rowan tree. Struggle past the rowan and take the good crack on the right to finish.

The main roofed buttress presents the most impressive section of the crag. A large rowan tree grows at its base. Behind the rowan is an overhanging crack or shallow corner slicing through the steepest section. To the right is a huge roof at about half-height. Right of this are huge blocks forming the base of the wall and a steep quartzy wall above, then follows a black slab with a steep orange wall above.

Jaggy Bunnets   13m   Severe 4a *   (1989)
In the centre of the slabby side wall 5m down and right of Woodworm is a big cracked groove. Climb this to a capping roof and climb twin cracks on its right to finish.

Jugs   15m   Very Difficult   (1989)
Climb the arete starting on its left side to a grass ledge. Follow the fine wide crack to the top.
Direct Start: VS 5a   (1961)
Climb the prominent wide overhanging crack 3 metres left of the rowan tree.

Just a Pech   15m   HVS 5a *   (1989)
Climb the easy wall behind the rowan *via* a thin crack to an awkward mantelshelf onto an overhung ledge. Climb onto the block on the left and follow two thin overhanging cracks to finish with another mantelshelf.

The terse route descriptions of the past had prevented a clear picture of the crag's remaining potential (as well as confusing any visitor) and so stagnated any possible activity. With more accurate information, a recent surge in interest has filled the remaining gaps with Katie Morag's First Steps, solo by Ben Ankers, Crash Test Dummies by Kevin Howett and The Mound of Venus by George Ridge.

MYOPIC'S BUTTRESS

This very steep compact wall was home to the aid brigade in the past and now provides a couple of very testing sport routes. It is situated well to the left of the Main Crag and sits just above the road. It is reached by a short walk right from the gate at the start of the track. A large beech tree grows close to the left-hand side of the crag. Descent is to the left.

Myopic's Corner   30m   HVS 5a *   (1959)
Behind the tree is a right-leaning overhanging corner. Climb this until an awkward pull gains a ledge on the left. Climb a hidden groove above on the left to the top.
Direct Finish: E2 5c *
Climb the overhanging and brutal-looking crack above the initial corner.

The Chopping Block   20m   7b **   (1996)
Climb a line directly up to and over the lower left-hand break going through the bulges in the front face of the buttress.

The Vibes   20m   7c **   (1991)
A difficult route through the higher, right-hand break through the bulges in the centre of the wall. Start at the overhanging rib at the right side of the wall. Go up the rib and onto the wall, then trend right and up with difficult moves until it is possible to climb leftwards through the break in the roof. Lower-off above.

Granola Head   20m   7c *   (1990)
Start just right of the small rib and climb up the bulging wall parallel with The Vibes to enter a steep tapering groove. Go up this and the very steep wall where it peters out. This is roughly the line of an old aid route called Coathanger.

Right of this are a couple of short sport projects.

IVY BUTTRESS

About 100 metres right of Myopic's Buttress is a complex little area of projecting walls and deep recessed corners which lost its ivy years ago. On the left is a smooth vertical wall with a large rotten tree stump below it. The arete of this wall contains an impressive hanging groove. The right side of the arete forms a deep corner (Ivy Crack) and further right again is the final corner line of Consolation Corner. The routes are described from left to right.

To descend, follow a path leftwards and descend past the base of Upper Buttress to go down a short gully and the open ground to the left of the crag.

Psoriasis   8m   E3 6a *   (1979)
This route takes the left edge of the buttress. Make a hard pull over the bulging start and move up to a horizontal crack (good RPs). Gain a flat hold in the angular niche above and pull desperately onto the slab to finish.

Sideline   15m   E5 6b *   (1987)
Climb the blank looking wall right of Psoriasis going diagonally right to a block forming an obvious crack near the top of the arete. Originally it was protected by a peg runner, but it is now a bold solo with a poor landing.
Variation: **Sharp End**   E6 7a   (1997)
A direct entry from behind the old tree stump with exceptionally hard moves up a small line of flakes.

Hot Tips   15m   E5 6c **   (1969/1980)
A tenuous struggle up the shallow hanging groove in the arete between Sideline and Ivy Crack. Entering direct is hard, stepping off the boulder reduces the grade to 6b. Protection is available if you can hang around long enough to place it, but the landing is appalling if you can't (it is possible to reach in from the right and pre-place the runner, obviously making it less tenuous).

Ivy Crack   15m   Mild VS 4b *   (1958)
The polished corner line gives a popular climb. After the initial difficulties it is possible to move left onto the rib to finish easily or to continue with difficulty up the corner to a tree belay.

Poison Ivy   15m   HVS 5b **   (1961)
To the right of Ivy Crack is another large corner which splits at half-height. Consolation Corner takes the right-hand main corner line. This route takes the left exit. Start at the base of the arete between the two corners. A problematic start up the right side of the arete gains a flake leading right to the base of the overhanging corner. Layback or jam to the top.

Poison Arete   15m   E4 5c   (1980)
Climb the arete in its entirety with thin moves at the top and only poor small RPs for protection (avoiding the temptation to reach into the corner of Poison Ivy).

Consolation Corner   30m   Very Difficult *   (1957)
A good route at the grade and now quite polished. Climb the easy corner to an impasse, then move out right and go up to a ledge. The corner above gives interesting climbing to a ledge and tree (possible belay). Climb the twin ribs above on the right to finish.

UPPER BUTTRESS

This sits above Ivy Buttress and provides good continuation climbs or, if you wish to walk to its base, gain it from the left side of Ivy Buttress by going up a short gully and traverse right. Twin corner cracks provide an obvious landmark. It is worth taking a belay at the base of the next routes as people have been known to fall down the gully below the path! Descend from the top by a long traverse to the left and go down a gully.

Left-Hand Edge   10m   HVS 4c   (1980)
Climb the left bounding rib of Left-hand Crack *via* a short right-facing groove and the slab above.

Left-Hand Crack   10m   E2 5c **   (1961/1974)
The superb curving corner crack gives a sustained, well protected climb (2 peg runners). It is possible to scuttle out right at the top of the corner, but it is arguably purer to exit directly. Finish up the rib.

Right-Hand Crack   5m   VS 5a   (1961)
Jam or layback the good-looking tapering crack to the right of the corner of Left-hand Crack to a floundering finish.

Hidden in the trees to the right, the next two routes are reached by a scramble up a mass of blocks to the recess of Duncan Hogg's Hole, one time residence of an old cattle rustler.

Mottled Rib   30m   Very Difficult *   (1980)
Left of the huge pointed boulder is a tree with a groove behind and above it. Climb the groove until it is possible to move left and go up to a ledge (possible tree belay). Ascend the rib above to finish.

Hogg's Hindquarters   30m   Very Difficult **   (1959)
A fine route with a strenuous start and a delicate finish. Start in the recess of Duncan Hogg's Hole beneath a steep groove. Either climb the groove direct or step off the large boulder into it. Climb the groove and exit right to a possible belay, then move back left and climb a wrinkled slab to the top.

The Trap   6m   HVS 5b   (1961)
Right of Hogg's Hindquarters is a steep little wall seamed with cracks. Climb it direct.

THE MAIN CLIFF

LEFT-HAND SECTION

About 100 metres right of the Ivy Buttress area and at a slightly higher level, is the left-hand section of the Main Cliff. The main features are a large slab capped by roofs and bulges on the left, with a slabby corner hanging above. The slab is bounded on the right by a giant arching flake. Right again is a prominent rib above which are short corners and ledges. Above these is a large gassy bay below a headwall. Right of the rib the wall is steeper and hidden by a big beech tree. Right of the beech tree the most obvious feature is the series of steep corners whose base is guarded by roofs. Wriggle finds a way through here. The wall continues rightwards as a more slabby affair with the occasional roof to terminate in the deep-set Hairy Gully. Descent is *via* a small path leading a long way left and under Upper Buttress.

1   Anon   20m   Difficult
Climb the slab *via* a vague crack line to a ledge. Traverse left into a wide corner which leads to the top.

2   Kestrel Crack   35m   Severe *   (1957)
A fine climb that ascends first the slab, then the huge flake and corner above. Start in the centre of the slabs at an indefinite crack.
1. 25m   Climb the crack line and move diagonally right to twin cracks, then into the big flake. Climb this to a grassy bay.
2. 10m   Finish up the easy slabby corner above.
Variation Finish I: HVS 5a *
From the bay move up, then go right to climb the front face of the steep wall to the right of the arete and gain a slim corner.
Variation Finish II: VS 5a
From high in the slabby corner move out right and climb an obvious short crack to the left of the arete.

3   Katie Morag's First Steps   45m   Mild VS 4b   (1992)
Start just left of a grassy corner, just left of Twisted Rib. Climb the slab to a small ledge. Move right and climb a thin crack to pull over a block and move up to an overhang (possible belay). From the left end of the overhang move up for 3m, then traverse right across a clean slab. Continue up to the left side of a smooth brown slab and climb steps until a delicate traverse can be made to a hanging ramp. Climb this to the top.

4   Twisted Rib   45m   Very Difficult **   (1957)
A wandering but interesting route finding the easiest way up this section of crag. Start at the obvious rib bounding the right side of the slab.
1. 15m   Climb the rib to a ledge, poorly protected. Move left into a short easy corner and go up to a tree, then move back right to a second long rock ledge and a huge flake belay.
2. 30m   Make a long rightwards traverse on disjointed ledges until below a slab. Climb this diagonally left to gain a grassy bay. Finish up the grooved slabby rib on the right.
Direct Finish: VS 4b   (1959)
From a belay in the grassy bay climb the brown shallow scoop in the top right-hand side of the headwall.

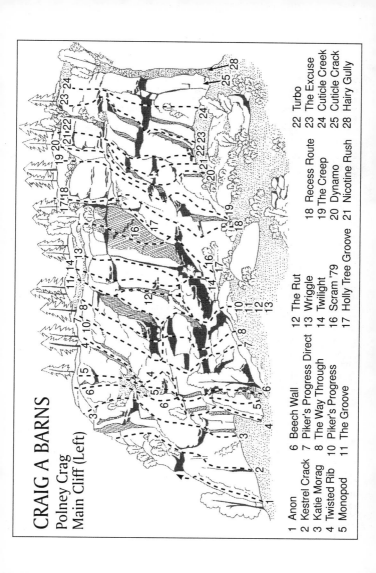

CRAIG A BARNS
Polney Crag
Main Cliff (Left)

1 Anon
2 Kestrel Crack
3 Katie Morag
4 Twisted Rib
5 Monopod

6 Beech Wall
7 Piker's Progress Direct
8 The Way Through
10 Piker's Progress
11 The Groove

12 The Rut
13 Wriggle
14 Twilight
16 Scram '79
17 Holly Tree Groove

18 Recess Route
19 The Creep
20 Dynamo
21 Nicotine Rush

22 Turbo
23 The Excuse
24 Cuticle Creek
25 Cuticle Crack
28 Hairy Gully

5   Monopod   35m   E2   (1986)
A direct line cutting through Twisted Rib. Start below the luminous green wall just right of the Rib, left of the beech tree.
1. 10m 5c   Boldly climb the centre of the wall by a long reach to a ledge.
2. 25m 5a   The corner behind leads past the ledge of Twisted Rib. Climb the bulging nose above on good holds to gain the grass bay. Climb the bulging headwall immediately right of the corner of Beech Wall.

6   Beech Wall   35m   Hard Severe **   (1959)
An excellent enjoyable route up the steep wall behind the beech tree, right of Twisted Rib.
1. 15m 4c   Climb the undercut corner and a further corner on the right to exit left at its top onto a ledge. Move up, then gain the long ledge of Twisted Rib. Belay on the huge flake on the left.
2. 20m 4a   Climb left and ascend the clean wall direct into the grass bay. Finish up the distinctive left-facing groove in the left-hand side of the headwall. Steep and awkward.

7   Piker's Progress Direct   35m   HVS 5a *   (1969)
The original route starts below the break in the roofs as for Wriggle. This gives a more direct and logical line, but it is difficult to protect. Start to the right of the beech tree below a break in the left-hand side of a line of overhangs. Climb the lower wall *via* a huge flake, then go up the steep wall leftwards (crux) to gain a break in the overhang formed by a block and pull strenuously into a short slabby groove on the right. Traverse right to the prow to join the original route and finish up the left side.

8   The Way Through   30m   E2 5b **   (1967)
A great little route up the centre of the double roofed wall between Piker's Direct and Wriggle. Steep with just enough protection. Start directly beneath the centre of the wall. Climb to the lip, then pull diagonally right through it onto the slab beneath the second roof. Take this at its biggest point on good holds, then go up to the cracked blocks below the prow. Pull over the overhang above the blocks at a thin crack, then finish easily.
Variation: E1 5b
From the lip of the first roof pull left into a scoop and exit easily.

9   The Porker   30m   E3 5b   (1979)
A more serious companion to the last route. Start just down and left of Wriggle. Climb the right edge of the overhanging wall (poorly protected) to gain the slab over the lip just right of The Way Through. Bypass the roof on the right and gain the cracked blocks under the prow. Follow The Groove until an exit can be made out left near the top.

    The next four routes have a common start at an obvious break in the lower roofs. Above, they diverge and climb separate grooves or cracks. Wriggle is painted at the base.

10   Piker's Progress   30m   VS 5a *   (1960)
Gain the break in the lower roof *via* a traverse in from the right. Step up into the overhung sentry box in the roof, then make hard moves up and right (peg runner) onto a wrinkled slab. Climb up, then go left to gain cracked blocks under the prow and at the base of the groove of The groove. Traverse left round the prow and follow the rib above to the top. A belay at the blocks will reduce rope drag.

11   The Groove   30m   VS 5a ***   (1960)
One of the best routes on Polney. Follow Piker's Progress through the roof and up to the cracked blocks. Climb the clean-cut groove on the right side of the prow to finish.

12   The Rut   30m   VS 5a **   (1960)
A direct line up the wall climbing the short hanging groove in the centre of the buttress. Follow Piker's Progress and The Groove through the lower roof. Head up into the short groove above which gives further hard moves and a strenuous pull out left into the final section of The Groove.

13   Wriggle   35m   VS 5a **   (1959)
A popular route which was the first to wriggle through the roof. Start as for Piker's Progress and once established on the lip traverse horizontally right across a wrinkled slab to the exposed right edge. Ascend this and follow the bottomless groove and crack on the right (which emanates from a holly bush under the roof) to the top.

To the right of the roofs where Wriggle and its companions start, the guarding lower roof relents at a groove whose base is infested with a holly bush. A slabby right-slanting ramp starts here and forms a right bounding edge to the steep concave wall above.

14   Twilight   30m   E1 5b **   (1980)
A splendid direct route crossing Wriggle. Start below the holly bush. Climb a steep slim groove just left and under the holly and pull out left through the roof onto the steep slab of Wriggle. Ascend directly up the wall on the line of a slight arete with pushy moves up the bulge near the top.

Piker's Variation   35m   HVS 5a   (1959)
Break out rightwards from just below the short groove of The Rut, go over a bulge and finish up the slight arete. This has been superseded by Twilight.

15   Wriggle Direct   30m   HVS 5a   (1978)
A prickly route following, in its entirety, the bottomless groove and crack up which Wriggle finishes, starting through the holly bush. It is better than it appears and is enjoyed by masochists.

16   Scram '79   30m   E4 5c *   (1979)
A fingery and serious route up the concave wall right of Wriggle Direct. Start up the slabby ramp of Holly Tree Groove to gain the base of the wall. Move up

directly to a peg runner in the centre of the wall, then climb the prominent black streak on the left *via* tiny pockets. Follow the streak as it kinks right and go up the centre to a point below the capping blocky roof. Finish directly over this.

17   Holly Tree Groove   30m   Very Difficult **   (1960)
Pleasant climbing up the diagonal ramp line. Start just right of the holly bush and follow the ramp under the concave wall through a short corner/niche to gain a ledge in the left side of a large recess. Finish up the chimney on the left.

18   Recess Route   30m   Very Difficult *   (1960)
This climb takes the wall to the right of the ramp of Holly Tree Groove. Start on a small elevated ledge containing a block, below a slight rib. Climb the wall going first left then right to enter the large grassy recess. Exit up the chimney out left as for the last route.

To the right is a short corner topped by an overlap. This continues as an intermittent line of small overlaps leading diagonally up and right.

19   The Creep   30m   Severe *   (1960)
Interesting but with only adequate protection. Start immediately right of Recess Route. Step into the short corner and climb the slab up and rightwards to a small sloping ledge below the right edge of the first overlap. Pull left through here on big holds, then climb up and right into the right side of the grassy recess. Exit up the shallow groove in the centre of the wall above.

20   Dynamo   30m   VS 5a *   (1980)
A parallel line right of The Creep. Start at the left side of an elevated grass ledge right of that route. The ledge can be gained by either scrambling up and right from The Creep or from the right below Hairy Gully. Climb a shallow right-facing groove in a black streak to gain a footledge on the right below the overlaps right of The Creep. Pull through the overlap direct at a slight weakness with difficulty, then step left and move up to the headwall. Climb a crack line in the headwall just right of the finishing groove of The Creep.

21   Nicotine Rush   30m   E2 5b *   (1980)
An eliminate line just right of Dynamo, poorly protected at first. Start from the grass ledge just right of that route to gain a scoop beneath the third overlap (thin). Pull over this on the left with further thin moves, then pass the overlap above through its left side and move up to the headwall. Bold moves directly up the centre of this feel more scary than smoking.

22   Turbo   30m   E2 5c *   (1983)
Another eliminate line, delicate and bold. Start immediately right of Nicotine Rush. Climb the fingery wall to gain the scoop under the overlap shared with that route. Follow the slight rib forming the right edge of the overlap (crux) to a second overlap. Pull over its right side and go up to the headwall to finish as for Nicotine Rush.

23   The Excuse   35m   E2 6a *   (1980)

This route finds a way through the overlaps above the raised grass ledge. Start at a small right-facing corner right of Nicotine Rush. Climb the corner and pull out left at the top below the overlap. Pull back diagonally right through the overlap to enter a shallow scoop above with difficulty. A slab leads to a large flake and the top.

Variation: E1 5b

An easier alternative moves left below the overlap and pulls into another more obvious scoop above the overlap.

24   Cuticle Creek   30m   Mild VS   (1966)

Climb the wall and the overlap between The Excuse and Cuticle Crack. A recent rockfall has left some loose blocks.

25   Cuticle Crack   25m   Severe **   (1960)

A classic struggle up the deep crack left of Hairy Gully. Follow the crack, then move right at a protruding jammed block in the side wall. Continue directly to the top.

26   Airy Arete   25m   VS 4c   (1965)

An enjoyable climb up the left bounding arete of Hairy Gully.

The next route lies on a buttress just above the finish of Cuticle Crack and it provides a good continuation pitch.

27   The Crescent   25m   Very Difficult *   (1960)

Climb a vegetated groove to a slab beneath an overhang. Turn this on the right and climb the obvious open groove and crack to an exit left at the top.

At the same level and further left are two short routes taking clean lines on an otherwise mossy wall. Both are Very Difficult.

28   Hairy Gully   25m   Moderate

The obvious gully is often used for descent, either by climbing or abseiling. Loose earth and stones at its top mean care should be taken not to dislodge them.

RIGHT-HAND SECTION

This begins immediately right of Hairy Gully. At the base of the centre of the wall is a large jumble of boulders. To the right, the crag is split into two tiers, the lower one being a fine smooth slab and the upper tier being undercut and topped by a roof. The upper tier continues rightwards as a steep wall of roofs to gradually degenerate into the hillside as a side wall.

29   Bollard Buttress   35m   Difficult *   (1959)

Climb the line of least resistance up the clean wall right of Hairy Gully with barely adequate protection.

30   Bollard Buttress Direct   35m   Severe *   (1959)
A harder climb which takes the wall 5 metres right of the normal route. Start at a thin crack with Bollard Buttress painted on it. Take the crack that leads to a shallow groove line, then climb a rib leading slightly right to the top.

The wall to the right is composed of an area of smooth rock split centrally by an overlap with a slim hanging groove over the lip. Starting at the level of the right end of the overlap, a right-facing brown corner leads up to a further roof.

31   Springboard   45m   VS 4c **   (1960)
A wandering climb, but full of interest. Start at the lowest point of the wall before the jumble of boulders and climb direct just right of a slight rib to a deep horizontal break under an overlap. Hand traverse right and enter the brown corner (it is possible to walk off onto the grass to the right here). There is no protection in the corner and it is hard to start and to move out left under the roof at the top onto a slab (the only 4c section). Climb left up an overhung recess to a slab which leads rightwards to the top.

31a   *Direct Variation:*   35m   E3 5c **   (1960/1978)
Excellent climbing, but poorly protected. Follow Springboard to the overlap. Climb up into the slim hanging groove over the lip, then go up it with difficulty to join the parent route on the slab.

31b   *Left-hand Finish:*   35m   Mild VS 4b   (1988)
Climb Springboard to the overlap, then follow the horizontal break left until an awkward move up leads into a scoop. Continue up the slabby wall to the top.

32   Live Wire   35m   E5 6a   (1980)
The main centre of interest is the left arete of the brown corner of Springboard. Follow Springboard to the overlap. Pull onto the smooth wall above (possible protection in small pockets). Span right onto the arete and make hard moves up it to gain a slight overlap. More hard moves over this lead to a junction with Springboard on the slab. Pull rightwards through the overlap above and follow the upper arete to the top.

In the upper part of the wall above the jumble of boulders (to the right of the brown corner of Springboard) is a huge deeply indented V-shaped scoop. A tree grows in its centre and slabs lead up to it. The headwall above is overhanging. An easy scramble up and right from the foot of Springboard leads to the grass ledge level with the brown corner. The following routes all start from this ledge.

33   Helter Skelter   25m   HVS 5a   (1980)
An eliminate line based on Chute, climbing the left side of the scoop. Start at the base of the brown corner. Climb to its top, then traverse right to the base of the quartz bulge of Chute. Move left and pull through the roof into a hanging ramp above. This leads left until it is possible to step right onto a slab leading left from the scoop.

The Chopping Block, Myopic's Buttress   (Climber, Neil Craig)

34   The Chute   25m   VS 5a *   (1961)
Start below the brown corner. Gain a slim groove in the slab on the right which
leads to the quartz bulge. Climb the crack in the bulge to gain the tree, then exit
out right under the headwall.

35   Space Scuttle   25m   E1 5b *   (1983)
Eliminate but enjoyable climbing just right of Chute. Start below the centre of the
slab. Gain a flake, pull over onto the slab and climb direct to short hanging
groove just right of the quartz bulge of Chute. Ascend the groove and go out
right onto Chute below the headwall. Climb this diagonally to the left on jugs,
doing as the name implies.

36   Pop   20m   HVS 4c *   (1978)
A poorly protected little line up the bulging wall and slabby rib right of Space
Scuttle. Start just right of the centre of the slab and climb grotty ground to gain a
large dubious flake below the bulge. Carefully pull through direct onto the slab
above and climb direct to the top.

   To the right of the rockfall the cliff forms a double tier. The next three routes
ascend both tiers and are amongst the best at Polney.

37   The End   45m   VS **   (1961)
Start at the base of the clean slab of the lower tier.
1. 15m 4b   Climb the left side of the slab under a left-facing corner. Either climb
the corner (4c) or the slab on its left to gain a standing position below a bulging
nose. Stand on the nose and finish delicately above to the ledge.
2. 30m 5a   The wall above is guarded by a steep bulge. Climb through this *via*
a slim right-facing groove with difficulty, then go up the slab to step right to
below the break in the largest part of the overlap. Pull through and climb the fine
slabs to the top.

38   Barefoot Beginning   45m   E2 **   (1980/1976)
A natural combination of pitches on each tier. Both are serious and high in the
grade on immaculate rock. Start at the base of the slab between The End and
the initial corner of Terminal Buttress.
1. 15m 5c   The easy slabs lead to an overlap. Climb the very thin flake above
to snatch out right for tiny sharp holds leading right to the arete. Stand on a small
ledge, then climb the right side of the arete to the ledge.
2. 30m 5b   Go up the short right-facing tapering corner slightly down and right.
Step up and left over the lip of the steep wall onto the slab. Climb directly to a
roof and pull over at obvious break right of The End, then finish easily.

High Performance, Upper Cave Crag   (Climber, Ken Johnstone)

39   Terminal Buttress   45m   Hard Severe *   (1959)
This route crosses The End on the halfway ledge. Start at the corner near the right side of the lower slab.
1. 15m   Climb the corner to the ledge.
2. 30m 4c   Climb leftwards through the bulge immediately left of the weakness of The End (crux) and gain a grass recess above. Step right and climb a crack in the overlap and follow slabs to the top.

40   Crash Test Dummies   15m   E3 5c   (1994)
The final piece of rock on the lower tier right of the corner of Terminal Buttress gives a natural first pitch to The Duel on the upper tier. Climb the steep lower wall *via* a flake to the overlap. Pull over in the centre and make thin moves directly up the slab to a quartz blotch.

41   The Duel Variation   30m   E4 6a *   (1980/late 80s)
Bold and strenuous climbing up the overhanging wall right of the second pitch of Barefoot Beginning. From behind a small tree, gain a large projecting wafer-thin flake. The route originally traversed a huge flake up and right from here, but this has long since fallen off leaving a blank wall. Instead move up from its top to an undercling, then go slightly left up the overhanging wall on quartz holds and move back right to reach a peg runner on the lip. Hard moves using a thin flake lead to the slab above.

42   The Mound of Venus   30m   E2 5c   (1994)
An eliminate but good route direct up the steep wall right of the black roof. Start at the lowest rocks, left of the beech tree. Climb to a deep horizontal break below the steep wall. Move up to good quartz holds, then pull onto the ramp above (junction with Carpet Beater). From the thin crack above make a long reach out left and traverse the lip of the roof to a projecting block. Easier climbing leads to the top.

43   Carpet Beater   20m   HVS 5a *   (1971)
This left-trending line between the roofs behind the tree is hard for the grade. Start at a short groove right of the tree. Climb this for 4m, then traverse left onto a large ramp between the roofs. Climb the thin crack up the short steep wall at the left end of the ramp onto another ramp below another smaller roof. Exit left.

44   Eschebaum   25m   Very Difficult   (1992)
Climb the short groove of Carpet Beater, then move up to and through the obvious broken flakes above to gain a short slab. Finish up the easy ridge trending right.

45   Spirochaete   25m   VS 4b *   (1969)
A nice enough route up the clean slab before the crag degenerates. Start just right of Carpet Beater at another small groove. Climb this and ascend the clean-cut layback crack to a grass ledge. Move rightwards into the middle of the slab, then go direct to the top.

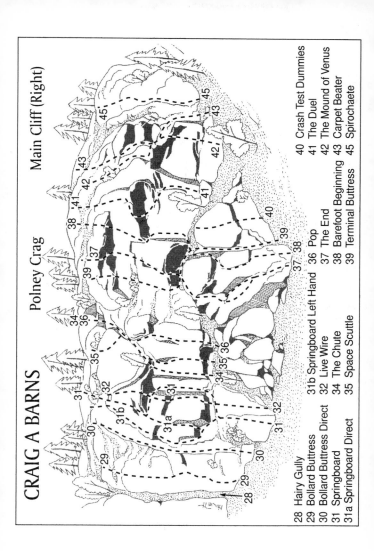

CRAIG A BARNS

Polney Crag   Main Cliff (Right)

28 Hairy Gully
29 Bollard Buttress
30 Bollard Buttress Direct
31 Springboard
31a Springboard Direct

31b Springboard Left Hand
32 Live Wire
34 The Chute
35 Space Scuttle

36 Pop
37 The End
38 Barefoot Beginning
39 Terminal Buttress

40 Crash Test Dummies
41 The Duel
42 The Mound of Venus
43 Carpet Beater
45 Spirochaete

46   Gitanes   20m   VS 4c   (1983)
Climb the blunt indefinite rib and small overlap 3 metres right of Spirochaete.

Girdle Traverse   180m   VS 4c   (1960)
A long and interesting traverse rightwards from Kestrel Crack to The End!
1. 20m   Follow Kestrel Crack until just below the flake. Traverse right to the large flakes on Twisted Rib.
2. 20m   Continue hard right to the cracked blocks on Piker's Progress.
3. 35m 4c   Descend diagonally right to the base of the short groove of The Rut. Descend a little and move rightwards to join Wriggle (crux) and climb up this to gain slabs above.
4. 45m   Continue by a long easy traverse descending slightly over sloping slabs to a belay on a ledge on Cuticle Crack.
5. 45m   Continue across Hairy Gully and the upper slabs of Springboard, before descending to a tree belay in the recess of Chute.
6. 30m   Traverse easily to the grassy bay on pitch 2 of Terminal Buttress.
7. 30m 4c   Traverse the slab on the right with difficulty until beneath the overhang and finish through the break as for The End.

LOVER'S LEAP   *(Map Ref 436 014)*

This is the large expanse of south-facing rock high on the hillside to the right of Polney Crag. It is nearly 60m high but the majority of the crag is heavily vegetated. However, the main routes climbing the pillar in the centre are worthy of more traffic and will remain clean with use. Solitude is almost certainly guaranteed. The easiest approach is to park as for Cave Crag and to follow the track beyond where the path for Lady Charlotte's Cave and Cave Crag branches off right, continuing round the front of the hillside until the crags can be seen on the hillside above. The main centre of interest is a large pillar of cleaner rock in the middle of the crag. A huge roof and corner bounds the right side.

HISTORY
Discovered and developed about the same time as Polney, this crag was until recently cloaked in thick forest and difficult to find. Local climbers John Proom and Ron Hockey were the first to climb here. Their ascent of Direct Route was exciting, for as Hockey led the second pitch a giant vibrating flake parted company, narrowly missing Proom. Ian G. Rowe was instrumental in most of the development of earlier routes. Later interest was dampened by the foliage and only Mal Duff persevered to produce a few routes, including Bullet whose first pitch had been done in the 1960s. The only other real interest since has come from Grahame Nicoll who climbed a direct start to Bullet in 1996.

Ash Tree Wall   25m   Very Difficult   (1960s)
This lies to the left of the main wall. Scramble up a wooded terrace and keep going left for 30 metres to where the angle of the rock eases. Climb between two ash trees, then finish up an obvious corner.

Tiff Off   55m   VS *   (1960s)
This climb takes the left side of the main wall starting at a very obvious crack.
1. 25m 4c   Climb the crack until a step left gains a groove which leads to a tree belay.
2. 30m 4a   Traverse left and climb a flake chimney to a ledge. The overhung groove above leads right to the arete and the top.

Central Route   60m   VS *   (1960s)
Sustained and delicate. Start at a recess at the base of the pillar.
1. 30m 4c   Ascend a few metres, then traverse right to a ledge. Hand traverse back left at a higher level to a sloping ledge. Continue traversing into a groove which leads to a grassy ramp and a ledge above.
2. 30m 4a   Climb the groove in the wall above, then step left when the wall steepens to climb a corner.
Variation Start: VS 5a   (1970s)
Start up the corner crack of the Direct Start to Direct Route, then move up left to join the normal route on the front of the pillar.

Bullet   60m   E1 *   (1983/1996)
A good line on the cleanest section of rock. It is described by the direct start to give a more sustained climb. The original route started up Central Route's Variation Start to the roof and moved right around an arete to climb a crack in the right side wall (5a). This direct line follows the arete all the way.
1. 30m 5b   Climb the prominent arete with moves to the right near an overhang, before moving back left to an obvious crack in the side wall. Pull onto the rib above and go up to a belay.
2. 30m 5b   Just right of the belay is a very thin crack running up to a small roof. Climb this, then follow corners through several bulges to the top.

Direct Route   60m   Severe   (1959)
Start 10 metres right of the obvious corner crack that lies the lowest point of the crag.
1. 25m 4b   Climb up and work leftwards over slabs to belay beside a large tree.
2. 35m 4a   Clamber through branches to a small ledge. Continue for a short distance up an open groove to gain a large flake/groove. This leads to a steep curving crack. At the top of the crack, step left and continue past a flake to an oak tree. Step left and continue up to the top.
Direct Start: VS 4b *   (1960)
This version transforms the climb into a fine route. Climb the obvious corner crack at the lowest point of the crag, then move right over clean slabs to the tree.

Jungle Jim   55m   VS   (1977)
Start 15 metres right of the corner of Direct Route at a pointed block.
1. 20m   Climb a wall direct to a corner, then go up this to a sloping forested ledge. Belay in a corner.
2. 35m   Climb to a stunted holly bush. Move right and go up a groove, exiting left onto a slabby bay. Continue diagonally right to finish up a heathery corner.

Twister   30m   Hard Severe   (1982)
A scrappy route about 15 metres right of Jungle Jim. Climb a left-slanting ramp
to a bush. Follow a weakness back right to a small white tree. Climb directly to a
large white tree.

Little Gem   20m   Severe   (1983)
Some 5 metres right of Twister is an open corner with a wide crack in the left
wall. Climb this to the white tree.

Hedgehog   20m   VS 4c   (1982)
Above the last two routes a ledge cuts across the face to the right-hand side
where there is an obvious cracked groove with a small cave at half-height. This
route climbs the groove to gain the rib above the cave.

   Worms (Very Difficult, 1982) takes a direct line on the small buttress at the
extreme top right of the crag.

CAVE CRAGS   *(Map Ref 439 108)*

The south-west facing Cave Crags, mostly hidden by the trees from the road,
give some of the best outcrop climbing in Scotland, especially Upper Cave. A
suntrap in the summer, it is steep enough to stay dry in any downpour and is an
easy walk from the carpark. However, the routes can seep after prolonged wet
weather. This part of the hill is criss-crossed by paths, installed originally for
Victorian tourists. These give easy access direct to the base of the crags — one
would almost think they were built with climbers in mind! However, the
Victorians were more interested in the scenery and the history, including the
origins of Lady Charlotte's Cave. Here, it is rumoured that a past Duke of Atholl
hid his lover.

ACCESS AND LAYOUT
After turning onto the A923 Blairgowrie road just out of Dunkeld, take the
second track on the left towards The Glack. Part way along this, before a gate,
there is a large carpark amongst the trees on the left. Take an obvious path from
here leading to a small overgrown forestry track. As this begins to descend,
branch off onto a small path on the right. The slender pocketed pillar of Even
Lower Cave Crag is obvious on the right after 100m. Just after passing a
stooped yew tree that partially blocks the path, Lower Cave Crag can be
glimpsed through the trees on the hillside above. The path continues across a
small stream before being completely blocked by a huge fallen tree. Lower and
Upper Cave Crags are reached by cutting up the slope just before the stream to
gain another path. This leads right to the base of Lower Cave Crag or left back
across the stream issuing from Lady Charlotte's Cave. Upper Cave Crag is
reached by skirting the cave on the left by a path which crosses the stream
again even higher and ascends the steep hillside through trees to meet another
old path. Upper Cave Crag is obvious on the right.

EVEN LOWER CAVE CRAG

As one walks towards Cave Crags, just after the small path branches off the track and before a fallen yew tree partially blocks it, there is a steep pocketed buttress about 20m above the path. There are two routes. Descent is by abseil.

Just for Laughs   20m   E2 5b   (1987)
Start at the overhanging crack in the centre of the face. Climb the crack to a ledge. Using pockets, trend up rightwards over the bulge above (crux), then step left and move up to a short crack. Finish direct on better holds.

Alternative Comedy   20m   E1 5b   (1988)
Follow Just for Laughs to the ledge below the bulge. Traverse diagonally left, then go right to the short crack near the top of that route.

LOWER CAVE CRAG

The lower tier of the two Cave Crags is partially obscured by trees that encroach right up to the crag in the vicinity of The Hood. However, there are some excellent routes in the middle grades on very steep rock with wonderful views as one emerges from the tree canopy. From Lady Charlotte's Cave a flat path leads right for 30 metres to the start of the crag.

HISTORICAL
Although there may have been some prior activity, the first recorded ascents came in the late 1950s from Robin Campbell and Paul Brian during the period when they were developing Polney and making tentative forays onto Upper Cave. The first route here was Cherry Tree Ridge. Perth JMCS members Ron Hockey and John Proom straightened this out, then made an attempt on the line of The Hood which failed and saw them abseiling into the trees and the dark. Campbell succeeded on this line after many attempts to give the classic route of the crag. Campbell dominated the free climbing here during the 1950s whilst others (including Ian G. Rowe) were using aid on steep lines that would go free during the 1970s. Dougal Haston paid a visit in 1959 and characteristically named his route to offend Scottish Mountaineering Club members. Come the 1970s attention was focused on Upper Cave Crag, but Hamilton's free ascent of Rowe's aid line Civer gave Lower Cave a local test piece. All the protagonists of the time made their mark on the crag: Alan Taylor, Rab Anderson, Pete Hunter, Mal Duff and Dave Cuthbertson. Anderson made a further visit in 1986 and climbed the steep Stay Hungry. He later returned and bolted it to produce a sport route whilst Kenny Spence produced another in a similar vein as a neighbour. Both lines of bolts were later removed.

LAYOUT
On approaching from Lady Charlotte's Cave, the first piece of rock encountered forms a steep prow overhanging the path. The side wall of the crag extends up the hillside from the path. It forms a short but steep bouldering wall at its

extreme left, gaining height as it descends to a vegetated corner. Below this is a clean lower wall (with a big grass ledge with trees above) ending in the prow. The front face of this prow is split by the hanging corner of Civer. Immediately right is a wet corner where the wall turns 90 degrees and is split by two horizontal roofs. This is slightly vegetated. The wall then turns the start of The Hood) beyond which are overhanging corners (Hood Direct and Fuck Face). The crag becomes scrappy after that and the path crosses a vegetated gully. Beyond here the crag rears up again as a well defined ridge (Cherry Tree Ridge). The routes are described from left to right as one approaches.

To descend, it is best to continue up the hillside above to the base of the upper crag and descend the access path.

The Cludge   35m   VS 4c   (1959)
Start at a short overhanging corner near the right end of the bouldering section of the side wall, just left of the vegetated corner. Climb the corner to a ledge (possible belay). Climb directly up the rib above until a rightward traverse can be made to a thorn tree. Continue right to finish up a further rib.

In the Shrubbery   35m   E1 5b *   (1979)
A climb of surprising quality up such a grotty part of the crag, the rib to the right of the vegetated corner right of The Cludge. Climb the vegetated corner, then traverse right on a slab under an overhang and move back left to a ramp. Traverse right to a small tree beneath a bulge, then pull over this and a second bulge before continuing up a rib to the top.

Secret Affair   HVS   5a   (1981)
Climb the clean wall forming the left side of the prow, going diagonally right to a stance on a big grass ledge. Ascend the wall directly behind the tree, then go up the slabby wall on the left.

Stay Hungry   10m   E4 6b *   (1986)
This route takes the nose of the prow left of Civer. Pull up a faint groove to a horizontal break (good nut and poor thread) and continue steeply to pull over onto the slabby wall above with difficulty, joining Secret Affair for a few metres below the grass ledge. Finish up The Stank.

Civer   35m   E4 6b *   (1959/1977)
The hanging corner in the front face of the prow gives a fierce test-piece. The corner succumbs with the aid of the hanging crack and a little oomph. Move right at an undercling (peg runner), then swing right and go up a crack to the big grass ledge. Finish up the second pitch of The Stank.

The Stank   35m   E1 *   (1959/1974)
A sustained route with a grotty first pitch leading to a good upper pitch. Start at the foot of a black corner right of Civer (often wet).
1. 15m 5a   Gain the corner from the left, then move up it for 6m until it is possible to move across the left wall to climb a small corner to a ledge.

2. 20m 5b   Step right and climb a groove to a ledge (peg runner). Traverse right to a bulge (peg runner). Pull over to a ledge and a large flake. Trend right to finish.
Variation Start:
The grotty first pitch can be avoided by climbing the first part of Secret Affair to the big grass ledge.

Kaituma   50m   HVS   (1978)
This route starts as for Stank, then climbs the right arete to join Cabaret.
1. 20m 5b   Climb Stank until it is possible to move right and climb an indefinite crack line in the right arete to reach a ledge shared with Cabaret. Climb a steep wall above before moving left to a shelf and a belay on the right.
2. 30m 4c   Climb the wide crack above, move left and go up the steep wall to the top.

Cabaret   40m   E1   (1979)
The next obvious corner right of Stank.
1. 20m 5a   Climb the corner over two small roofs to a shelf and belay under the roof.
2. 20m 5c   Pull onto the wall above, traverse right above the lip of the roof, then go up to gain the final rib of The Hood. Climb the crack of The Hood Direct to finish.

Wot Gorilla   40m   E1   (1980)
Very eliminate and now very overgrown with nature reclaiming every nook and cranny. Start under the large leaning roof below and right of Cabaret. Pull over the roof, the following one and the one above to the right of a slot to gain a ledge. Finish up Cabaret.

The Hood   35m   VS **   (1959)
An excellent route with wild exposure and only adequate protection. Start just to the right of the lower leaning roof of Wot Gorilla just before the crag turns an arete.
1. 20m 4b   Bypass the leaning roof and ascend to the steep leaning wall above. Traverse right along a juggy break below the steep wall and turn the arete onto a ramp. This leads back left. From its top, step right to gain ledges and easy ground leading up to a large roof. Bypass this on the right to a ledge below an overhanging corner.
2. 15m 4c   Step up onto the slab and traverse left to the arete (delicate). Climb up to the base of an obvious overhanging crack (The Direct Finish) and swing out left to finish up a slabby rib.

The Hood Direct   35m   HVS *   (1963)
Start just around the arete to the right from the normal route at a short leaning corner cutting through the overhanging walls at the base.
1. 20m 4c   Clamber out of a tree and go up the short corner past the lower roofs to below a bigger roof. Traverse awkwardly left to gain the base of the

ramp on the normal route. Follow this to the left, then step right onto easy ground at a large roof. Bypass this on the right to a ledge.
2. 15m 5a   Follow The Hood onto the slab and climb leftwards to beneath the overhanging crack. Finish strenuously up this crack on painful jams.

Fuck Face   35m   HVS **   (1959)
Good climbing up the smooth corner right of The Hood Direct.
1. 10m 5a   Gain the corner from the left and climb it by thin bridging to pull onto a large slabby area.
2. 25m 4c   Pull onto the steep wall on the right (peg runner) and climb through onto the easier wall above. Trend right and go up to finish.

The following five routes are of poorer quality on flaky and sometimes vegetated rock.

The Stripper   30m   HVS   (1978)
An eliminate line left of Grappler's Groove.
1. 20m 5b   Climb the small groove in the arete and continue to join Fuck Face. Move left to belay on The Hood.
2. 10m 5a   Climb 3m above the belay, then traverse the steep slab on the right to the arete. Finish up this.

Grappler's Groove   30m   Hard Severe
A rather useless climb up the next obvious groove line. Start the at right arete of the groove. Climb this for 3m, enter the groove and go up the flake in the overhang. Pass a tree and continue up a groove to a ledge. Traverse left above the overhang and take the wall to the top.

Shikari Rib   25m   HVS 5a   (1979)
Climb the hanging corner and rib between Grappler's Groove and Grot to a ledge beneath an overhang. Move slightly right over the overhang on small but good holds and finish by steep but easy ground.

Geronimo   20m   E1 5a   (1979)
A worthwhile but poorly protected climb. Start at the top of a grassy ramp 7 metres right of Shakiri Rib. Climb direct to the overhang. Delicate moves left reach good holds on the overhang. Pull over, step right and climb up parallel to Shakiri Rib.

Grot   35m   Severe   (1959)
A climb which lives up to its name! Climb the slab right of Geronimo to a steep wall. Traverse left for 3m and go up to a ledge. Traverse right and garden your way to the top.

To the right, across a vegetated gully, is a more open area of cliff where there are some worthwhile climbs. The most obvious feature is the steep corner of Cherry Tree Ridge Direct. The steep wall to its right is taken by Dhias and Dram.

Cherry Tree Ridge   35m   Difficult *   (1959)
This climb follows the indistinct rib just beyond the vegetated gully. Start at its foot and climb easy rock steps between grass ledges which form the rib to below a steep corner (possible belay). Turn the corner on the left and continue to the top.
Direct Finish: Severe *   (1959)
Climb the fine corner avoided by the original to a ledge, then step right and go up the edge to finish.

Paramour's Rib   25m   E1 5a *   (1976)
Bold and airy climbing directly up the right edge of the upper corner of the direct finish to Cherry Tree Ridge. The protection is poor even with Friends.

Dram   35m   E1 5b   (1979)
Immediately right of Paramour's Rib is a scoop in the bulge with a shallow crack in it. Climb this (technical) and trend left to the top.

Tremendous Applause   35m   E1 5b   (1979)
Climb the lower grassy wall 3 metres right of Dram to reach a cracked groove in the bulging wall. Go up this and the easier crack above to cross the roof at the top by a V-groove.

Dhias   35m   HVS 5a   (1979)
A steep pitch on large but suspect holds. Start at the end of the buttress beneath a bulging wall. Climb the wall to a niche on the left. Continue trending left into Tremendous Applause, then move rightwards to climb the slabby headwall.

UPPER CAVE CRAG

This crag has been a forcing ground for some of the hardest routes of their time and the traditional routes are generally intricate, bold and technical. The sport routes that have been put up here are stamina climbs with brilliant enjoyable moves. Marlina and Silk Purse are two of the finest sport pitches to be found anywhere. Once established on a route, the exposure feels a lot greater than it should. As an added bonus the bouldering at the base of Upper Cave Crag is excellent – a rare commodity in these parts.

HISTORICAL

Until the late 1950s and early 1960s, Upper Cave Crag, being steep and intimidating, was generally ignored for others in the area. In 1959 and 1960, Paul Brian and Robin Campbell climbed many of the fine easier lines including The Ramp, but the best early effort was Ferranti club member Pete Smith's ascent of Coffin Corner. During the 1960s the crag became the forcing ground for many difficult aid routes, including Rat Race in 1963 from Brian Robertson and J. MacLean and Green Cheese by K. J. Martins in 1969. Also that year, the steep central section was climbed *via* the use of aid bolts by Brain Forbes and G. Millar to give Fall Out. In the same period many natural lines were climbed mainly free with recourse to a few aid points, for example Squirm and Corpse by Neil MacNiven.

The 1970s brought a dramatic rise in free climbing standards. Many of the easier natural lines were relieved of their aid. Mick Couston pointed the way with a free ascent of Gnome. Then in 1976, Murray Hamilton from Edinburgh freed Corpse, Squirm, Squirm Direct and Rat Race. This latter route in particular was a major breakthrough being one of Scotland's hardest free climbs at the time. Pitch 1 (the crux) was completely freed, but pitch 2 required a point of aid on a new direct finish over the upper roof. The first completely free ascent was later made by visiting American, Mike Graham.

Also in 1976, Derek Jamieson climbed Tumbleweed, so named because he fell from the top at one point clutching handfuls of heather (and was still clutching them as he bounced off the slab below). Dave Cuthbertson teamed up with Hamilton to free Ratcatcher and Hang Out. This powerful partnership went on to add Marjorie Razorblade the following year. Well named and until the establishment of the sport routes here, it was the most fallen-off route on the crag despite its relatively lowly grade.

In 1978 Jamieson and party established Warfarin, freeing the original second pitch of Rat Race in the process. The highlight of the year was Cuthbertson's on sight free ascent of Coffin Arete as High Performance. He went on to dominate development through the late 1970s and early 1980s. He freed Mousetrap over two days of effort, working the moves out and down-climbing rather than taking falls, and grading it as technical 6c – one of the hardest routes in 1979. Whilst doing this the left arete seemed possible. An initial on sight attempt resulted in a big fall from the top of the arete before Morbidezza was finally conquered. This superb pitch was graded E4 at the time, but has since been confirmed as Scotland's first E5. Bear in mind that Cuthbertson would not have had the benefit of the peg later placed for an ascent of In Loving Memory. John (Spider) Mackenzie made the second ascent in 1983 and Gary Latter ticked the fall during the third ascent.

At the left end of the crag Pete Hunter top roped Gotterdammerung prior to leading it. Cuthbertson made the on sight ascent, then added Voie de l'Amie. The 1980s kicked off with Lady Charlotte from Cuthbertson, who regarded it as Scotland's first E5 at the time. The superb Pied Piper was added shortly after, followed by a free ascent of Rat Race Direct and the bold arete of Laughing Gnome.

The hardest traditional route was again from Cuthbertson when he completely free climbed Green Cheese to give In Loving Memory. This was repeated in 1984 (along with Lady Charlotte and Laughing Gnome) by Gary Latter, but it had to wait 7 years before an on sight ascent from Grant Farquhar. Using the old aid bolt stubs for protection, Cuthbertson and Latter freed Fall Out over two days in 1982.

During the second half of the decade, the advent of sports climbing led to the bolting of the steep central wall. Duncan McCallum's Rattle Yer Dags was the first route to be done, taking the line of the old aided girdle using one new bolt to replace a clutch of old ones. Hamilton flashed the second ascent before Cuthbertson superseded it by gaining the diagonal crack *via* the wall below (using two further bolts but still requiring natural gear) to create Marlina.

Hamilton was again quick to repeat this, using a line of better holds to the left at one point. This left-hand variation was later bolted, and others added where Cuthbertson had used gear, by Steve Lewis who made the first redpoint. Later in 1986 Hamilton re-bolted and re-climbed Fall Out in two pitches, adding a direct start and finish, whilst Ronnie Bruce climbed Bailed Out with one rest, later eliminated by Mark McGowan.

The following year Graeme Livingston created the hardest pitch when he linked Fall Out Direct's pitches together with an extra bolt to "make a Silk Purse out of a pig's ear". Silk Purse was repeated by Cuthbertson before he straightened out his own Lady Charlotte. Mark McGowan added Ultima Necat to the bolt wall using a peg runner. This was later replaced with a bolt prior to the second ascent by McCallum. McGowan also removed some bolts from Euan Cameron's Cushionfoot Stomp before re-climbing and renaming it, All Passion Spent.

Grant Farquhar added Necrophilia in 1988 and Post Mortem in 1990. Around this time Livingston soloed Marlina Left-hand after much practice whilst Glen Sutcliffe and Alan Taylor made the first on sight flashes. Carol Hamilton made the first female ascents of this and Silk Purse. Marlina has now become Scotland's most popular sport route.

During the 1990s the bolt routes received much traffic and everyone believed the crag to be worked out. However, Anderson, Johnnie May and McCallum proved them wrong by finding, cleaning and bolting Hamish Teddy's Excellent Adventure which was first red-pointed by McCallum. The climbing (and the name!) and the fact that it is now the easiest way up the bolted section, made it an instant classic. Further additions have concentrated on some bold routes on Morningside Wall by Kevin Howett and sport routes on the nearby Sinner's Wall from George Ridge and Janet Horrocks.

LAYOUT

There are several separate walls and facets to this crag. Morningside Wall lies hidden in the trees 200 metres along the path to the left of the main crag. Up and right of this in the broad open gully that defines the left side of the main crag is the steep and compact Sinner's Wall. On walking rightwards the first part of the Main Wall is encountered with the line of The Ramp cutting from right to left being the main feature. There is a steep bouldering wall below this ramp and the big wall of Lady Charlotte is above. Right of this a larch tree grows close to the wall and immediately to its right is the deep open corner line of Mousetrap. Beyond this the steep central bolted sports wall (capped by roofs) is bounded on the left by the vertical crack line of Rat Race and on the right by the triangular niche of Squirm Direct and an arete in the upper half. A more broken but still steep section continues into the obvious Coffin Corner with the steep prow of High Performance defining the right edge.

Below this prow is a huge boulder forming a cave of sorts with an entrance in its right side. Above here is a short overhanging crack that is Marjorie Razorblade. The crag now turns to face due south and forms a large slab taken by Noddy which has a steep side wall to the right.

MORNINGSIDE WALL

A short but steep wall running diagonally right up the hillside. A large tree obscures the left-hand section, where an overhang sits above a sloping ledge. In the centre of the wall is an obvious left-facing corner. Right of this the base of the crag rises steeply to a small recess with pointed boulders. Directly above is a hanging groove and arete. Leading out right is a groove/ramp. The routes are described from left to right.

Hot Line Direct   25m   E2 5b   (1979)
A loose and poorly protected route. Start just right of the large recess at the lowest part of the wall. Climb the wall on obvious flaky holds to the ledge beneath the overhang of the normal route and finish up that.

Evening Hot Line   25m   E1 5c   (1979)
Start behind the tree. Climb the wall to a ledge, then go left along this to beneath an overhang. Surmount its right side to gain a small recess and finish up steep but easier ground. There are some loose flakes on the crux.

Morningside Warm Up   20m   HVS 5a   (1979)
The obvious left-facing corner in the middle of the wall. Gain the flake crack and climb this (crux) into the corner. Follow the corner and move out right at the top to a tree belay.

Sweaty Time Blues   20m   E3 5c   (1995)
This climb takes the wall right of Morningside Warm Up, starting just right of that route, climbing slightly right then left to reach big quartz holds below the upper bulging wall. Pull through direct and right to gain a slab to finish.

Working up a Sweat   20m   E5 6b *   (1995)
The conspicuous hanging arete to the right. Start off a huge pointed block and climb a small undercut flake to gain the base of the arete. Move up this, then continue to beneath a small roof and step left into the final slabby corner of Sweaty Time Blues. Protection is strenuous to arrange.

Chopping and Changing   20m   E1 5c *   (1995)
Climb the ramp leading out right from beside the last route. Pull through the bulge above *via* the flake, then tackle the final leaning wall direct.

SINNER'S WALL

This compact and steep wall lies hidden in the left side of the tree-filled open gully between Morningside Wall and Upper Cave Crag's Main Wall (above Morningside Wall). There are four sport routes giving entertaining warm up exercises for the bigger meat on the main crag.

Generous Offering   E3 5c *   (1996)
Climb easily up the lowest rocks at the extreme left edge of the wall to a deep
break line. Gain holds just right of the arete and pull up past a spike to a good
thread. Enter the hanging groove above and exit direct through the final bulges
on jugs. Very strenuous.

The line directly up the centre of the highest bit of crag is a project.

Six Fours-les Plage   6b   (1995)
Climb from the base of the central fault line directly through the bulge above.

Fear of the Dark   6b   (1995)
Follow the central fault/crack.

Father Figure   6b+   (1995)
Pull through the steep bulges just right of the fault and go straight up.

MAIN WALL

The routes are described left to right as one arrives at the crag. The descent
from the top of most routes follows a path leftwards (facing in) to descend down
the open gully on the left side of the crag.

The following five routes lie on the bouldering wall below The Ramp.

Left Edge   40m   Mild VS 4b   (1959/60)
A poor route up the side wall. Start at the left-hand edge of the wall. Climb the
shallow groove left of the arete to a small corner, go up this to a ledge and finish
up a pleasant rib above.

1   Hos   30m   HVS 5a   (1980)
From the toe of the arete gain a groove in the right side. Ascend this with a step
left to follow the arete to join The Ramp and finish up its top pitch.

2   Sore Fingers   25m   E1 5b   (1983)
Climb directly up the bulging wall to the right of Hos. Scrappy climbing then
leads to The Ramp.

3   Lilly White Lilleth   15m   HVS 5b**
Climb the short hanging groove in the middle of the wall with surprising difficulty.

4   Sidewinder   40m   Severe   (1974)
Start at the shallow groove in the right side of the bouldering wall. Climb up and
right to another groove, then move up this and turn the overhang on the left.
Step back right and go up a rib to the belay platform of The Ramp. Continue up
its top pitch.

5   The Ramp   40m   Hard Severe *   (1957)
One of the few good lower grade routes on Upper Cave Crag with a steep and bold top pitch.
1. 20m   Climb easily up the large obvious ramp to a large belay platform.
2. 20m   Climb the crack above to the top of a pinnacle. Either step left and climb a sandy groove or continue directly up the steep wall. Both options are hard to exit.

The next six routes all start from the large platform of The Ramp.

6   Lilly Langtry   25m   E2 5b *   (1978)
Steep and fairly well protected up the groove to the right of the top pitch of The Ramp. Climb the groove past a small tree. Either step left, then go up and right to a recess under a bulge, or continue directly up the groove to the same position (harder). Surmount the bulge and continue to the top.

7   Ring Piece   25m   E5 6a   (1995)
An eliminate line up the area of rock left of Gotterdammerung. Start up that route to the block in the black bulge. Traverse left to a peg runner and continue directly up with difficulty to a serious finish, moving right and up left at a bulge to exit close to Lilly Langtry.

8   Gotterdammerung   25m   E4 5c   (1979)
Strenuous climbing on suspect rock in the lower half and serious in the upper half. Start below a small flat-topped rib formed by twin right-slanting grooves right of Lilly Langtry. Climb the rib, then follow the groove to a recess beneath a black bulge formed by a block. Pull over this directly and continue up and slightly left before climbing directly to the top.

9   Voie de l'Amie   35m   E3 5c **   (1979)
The meat of this route is the short but sensational thin crack in the headwall above the small ledge of Hang Out. Follow Gotterdammerung to the black bulge. Make an exposed hand traverse right into Hang Out and the small ledge. Attack the thin crack above and slightly left (often wet).

10   Hang Out   35m   E2 5b *   (1972/76)
An exposed trip across the right-trending scoop. Start from the right end of the platform. Move up and right to gain the scoop (serious) which leads to a small ledge (possible belay). Traverse right into a short corner to finish.

11   The Pied Piper   65m   E3 ***   (1980)
A superb traverse that is both sustained and committing. Start from the right end of the platform.
1. 40m 5c   Scuttle across the horizontal crack to a junction with Ratcatcher (peg runners). Step down, then ascend to the spruce tree. Climb the tree, then move up and right to join Morbidezza on the arete. Traverse into the big corner of Mousetrap and across to the hanging stance below the big roofs on Rat Race.
2. 25m 5b   Follow Warfarin up and right under the capping roofs to finish.

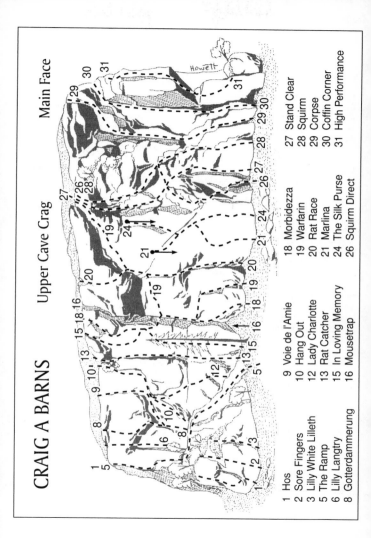

CRAIG A BARNS

Upper Cave Crag   Main Face

Howett

1 Hos	9 Voie de l'Amie
2 Sore Fingers	10 Hang Out
3 Lilly White Lilleth	12 Lady Charlotte
5 The Ramp	13 Rat Catcher
6 Lilly Langtry	15 In Loving Memory
8 Gotterdammerung	16 Mousetrap

18 Morbidezza	27 Stand Clear
19 Warfarin	28 Squirm
20 Rat Race	29 Corpse
21 Marlina	30 Coffin Corner
24 The Silk Purse	31 High Performance
26 Squirm Direct	

Halfway up the first pitch of The Ramp, the short corner and shallow scoop left of Lady Charlotte has been climbed (**One Size Fits All**, E4 6a)

12   Lady Charlotte   40m   E5 ***   (1980)
An excellent excursion up the big steep wall above the ramp. Protection is adequate but difficult to locate. Start 5m up the ramp below a small right-trending groove. The original second pitch is described, but it is perfectly logical to finish up the thin crack of Voie de l'Amie.
1. 20m 6a   Climb the wall right of the groove and move left to a good footledge at its top. The pocketed wall above leads slightly left to better holds and protection in the horizontal crack of Pied Piper. Gain the hanging flake above and follow it to exit left at its top onto the final few metres of the scoop of Hang Out, and so to the small ledge.
2. 20m 5c   Step down the scoop and reverse the traverse of Voie de l'Amie. Pull over the black bulge as for Gotterdammerung and ascend the wall up and right to a small niche. Finish up the thin crack above (serious).
Direct Variation: 35m   E5 6a **   (1987)
A direct one pitch version with added clout. Follow the original route to the top of the hanging flake. Make a move up to gain a good pocket which allows a move right to a hidden peg runner in a small groove. Climb to the small ledge and finish up the thin crack above and left as for Voie de l'Amie.

13   Rat Catcher   35m   E3 5b ***   (1969/76)
This excellent but serious route takes the shallow fault left of the tree. Start below a small corner. Climb the wall and the corner to a small ledge. Ascend right, then go back left (serious) to meet the Pied Piper and welcome peg runners. The groove above is less taxing on the brain until an exit can be made out right at the top.

14   Necrophilia   40m   E5 6a   (1988)
A contrived pitch giving very sustained and bold climbing. Start up Rat Catcher and follow the groove until level with the peg runner of In Loving Memory. Step down and traverse horizontally rightwards to the peg (Sexy Lady in reverse) and move right to the arete of Morbidezza. Follow this to where it moves left below the cracked block. Gain and finish up the ragged crack directly above.

15   In Loving Memory   35m   E6 6b **   (1969/81)
Hard bold climbing up the centre of the headwall above the spruce tree. Start up the wall behind the tree, then climb the tree itself and traverse right to the arete and junction with Morbidezza. Step back left and go up to a peg runner. Climb the wall direct to a small niche (hidden RP placement above) and continue (crux) to a huge jug. Move up left to finish up a small right-facing corner.

16   Mousetrap   35m   E4 6b *   (1960/79)
The huge, often wet, open corner right of the spruce tree succumbs with ease apart from a short very hard section through the bulge near the top. It is protected by two peg runners.

17 Sexy Lady 40m E4 6a (1980)
An eliminate but enjoyable wander taking a counter diagonal line to Necrophilia. Start as for Warfarin until into the corner of Mousetrap, then go up this to below the bulge where it is possible to move out left to the arete. Step left and move up to the peg runner of In Loving Memory. Traverse horizontally leftwards into Rat Catcher and finish up this.

18 Morbidezza 35m E5 6b *** (1979)
Another bold route in a wild position up the left arete of the corner of Mousetrap. Start 3 metres right of Mousetrap below an impending blunt rib. Hard bouldery moves (technical crux) lead to a scoop. Move left into the big corner and go up this until just below the bulge (peg runner). Traverse left onto the arete, move up the arete (reaching left to clip the peg runner on In Loving Memory), then move left to finish up the left side of the large cracked block.

19 Warfarin 50m E2 *** (1978)
A tremendous excursion across the central area, bold and surprisingly delicate. Start beneath the short right-facing corner between Mousetrap and the crack of Rat Race.
1. 25m 5c   A boulder problem start leads into the corner (peg runner at its top). Traverse left into the big corner of Mousetrap and follow this for a few moves until it is possible to traverse back right under the roofs to a hanging stance (old peg belay and good natural gear).
2. 25m 5b   Climb the slabby wall to a corner under the capping roofs (peg runner). Continue traversing right (peg runner) under the roof, moving up at the end to finish.

20 Rat Race 45m E4 *** (1963/78)
A magnificent route with two exhilarating but contrasting pitches. Start below the obvious overhanging crack in the steep central wall.
1. 20m 6a   Climb the pod (or its left edge) and crack (peg runner) to a niche. Continue up the crack (peg runner) past an overhang to a hanging stance on the left (peg belay). Strenuous.
2. 25m 5b   Climb the slabby wall to a corner under the roof (peg runner). Traverse hard under the roof rightwards for 3m (peg runner) and pull left through the roof on large flat holds. Continue directly to the top.
20a *Direct Finish:* 25m E4 6a ** (1966/80)
A harder finish through the roof directly above the belay. From the corner under the roof, move left to pull awkwardly onto the wall above (peg runner), then go up to the top.

THE SPORT WALL

The steep area of rock right of Rat Race was the scene of explorations into sport climbing over a period of several years. The routes evolved almost piecemeal leading to an assortment of seven different interconnecting lines based on the original two that were bolted (Marlina and Fall Out) and all starting as for either of these two routes. Over time the best lines have become better understood and some bolts re-positioned. The following descriptions are now recognised as the main routes. They are all excellent stamina climbs.

The most obvious feature is a left-slanting crack starting halfway up the wall and leading to a lower off below the roofs (the entirety of a now superseded route, Rattle Yer Dags). With a little imagination, various combinations of these routes can be made to give extra fun after the main lines have been ticked.

21 Marlina 20m 7b+ *** (1986)
Start up the left-hand line of bolts, just right of Rat Race. From the second bolt, go up left to a flange (bolt), then traverse right to good holds and clip a high bolt in the centre of the wall. From the end of the hand rail, a hard move up and right gains the foot of the crack (bolt) and a shake out for the strong. Hard moves up the crack lead to smaller holds and a final technical section before the lower off. It is eminently feasible to fail mere centimetres from the chain.
Marlina Original: 20m 7b+ ** (1986)
Move directly up the wall between the second and third bolts.

22 Ultima Necat 20m 7b+ ** (1987)
Follow Marlina to the fourth bolt. Step left and climb directly up the wall to the lower off of Marlina.

23 Hamish Teddy's Excellent Adventure 25m 7b+ ** (1992)
The extra meat of this route takes the arete above the start of the diagonal crack. Although this is slightly easier than the finish to Marlina, it is still a real pumper. Climb Marlina to the start of the diagonal crack. Move up right and make a couple of very steep moves to reach a good shake out on the arete. Pull back left and climb a crack on good holds on the left side of the arete. Lower off as for Silk Purse.

24 The Silk Purse 25m 7c+ *** (1987)
The right-hand bolt line. At the fourth bolt hard moves lead up and left to join Marlina at the base of the diagonal crack. Follow this past another bolt, then step right and climb the shallow scoop above precariously to a lower off.
Variation: **Fall Out Direct** 30m 7b+ * (1986)
At the fourth bolt use a pinch to move right to join Squirm Direct (peg runner, thread and possible belay), then move up left into the diagonal crack and finish up the shallow scoop.

25 Fall Out Original 25m 7b * (1982)
Not strictly a sport climb and rarely climbed. Start at a thin crack leading to the slanting niche of Squirm Direct, immediately right of the bolts of the direct version. Bouldery moves lead to the niche. A long reach up and left joins Fall Out Direct at its third bolt. Follow this to the fourth bolt, then go up right (crux) to Squirm Direct (peg runner, thread). Move back left to the base of the diagonal crack, then follow Hamish Ted's to the good shake-out. The original route moved right from there to finish up the black groove of Stand Clear, but it is better to finish up Hamish Teddy's Excellent Adventure.

The Crossing (E4 6b) is a low-level diagonal traverse of the Sport Wall, requiring some natural gear. Start up Fall Out and from the niche move up to the third bolt. Hard moves up and left lead into Marlina. Step left, then follow Marlina Left-hand and go left again into the niche on Rat Race and finish up this. An attempt on this would prove rather anti-social during a busy day.

The wall now becomes more broken with ledges, short hanging corners and niches. Its angle however does not relent. **Baled Out** (E4 6b) is an eliminate line squeezed up the shallow groove between Fall Out and Squirm Direct. Starting up Fall Out's thin crack and niche, it moves up and left into an awkward shallow groove to reach a belay on Squirm Direct.

26   Squirm Direct   30m   E3 *   (1960/69/76)
Superb technical climbing up the slanting niche which bounds the right side of the Sport Wall. Start below and right of the niche in a groove.
1. 15m 5c   Climb the groove and transfer left into the slanting niche. Go up this (peg runner) and exit leftwards with difficulty to gain a shallow recess below the prow (peg runner, thread and possible belay). Continue up right to the ledge and belay of Squirm.
2. 15m 5c   Squirm up the ribbed slab on the left (peg runner) to reach a small ledge. Move back right and finish up a steep groove with a dead tree.

27   Stand Clear   30m   E2 5a   (1978)
A serious outing on flaky rock. Start just right of Squirm Direct. Climb a shallow groove and go over a small overhang. Continue leftwards, crossing Squirm Direct into a groove. Climb this until it is possible to move left onto the arete. Ascend the brown groove on the right side of the arete to the top.

28   Squirm   30m   E1 *   (1960/76)
A worthwhile climb with one short hard section in an exposed position. Start below the scooped wall, right of Stand Clear.
1. 15m 4b   Climb the brown scoop and rib to belay on a large ledge.
2. 15m 5c   Move left and squirm up the smooth hanging ribbed slab (peg runner) to reach a small ledge. Continue leftwards on large flakes to an airy finish at the top of the arete.

29   Corpse   35m   E2 5c **   (1960/76)
A fine pitch, technical and surprisingly exposed. Start beneath a right-facing corner, hanging in the upper wall left of the obvious Coffin Corner. Climb easily up ribs to a ledge at the base of the corner. Follow it (peg runner) to a hanging glacis under the final steep wall (pegs). Traverse right and climb the awkward crack (crux) to the top.
Left-hand Finish: E2 5b   (1980)
From the hanging glacis, hand traverse boldly left to finish up the vegetated groove on the left.
Variation: **Post Mortem**   E4 6b   (1990)
A stiff direct finish directly up the steep wall above the glacis (2 peg runners).

30 Coffin Corner 30m HVS 5a ** (1960)
The best line on the crag gives awkward thrutching up the off-width corner crack. A choice of lines leads up to the base of the corner. Follow it with reasonable protection, exiting right near the top or finish direct if so inclined.

31 High Performance 20m E4 6a ** (1960/78)
Gymnastic moves over the roof and prow right of Coffin Corner. Start on top of a huge boulder, gained through the cave beneath. Gibbon out across the roof crack to a flat hold on the lip (peg runner). Pull up, then step right and climb an awkward groove (peg runner) to the top.

32 Death's Head 35m E1 5b * (1976)
Deceptively steep climbing up the shallow cracked groove right of the prow of High Performance. Start through the cave and get onto the top of the boulder. Climb the groove until it bulges, then step right onto the edge and go up and back left to below a flying groove on the left. Follow this worryingly to finish. Avoiding the step right onto the edge by climbing the cracks through the bulge direct is 5c.

33 Crutch 30m Severe ** (1959)
An interesting and exposed route following the groove above the entrance to the cave. Start 3 metres right of the cave at a left-slanting ramp. Ascend the ramp to a ledge, climb the corner above, then move leftwards across the slab to finish up the central groove.

34 Marjorie Razorblade 25m E3 ** (1977)
Excellent well protected jamming up the short S-shaped crack right of the corner of Crutch.
1. 15m 5c Ascend the lower wall and the crack to a ledge.
2. 10m 5a Move left and climb the overhanging corner to finish.

35 Noddy 30m Moderate (1957)
This climb ascends the vegetated slabs round the corner from Marjorie Razorblade. Start nearly in the centre of the slabs and take a botany tour diagonally left to the top. It is a very handy descent route (with care) from the Coffin Corner area.

36 Flook 35m Very Difficult ** (1959)
A very amenable route up the corner formed by the slab and the steep right-bounding side wall. Climb the steepening corner until a left traverse can be made to finish up a steep broken wall on the left side of the capping wall.

The following routes climb the steep side wall. The most prominent feature is the lone holly bush in the centre of the wall growing from the upper of two diagonal breaks.

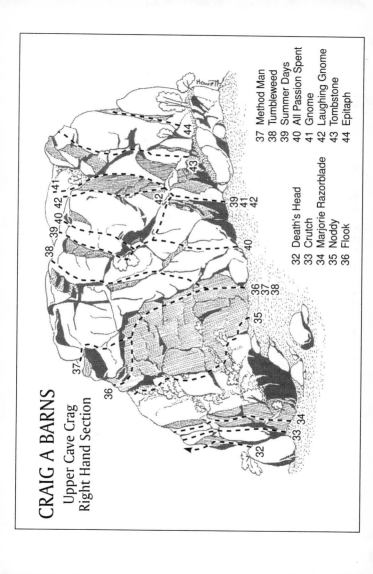

CRAIG A BARNS
Upper Cave Crag
Right Hand Section

32 Death's Head
33 Crutch
34 Marjorie Razorblade
35 Noddy
36 Flook

37 Method Man
38 Tumbleweed
39 Summer Days
40 All Passion Spent
41 Gnome
42 Laughing Gnome
43 Tombstone
44 Epitaph

37 Method Man 30m E3 5b   (1996)
Start up Flook to the top right-hand corner of the slab. Step up onto a ledge and climb direct up the slight arete past a roof before traversing left on big jugs below the capping roof. Poorly protected.

38 Tumbleweed 35m E2 5b *   (1976)
Steep and fingery with barely adequate protection up the left side of the wall. Start by climbing Flook for 6m before pulling onto a ledge in the lower break on the wall below the holly. Follow the overhung gangway on the left to a ledge at the foot of the corner demarcating the left side of the wall (peg runner). Step right and climb a slim groove and wall rightwards on pockets to finish.

39 Summer Days 25m E3 5c *   (1978)
Steep climbing above the holly with the crux negotiating the bush. Start as for Gnome by climbing the steep cracked arete forming the right side of the wall. Follow the upper diagonal break leftwards to the holly bush. Swing on it, sit on it, then stand on it. Finish up the crack and groove above.

40 All Passion Spent 25m E4 6a *   (1987)
This bold route forces a way powerfully up the richly pocketed wall and shallow hanging groove right of the holly bush. Gain the holly from directly below. Step right down the break and climb the wall direct past 2 peg runners on improving holds to enter the groove. Pull out right to finish.

41 Gnome 25m E1 5c *   (1960/74)
A steep little corner round the arete from the last routes provides the main feature of this route. Start at the base of the arete. Climb the lower blunt and cracked arete until it is possible to gain a ledge on the right below the corner. Struggle with the corner (peg runner) to an easy finish.

42 Laughing Gnome 25m E5 5c *   (1980)
This climb follows the arete in its entirety; the difficulties are short but serious. Climb the lower cracked arete to the ledge on the right, then launch out leftwards up the ludicrously overhanging upper arete.

43 Tombstone 20m E2 5c **   (1978)
Steep jamming and bridging up the next corner right of gnome. Start by scrambling rightwards to a belay ledge below the corner. Follow the crack to a triangular overhang, pull over and continue directly up the corner and crack to the top. Deceptively steep.

44 Epitaph 20m E1 5b   (1978)
Climb the vertical crack in the short right wall of Tombstone, then continue up the easy slab to finish.

NEWTYLE QUARRY   (Map Ref 045 413)

This slate quarry is unique in Scotland and the closest thing there is here to the more famous Welsh and Lakeland versions. Although it does not compare, it is worth a visit to savour a similar feeling of insecurity. It is erroneously known by climbers (visitors and locals alike) as Birnam Quarry, but in fact the quarry of that name is a pile of choss on the other side of the river to the west of the A9, on the flank of Birnam Hill (Shakespeare wrote about it in Macbeth – the hill not the quarry). The rock is a grey slate lying at an average angle of 65 degrees with virtually no frictional properties, little in the way of good natural protection, but high on excitement. The quarry is a sun trap in the late afternoon and evening and it dries very quickly after rain. It never, however, sees the sun in winter and seeps after prolonged rain.

ACCESS and LAYOUT
From the centre of Dunkeld take the A984 Coupar Angus road along the east shore of the river Tay. After 2km there is a small estate of modern bungalows on the left (Dean's Park). The quarry is in the trees to the right of these and the available parking is limited. Immediately right of the entrance to the estate is the old entrance to the quarry, now overgrown and blocked by an iron gate (parking for two cars here). Follow the path behind the gate passing slate waste tips and bearing left through the trees into the quarry.

At the entrance there is an isolated piece of rock on the right – a narrow slab guarded by a bulge and nettles (Doorjamb Slab). Its left side is an overhanging wall cutting diagonally up the hillside. The slab is split centrally by a fine crack (Spandau Ballet). To the left of this the quarry floor is formed by a huge fan of scree emanating from the base of the main slab up to the right. This consists of a smaller subsidiary slab on the right side (The Outhouse Slab), the main slab then ripples up and left culminating in a half-hidden cave known as The Tube. There are roofs above the cave entrance.

The easiest descent is by walking down to the left.

DOORJAMB SLAB

Spandau Ballet   30m   E2 5c **   (1981)
An excellent climb up the thin crack in the centre. It is hard but well protected.

In the overhanging left side-wall of the slab is a bolted sport project.

PANTILE SLAB

Some 100 metres right of the main quarry, level with the top of The Outhouse Slab, is a small but clean slab slanting up the hillside.

Pantile Headlap   15m   E2 5b *   (1997)
Climb the slab using the obvious crack to a narrow ledge at half-height. Move left and boldly climb the upper slab to the top.

THE OUTHOUSE SLAB

This is easily reached by walking up the hillside close into the overhanging retaining wall of Doorjamb Slab, or by going up the centre of the scree fan and following the base of the main slab right to descend a little to the base of the outhouse.

Flashdance   20m   E3 6a   (1983)
This route follows the obvious incipient crack line up the slab.

THE MAIN SLAB

Walking up the centre of the scree fan one arrives below the lowest point of the slab. This section has three ripples running across diagonally from left to right. Above these and at about half-height there is a horizontal overlap which curves down into slight grooves at the left side. A further overlap above and left of here curves down at the left side before reaching the cave entrance of The Tube. A prominent crack starts near the right side of the slab and goes diagonally up to the overlaps (Counting Out Time). The routes are described from right to left.

1   Counting Out Time   30m   E3 5c **   (1979)
An excellent sustained route up the big crack on the right side of the slab. There is good protection in the crack and a peg runner near its end just below the overlap. From this move up left to the overlap and pull through boldly and with difficulty, passing a small sapling, to gain thin cracks. Follow the obvious line horizontally right to a ledge and tree belay. Escape off to the right.

2   Compulsive Gambler   45m   E5 6a ***   (1986)
A stunning and serious route up the centre of the slab parallel with Counting Out Time. Start at the lowest point of the slab. Follow a thin crack to the first ripple, then move into a further crack on the right passing through the second and third ripples to reach a scoop under the overlap. Step right and clip the peg runner on Counting Out Time, then follow this up left through the overlap. Continue direct up the upper slab following a thin crack past 3 peg runners, finishing slightly right then back left at the top. RPs and small rocks are needed.

3   Slateford Road   25m   E2 5b **   (1979)
A good but poorly protected wander across the slab from left to right following a line above the overlap. Start at the foot of twin curving corners which run into the main overlap. Climb the corners going diagonally right and into the overlaps. Undercling right and gain a scoop above the obvious break in the overlap. From the top of the scoop exit right and traverse hard right across the slab to the ledge and belay of Counting Out Time.

4   Atomic   30m   E3 5c *   (1980)
Climb as for Slateford Road up the corners to the overlap. Make committing moves up and left to enter the base of a left-facing corner, then go up this to a further overlap (peg runner). Continue direct to gain a crack leading to a tree belay.

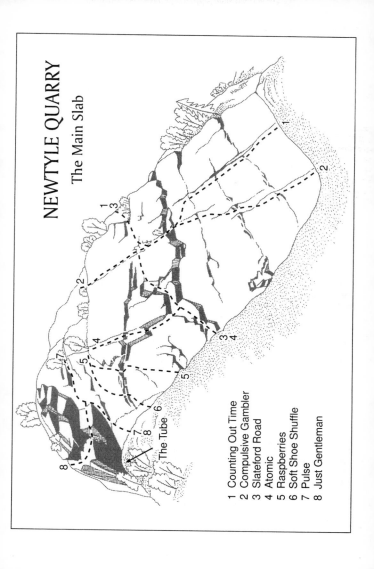

NEWTYLE QUARRY
The Main Slab

The Tube

1 Counting Out Time
2 Compulsive Gambler
3 Slateford Road
4 Atomic
5 Raspberries
6 Soft Shoe Shuffle
7 Pulse
8 Just Gentleman

5   Raspberries   30m   E3 5b **   (1980)
Poorly protected climbing up the slim left-facing corner to the left of Atomic. Start in the centre of the blank slab beneath the right end of a large block in the overlap above. Boldly go up the slab to the block. Traverse 2m left under this (protection in the borehole above the overlap) to move over and up to the slim corner. Follow this, then traverse right to the tree belay.

6   Soft Shoe Shuffle   25m   E1 5a *   (1981)
Start towards the left-hand side of the slab where the overlap curves down to meet a grassy diagonal break. Pad diagonally up and right under the overlap until it is possible to pull through. Move left with difficulty, then follow a right-trending fault (peg runner) to step into Raspberries above its slim corner.

7   Pulse   35m   E2 5b *   (1981)
Climb directly up to the broken corner which marks the boundary of the slab, then layback it all the way until it bulges and a horizontal traverse line leads right to the higher of two trees. Escape above or to the right.

8   Just Gentleman   35m   E3 5c   (1981)
Follow Pulse until moves left across the slab between the roofs and the lip of the cave reach a series of rising ledges which lead to the top. Serious and loose.

An eliminate half girdle has been climbed from Pulse. **Marguerita**, E1 5a (1979) follows Pulse for 10m, then takes an obvious rising ramp rightwards to a birch tree belay (superseded by Raspberries). An unenticing right to left girdle traverse (**The Fringe** 60m E4 6a) has been climbed above the overlap. It starts up a chossy crack/corner line in the extreme right end of the slab right of Counting Out Time and goes to a belay tree on the edge of the slab. The main pitch traverses left to a peg runner, steps down onto a sloping foothold and makes a hard reach left to a small ledge (Hex 6). Step up and left to gain Atomic and belay in the tree. A final pitch (5b) reverses Soft Shoe Shuffle down and left into the corner of Pulse which is followed to its belay tree. Abseil off. A wandering route called Desmond Decker started up the girdle and finished up Compulsive Gambler but has now been superseded by the latter.

THE TUBE

There are two bolted sport routes emanating from the bowels of the earth. All were manufactured by modern-day quarrymen carrying on the traditions of crafting slate for use on roofs! All are, as yet, projects.

CRAIG LAGGAN   *(Map Ref 994 416)*

Previously known variously as Craig Vinean or Farm Crag, this impressive and steep south-facing crag lies directly above Kennacoil Farm on the southern slopes of Creag Bheag. Craig Vinean is the smaller outcrop in the forest to the east of Craig Laggan. The rock is similar to that at Cave Crag, but it is not as solid, there is more vegetation and the present farmer will not allow climbing as it is so close to his house. As a result there is still lots of potential for new routes, but as this would involve extensive cleaning it is both impractical and probably impossible. The routes are included for reference if the situation ever changes.

ACCESS and LAYOUT
Follow the A822 off the A9 at the Dunkeld junction for 3km. Take the small road sign-posted to Rumbling Bridge immediately beyond which the crag is obvious on the hillside above the farm. The crag has two steep walls, separated by a vegetated gully. The left-hand section is very steep, split in half by a ledge. The very steep bulging wall above the ledge is unclimbed. The right-hand side is defined by more obvious lines. On the right is a prominent rib separated from the main crag by a dirty unclimbed groove. The routes are described from left to right.

Chrysalids   30m   VS 5a   (1980)
Climb a thin crack in the left-hand corner of the crag passing a V-shaped block to a ledge. Pull onto the ramp directly above and continue up the scoop on the left.

Trouble with Lichen   30m   E1 5a   (1980)
Aptly named. Start 4 metres right of Chrysalids at a feint crack. Follow this to a sloping ledge, then go over the bulge above to a further ledge. Climb the short wall above moving slightly left to reach a large tree.

Goliath's Granddad   30m   Very Difficult   (1978)
Follow an obvious rising traverse line starting 4m left of Chrysalids, cross it at the scoop and continuing for 5m until moves up and left on broken ledges gain the tree.

Granddad's Groove   30m   HVS 5b   (1978)
After a strenuous, fingery start the difficulties ease. Start 5 metres right of Trouble with Lichen directly below a corner. Climb the right wall of the corner, then enter the upper corner by a traverse and finish up this.

Powerplay   25m   E3 5c   (1980)
A steep and strenuous route with only adequate protection. Start at the foot of an obvious crack formed by a huge block at the right end of the overhanging section. Climb the crack and step left onto a loose ledge. Pull onto the flange above and layback the arete to gain a hanging loose block. Use this gingerly to pull over the small roof and go up to a large ledge below the steep headwall. Follow this to the left and finish up Goliath's Granddad.

Nomad   30m   Very Difficult   (1980)
Start beneath the right end of the half-height ledge. Climb the broken wall to the ledge and follow it to the left to finish up Goliath's Granddad.

The Wiper   25m   Hard Severe   (1980)
Start beneath an open book corner overlooking the vegetated gully that bisect the crag. Climb the wall to a small grassy patch. Graze up this to the corner to finish.

General Woundwort   35m   E2 5b   (1980)
Sustained and committing climbing up the hanging groove in the wall to the right of the vegetated gully. Gain the groove and at the roof move left for a few metres, then go back right to a less steep wall. Climb the wall to finish up a corner.

Misconception   35m   VS 5a   (1978)
A steep interesting route, but with some suspect rock. Start at the foot of the central groove. Make some difficult moves to gain the groove proper and climb this to a ledge on top of a pillar. Ascend directly above (loose) to a niche, then climb a crack in the roof above to reach the top.

Lettuce   35m   VS 4c   (1980)
Start as for Misconception to the foot of the groove. Traverse right and climb the crack which forms the right side of the pillar. At the top of the pillar join and finish up Misconception.

The Snare   30m   E2 5b   (1980)
A good but rather worrying route taking the line of the obvious forked lightning flake crack right of Misconception. Scramble up to a ledge 5 metres right of that route. Climb the short steep wall to gain the flake. Follow this onto a slab, then move diagonally left on the slab to reach the top of the pillar. Pull through the roof rightwards on large flaky holds to gain a ramp that leads to the top.

Rainbow Warrior   35m   E1 5b   (1980)
An excellent route which follows a curving line rising from the groove of Larceny. Start as for that route at the slabby open groove. After 5m break out onto a short steep wall on the left which leads to a niche. Continue trending left to the top.

Larceny   30m   VS 4c   (1978)
A good climb that will improve with traffic. Climb the slabby-looking open groove that is topped by a holy tree. Turn a small roof on the left to finish.

Convergence   30m   VS 4c   (1978)
Start 3 metres right of Larceny and climb the wall to gain the foot of a very small left-slanting groove. Follow this to a small niche below the holly tree on Larceny. Climb the roof *via* a thin crack and tree to finish.

Rib Cage   30m   VS 4c   (1980)
Start as for Convergence, but trend rightwards up the wall to a ledge with loose blocks. Move right along the ledge almost to the tree-filled groove. A thin sharply defined ramp leads through the roof overlooking the groove before going left to the top.

Spare Rib Direct   20m   VS 4c   (1990)
A rib bounds the right side of the vegetated groove, giving the line of the route.
Start just right of the vegetated groove and climb the rib direct on steep suspect
rock. Finish over bulges on the left arete just left of Spare Rib.

Spare Rib   25m   Severe   (1980)
Start on the right side of the rib and traverse left onto front of it above the steep
initial wall. Continue up the slabby central section direct, turning bulges at the
top on the right.

The next routes climb the short steep wall right of the rib of Rib Cage.

Sirius   15m   E2 5c *   (1995)
Climb the short leaning wall centrally *via* a thin groove, then take the headwall
above directly.

Razor Flake   10m   VS 4c   (1990)
On the right of the steep wall climb to a conspicuous corner crack. Climb this
with a tricky move to exit onto slabs to finish.

CRAIG RUENSHIN   *(Map Ref 041 403)*

This lies on the north-east flank of Birnam Hill near Dunkeld (on the west side of
the A9) at about the same level but left of Birnam Quarry and below the more
obvious but scrappy Rohallion Castle Crag. From the carpark 300 metres down
the Bankfoot turning from the A9, walk under the railway and the crag lies 5
minutes walk through the trees above. It has a short overhanging east face and
a slabby moss-covered north face.

Larch Crack   35m   Very Difficult   (1968)
Climb a line up the right side of the mossy slab.

The Hinge   35m   VS 4c   (1968)
Climb the centre of the slab.

Victoria's Chimney   30m   VS 4c   (1968)
The chimney on the east face.

Eye of Newt   10m   E4 6b *   (1995)
Climb the left-hand crack line on the east face, starting from a tree stump.
Sustained, with a peg runner.

Strathearn and Strathyre

The large glen of Strathearn runs from west to east almost defining the boundary between the central belt area and the Highlands. Indeed the Highland Boundary Fault (a geological distinction between the two) follows roughly the same line at this point. Small radiating glens feed into Strathearn and it is in these that the bulk of the climbs are found, the most important being Glen Lednock and Glen Ogle. The waters originating in Glen Ogle at Lochearnhead and neighbouring Glen Ample drain into Loch Earn from where the River Earn flows east into the North Sea. Strathearn is very like the Lake District without the crowds and is designated a National Scenic Area.

Strathyre lies between the outflow of Loch Voil and the head of Loch Lubnaig, with the village of Strathyre at its south end. Loch Lubnaig Crag between Strathyre village and Callander and a large but disappointing crag at the head of Kirkton Glen (Leum an Eireannaich) in the upper reaches of the strath (above Balquhidder village) are detailed in the SMC *Lowland Outcrops* Guide. Some of the other crags in the upper reaches of the strath have seen recent development, particularly of sport routes, and they are most conveniently grouped with the Glen Ogle climbs and so are described here.

Despite Glen Lednock attracting visits from all the major protagonists of the seventies and early eighties, the area's climbing has been regarded as something of a backwater and had become neglected. A recent reawakening has occurred with the Glen Lednock routes now being recognised as deserving more attention from visitors, indeed some are of the highest quality, and recent developments in Glen Ogle and the surrounding area have brought this particular nook to the forefront as Scotland's "premier sport climbing venue". And of course there is a good selection of cake shops and cafes — all very civilised.

HISTORY

The first recorded climbing in the area concerned Glen Lednock when Robin Campbell visited Balnacoul Castle Crag after reading a note in an earlier SMC Journal. He dragged various people along from Stirling University including J.Monan and Peter Murray-Rust. Carcase Wall, which Campbell led throughout, was the only route of any consequence from these explorations. Other routes from this period were the main gully/chimney lines, including one they named Central Groove. The following year attempts were made on various lines on the crags on this hillside but the only successful ascent was from Robin Campbell with Spare Rib. Les Brown became resident in Scotland at this time and he (and Ian Rowe, amongst others) failed on The Great Crack, which was rapidly gaining a reputation.

No Place for a Wendy, Balnacoul Castle, Glen Lednock   (Climber, Lawrence Hughes)

Through 1973 and 1974 the SMC Journal records that 'mysterious' naval personnel from Rosyth had developed Balnacoul Castle. Of these 'aliens' Ian Conway and Dick Baker were particularly active and wrote that 'the area is reaching maturity, perhaps surpassing Craig a Barns in importance'! Squirrel Club members were also active here about this time, but it was Conway who made the first ascent of The Great Crack with one nut for aid, an impressive achievement. Also an unidentified 'Central Groove' succumbed to 'unethical attacks' with pegs by unrecorded persons.

Ed Grindley, who was teaching in Stirling at the time, paid a visit and snatched the free ascent of The Great Crack (E3) as well as the corner to its left, called Chancers, both in 1975. A few years later Murray Hamilton climbed No Place for a Wendy (E3), typically nabbing the best route in the glen and perhaps one of the best outcrop routes around these parts. The earlier gully/chimney line of Central Groove was confused with other lines including the one that received an aided ascent. Dave Cuthbertson, searching for the potential of a free ascent of this 'Central Groove', looked at the clean red corner on Central Buttress, but it turned out to be a bit loose and the right arete proved more enticing. The result was Gabriel at E4. The Corner was finally done free by Rick (the stick) Campbell in 1992 at a surprisingly lowly grade of E2 and the name Central Groove retained, although it is undoubtedly not the groove of previously recorded ascents.

In 1979 the development of Creag na h-Iolaire (Eagle Crag) proceeded at a fast pace with Ian Duckworth and Neil Morrison being most prominent. All these routes were undergraded as the first ascensionists were basing the grades on Northumberland routes and were new to the new-routing scene. Development in this quiet backwater was also not without incident, such as Morrison nearly coming to grief when he fell from Disco Duck and rolled down the hillside below becoming wrapped up by his rope. Kenny Spence visited Lednock with John (Spider) McKenzie and Duncan McCallum (later to be involved in developing sport climbing in Glen Ogle). Spence's Diamond Cutter on Creag na h-Iolaire in particular is worthy of greater praise.

Graham Little and Kevin Howett started the development of Glen Ogle in 1990 and 1991 with several bold routes on Beinn Leabhainn and Creag nan Cuileann in the company of Bob Reid and Tom Prentice. At the latter crag Little climbed the inaugural route Pruner's Groove (E1), whilst Howett found the serious Mind Bogle (E5), and Prentice completed The Harder They Fall (E4), after falling through, and demolishing, a small tree that had clung to life below the crux. Rab Anderson and Rick Campbell paid the crag a visit and after repeating some of the routes, shared in the ascent of the final (and hardest) line here, the thin roof crack of The Bigger They Fall (E5 6c). At the same time (1992) Paul (the stork) Thorburn discovered the Diamond Buttress on the 'dark side' of the glen and, with Johnnie May, saw the potential for its development as

Electrodynamics, Strathyre Crag   (Climber, Rab Anderson)

a sport venue. Thorburn made attempts on the line of Off the Beaten Track (finally climbed in 1993 at 8a) whilst Campbell and Anderson climbed the gear route of Sugar and Spice (E3). Anderson was then successful on the first of the sport routes to be completed, producing Metal Guru (6c) and Children Of The Revolution (7b).

All the gear routes in the glen generally remained unpopular, partly due to a lack of information. However, the dust from the drills had hardly settled when Glasgow and Edinburgh climbers who had heard the rumours were making visits. Over the next two summers Anderson along with Dundee Climbers Neil Shepherd and George Ridge really got started on the rapid development of the crags, and with additional input from Andy Banks, Janet Horrocks, Chris Anderson, Thorburn, Iain Pitcairn and McCallum, managed to produce over eighty routes on both The Dark Side and The Sunny Side. Glen Ogle has become accepted as a legitimate venue for sport routes although some of the higher crags are certainly at the boundary of what constitutes a low-lying or mountain crag. Their proximity to the road is probably the most important factor and future expansion onto nearby crags that are definitely mountain in character should hopefully be resisted.

Meanwhile, Howett was quietly developing a couple of small buttresses in nearby Balquhidder (although signs of previous activity were found). In the company of Ridge and others he produced some short but very sustained and serious lines on Bleating Wall which should appeal to the connoisseurs of imaginative protection. Thorburn and Pitcairn discovered Strathyre Crag and this was rapidly developed as a sport venue with Anderson as the main protagonist.

In 1994 Thorburn ventured over the top of the hill from Ogle to discover the extremely impressive wall on Creag Mac Ranaich. He and Rick Campbell produced a couple of very hard routes with the necky Sidewinder from Campbell in 1994 and the very overhanging Toiler on the Sea from Thorburn (both E6) in 1995. Finally some re-awakening of interest was occurring in Glen Lednock during 1995 and 1996. The 'Dundee Pig Farmers', Craig Adam and Gordon Lennox, were filling in the gaps on both Balnacoul Castle's myriad of crags and Creag na h-Iolaire. Their best find was Hanging Buttress on the former where they climbed a prominent crack on sight, using one nut for aid. At the same time Howett and Lawrence Hughes (fresh from completion of his Highers) were sniffing about in the area. Hughes made a free ascent of the crack and re-named it Hormone Warrior (E4), then added another strenuous E4 (Huckleberry Thin) next to it. This same pair developed The Hideaway Crag with the best line being the steep Hide and Sneak (E5) from Howett. Lennox and Adams continued to add several lines on several new crags on Balnacoul Castle with various partners throughout 1996. All were led on sight and the hardest was Rough Cut (E4), again using several rest points to allow cleaning. Thorburn returned to Creag Mac Ranaich to add Complicity (E5), and finally in 1997, just as the text for the guide was being finalised, Howett produced Solutions to a Small Problem (E5 6b) at Balnacoul Castle.

STRATHEARN

The A85 links Perth with Lochearnhead through the length of the strath and Lochearnhead itself sits at the junction of the A85 and the main A84 route north from Stirling to Fort William. There is a bus service running from Perth to St Fillans, stopping at Comrie from where Glen Lednock can be reached. There is also a 'Trundler' bus service running round the Loch Earn area. However the easiest way to travel is by car.

AMENITIES
There are a few organised campsites and caravan parks in the area although none are popular with climbers as most visit on a day basis. There are also some very good cheap B&Bs and hotels. The only bunkhouse style accommodation to date is Braincroft, between Crieff and Comrie (Tel. 01764 670 140) which would be very handy for visitors from further afield. Otherwise discrete camping or bivouacking is possible in those areas away from habitation. Comrie and Crieff both have a good selection of cafés, chip shops and summer diversions such as the Comrie Fortnight and the Crieff Highland Games in August.

GLEN LEDNOCK

The Highland Boundary Fault and the River Earn cross each other at the charming little village of Comrie where there is an Earthquake House (testifying to the instability of the area). From the flanks of the Munro, Ben Chonzie, Glen Lednock runs south into Comrie.

A single track road signposted to the glen turns off from a sharp bend by The Deil's Cauldron restaurant, just before leaving Comrie when going west. The crags are about 12km from here, halfway up the glen between the farms of Funtulich and Invergeldie. The road continues to the head of the glen at a hydroelectric dam (good discrete camping).

There are two main crags languishing in an open, tranquil situation either side of the glen. On the right-hand side when driving up (the east side) and quite close to the road, is Creag na h-Iolaire (Eagle Crag). On the opposite side of the glen (the west side) and almost facing Eagle Crag, are a series of small buttresses scattered across the hillside of Balnacoul Castle. The largest is the rightmost crag, whilst lower on the hill and virtually the leftmost crag is Ballindalloch Crag, close to a farm of the same name.

CREAG NA H-IOLAIRE   *(Map Ref 270 749)*

Creag na h-Iolaire (the crag of the eagle) is the craggy hill on the east side of the glen, clearly seen in the distance after the road emerges from the trees into the glen proper. The crags of interest are those at the lowest western end of the hill, just above the road and have assumed the name of the hill itself as far as climbers are concerned. A very mellow aspect with plenty of sunshine well into the evening in summer (and often in condition throughout the winter) make this a popular venue with locals. The rock is a coarse-grained red granite very similar to that found in the north-east of Scotland. The climbs used to have a reputation for being grossly undergraded but hopefully this has now been rectified and visitors will be less likely to leave with bruised egos or bums.

APPROACH AND TOPOGRAPHY
About 500 metres beyond Funtulich, where the road is unfenced, there is space to park almost directly below the crag (before a cattlegrid). There are three separate buttresses. The lowest is short but long and steep. To its right and slightly higher on the hillside is Central Wall which is a smooth black wall. Up and right of this is the much more daunting High Wall which lies diagonally up the hillside. There is also some good bouldering, especially on Central Wall.

LOW WALL

This is divided into three separate sections by grassy areas. On the left is a buttress composed of a slab leading to a roof. A tree-infested bay separates it from a more alluring buttress, an overhanging wall rounding off into a slab. At the highest point of this a finger crack cuts up the slab (the line of Premiere). A grassy rake (Difficult), which can be used as a descent, defines the left side of this buttress and separates it from the right-hand section. This presents a long shorter wall which is all overhanging, the most obvious feature being a deep corner recess towards the left side (The Strangler), another more open reces to its right and a smooth wall at the right-hand end (Cranium Wall). The routes are described from left to right.

By the Way   20m   VS 4c   (1979)
This climb is unfortunately often wet and takes the slab and roof of the left-hand buttress. Go through the roof *via* a large hold, then climb the slab above.

The following routes are all on the more impressive central buttress.

1   Deuxieme   15m   Mild VS 4b   (1979)
The main part of the buttress is defined on the upper left by a corner. Start at a rib bounding the left edge of the buttress below the corner. Climb the rib, stepping right into the corner which leads to the top.

2   Premiere   20m   VS 5a **   (1979)
Start just right of the rib and climb direct to the base of the corner. Step out right onto the front of the buttress and climb a finger crack up the left edge in a fine position to the top.

3   Junior's Jinx   20m   E1 5b **   (1979)
Good climbing direct up the steep twin cracks to join Premiere below the finger crack.

GLEN LEDNOCK

Creag na h-Iolaire

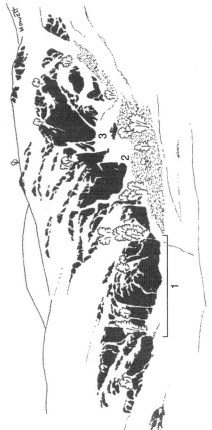

1 Low Wall
2 Central Wall
3 High Wall

4   Lenny's Jinx   10m   E2 6a   (1995)
Climb cracks on the right side of the overhanging wall right of Junior's Jinx, until it is possible to step right onto the arete and finish direct up cracks.

5   Strategies for Survival   20m   E1 5b *   (1979)
Another enjoyable climb up the right edge of the buttress. Start at an easy grassy rake which descends from the right. Go up the rake until it is possible to pull out left onto the arete, which leads to the top. Alternatively, the finger crack further left can be gained to finish if wished.

An easy grassy rake separates this central buttress from the longer right-hand section. This begins with a clean steep rib whose right side is formed by a recessed corner. Right of this the wall is undercut with a right-slanting diagonal crack above.

6   Oddball   12m   Very Difficult   (1979)
At the extreme left side a series of corners and ledges lead up to the rake.

7   Time for a Sharp Exit   12m   E2 5c   (1995)
Climb the arete to the left of the groove of Get a Grip, then go up the wall above directly. Somewhat eliminate.

8   Get a Grip   12m   E2 6a **   (1979)
An excellent and hard route up the centre of the rib. Climb the lower wall to a horizontal crack. Pull into and climb a shallow groove with a hard move near the top. Tree belay.

9   The Strangler   12m   E2 5c **   (1979)
Exceedingly steep, crotch-wrenching bridging up the recessed corner — good route for aspirant ballet dancers. The difficulties only end after the final pull over the lip into the groove above.

10   Bear Cage   12m   E2 5c   (1988)
Climb straight up through the overhangs above the start of the diagonal crack of Sultans of Swing. Finish to the left.

11   Sultans of Swing   12m   HVS 5b **   (1979)
This strenuous route climbs the diagonal crack. Start from the right edge of the recess of The Strangler. Gain the crack and follow it to a slight niche. Climb the wall above exiting out right near the top to a tree belay.
11a   *Direct Start:*   E1 5b   (1979)
Gain the slight niche from the large recess on the right by thin tenuous moves.

12   The Branch   12m   HVS
Climb the shallow corners to the right of the Direct Start to Sultans of Swing, finishing at a tree.

13   Power Pinch   10m   E3 6a   (1995)
Climb up the left arete of Cranium Wall, moving right to follow a hairline crack to the top.

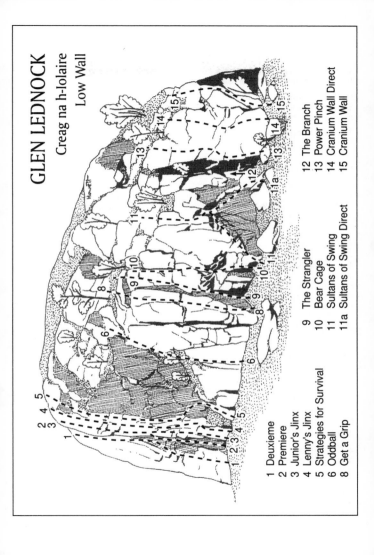

GLEN LEDNOCK

Creag na h-Iolaire
Low Wall

1 Deuxieme
2 Premiere
3 Junior's Jinx
4 Lenny's Jinx
5 Strategies for Survival
6 Oddball
8 Get a Grip

9 The Strangler
10 Bear Cage
11 Sultans of Swing
11a Sultans of Swing Direct

12 The Branch
13 Power Pinch
14 Cranium Wall Direct
15 Cranium Wall

14   Cranium Wall Direct   10m   E2 5c   (1994)
A line straight up the middle of the overhanging wall. Climb into the L-shaped niche (peg runner) and finish slightly rightwards.

15   Cranium Wall   10m   HVS 5a *   (1980)
Start at the right end of the steep wall before it degenerates. Climb up to an overhang on the right. Move right, then continue direct to finish.

16   Rucking with Rosie   15m   VS 4c   (1995)
Climb a crack up the wall on the other side of the tree right of Cranium Wall.

CENTRAL WALL

This wall has excellent clean and compact granite giving generally thin climbing with only just enough protection. The wall is split in the centre by a sloping rock ledge. The steep wall above the ledge has a fine thin crack up the centre. A short corner leads to the right end of the ledge. Right of this the wall is shorter but continuous and split by an overlap.

1   Black September   20m   E4 6a **   (1979)
An excellent and difficult climb up the thin crack in the highest part of the wall. Start in the centre of the lower wall directly below the upper crack. Climb the lower wall at its highest point to gain the sloping ledge. Climb directly up between twin cracks above and left, and a tiny vertical seam (protection — difficult to arrange) by desperate moves to gain small incut holds below the thin upper crack. Finish up this with less hassle.

2   Jessicated   20m   E2 6a   (1980)
Just left of the short corner in the centre of the lower wall are twin diagonal cracks. Climb these to the ledge. Pull through the bulge near its right end and ascend the wall and shallow corner to the top.

3   Tigger   25m   VS 5a **   (1979)
A wandering route that finds the easiest line up the wall. Start below the corner in the centre of the wall. Climb this to the midway ledge. Traverse this down left beneath the bulging upper wall to gain a slab on the left side. Delicately ascend this up and left following the junction between the slab and the steep wall to finish up a slim corner.

4   The Disco Duck   20m   E3 6b *   (1980)
A quacking good route with deceptively steep and fingery climbing up the left side of the wall to the right of the corner. Start at a feint vertical crack line just right of the corner. Desperate moves gain the break below the overlap. Step right and pull over in the centre, then go back left onto the left edge. Flap your way up this to the grass ledge above. Go diagonally left through a break in the overhangs to join Jessicated to finish. Belay well back.

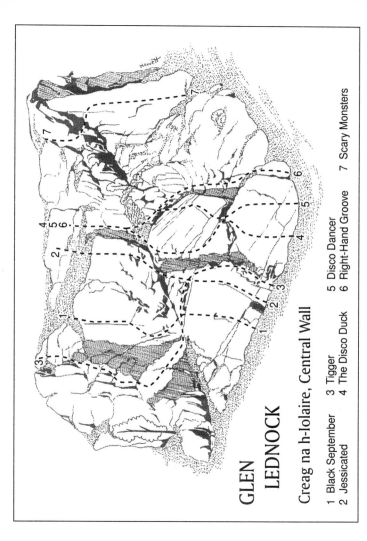

GLEN LEDNOCK

Creag na h-Iolaire, Central Wall

1 Black September   3 Tigger   5 Disco Dancer   7 Scary Monsters
2 Jessicated   4 The Disco Duck   6 Right-Hand Groove

4 Perishing 25m E4 6a (1983)
Follow No Cruise past the bulging section (where Sidewinder crosses), then step right along a ramp. Climb the steep wall above to a flake, then go up and right to a ledge system. Move back left and step up to a roof. Pull round this on the right to reach good holds and tree belay on the left.

5 Pleasure Cruise 15m Severe (1995)
Located on the small wall on the right-hand side of the main wall, this route follows the diagonal crack above the cave.

6 Dying Breed 12m VS 5b (1995)
Climb directly out of the cave and follow a flake to join Pleasure Cruise.

BALNACOUL CASTLE *(Map Ref 735 271)*

Balnacoul Castle is the name given to the craggy hillock on the west side of the glen opposite Creag na h-Iolaire. There are outcrops all over this area but the main ones are located at the lower right-hand side and form Great Buttress and its neighbours. The rock is a form of schist, generally smooth but with excellent crack and corner lines. Great Buttress in particular gives very steep long pitches. Unfortunately it only sees the sun up until mid-afternoon in summer and takes some time to dry out after the winter.

Approaching the crags direct would involve wading across the river. From the parking area for Creag na h-Iolaire it used to be possible to follow the dry stane dyke running to the river. As of 1996 there are new areas of tree planting and new fences and it is no longer possible to access from here. The best approach (preferred by the farmer and one involving dry feet) is to continue up the road towards the dam, go through a gate by the farm houses and to take a left branch of the road (signposted 'private, locked gate') to park just beyond a bridge over the river. Walk back along the west bank of the river to Great Buttress in 15 minutes.

The series of crags making up Balnacoul Castle lie in a diagonal line up and left across the hillside starting with Great Buttress. The climbs and the crags are described from right to left as one approaches.

GREAT BUTTRESS

This brilliant chunk of rock is acutely overhanging throughout its upper half with striking natural lines, the most obvious being the vertical central crack of The Great Crack. The only belay at the top is in the slab of rock well back from the edge. Descent is to the left.

Spare Rib 30m Severe (1972)
Climb the nearly separate rib on the right of the main buttress. There is an awkward start and a spectacular hand traverse at 20m.

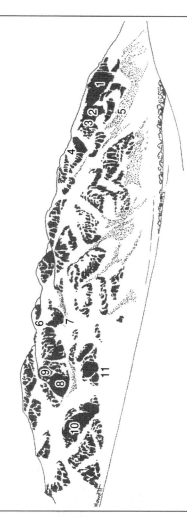

GLEN LEDNOCK
Balnacoul Castle

1 Great Buttress
2 South Buttress
3 Lunar Buttress
4 Superlative Buttress

5 Base Crag
6 Forgotten Crag
7 Hanging Buttress
8 Weeping Wall

9 Diamond Buttress
10 Ballindalloch Crag
11 Lower Buttress

1   Piggies Paradise   40m   E2 5b *   (1979)
A good steep route with an exposed finale. Start by scrambling up the right side of the buttress to belay on a slab below the obvious groove of No place for a Wendy. Climb the initial groove and step up left as for that route. Pull steeply right and climb a flake in the arete leading to a ledge on the right wall with a large block. Continue up flakes and the final overhanging groove.

2   No Place for a Wendy   45m   E3 5c ***   (1978)
A stunning route up the out-there groove in the right arete of the buttress. Start by scrambling up the right side of the buttress to belay on a slab below the obvious groove. Climb the initial groove and step left into the base of the main groove line. Follow this with your feet higher than your hands at times in a stunning position to the top.

3   Wendy's Day Out   45m   E4 6a *   (1985)
An eliminate squeezed up the hanging groove between No Place for a Wendy and The Great Crack. Start below No Place for a Wendy below a short crack.
1. 20m 5a   Climb the crack for 3m, then move left to a sloping ledge. Traverse a couple of moves further left to a corner crack which leads up to beneath the steep upper wall (peg belay).
2. 25m 6a   Climb the impending wall behind the stance and go over a small overhang into a smooth groove (crux). Climb the overhanging groove leftwards to reach The Great Crack and finish up this.

4   The Great Crack   45m   E3 **   (1974/75)
The blatantly obvious wide crack gives a good route, low in the grade.
1. 20m 5b   Climb the corner and crack through the overhang in the lower wall, then continue until moves up and right lead to the peg belay shared with Wendy's Day Out.
2. 25m 5c   Follow the crack to the top.

5   The Chancers   45m   E3 *   (1975)
A bold and technical climb up the deep corner bounding the left side of the main section of the buttress. Start at the foot of a corner to the left of The Great Crack.
1. 30m 5c   Climb the corner for 20m until level with a gangway on the left. Swing right to the foot of a steep thin corner crack which leads to a big ledge in the base of the deep upper corner.
2. 15m 5c   Climb the open book corner to the top of the prow and finish up a steep crack.

6   Les Alpinists Deshabilles   65m   E1   (1980)
A loose, unpleasant and poorly protected climb up the vegetated corners on the left side of the buttress. Start as for The Chancers.
1. 40m 5a   Climb the corner to a perched block on the left. Gain the top of the block and follow a gangway leftwards. Go up a short wall to belay in a corner on a large grassy ledge.
2. 25m 5a   Climb the corners above and follow a left-trending ramp to belay at a tree.

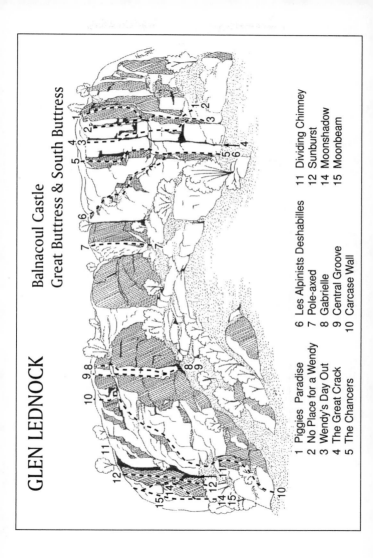

GLEN LEDNOCK

Balnacoul Castle
Great Buttress & South Buttress

1 Piggies Paradise
2 No Place for a Wendy
3 Wendy's Day Out
4 The Great Crack
5 The Chancers
6 Les Alpinists Deshabilles
7 Pole-axed
8 Gabrielle
9 Central Groove
10 Carcase Wall
11 Dividing Chimney
12 Sunburst
14 Moonshadow
15 Moonbeam

There are two short isolated overhanging aretes at a higher level between Great Buttress and South Buttress. The right-hand arete gives one impressive route. It is best to approach the base of the route by abseil.

7   Pole-axed   15m   E4 6a **   (1993)
Climb the strenuous arete starting up a short groove on the left.

SOUTH BUTTRESS

To the left of Great Buttress is a larger but less impressive buttress. The most prominent section is on the upper right side of the buttress where a distinctive overhanging corner splits pink-coloured rock (Central Groove). The buttress extends further down the hillside than Great Buttress but a large rake extends leftwards from the steep broken ground left of Great Buttress into the centre of South Buttress. This gives access to the overhanging corner. The steep chimney on the left of this buttress is Dividing Chimney with Lunar Buttress beyond. The best descent is to walk right and descend between Lunar Buttress and Superlative Buttress.

8   Gabrielle   30m   E4 6a *   (1979)
The right arete of Central Groove is only adequately protected. Start directly below the groove. Climb a smaller corner to a ledge, then step left and climb grooves to a ledge below the main groove. Regain the groove on the right and climb up to a thin diagonal crack. Continue up the arete mostly on the left side, stepping right at the top.

9   Central Groove   30m   E2 5c **   (1992)
Follow Gabrielle to the ledge below the groove, then climb it directly.

10   Carcase Wall   90m   Severe **   (1971)
This route climbs the entire height of the buttress. Start at the lowest rocks.
1. 30m   Climb a crack to two small trees. Transfer to another crack on the left which leads to a niche. Continue over grass to a tree.
2. 40m   Move up to the base of the steep wall and climb strenuously to a flake. Trend right a grass ledge below cracked overhangs.
3. 20m   Move right to reach a slab on the right side of the overhangs. Traverse delicately round the corner on undercuts, then continue to the top.
Direct Finish: VS 4c   (1971)
Climb the overhangs above the belay of pitch two direct. Loose.

LUNAR BUTTRESS

To the right of South Buttress is a large bay extending steeply up the hillside. The upper wall is split by a deep chimney and the left wall extends nearly back down to the path. This constitutes Lunar Buttress. Descend by walking right and going down below Superlative Buttress.

11 Dividing Chimney 25m Severe (1974)
Climb the chimney.

12 Sunburst 30m E2 5b *
Start a few metres right of Moonraker at the foot of a thin crack, which gives a steep but well protected climb.

13 Moonraker 30m VS 4c (1974)
Start beneath the chimney on the right-hand wall of the steep buttress. Traverse the overhanging wall leftwards to the arete (peg runner). Go up this, then traverse left into Moonbeam. Make a couple of moves up the groove, then traverse right into the middle of the face. Climb direct to the large roof above. Bypass this on the left (peg runner) and continue to the top.

14 Moonshadow 40m E1 5b *
Sustained and strenuous climbing up the wall right of Moonbeam. Start as for that route beneath an overhang below the steep buttress left of the chimney. Climb a short steep wall to a ledge, then move right and climb the overhanging wall. At its top traverse right for 5m to the foot of a groove on the wall overlooking the steep chimney (shared with Moonraker). Climb the groove to the overhang above. Move left around this and go up to a large roof. Traverse left and finish as for Moonraker.

15 Moonbeam 35m VS 4c * (1973)
A good steep route with ample protection. Start as for Moonshadow beneath the overhang under the steep buttress. Climb the short steep wall to a ledge, then move right and climb the overhanging wall to a ledge below a groove. Go up the groove to a small overhang. Move awkwardly left and continue direct to top.

16 The Grafter 25m VS 4c * (1974)
Steep and well protected climbing following a wall and corner crack on the clean area of rock at the bottom left end of the buttress. Climb broken rock to a ledge below the corner. Go up the thin crack in the corner, then traverse left until it is possible to head back right to the foot of another corner. Exit from the corner *via* the crack containing an old tree stump.

17 Lunar Groove 35m VS 4c (1974)
Overgrown and messy. Start at a short corner below a slab between The Grafter and Percy Thrower. Climb the corner and the slab to take a prominent left-trending groove. Go up this passing two small trees to an overhanging crack which leads to tree. Climb a slab and a short wall above to finish.

18 Percy Thrower 20m Very Difficult (1973)
Scrappy climbing from the rowan tree at the lowest point of the buttress following a left-trending shallow fault to a slab and finishing up a wide chimney.

SUPERLATIVE BUTTRESS

This is the long buttress which tapers up and rightwards above Lunar Buttress. The crag is characterised by green rock at its left end, a tree-filled corner in the centre and a cave-like recess towards its right end. The climbs are described left to right as one approaches. Descent is best to the left.

Humdinger   25m   E1 5b **   (1974)
An exposed and sensational climb for its grade. Start at the left-hand end of the crag beneath an overhanging arete. Climb a crack just left of the arete, then continue up a groove to a ledge. Pull up the steep wall and step left into the base of a hanging groove (peg runner) which leads to the top.

Little Brahma   25m   VS 4c *   (1974)
Start to the left of the tree-filled corner. Traverse left on a grassy ledge to a short groove. Step left onto a slab and go up the wall trending first left then right to the base of a right-sloping crack. The crack leads to a niche to finish.
Direct Finish: HVS 5a   (1974)
From the base of the crack climb directly up the steep wall to finish at a tree.

Sweat   15m   HVS 4c   (1974)
Climb the tree-filled corner.

Barnstormer   20m   VS 4c *   (1974)
Start on the right side of the buttress at a slab below a large roof. Move up to the roof and traverse left to a sloping ledge below a short corner. Climb this, moving left to finish up a slab.

BASE CRAG

This small crag is hidden amongst trees underneath the main section of South Buttress, almost directly below the start of Carcase Wall.

White Lines   10m   VS 4c   (1996)
Climb the obvious snaking flake crack on the right-hand side of the crag. Continue over a short headwall to a choice of trees for a belay.

HANGING BUTTRESS

Continue walking in the same general line across the hillside to the left of Superlative Buttress and over a rise, then drop into a large grassy bay. Protruding from the centre of this bay is a nondescript wall with a slightly shattered appearance. A conspicuous diagonal crack slices through its right-hand side. Closer inspection reveals the crag's acute steepness and although the routes are reasonably well protected they are all extremely strenuous. A belay exists in a small outcrop well back from the top. The routes are described from right to left. To descend, from the belay take a small descending ramp rightwards into the bounding gully.

Hormone Warrior   20m   E4 6a **   (1996)
The immaculate diagonal crack. Start off the boulder at the foot of the crag and climb past a small bush. Gain the base of the crack and follow it to a juggy exit. Scramble up to a belay.

Pump up the Groove   20m   E5 6a **   (1996)
A line directly up the centre of the wall. Start just left of the boulder at the base of the crag. Climb pockets to gain a quartz niche. Exit from the apex of this and step up and right to gain a shattered crack line leading strenuously to easy ground. Finish up a left-slanting groove.

Huckleberry Thin   20m   E4 5c *   (1996)
This route takes a line up the shattered left side of the wall. Start just left of Pump up the Groove and climb to the base of a brown triangular niche. Climb the wall on its left and pull into a big hold at its top. Continue direct on big holds to finish by pulling out right onto a ledge at the top. Step right and finish up the diagonal groove of Pump up the Groove.

WEEPING WALL

Continue down and left from Hanging Buttress to the boulder field at the base of a large and complex wall. The lowest section gives the wall its name, with a blackened wall being most prominent. Above and right of this is a steeper wall forming a soaring arete (Diamond Buttress). Descent is awkward. Either abseil from the belay tree or scramble above past the left side of Diamond Buttress to the top and descend well to the left down past Hanging Buttress.

Bruised and Battered   12m   E1 5b   (1996)
Climb directly up the black wall to a halfway ledge. Go up and right and gain a hanging groove formed by a suspect flake and block. Finish up this with care. Belay on a tree 15m back.

DIAMOND BUTTRESS

This is the square-cut, overhanging wall that sits directly above and right of Weeping Wall. Its most prominent feature is an impressive overhanging arete. The right-hand side wall is split by a crack. Approach the base of the wall by an unpleasant scramble from the right.

Rough Cut   20m   E4 6a   (1996)
The crack in the right wall is well protected but very strenuous.

The following crags lie at a slightly lower level than the main group. They lie close to Ballindalloch Farm, from where they are most easily reached.

BALLINDALLOCH CRAG   (Map Ref 736 265)

This is the lowest and virtually the most southerly of the outcrops on the hill and not far above Ballindalloch Farm. Approach from the end of the track from the farm, heading up and right from a small steading. The crag is characterised by a large pale section of rock in the centre. On the left-hand side of the crag are two prominent left-facing corners. The routes are described form left to right.

Solutions to a Small Problem   20m   E5 6b ***   (1997)
Start below the superb thin hanging crack in the left hand wall of Jungle Warfare. Climb up under the guarding roof, then pull through at an obvious jug and go up the slight groove to the overlap. Pull right into the base of the crack and climb it with difficulty to the top. Block belay above.

Jungle Warfare   25m   HVS 5a   (1985)
Start below the left-hand corner. From the top of a large boulder climb a short wall to reach a ledge. Move right into the corner, then climb this with increasing difficulty to reach a horizontal break under a roof. Swing right to turn the roof, then traverse back left to finish up a series of short grooves.

Bridget Midget   25m   E1 5b   (1996)
This route climbs the right-hand corner.

Zig and Zag   50m   HVS   (1996)
1. 25m 5a   Climb the bulging wall in the middle of the crag to gain the obvious diagonal ledge that splits this section from right to left.
2. 25m 4c   Traverse the ledge leftwards to near its end and climb the wide crack in the back corner. Belay well up the hillside above.

LOWER BUTTRESS

To the right of Ballindalloch Crag and at the same level is a two-tiered buttress. The upper tier lies slightly up to the right of the larger lower tier.

Drunk and in Charge   10m   E1 5c   (1996)
Climb the main hanging crack in the centre of the wall of the upper tier.

The following routes are on the lower tier and are described from right to left.

Feet Don't Fail me Now   25m   E1 5a   (1996)
Gain the overlap that lies behind the tree at the base of the crag by a mossy gully on the right. Traverse under the lip of the overlap, pull over on big holds

and climb boldly to reach the crack line in the wall above. Head right at the top to belay on stakes.

No Digidy   25m   E2 5b   (1997)
Start left of the smaller tree at the base of the crag, just right of a groove. Climb diagonally up and right into the centre of the wall. Pull over the overlap and move left to climb a shallow groove immediately right of the larger one taken by Optical Illusion. As it steepens make hard moves up and right to finish in a hanging crack in the steeper central prow.

Optical Illusion   25m   E2 5b   (1996)
Climb a groove on the left of the buttress to the overlap. Cross this as soon as possible and climb the groove on the left.

THE HIDEAWAY CRAG   *(Map Ref 723 287)*

This innocuous-looking crag lurks on the hillside level with but to the west of the dam at the head of the Glen. Park as for the dry walk option to Balnacoul Castle, just over the bridge. Walk along the tarmac road, through the locked gate and continue until the road crosses the river. The crag lies directly above on the right. The crag's most impressive feature is its very overhanging lower right-hand wall. This is bounded on the left by a steep groove, followed by a slim buttress split at half-height by a roof. The wall below the roof is vegetated and a large tree grows at its left-hand base. The routes are described from left to right. The descent is well over to the right.

Goldie   20m   E2 5c *   (1996)
This route is on the slim buttress on the left. Start below the more scrappy buttress to the left again, just left of the large tree. Climb up a bulging wall into a hanging groove which leads rightwards into the vegetated fault that forms the left side of the slim buttress. Cross this and traverse out right across the lip of the roof and pull onto the slab above. Continue more easily to finish.

International Colouring-in Contest   20m   E4 6a *   (1996)
A line up the left edge of the overhanging wall. Start right of the fault which divides the two main buttresses, below a hanging flake. Move up to the flake and wildly gain good holds above it. Swing onto the wall above and follow the cracks in the slab to the bulging headwall. Exit left.

Hide and Sneak   20m   E5 6a **   (1996)
The left-slanting weakness through the centre of the overhanging wall gives another good, hard climb. Follow the fault diagonally left to gain a large protruding hold at the lip. Pull into a groove above on the left and so to the left side of the upper roof. Pull up and right into a hanging niche above the roof and exit left onto a large flake which is quitted to finish round rightwards of a huge block at the top.

GLEN OGLE

The many buttresses either side of the glen must have been considered as worth a look by decades of climbers passing north to Glen Coe and Ben Nevis, but it wasn't until the 1990s that curiosity got the better of two different groups. One explored the crags on the east (sunny) side above the road, recording routes on the one closest to the road, whilst the other group began hunting for sports venues amongst the numerous walls scattered above the old railway track on the west (dark) side. A change was as good as a rest, and development of sports climbs later spread to the east side too. After just two years of development, Glen Ogle now has the largest concentration of sports climbs of any one area in Scotland.

There will doubtless be those who will be amazed at 'Scotland's Premier Sport Climbing Venue' — amazed at the tiny stature of the cliffs! However, what they lack in height they make up for in steepness and, more to the point, the deviousness of the climbing; what at first sight would appear to be trivial can give a sharp blow to the arms and ego. For those who come and shake their head in disbelief, then they can take a hike over the hill to Creag Mac Ranaich — steep and high, or concentrate on the fine crag of Creag Nan Cuileann.

AMENITIES

The mobile café in the carpark at the head of the glen offers excellent sustenance for the weary and dilapidated who have reached the point where they cannot lift their arms above their heads or drive very far. Otherwise Lochernhead itself has a good basic café, an excellent pub and a more expensive loch-side restaurant.

BIRD NESTING INFORMATION

The glen is inhabited by numerous species of birds during the nesting period. Their nesting success is monitored by a local group of volunteers. There have been thefts of eggs and young in the past. Climbers should make every effort not to disturb any such birds by climbing close to the nests and it is recommended that you contact the Mountaineering Council of Scotland for up to date information about any restrictions. It is important to respect this voluntary arrangement of possible restrictions in order to ensure continued access for climbing.

THE EAST SIDE (THE SUNNY SIDE)

The two crags with traditionally protected climbs are described first, starting at the top of the glen.

BEINN LEABHAINN   (Map Ref 567 282)

This crag lies directly below the TV Mast at the head of the glen. It is reached from the layby at the summit of the pass where a forest track leads off

GLEN OGLE
The Sunny Side

Parking Layby

Parking Layby

1 Roadside Wall
2 The Asteroid
3 The Gap
4 Overlord Buttress

5 Bournville
6 Creag nan Cuileann
7 The Terraces
8 The Gallery

rightwards and up the hill to the mast. The left-hand side of the crag, as seen from the carpark, is a blocky buttress, the right constitutes a wide slab. One route exists so far on the slab.

Ex Officio   30m   HVS 5a   (1990)
Climb the centre of the slab with a strenuous finish.

CREAG NAN CUILEANN   (Map Ref 568 273)

This south-west facing crag is the closest to the road on The Sunny Side, on the lowest southern slopes of Meall Buidhe near the top of the glen. Its true size is hidden from view and its stature only becomes apparent on reaching its base. The routes are on excellent clean schist. Parking for two cars is possible on the side of the road on a small gravel layby slightly beyond the crag near the head of the glen. From here it is best to follow the small stream on the left of the crag and to contour right to it; 15 minutes.

The wall is undercut along its length with a holly bush sitting under the centre of the roof. Just right of centre a vertical shallow groove splits the crag whose base is guarded by roofs. A dead tree sits at its base. The climbs are described from left to right. The routes finish on a big ledge. Exit this with caution to the left, then descend either side of the crag.

Merlyn's Flight   30m   E3 6a *   (1992)
This route takes the obvious break through the roof at the left side. Start just right of the short hanging corner formed by a block under the roof. Climb into the corner under the roof. Exit out left on a horizontal crack and just before its end climb the crack above onto the slab. Take a more or less direct line to the top.

The Bigger they Fall   30m   E5 6c **   (1992)
The thin crack through the roof right of the holly bush and left of Pruner's Groove. Gain the crack direct and struggle up it onto the slab. Move up left to a small isolated overlap. Pull over direct and boldly continue to a quartz niche and a pocketed wall which leads to the top.

The Harder they Come   30m   E4 5c **   (1991)
A bold route up the centre of the highest section left of The Bigger they Fall, starting right of that route. Start directly behind a dead tree just left of the roofs of Pruner's Groove. Gain a thin crack above the roof which leads to a small holly bush in Pruner's Groove. Pass the tree, then traverse hard left on an obvious line to the remains of a sapling in the centre of the wall. Climb the thin crack above with difficulty to gain a deep horizontal slot on the left. Stand in this, then continue direct with a final exit out left.

Pruner's Groove   30m   E1 5c *   (1991)
The central fault on the crag. From just right of the dead tree at the base, climb up and right through the roof with difficulty to gain a small ledge with a holly tree below the groove itself. Follow the groove with interest.

Mind Bogle   30m   E5 6a *   (1991)
The line between Pruner's Groove and Poison Ivy, although escapable into the former at half-height, provides strenuous and serious climbing. Start under the stepped roofs right of Pruner's Groove. Climb the initial wall to beneath the roofs. Pull out left through the arete of the lower roof to gain the base of a prominent white break that leads left. Go up to join Poison Ivy at the crack, then step hard left into the break and follow it with difficulty to pull onto the wall just right of Pruner's Groove. Continue direct about 3m right of Pruner's Groove through the bulges near the top. Friends are essential.

Poison Ivy   30m   E3 5c **   (1991)
The prominent crack line splitting the wall right of Pruner's Groove. Start below the roofs below the crack just right of Mind Bogle. Ascend into the roofs and go out left to the base of the crack. Climb it to a small shelf near the top and exit right onto the grass ledge.

THE SPORT CRAGS

These lie scattered on the outcrops of Creag na h-Oisinn and Meall Buidhe. They were overlooked at first in the general search for steepness, but the many buttresses on The Sunny Side of the Glen came under scrutiny in 1994. The rock turned out to be far better than across the road, but usually nowhere near as steep. Other plus points (!) are the quick-drying rock, the remote feel of the climbing, the breeze (midges!) and most importantly it gets the sun! In fact it gets lots of sun. The crags are described with The Warm-up first (isolated and nearest to Lochearnhead), then the others in order when approaching from Roadside Wall. Refer to the layout diagram on page 331 for a clearer picture.

THE WARM-UP   (Map Ref 582 261)

Park in the lowest pull-out on the south of the glen, beyond Glen Ogle Farm House. Walk up the hill to the crag. The routes are described from left to right.

Ultraviolet   10m   6b+ *   (1994)
Climb the bulging wall, then trend right to a shared lower-off.

Outshined   10m   6a+ *   (1994)
The groove just to the right.

Burnt Offerings   10m   6b+ **   (1994)
The line of bolts to the right of the previous route is a project. This route follows the diagonal crack to near its end, then goes direct to a lower-off.

Face the Heat   10m   7a **   (1994)
Climb directly up the wall on small pockets. A pretty crimpy route.

Infrarete   10m   6b+ *   (1994)
The arete, of course!

Under the Same Sun   10m   6b+   (1994)
Starting from the rock scar, make thin moves up the slab.

Burn Baby, Burn   10m   6a+   (1994)
Climb the hanging groove to the slab, then tackle the overhang above.

Burn it up   10m   6b+   (1994)
An eliminate up the wall just right. Find the one-finger pocket and crank.

ROADSIDE WALL   (Map Ref 577 266)

This has the easiest walk to any of the Ogle crags! Head up the hill from the
Viaduct parking space towards the nearest pylon. Aim for a large boulder, then
go up to the crag. Only two lines have been climbed so far, but there is space for
more.

Don't Fight the Feeling   10m   6b *   (1994)
Climb the barrel-shaped wall in the centre of the crag.

   The hanging slab on the right side of the crag is a project.

Hold the Press   10m   7a *   (1995)
Boulder up to beneath the small roof, pull over and climb the right edge of the
slab.

THE ASTEROID   (Map Ref 578 265)

This is the black slab easily seen from the road lying above and right of
Roadside Wall. Slog up the hill from the Viaduct parking space to reach the slab.
There are 4 routes on the slab giving pleasant climbing at about 5+ and 6a, but
they are not very well equipped.

THE GAP

Right of The Asteroid is this small clean wall hidden in a recess.

Beggars Banquet   10m   6b+ *   (1994)
The left-hand line. Climb to the quartz, pull through the overhang and continue
up the wall.

Chimera   10m   6b+ **   (1994)
From the quartz, go right then move up to the ledge. Precariously bridge up the
shallow groove to the lower-off.

OVERLORD BUTTRESS

From The Asteroid, contour left (up the glen) and slightly up. This is the steepest
crag found so far on the east side of the glen and a superb place to climb, being

unbelievably tranquil and a fine place to spy on the antics of the fools across the glen climbing in the shade! The routes are described from left to right.

Restless Souls   10m   7a **   (1995)
The left side of the buttress looks easy, but it is very steep! A long reach helps.

A project follows Restless Souls to the second bolt, then goes right and up.

Overlord   12m   7b *   (1994)
Very steep and powerful climbing! Finish right to the Overkill lower-off.

Overkill   10m   7a+ **   (1994)
The right side of the wall has generally good holds — if you can find them!

Over the Top   10m   6b+ *   (1994)
Good, varied climbing, from very steep to slabby, with the crux somewhere between the two.

Pullover   10m   6b+   (1996)
Climb left of the first two bolts, or right (slightly harder), and pull over awkwardly onto the slab. Move left beneath a heathery ledge to the lower-off of the previous route.

BOURNVILLE   *(Map Ref 570 273)*

From Overlord, drop down the hill a bit, then continue up the glen for a minute or two. An excellent wee crag, giving fingery, pockety, vertical climbing. The much larger crag to the left of this wall is Creag nan Cuileann which is described earlier and contains the gear routes. The routes are described from right to left.

Voodoo Ray   8m   6b   (1994)
Start just right of the small niche. Climb the pocketed wall until forced to use the arete. It is 7a without the arete.

The Greenhouse Defect   8m   6b **   (1994)
Start just left of the cave. Nice moves on pockets and edges, with one thin move near the top.

Sorry Tess   8m   6b   (1994)
There are a couple of thin moves between the first and second bolts, then much more user-friendly holds.

Hot Chocolate   8m   6b **   (1994)
The wall between the brown and white streaks has thin moves on perfect rock.

Sudden Alchemy   8m   6b *   (1994)
Take the line up the highest bit of the crag.

Fingers of Fudge 8m 6b+ (1994)
This route lies further left again.

Chocaholics 8m 6a+ (1994)
Take a line up to and through the small overlap on the left end of the crag.

Half Covered 8m 6b * (1994)
The leftmost line is unfortunately split by a ledge.

THE TERRACES

These are slightly lower than The Gap and about 100 metres to the right. There is lots of potential for short routes.

Unnamed 8m 6b+ (1994)
Climb the obvious short steep arete on its left side.

THE GALLERY

This gently overhanging pocketed wall is situated above The Terraces and is gained *via* a path up the slope to the right. From left to right, the routes are **Mona Sleeza** (6a+ * 1994), **Modern Tart** (6b+ * 1994) and **Art Attack** (7a+ * 1994 — the pocketed wall to the right).

THE WEST SIDE (THE DARK SIDE)

The routes lie on the multitude of crags of Sgorrach Nuadh and on the slopes of Meall Reamhar. With the exception of the Project Crag and Bond Buttress which are long and steep, the routes here are short and steep. In general the crags only get the sun in the early morning so make the effort for 'Alpine' starts. They are also a playground for midges and when there is no wind, be prepared for the worst and invest in a midge head protector or some running shoes. The routes take some time to dry out — a useful indicator that all is well is the appearance of a white streak left of centre on The Diamond.

Some routes here have the first bolt a bit too high for comfort and have been climbed as stick-clip starts. These should be fairly obvious, except to impetuous youths.

TOPOGRAPHY

Most of these crags are situated above the viaduct halfway up the glen. The Project Crag is separate from the others and can be found above the huge jumble of fallen boulders that stretches down the hillside from the far southern section of cliff, closest to Lochearnhead.

GLEN OGLE

The Dark Side

The Viaduct Crags

1 The Diamond
2 Buzzard Wall
3 The Rave
4 The Galleon
5 The Underworld

6 The Cascade
7 Far Beyond
8 Down Under
9 Bond Buttress
10 Concave Wall

THE PROJECT CRAG

This is characterised by a huge roof and sitting above a massive boulder field at the furthest southerly end of the cliff line on the west side. It is most easily approached from a large parking area on the east side of the road opposite the crag (as for The Warm-Up – see Glen Ogle East). Cross the road and follow a track that crosses the Ogle Burn and twists up to the old railway line. From here slog up the hill to the left of the boulder field beneath the crag. Seriously, it is nowhere near as bad as it looks or sounds! There is much potential here in the harder grades. There are 4 lines that have been equipped for a number of years now but none have been climbed.

THE VIADUCT CRAGS   (Map Ref 569 265)

These are the lowest crags above the viaduct. Approach from a layby opposite the viaduct (which is the one lower than that for Creag Nan Cuillean). There is space for about 4 cars. Face your car downhill to make life a lot easier when you want to rejoin the road. An obvious path leads down to a wooden bridge over the Ogle Burn, then go up to the viaduct. From here cross the fence and follow the path up and right to join the crags at the most impressive section (The Diamond) at the left-hand side. The crags continue rightwards as two tiers, the lower being smaller, and both terminate just after a waterfall.

THE DIAMOND

The largest of the crags at this level. It is almost worked out and offers some of the hardest routes in the glen. The routes are described from left to right.

1   Midge Patrol   12m   6b *   (1993)
A fun wee route, steeper than it looks, and a good warm-up for the harder stuff.

2   Project
A boulder problem up the black wall.

3   Project
Another boulder problem wall.

4   Easy Over   12m   7a *   (1993)
Climb a steep pocketed wall to a roof, and go over this on jugs (thank God!). Move left and go up a slab to the lower-off.

5   Digital Quartz   15m   8b   (1994)
Use the quartz boss to climb the wall (crux) to the traverse of Children of the Revolution. Move up and right, then climb direct up to a lower-off.

6   Project
This will climb up the wall to join the second bolt of Children of the Revolution, then finish direct up the wall.

GLEN OGLE

The Viaduct Crags, The Diamond

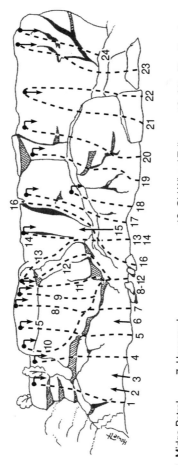

1 Midge Patrol
2 Project
3 Project
4 Easy Over
5 Digital Quartz
6 Project

7 Unnamed
8 Spiral Tribe
9 Off the Beaten Track
10 Children of the Revolution
11 Chain Lightning
12 One in the Eye for Stickmen

13 Old Wives' Tail
14 Metal Guru
15 Project
16 Sugar and Spice
17 Gross Indecency
18 Trossach Trundler

19 After The Flood
20 Arc of a Diver
21 Climb and Punishment
22 Wristy Business
23 Raspberry Beret
24 Ship Ahoy

7   Unnamed   15m   7c+ **   (1994)
Climb the previous project route to the horizontal, then finish up Digital Quartz.

8   Spiral Tribe   15m   8a+ ***   (1993)
Climb straight up from the first bolt of Children of the Revolution.

9   Off the Beaten Track   15m   8a ***   (1993)
Fine technical moves up the wall just left of the arete.

10   Children of the Revolution   18m   7b **   (1992)
Start under the right arete and head diagonally left almost to the cave. From just
right of the cave climb straight up to a lower-off.

11   Chain Lightning   15m   7b+ ***   (1993)
Groovy moves up the right arete. It is usual to clip the second bolt from the first,
then step down to prevent a knee-capping !

12   One in the Eye for Stickmen   15m   7a *   (1993)
A line of resin bolts right of the Chain Lightening, powering through the roofs.

13   Old Wives' Tail   15m   6b *   (1993)
Start up Metal Guru to the second bolt, then take the left-trending ramp.

14   Metal Guru   15m   6c **   (1992)
The thin crack up the vertical wall right of the main face often spits out weaklings
at the top!

15   Project
The wall between the two cracks.

16   Sugar and Spice   15m   E3 6a   (1992)
The obvious wide crack just left of Gross Indecency is the only established gear
route on this side of the glen.

17   Gross Indecency   15m   7c   (1993)
Hard moves from the flake lead to the ledge. From here take the wall just right of
the wide crack to an interesting finish.

18   Trossach Trundler   10m   7b+   (1993)
Bouldery moves up the line of the resin bolts to the ledge. Tough!

19   After the Flood   12m   6c *   (1993)
Another line of resin bolts. The third bolt can be hard to clip, and the lower-off
too if you are short.

20   Arc of a Diver   12m   6c **   (1993)
A steep start to the ledge with the crux on the headwall.

21   Climb and Punishment   12m   7b+   (1994)
A bouldery start leads to the ledge, from here turn up the power.

22   Wristy Business   10m   6c+ *   (1993)
Climb the cleaned groove to the ledge, then the deceptive wall above.

23   Raspberry Beret   10m   6b+ *   (1993)
The nicely featured wall, starting from ledge.

24   Ship Ahoy   8m   6b   (1993)
The wall right again is a bit scrappy and a bit of a scrap.

BUZZARD WALL

About 50 metres to the right and slightly higher is a small buttress. In recent years buzzards have taken residence in the cave to the right of the two routes here. Please avoid disturbing them during the nesting season.

Cut Loose   8m   7a+   (1993)
The central line takes the widest section of the roof using the flake.

Hang Free   8m   7a+   (1994)
The line to the right through the V-shaped roof.

THE RAVE

This is the steep wall that lies above Buzzard Wall.

The Edge of Ecstasy   8m   6c *   (1994)
Climb the left side of the arete, taking the slab.

Rush   8m   7a **   (1994)
The right side of the arete, following the crack for part of the way.

Raving Lunatics   8m   7b *   (1995)
A powerful sequence to the right again.

Recreational Chemistry   8m   6c+   (1995)
A short and thuggy route to the joint lower-off with Raving Lunatics.

THE GALLEON

Back down at the main level, and 10 metres to the right, you're at the continuation of cliffs from the Diamond. Don't let the lack of height put you off as the routes pack a lot in.

1   Weigh Anchor   8m   6b+   (1994)
The wall left of the corner with the crux through the roof.

2   Frigging in the Rigging   8m   6c *   (1994)
Easy climbing up to the roof, then a horrible thrutch.

3   Slave to the Rhythm   8m   7a+ **   (1993)
Start right of the corner. Go up through the bulging wall on ever worsening holds to the lower-off.

4   Rum Ration   8m   7a+ *   (1993)
Climb to the roof left of the groove, then go right into the groove. Climb up and back left to the lower-off.

5   Blithe Spirit   8m   7a ***   (1993)
The right-hand side of the groove gives a brilliant route.

6   Get a Grip   8m   7b *   (1993)
The line right again is fingery towards the top.

7   Eat Y'self Fitter   8m   6c **   (1993)
The line of jugs to a big staple bolt lower-off.

8   Infinite Gravity   8m   7a+   (1994)
Bouldery to start, with sharp holds.

9   Fight Fire with Fire   8m   7c **   (1993)
Powerful and crimpy, and that's just to get off the ground. If you manage the first few moves, persevere – it does get slightly easier.

10   Waiting for a Train   8m   6c *   (1993)
Steep and short with good holds, following a left-slanting crack.

11   The Pack Horse   8m   6c ***   (1993)
The pocketed wall right again is juggy and thuggy!

12   Horrid   8m   6c   (1993)
The scoop at the right end of the wall is fingery and ...?

Further along, just before the gully separating this wall from The Cascade sector, the crag gains height again to give two wimpy slab routes (after steep starts).

13   Don't Pass Me By   10m   6a+   (1994)
At last, a chance to rest your arms!

14   The Guilt Trip   10m   6c **   (1993)
The bulging wall guarding the slab only succumbs to crimping with reckless abandon!

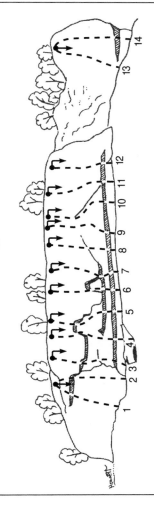

GLEN OGLE

The Viaduct Crags, The Galleon

1 Weigh Anchor
2 Frigging in the Rigging
3 Slave to the Rhythm
4 Rum Ration
5 Blithe Spirit

6 Get a Grip
7 Eat Y'self Fitter
8 Infinite Gravity
9 Fight Fire with Fire
10 Waiting for a Train

11 The Pack Horse
12 Horrid
13 Don't Pass Me By
14 The Guilt Trap

THE UNDERWORLD

This crag is down below The Galleon and offers the ultimate in micro-routes which are best described as bolted bouldering!

Carsonagenic 6m 6a   (1994)
Climb the left-hand line, starting direct to avoid the choss on the left.

The next line of bolts is a project, very eliminate but with very thin moves.

Hanging out the Smalls 6m 7a **   (1994)
Superb thin climbing, over all too soon.

Under Where? 6m 6b   (1994)
Quite juggy but, typical mica schist, hard to read.

XX 6m 6c   (1994)
A quick pull past some flakey rock leads to a thin move or two.

Satan's Slaves 6m 6a   (1994)
Here again poor rock beneath the real stuff slightly mars a fine route.

Maniaxe 6m 6b   (1993)
The right-hand bolt line has a boulder problem start direct to the first bolt.

Under Mind 6m 6b+   (1994)
Start from the cave to the right pull to a large protruding hold, then go up to even better holds.

THE CASCADE

This steep crag lies back up at the main level and 20 metres to the right of The Galleon.

1   Hive of Industry 6m 7a+ **   (1993)
The left arete of the wall is ridiculously short and ludicrously steep.

2   Gotta Sin to Be Saved 8m 7b *   (1993)
Climb direct to the lower-off of Paradise Road.

3   Paradise Road 9m 6c **   (1993)
Follow the obvious left-slanting line. Don't mess up the third clip!

4   Short Sharp Shocked 10m 6a+ ***   (1993)
The left edge of wide diagonal crack gives a fine pump-out for the grade. Aptly named.

5   The Age Old Problem Rears its Ugly Head 10m 7a   (1994)
Float up the hard moves through the overhang and headwall.

GLEN OGLE

The Viaduct Crags, The Cascade

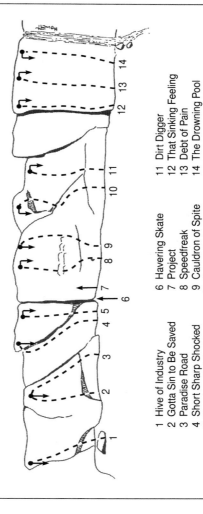

1 Hive of Industry
2 Gotta Sin to Be Saved
3 Paradise Road
4 Short Sharp Shocked
5 The Age Old Problem
6 Havering Skate
7 Project
8 Speedfreak
9 Cauldron of Spite
10 Stone Junky
11 Dirt Digger
12 That Sinking Feeling
13 Debt of Pain
14 The Drowning Pool

6   Havering Skate   10m   6b+ *   (1994)
The groove-arete-crack thing.

7   Project
This looks hard, but the final product will be marred by the gluing up of a hold.

Unfortunately the next two routes take longer than the rest to dry out, but they are well worth seeking out when they are in nick.

8   Speedfreak   10m   7b *   (1993)
From the big pocket gain the one finger pocket. Use this to gain good edges and so to the lower-off.

9   Cauldron of Spite   10m   6c *   (1994)
Start just right of Speedfreak. From the pocket of that route, head up and right to the horizontal, then fire for the quartz boss. Easier ground leads to Speedfreak's lower-off.

10   Stone Junky   10m   6c   (1993)
Follow the diagonal crack to two-thirds height, step right and go up the wall above direct.

11   Dirt Digger   10m   6b+   (1993)
The line right again is surprisingly good.

The wall to the right has a waterfall flowing over it for much of the year which may or may not affect the following four routes. If they are dry, do them!

12   That Sinking Feeling   10m   7a   (1994)
The left arete.

13   Debt of Pain   10m   7b *   (1994)
Right of the arete.

14   The Drowning Pool   10m   7b *   (1993)
Start just left of the waterfall, or in it depending on the weather. Slap for the (very rusty!) chain unless you fancy the alternative.

FAR BEYOND

Continuing along past the waterfall is a short wall with a roof. The right end of this roof forms a steep groove.

Submersion   6m   7a+   (1995)
Just right of the fall and similar to the route on its left.

The next four lines are abandoned projects.

Far Beyond Driven   6m   6b+ **   (1994)
Climb the steep wall using various contortions.

Driven to Distraction   6m   6b+ *   (1994)
Start right of the arete. Climb to the left end of the large block, then go up and left.

HyperHyper   6m   6b   (1994)
Climb to the right end of the block, then follow the crack to the lower-off.

DOWN UNDER

Below the Cascade lies a further wall.

The Bends   8m   7a+ **   (1993)
The centre of the leaning wall features a peculiar square hold.

The next line of bolts is a project.

Nitrogen   8m   6b+   (1994)
Climb direct to the second roof, then go left and up to the lower-off.

BOND BUTTRESS

An impressive buttress with only one route so far. At 25m high, it is twice (or more!) the height of most of the other Ogle crags. From The Diamond hike up the hillside to the left until you find a big buttress with an obvious bolted groove. The big arete leading to the groove is a bolted project.

Scaramanga   20m   7a+ ***   (1993)
The groove on the right side of the crag gives a classic outing.

CONCAVE WALL

Well right of The Waterfall Wall and further up the hillside near the northern end of the line of cliffs is yet another obvious steep wall. It is slightly disappointing in that the wave of rock on the left isn't as big as it looks from the road. There is one project up the spectacular arete.

GLEN KENDRUM

There are two short rivers that drain into the head of Loch Earn, one the Ogle Burn, the other the Kendrum Burn, just to the west. The following crags are at the head of this latter stream.

CREAG MAC RANAICH   *(Map Ref 549 250)*

A number of south-east facing mica-schist crags lie just under the summit of Creag Mac Ranaich on the eastern and southern slopes of the hill at the head of Glen Kendrum. They range from 15m to 45m in height . The rock is a softer version of the other schist crags in the area, but it is studded with garnets (rather like the Sierra Nevada in Spain). There is abundant lichen and some loose flakes and the crag is high up, but it has so far offered two very hard adventurous climbs and has potential for much more. The most impressive crag lies high on the southern end of the east face and the other developed cliff, The Pyramid, lies 200 metres to the north at the same level.

   The easiest approach is from the head of Glen Ogle. Park in a layby next to the plantation on the west side of the road just south of the head of the glen. Walk back along the road to gain a slight path which crosses the old railway line and picks up an ATV track that follows the line of a burn in a shallow valley up the hillside leading to a col. The crag can be seen across the corrie on the right. Contour round and ascend steeply to the base. Alternatively, it is possible to approach from the south along a track up Glen Kendrum which, although less taxing, is longer with extra height gained. One also has to park and approach through the farm, so please respect their privacy.

BIRD NESTING INFORMATION
The glen is inhabited by Schedule One species of birds. Their nesting success is monitored by a local group of volunteers and the landowner. Climbers should make every effort not to disturb any such birds by venturing close to the nests during the nesting period of February to the end of July. It is recommended that you contact the Mountaineering Council of Scotland for up to date information about any restrictions. It is important to respect this voluntary arrangement of possible restrictions in order to ensure continued access for climbing.

THE MAIN CRAG

This is characterised by a large central vegetated corner (unclimbed) with an overhanging left wall split by an impressive crack line. The right wall is less steep but bounds a colossal overhanging prow.

Toiler on the Sea   50m   E6 **   (1995)
This route ascends the disjointed but impressive 1 in 3 overhanging crack line up the three-tiered wall right of the vegetated corner. Start 5 metres left of the corner.

1. 10m 6b   Climb to a pod in the diagonal crack. Follow this leftwards to a niche and pull onto the grass ledge with difficulty. Bold and technical.
2. 20m 6b   Climb the crack above into a niche (rest) and make a hard mantelshelf straight above to finish.
3. 20m 6b   Climb the groove above to a spike and rest, then a crack and a strenuous groove (Friend 4 essential) lead to good holds. Finish direct through the bulges above (some hollow rock) to finish on a heather ledge. Peg belay 15m back.

Sidewinder   65m   E6 **   (1994)
This route climbs the left wall of the impressive prow and although very bold it is never too hard. Start on blocks just right of the arete.
1. 50m 6a   Step off a boulder and follow jugs up the arete to a belly flop onto a ledge. Gain the ledge above, ascend the groove (peg runner) and swing left around the arete to a flake shield. Climb straight up (crux) past a scarred flake to protection in a smaller flake above. Continue up, then traverse right under an overlap and make a hard move to gain a standing position above the steepening. Move left along the lip of the overlap to place a runner, return right and finish direct. Poor belay.
2. 15m 4c   Continue up the middle of the small wall above to reach a belay at the back of the heather ledge.

Complicity   30m   E5 6a *   (1996)
This route climbs the wall just left of Sidewinder. Start at the toe of the slab and climb a small right-facing corner to gain a flake above (peg runner). Move up to a thin crack and follow this to a sloping ledge. Climb flakes on the left, then move back into the centre of the wall to finish up a short diagonal crack.

THE PYRAMID

A deceptively steep and compact crag with an obvious central corner.

Charge!   20m   E4 6b *   (1995)
The book-shaped corner. Gain a flake line from the right and climb to its top. Climb the corner with difficulty to pockets, then better holds lead left round a bulge to easy ground left of the arete. Spike belay 20m back.

STRATHYRE

There are numerous small crags along the length of Strathyre. The ones detailed here lie in the upper part of the strath in the area known as The Braes of Balquhidder, the resting place of the notorious highland hero (or brigand depending on your allegiances), Rob Roy. The large crag at the head of Kirkton Glen above Balquhidder village (Leum an Eireannaich) is detailed in the SMC Lowland Outcrops Guide. It is not described here but what are described are the more recently developed crags, both gear and sport types, which can be easily combined with a visit to Glen Ogle.

Despite the acres of sitka plantations the strath is very picturesque, especially in its upper reaches around Loch Voil. It is a great place to mellow out, with an excellent hotel near the head of the strath that does great cream teas (in Scotland!). The Kingshouse Hotel and its Rambler's Bar are at the east end on the main road. There is also a cafe in the Stronvar Castle and another great cafe in Strathyre village itself (as well as a good ale house).

Strathyre village has a good caravan and camping site on its southern outskirts, otherwise accommodation is available from B&Bs, hotels and discrete wild camping.

The following crags are concentrated around the Braes of Balquhidder area.

CREAG NAN SPEIREAG *(Map Ref 491 211)*

This hill lies near the west end of Loch Voil. It contains several small buttresses scattered all over its southern flanks. The crags that have been developed lie just above the tree line only a short walk from the road.

CRAIGRUIE *(Map Ref 499 203)*

The climbing is on one of the lower south-facing buttresses just above the farm of the same name. The crag is composed of rather soft and smooth mica-schist, and therefore was developed as a sport crag. There are at present only two routes, but there is scope for more. The crag presents a flat wall, steep at the left side and less so on the right.

Take the Balquhidder turn off from the A84 at the Kingshouse Hotel. Follow the road past Balquhidder and Rob Roy's Grave until crags appear on the right above the farm of Craigruie. From a gate near the entrance to the farm head up across the field and into open pasture heading left to the crag.

An Dialtaig   15m   7b+   (1992)
This is the only route on the steep left side of the wall. Climb carefully to the rather high first bolt and finish powerfully through the bulge.

There is an abandoned project directly up the centre of the less steep section, but it is surprisingly blank.

Dirty Deeds   10m   6a+   (1993)
Done on the cheap, this is the line up the right side of the wall.

BLEATER'S WALL *(Map Ref 483 202)*

Situated further along the flank of Creag nan Speireag above the charming house of Rhuveag, this is the lowest south-facing wall — almost worth ignoring until encountered close up. It offers short but very fingery and intricate climbing on good rock, protected by RPs and Tricams (two 0.5s essential). The wall gains height from the left to form a prow on the right. Two distinctive cracks, one vertical and the other diagonal, meet in an inverted V. To the left of the large diagonal crack is a smaller diagonal flake crack. The routes are described from right to left.

There is limited parking on the side of the road about 200 metres beyond Rhuveag, just as the road drops back down to the loch side. Head up through the trees and go leftwards, crossing a small stream to gain the base of the lowest crag.

The Blind Buddha of Balquhidder   20m   E4 6a   (1993)
Climb the blank-looking wall between the right arete and the vertical crack. The lower wall is unprotected with the crux getting established on the slab above.

The Old Boy Network   20m   E1 5c *   (1993)
Climb the right-hand vertical crack to a junction with the diagonal crack at the small sapling, then wander up easy ground to the top.

Flapping Around   20m   E2 5c *   (1993)
Take the left-hand diagonal crack to just above where it joins The Old Boy Network, then climb the bulge on the left *via* a short flake and go up left onto the upper wall. Finish direct.

Bleating Heart   20m   E5 6a **   (1993)
A good route up the centre of the highest section of the wall. Start just left of the base of the diagonal crack. Climb up to the right end of the fainter diagonal flake crack. Pull over the bulge above leftwards and climb up and right to a big quartz blotch. Hard moves gain better holds above in a slight ramp which leads out left onto the slab above. Follow the slab up right and pull over the bulge to the top.

Scruff   15m   E4 6a **   (1993)
This route wends a thin and intricate line left of Bleating Heart with slightly better protection. Start 3 metres right of the base of the large diagonal crack. Climb direct through the centre of the smaller flake crack above, moving right above it to good quartz pockets. Go up and left through the bulging nose and back right above it to gain holds in the final scoop (small Rock in a finger pocket in the scoop). Finish above on good quartz jugs to gain the slab. Belay in the crack at the back of the slab.

Guissers and Ghouls   10m   E3 5c **   (1993)
A direct line left of Scruff, between the central and right-hand moss streaks. Start from the obvious small flat boulder at the base of the crag. Climb directly up the wall to a horizontal slot. Move up and slightly right *via* quartz holds to a small flake and good Tricam above. Continue direct with thin moves to finish onto the slab.

Skin-up   10m   E1 5c *   (1993)
Climb a line up the clean area between the central and the left-hand moss streak with thin moves to start and good protection once found.

Wondr'ing Aloud   8m   VS 5a   (1994)
Climb a small flake at the left end with hard moves to pull over onto the slab.

THE BIGG WALL   (Map Ref 483 202)

This is the largest-looking crag on this section of outcrops, lying just 100m above and right of Bleater's Wall. It is generally slabbier than the other crag and offers two middle grade climbs.

Escape from Drudgery   25m   HVS 5a   (1993)
A line at the left end of the wall. Start at a big flake. Climb this, then go right into a short hanging corner. Exit from this out left onto ledges, then trend back right before finishing direct.

The Slippery Slope   30m   HVS 4c **   (1993)
An excellent route up the right side of the wall. Start about 15m up from the base and take an easy line of big holds diagonally out left above the steep lower section to reach a scoop. Pull up to the horizontal overlap and gain the diagonal crack above. Hard moves lead up the wall above to another bulge. Blind climbing up the superb wall above gains easy ground.

STRATHYRE CRAG   (Map Ref 555 183)

This south-east facing schist crag is short but very steep and has been developed as a sport venue. It can be clearly seen as a spur low on the hill on the other side of the strath from the main A84 road when travelling north of Strathyre village. A local outdoor centre have been using the crag for abseiling for some years and due respect should be shown to their use of it in the future.

Travelling north on the main road through Strathyre village, turn left immediately beyond the small newsagent's shop and go over the humpbacked bridge. Follow the single track road right through the trees for 3km to just beyond a house on the right (Bailefuill). Beyond a stand of mature pines is a small clearing on the left where the small lower crag becomes visible. The main crag sits directly above it. A small path leads through the large mature pines and up to the left side of the crag. Parking for three or four cars is available on the right opposite a forestry track leading off left 200 metres further along the road. The routes are described from left to right.

Power Sink   10m   7b   (1994)
The short wall to the left of the prominent arete is short and to the point.

Electrodynamics   10m   7a ***   (1993)
The prominent left arete — one to fly on — or off!

Bridging the Gap   10m   6c+ *   (1994)
The prominent groove leads to the lower-off on the previous route.

Short Circuit   10m   6b **   (1993)
The slim groove beside the main groove (common start).

Crossed Wire   10m   6a+   (1996)
Swing around right from the first bolt on Short Circuit and climb the groove.

Clam Chowder   10m   7a *   (1994)
Climb the wall to the right through a ledge.

High Tension Lead   10m   7c *   (1994)
The fingery wall leads to a finish up Static Discharge.

Static Discharge   10m   7b ***   (1993)
The central line through the diagonal crack proves very reachy.

Project
The line through the crack.

All Electric   10m   7b+ **   (1996)
The line straight up from the base of the crack, sharing the first two bolts of that route and the lower-off of Circuit Breaker.

Cracking the Lines   10m   7b *   (1994)
Climb the obvious crack from its base to finish up Static Discharge. In other words — the short man's version.

Circuit Breaker   10m   7b *   (1994)
The short steep leaning wall and the less steep wall above.

Power Surge   10m   6c *   (1993)
The leaning wall and the scoop on the right.

Spark Thug   10m   6b *   (1994)
Climb the short corner and wall to the lower-off shared with Power Surge.

Addendum

The following routes were received too late for inclusion in the main body of the guide.

ARDNISH PENINSULA

This rugged peninsula lies to the west of Loch Ailort. It holds a number of small crags and can be accessed by a good path leading from Polnish to the beautifully situated bothy at Peanmeanach ruins.

PARADISE WALLS   *(Map Ref 719 806)*

This is the name given to the short walls just north-east of the Peanmeanach ruins. The rock is immaculate gneiss although only 25m high on average. The main feature seen from the bothy is a steep west-facing wall turning round to the right to form a larger disjointed slab which has a distinctive clean rib in its lower half. The walls continue rightwards in two distinct sections. The first is in two tiers, the lower being short but very steep with striking thin flake cracks. A big heather ledge runs in from the right above this wall, above which is a clean brown wall on the right and a distinctive barrel-shaped arete to the left. The second section lies some 100 metres to the right and has a prominent hanging slab in its central section.

Lost Rib   30m   Very Difficult *   G.E.Little   28 May 1989
Climb the distinctive clean rib of the highest section and short slabby walls above.

Interlude   30m   Severe   G.E.Little   19 Sep 1997
Climb the slabby face to the right of Lost Rib to a ledge. Surmount a tricky quartz wall, then follow easier ground to finish.

To the right of the slabby face holding Lost Rib is a bay holding an oak tree. Immediately right of this tree is the left-hand of two distinct and separate walls.

Forbidden Fruit   50m   E2 5c *   G.E.Little, K.Howett   19 Sep 1997
A line up the left side of the right-hand section, going up both tiers. Start below the left arete of the steep lower wall, just right of the oak tree. Pull onto a flake and gain a small sloping ledge above. Hard moves up the thin cracks in the arete above lead to a huge jug. Pull up onto the heather ledge (possible belay). Climb the obvious corner crack on the left to a step left at the top of the wall to reach a good hold to pull over on. Continue more easily to the top.

Puffing and Padding   25m   E2 5c **   K.Howett, G.E.Little   19 Sep 1997
A climb up the immaculate hanging slab in the right-hand wall some 100 metres
to the right of the previous route. Start below the slab by two diagonal cracks
that bisect to form an X. Make a steep pull into the X, then go leftwards up the
diagonal break to gain a thin vertical crack which leads to a peculiar boss of rock
sitting at the base of the slab. Make one move up the slab, then climb diagonally
right to gain a thin vertical crack which leads to a bigger diagonal crack. Follow
this leftwards to the top.

FLYING ANT BUTTRESS   *(Map Ref 693 807)*

This slabby face lies on the southern flank of a distinctive little dome, near the
remote western tip of the Ardnish Peninsula. Both recorded routes lie on the
clean section to the left of the obvious vegetated chimney which divides the
roughly triangular shaped face. The sandy beach nearby (Map Ref 700 806) is a
real bonus.

Antidote   30m   VS 4b   G.E.Little, A Walker   4 Aug 1997
Start at an oak tree at the foot of a clean slabby groove left of a vegetated
chimney. Climb up and left onto a messy slabby rib and follow this without
protection to the start of a thick quartz band. Climb this to the top.

Antigravity   30m   E2 5c **   G.E.Little, A.Walker   4 Aug 1977
Start up Antidote in the slabby groove and follow it with difficulty to a roof.
Layback its left edge and go straight over a smaller roof to the steep slab above.
Go up and right to a good rest and continue slightly leftwards to the top.

CRUACH AN AONAICH   *(Map Ref 732 802)*

The crag lies 100m up the hillside of Cruach an Aonaich above the shore of
Loch Ailort. It is best approached by walking along the shore or by boat. There is
scope for more routes.

Isis   50m   VS   I Sykes, C.Philipson   1997
Start in the centre of the crag below a grassy recess.
1. 25m 5b   Climb up for 3m until it is possible to traverse right and step down
onto a nose. Climb the slab above which steepens to a recess below a steep
groove. Climb this and the slabby corner above to a grassy belay.
2. 25m 4b   Move left up slabs to a steep wall. Climb this up a crack on the left to
the final easy slab.

LOCH NESS

INVERFARIGAIG   *(Map Ref 525 237)*

These routes are on the crag visible above the road in the valley down to Loch Ness near Foyers. They have been climbed on before, particularly by Clive Rowland and Richard McHardy, but not written up. The assumption therefore is that the following are new:

Wild Roses   60m   E2   D.Cuthbertson, I.Sykes   30 Apr 1997
A diagonal ledge crosses the lower part of the south face of the crag which turns into a steep diagonal crack. There are two rowan trees on the ledge below the crack. Start directly below the rowan trees at the foot of the crag.
1. 20m 5a   Climb broken rocks into a slanting groove until it is possible to break right over an overhang. Follow the groove to a rowan tree and belay on a ledge at the foot of the steep crack. This can also be reached by traversing in along the ledge.
2. 40m 5c   Climb the crack above the tree, steep on good holds, until it is possible to step left round a bulge and onto a perch below the final wall. Climb directly up on small holds to the top.

Cracked Wall   45m   HVS   D.Cuthbertson, I.Sykes   3 May 1997
Start on the diagonal ledge that crosses the south face.
1. 10m 4b   Traverse to the rowan tree belay between the pitches of Wild Roses.
2. 35m 5a   Move steeply right and go up delicately until it is possible to climb the obvious cracks on the right arete of the buttress. Either abseil off (better) or climb easy rocks to the top.

Fat Cat Corner   20m   E1 5b   D.Cuthbertson, I.Sykes   3 May 1997
Start on the beginning of the diagonal ledge splitting the south face. Climb the obvious overhanging corner to the right of the cracked wall.

Omega   60m   E1   O.Clem, I.Sutherland, I.Sykes   15 Jun 1997
Start at the foot of the crag below the crack of Wild Roses at broken rocks beneath the overhanging ivy corner. The route follows a left-trending diagonal crack line until it is possible to break up the walls above.
1. 15m 4c   Climb broken rocks into the corner, then go up left onto a ledge with bollards. Traverse a gangway leftwards until below the obvious groove.
2. 45m 5b   Climb a bulge into the steep groove. Go up this with difficulty, then follow the obvious crack up the nose of the buttress until it is possible to move left onto the slabs above.

CREAG DUBH

SPRAWL WALL *(Map Ref 672 959)*

Yes, Yes!   30m   E7   D.Cuthbertson, J.George   Sep 1997
This potentially serious route climbs the wall between Instant Lemon Direct and Jump so High. From the right-hand end of the ledge common to Instant Lemon a vague crack, containing a niche low down, runs the height of the lower wall. Start 2 metres left of this at a thread belay.
1. 14m 6b   Climb the pale wall to a small overlap and step right into the niche. Continue steeply on good holds for about 3 metres (protection in a succession of three thin cracks to the left, the third being in the black wall above an obvious handrail which runs across the width of the face). Stand on the handrail and reach left for a small hold and so to a poor peg in a little left-facing corner. From the top of the corner, rock over and make a long reach left for a good finishing jug. Continue up and right to a belay at the thin crack of Jump so High.
2. 16m 6a   Climb a thin crack which lies 2 metres left of and parallel to Jump so High. Where the crack peters out go left and up to a large recess and protection (bold). Continue to finish up the right side of a corrugated overhand as for Instant Lemon.
The Yes No! Variation   E5/6 6a
This circumnavigates the crux by going left on the handrail to gain a small stepped left-facing corner. Go up this to join Instant Lemon at the ledge, then move right to join the normal route.

LAGGAN

BINNEIN SHUAS   *(Map Ref 468 827)*

Creepy Aardvark   30m   E3 5c   J.Andrew, C.Pasteur   2 Aug 1997
Start at the top of the first pitch of The Keep. Climb steeply up the wall left of The Keep (bold) and pull onto a slab above. Climb the overhang above 5 metres left of The Keep by a layback flake and an exciting pull onto the Kubla Khan slab. Finish as for The Keep.

TAPERED CRAG   *(Map Ref 474 812)*

This fine little crag lies on the opposite side of Lochan na h-Earba from Binnein Shuas. Approach as for Binnein Shuas, but carry on round the south-west side of the lochan and slant up the hillside. The crag is marked by a tapering left-hand side, a severely undercut base in the centre, and a grassy terrace at the base of the right-hand side. The rock is superb pegmatite, but because of its compact nature it provides only sparse protection. Descend from the northern end of the crag.

Drifter　25m　HVS 5a　　　　　W.Jeffrey, N.Williams　Jul 1994
Start towards the left-hand side of the crag at a beak of schist. At the top of the crag and slightly right there is a prominent boulder. Make hard moves to get established in a crack which curves a long way leftwards. Finish up a steep scoop to a grassy ledge.

Crystal Maze　40m　E2 5b　　　　W.Jeffrey, N.Williams　22 Jun 1996
Start in the centre of the crag where it is deeply undercut. Make a high step up to reach a long left-slanting traverse line which leads to a small ledge with a corner above. Step right on small holds to reach a crack, and follow this trending up left. Where the crack fades continue until a traverse right can be made to another crack. Climb this to a grassy ledge and move left up a slabby wall to finish on a large terrace.

Gallus Besom　40m　E1 5b　　　　W.Jeffrey, N.Williams　17 Oct 1994
Start towards the left-hand end of a higher grass ledge on the right-hand half of the crag. Move up and left and make some difficult moves to reach a ledge and recess. Step right and move up to a slight bulge. Continue more or less straight up with poor protection until the difficulties ease at a horizontal crack. Further thin moves on slabby rock, sometimes wet, lead to a large terrace.

DIRC MHOR

Nature's Raw　45m　E1 5b **　K.Howett, G.Nicoll　28 Sep 1997
This route climbs the excellent grey wall right of Carry On up the Kyber. Scramble up to underneath the short corner immediately right of that route. Climb the corner passing a perched flake with care to reach a sharp flake forming the top of the corner (do not exit onto the ramp above). Step immediately right into the centre of the face and climb up then right to gain a slight recess near the top right-hand side. Finish onto the easy slabby rock and junction with The Kyber. Finish up its final short corner. It looks blank, but it is covered in good holds and protection.

STRATHTAY

WEEM ROCK

One Peg One   7b   N.Shepherd, D.Pert   17 Sep 1997
This is the leftmost line on the steep side wall. Move up to the hanging corner, then fight on using pockets and sidepulls.

The Real McKay   5+   D.McKay   May 1997
A pleasant route up the arete right of The End of Silence. Finishing direct to the lower-off requires the use of some loose rock, but this is easily avoided on the left by climbing the final crack of The Last Temptation.

Boomhead   6a+   N.Shepherd, G.Ridge   24 Aug 1997
Climb the wall to the right of On the Tick List to the overlap, pull over, then go up to a huge loose flake. Skirt the flake on the right, step onto the flake and finish direct. All a bit unnerving.

   A tree and bush-filled corner line lies to the right, beyond which is another fine series of routes.

The Soup Dragon   5   J.Horrocks, I.Watson   20 Sep 1997
A pleasant easy route. Avoid some obviously loose blocks just after crossing the upper roof by climbing the wall to their right.

Scooby Snacks   6a   G.Ridge, D.Johnson   21 Aug 1997
The concave slab is very nice.

One Step Beyond   6a   I.Watson, C.Miln   24 Aug 1997
Pleasant slabby climbing leads to a steep finish.

The Trial of Brother Number One   6a+   C.Miln, I.Watson   7 Sep 1997
Climb the orange wall, finishing direct from the last bolt and so avoiding a worryingly loose rock out to the right. The finish is surprising – no grabbing the chain before clipping it!

The Llama Parlour   6c   J.Horrocks, G.Ridge   28 Sep 1997
Climb the short steep wall left of the steep corner.

The Protection Racket   6a   D.Johnson, G.Ridge   21 Aug 1997
This is the overhanging corner.

List of First Ascents

The details here are as accurate as has been possible to compile to this date. If anyone can shed light on inaccuracies, additions or interesting details concerning first ascents please send them to the SMC. FFA is the abbreviation for first free ascent.

GLEN NEVIS

1946	16 Feb	Hangover Buttress Edge	J.Ness, B.Ellison

G.Band, of Everest fame, was seen placing the first peg at Polldubh, possibly on Styx Buttress in 1947.

1947		Cavalry Crack	J.Ness, J.Wynne
1947		Left Pine Ridge	Lochaber MC Party
1947		Pinnacle Ridge	J.Ness, D.Duff
1947		Sheep Fank Rib	J.Ness, J.Wynne
1947		Sheep Fank Wall	J.Ness, J.Wynne
1950	11 May	Hamlet Edge	J.Ness, A.Burgon
1950	11 May	Secretaries' Crack	J.Ness, A.Burgon
1950	25 May	Severe Crack	J.Ness, A.Burgon
1950	1 Jun	Pine Wall	J.Ness, A.Burgon
1950	12 Jul	Route 1	J.Ness, A.Burgon
1950	23 Sep	Tiptoe	J.Ness, M.Hutchison, R.Corson
1950	28 Sep	Staircase	J.Ness, A.Burgon

Jimmy Ness's article 'Rock playground of Lochaber' was published in the 1951 SMC Journal.

1953		Flapjack Gully, Galax, Toadal	F.Moralle, D.Lawson
1953		Route I, Route II	H.Gartside, B.Collinson, B.Bellamy, R.Wallace, T.Freeman

1957 saw the start of a 3 year period of exploration, mainly by RAF personnel, in particular the Kinloss MRT, with Ian Clough, Terry Sullivan and Eddie Buckley accounting for many superb lines throughout Polldubh.

1957	1 Sep	Route II	I.Clough, R.Mason, P.Hannon, O.Cook
1957	1 Sep	Route III (aid)	I.Clough, R.Mason, P.Hannon, O.Cook

FFA by K.Howett, C.Henderson on 16 Feb 1985 and renamed Mousplay as Ed Grindley had shown an interest in it, but as he was away the 'mouse doth play'.

1958	8 Apr	Nutcracker Chimney	R.Wilkinson, D.Pipes
1958	8 Apr	Diagonal Crack	R.Wilkinson, D.Pipes

FFA: A.Fulton, B.Chambers, 1968.

1958	28 Jun	Doomsday	I.Clough, J.Alexander

FFA: K.Schwartz, 1968

1958	28 Jun	Damnation	I.Clough, J.Alexander
1958	29 Mar	Creag Lough Grooves	T.Sullivan, I.Clough

The third pitch required combined tactics and 2 points of aid. FFA by J.A.Austin, J.M.Austin in 1962.

1959	5 Apr	Mechanic's Institute (aid)	I.Clough, A.Lakin, A.Parkin

Used extensively for pegging practice, it was later free climbed but pegged ascents continued which rendered the route unclimbable. Then in the 1980s the bulk of the line fell down and was only climbed again in free form in 1992 by Paul Newton at E5 6c, after being practiced on a top rope to produce People will Talk.

1959	5 Apr	Resurrection	I.Clough, A.Lakin

1959	5 Apr	The Paunch	I.Clough
1959	11 Apr	Fidelity	I.Clough, T.Sullivan
1959	11 Apr	Iche	T.Sullivan, I.Clough
1959	11 Apr	Kinloss Grooves	I.Clough, T.Sullivan
1959	11 Apr	Enigma	T.Sullivan, I.Clough

Now included as the second last pitch of Autobahnausfahrt.

1959	20 Apr	Burma Road	I.Clough, E.Buckley

Now a grade harder than the original 'fight through the subsequent jungle'.

1959	20 Apr	Dental Groove	I.Clough, E.Buckley
1959	20 Apr	Pandora	I.Clough, E.Buckley
1959	21 Apr	Vampire	I.Clough, E.Buckley
1959	21 Apr	Secretaries' Direct	I.Clough, E.Buckley
1959	21 Apr	Hawk's Nest	I.Clough, E.Buckley
1959	22 Apr	Wanderlust	I.Clough
1959	2 May	Hot Tin Roof	T.Sullivan, I.Clough
1959	3 May	Storm (3 pts aid)	I.Clough, T.Sullivan

FFA by J.A.Austin, J.M.Austin in 1962. The True Finish was added by John Taylor and K.Schwartz in the 1976.

1959	3 May	Flying Dutchman	T.Sullivan, I.Clough
1959	3 May	Degradation	I.Clough, T.Sullivan
1959	3 May	Phantom Slab	T.Sullivan, I.Clough
1959	22 May	Heatwave	I.Clough, J.Pickering, R.Henson, P.Brocklehurst, R.Porteous
1959	22 May	Last Word	I.Clough
1959	29 May	Tutor's Rib	I.Clough
1959	29 May	Drizzle (2nd pitch)	T.Sullivan
1959	28 Jun	Repton Slab	E.Buckley, I.Clough
1959	28 Jun	Spike Wall	I.Clough, R.Henson, P.Brocklehurst, R.Porteous
1959		Left Wall, Quartzite Wall, Edge Diedre	I.Clough

Ian Clough's article 'Haunt of the Tiger: A Record of Recent Developments on Polldubh Crags', with a sketch map of the main buttresss, was published in the 1960 SMC Journal. It contained the following observation 'though possibilities for good climbs still exist, most of the best lines have been climbed'. The early 1960s however, see further development, with RNAS Lossiemouth personnel and Ken Johnson in the forefront.

1960	22 Mar	Sunset Boulevard, Sundowner	I.Clough, J.Davis, G.Gargett, R.Mathews, D.Ducker
1960/61		Shag, Bardhinaghi, Black Slab Edge	K.Johnson
1960/61		Eigerwand, Fly, Gambit, Promises	K.Johnson
1960/61		Quartz Wall, Wren's Delight, Ant's Walk	K.Johnson
1960/61		Spike Direct	K.Johnson
1963	1 Jan	Steall Waterfall (winter)	I.Rowe (solo)
1963	Jul	Fang (aid)	W.Skidmore, P.MacKenzie, J.Crawford

FFA by E.Grindley, I.Nicolson on 19 Apr 1978.

1963		Gambit	H.Brown, R.Rankin, R.Grant, J.Sutton
1963		The Old Wall	I.Jones and party
1963		McGonigal's Groove	J.Grieve, D.Smith
1963		White Goat	J.Grieve, R.Grieve

1963		Triangular Wall	J.Grieve, R.Grieve
1963		Two Pines	K.Johnson, F.Munday
1963/4		Tear, Fred's Delight, The Traverse, SW Girdle	K.Johnson
1964		Canine, Bitch, Howl	K.Johnson, A.Williamson
1964		High King Hole	J.Hinde
1964		Vampire Direct	K.Johnson, F.Munday
1964		Clapham Junction Direct Finish	K.Johnson, F.Munday

The crack had previously been much used for pegging practice.

1964		Dirty Sheet, Chimney Crack	K.Johnson
1964		Tip Toe Direct	K.Johnson, F.Munday
1965	2 May	Dundee Weaver (aid)	R.Gray, G.Low

FFA: K.Schwartz, A.Fulton 1967

1965		Ethmoid (aid)	I.Sykes, I.Sutherland

FFA: D.Griffiths, I.Griffiths 23 Apr 1988. Renamed Hot Spots after some of the holds were dried off with a blowtorch.

Ken Johnson's unpublished guide was written in 1965 and the crags were 'popular throughout the summer mid-weekly evening meets' of the Lochaber JMCS members.

1967		Hodad	I.Jones, J.Grieve

Klaus Schwartz, equiped with bendy vibram-soled Hawkins 'Cairngorm' boots appeared in 1967, spearheading a 10-year campaign of new routing, with fellow Loch Eil instructors, centre students and domestic staff in tow. The unorthodox footwear may account for some of the aid used as everyone else was wearing 'PAs' at the time.

1968	15 Jun	Rubberface	K.Schwartz and party
1968	7 Jul	Kaos (aid)	K.Schwartz, P.Logan

FFA by K.Spence in 1980.

1969	5 Apr	Black Horse, Ariom	K.Schwartz, M.Horsburgh
1969	6 Apr	Kraut (1PA)	K.Schwartz, S.Crymble, B.Wright

FFA: K.Spence, 1970.

1969	7 Apr	Why	K.Schwartz
1969	17 Apr	Sprauchle, Half Sheet	B.Wright, K.Schwartz

On the latter route, a 10 Shilling note (half sheet) was dropped, the shock of which necessitated a rest point. FFA K.Johnson.

1969	19 Apr	Three Pitch Climb	A.Fulton, K.Schwartz
1969	19 Apr	Panda	K.Schwartz, A.Fulton
1969	20 Apr	Two Pine Gully Edge	K.Schwartz and party
1969	May	Zelos	A.Fulton, B.Chambers
1969	13 May	Black Friday (aid)	K.Schwartz, B.Wright

FFA: M.Hamilton, J.Fantini, 1981.

1969	21 May	South Diagonal	S.Crymble, A.Fulton
1969	29 May	The Web (aid)	K.Schwartz, B.Wright

FFA: E.Grindley, W.Todd, 5 Jun 1976.

1969	28 Jul	Secretatries' Super Direct	A.Fulton, K.Schwartz

The first pitch was added by K.Schwartz, J.Mount on 19 May 1973.

1969	8 Aug	Cucumber	S.Crymble, M.Horsburgh, K.Schwartz
1969	2 Sep	Autobahnausfahrt (some aid)	K.Schwartz, B.Chambers

FFA: (of pitch 4, as Autoroof) by K.Spence, R.Anderson in 1981.

1969	13 Sep	Shakespeare Wall	K.Schwartz, M.Horsburgh
1969	16 Sep	Central Route	B.Chambers, K.Schwartz
1969	11 Oct	Nosbulgia (1pt aid)	K.Schwartz, B.Chambers

FFA: M.Hall, 1970s.

1969	11 Oct	Cervix	K.Schwartz, B.Chambers
1969	12 Oct	Calluna	K.Schwartz
1969	29 Oct	Tomag (aid)	A.McKeith, B.Wright
1969	29 Oct	The Long Crack	D.Nicol and party
1969	29 Oct	Foursome	J.Telfer, A.Hall, A.Gaskell, T.Campbell
1969	29 Oct	Twitch	J.Cunningham and party
1969		Stretcher Lower	K.Schwartz, B.Chambers

Achdalieu, Cracians, Gaers, Hot Eye, Rump and Windfall were climbed in the 1960s and 1970s by K. Schwartz, and Loch Eil Centre parties. The routes showed signs of possible previous ascents.

1970	23 Jan	Palpal	K.Schwartz
1970	24 Jan	Waznusmoles	K.Schwartz, S.Crymble

FFA by W.Todd, E.Grindley on 7 June 1976.

1970	24 Jan	Sodafarl	S.Crymble, K.Schwartz, J.Grue
1970	13 Feb	Boorock, Por Ridge, Hospital Wall	K.Schwartz
1970	15 Feb	Zelos (pitch 2)	K.Schwartz
1970	27 Feb	Anonymous	S.Crymble, K.Schwartz
1970	27 Feb	Wee Wire	K.Schwartz, S.Crymble
1970	28 Feb	Pal	K.Schwartz
1970	29 Jun	Crybaby (1pt aid)	K.Schwartz, M.Horsburgh

FFA K. Schwartz and Loch Eil party 1972.

1970	20 Jun	Wilhemstrasse 71 (HVS/A2)	K.Schwartz, B.Chambers

FFA: as Quality Street by P.Whillance and M.Hamilton in 1981.

1970	23 Jun	Mouseface	K.Schwartz, M.Horsburgh

A dead mouse adorned a vital hold.

1970	7 Jul	Albatross, Fossil Bluff, Penguin	K.Schwartz, M.Horsburgh
1970	7 Jul	Pinguin, Seal	K.Schwartz
1970	10 Aug	Fibrillation	K.Schwartz, B.Chambers, Loch Eil Centre party.
1970	10 Aug	Frenzy, Palpitation	B. Chambers, K.Schwartz
1970	10 Aug	Gradation	K.Schwartz, Loch Eil Centre party
1970	26 Aug	Black Goat	K.Schwartz, Loch Eil Centre party.
1970		Kitchen Rib 85	S.Crymble
1970		Thirst	I.Sykes and party
1970		Steall Slabs	W.Anderson, S.Barr

The first published guidbook to the glen was done by Klaus Schwartz and Blyth Wright and published independently in 1970 (printed locally by Nevisprint).

1971	7 Feb	Wilhelmstrasse Direct Start (aid)	K.Schwartz, M.Horsburgh

Now the start of Quality Street.

1971	3 Apr	Nameless Rib, Appendix	K.Schwartz, M.Horsburgh
1971	Jun	Croch (A2), Druim	I.Sutherland, I.Sykes
1971	17 Aug	Wutz	K.Schwartz, M.Horsburgh
1971	17 Aug	Alfonselli	K.Schwartz, M.Horsburgh

FFA by K.Schwartz, Loch Eil Centre, 4 Nov 1974.

1971	22 Aug	The Strip	K.Schwartz, J.Mount
1971	Sep	Patdoug, Pinelet	Loch Eil Centre party
1971	3 Oct	The Strip Direct Start (2pts aid)	K.Schwartz, J.Mount
1971		Boggle	D.Regan, Loch Eil Centre
1971		Diamond	M.Hall
1971		Hircine	K.Schwartz, M.Horsburgh
1971		Liaison Dangereux	B.Wright, Glenmore Lodge party

1971		Nota Route	J.Mount, Loch Eil Centre
1971		Marie Celeste	C.Burgess, K.Donnan, L.Morris, G.Skelton
1971		Tee	M.Hall
1972	27 Feb	Airlift, Blow, Chick	K.Schwartz and party
1972	18 Mar	Nowire	Loch Eil Centre
1972	13 Jul	Lismore Avenue	M.Horsburgh, K.Schwartz
1972	6 Oct	Goldener Oktober	K.Schwartz
1972	6 Oct	Knucklebuster	B.Chambers, K.Schwartz
1972	11 Oct	Withering Crack	K.Schwartz, J.Mount

FFA by E.Grindley, C.Grindley on 16 May 1978.

1972	20 Oct	Rhubarb, Horsi	K.Schwartz and party

Comment in the SMC Journal 1972: "The resources of these very popular crags are seemingly inexhaustible. Ours however are not. This year we will publish only a selection ... next year we will be more ruthless."!

1973	18 Mar	Andrea's Visit	J.Mount, K.Schwartz

FFA by A.Taylor, R.Anderson in 1981.

1973	16 May	Hyphen	K.Schwartz
1973	19 May	Ascension	K.Schwartz, J.Mount

FFA by N.Colton, R.Carrington on 5 Jun 1976.

1973	5 Oct	Ord, Staythere	K.Schwartz, J.Mount
1973	14 Oct	Heulsuse	J.Mount, K.Schwartz
1973	28 Oct	Pich	J.Mount, K.Schwartz
1973		Wee One	J.Mount, B.Chambers

FFA by M.Hamilton, K.Spence 1980

1973		Wee Two	A.Gray, J.Mount

FFA as Cubsville, G.Latter, D.Cuthbertson (both led), 3 May 1985.

1973		South Crack	A.Kimber, J.Mount

FFA by M.Hall, E.Grindley on 27 May 1978.

1974	12 Apr	Grope	Loch Eil Centre
1974	11 Oct	Malaw	Mr and Mrs Roobottom
1974	3 Nov	Dead Pine, Isit	K.Schwartz, C.MacQueen
1974	4 Nov	Omalegs, Singer	K.Schwartz, R.Morrow
1974	4 Nov	Clach, Sheslept	K.Schwartz, R.Morrow
1975	4 Jan	Nuts	A.Gray, K.Schwartz

FFA by E.Webster on 5 Apr 1981.

1975	7 May	Trottoir	K.Schwartz, D.Wilson
1975	14 May	Knees	Loch Eil Centre
1975	19 May	Double Black	K.Schwartz, H.Schwartz
1975	May	Neck, Break	N.Williams

Both lines were top roped prior to being led.

1975	22 Jun	Schnooks, Schnooful	K.Schwartz, R.Morrow
1975	2 Jul	Duskscreams	K.Schwartz, C.MacQueen
1975	17 Jul	Route II½	K.Schwartz, S.Orr and party

FFA by E.Webster on 5 April 1981 and renamed Friends.

1975	17 Jul	Route III½	S.Orr, T.Wise, K.Schwartz

FFA by E.Grindley on 3 Apr 1982 and renamed McAlck. 'Route III½ without pegs or trees for aid (all removed)' was the entry in the new route book.

1975	25 Sep	Cling	Loch Eil Centre party
1975	8 Oct	The Gutter	K.Schwartz
1975	8 Nov	Heather	R.Morrrow, K.Schwartz
1975	9 Nov	Cigol, Pink Plastic Bag, Samantha	K.Schwartz.

1975	9 Nov	Middlelast	K.Schwartz
1975		Dragon	A.Wielochowski
1975		Groanangasp	A.Wielochowski, N.Williams

FFA, with the top pitch straightened out, by D.Cuthbertson, G.Latter in May 1982 and renamed Exocet.

1975		Monster	A.Wielochowski, P.Webster

FFA by D.Cuthbertson, A.Moist on 16 Jun 1985.

1975		Scorpion	A.Wielochowski, N.Williams
1975		Tarantella	A.Wielochowski and party
1975		Titus	A.Wielochowski, N.Williams
1975		The Sting	A.Wielochowski, N.Williams
1975		Hush Puppy	N.Williams, A.Wielochowski
1975		Mental Block	N.Williams
1975		Pete's Corner	P.Webster and party
1975		Steerpike	N.Williams, A.Wielochowski

A point of aid was used. FFA: D.Cuthbertson, G.Latter 1982.

1975		Stonetrap, Hang	K.Schwartz, R.Smith
1975		Soldier, Roundabout	K.Schwartz, R.Morrow
1976	2 Mar	Rubberface (direct)	E.Grindley
1976	17 Apr	Foil	K.Schwartz, S.Orr

FFA by E.Grindley on 22 Apr 1978.

1976	20 Apr	Maintenance	K.Schwartz, R.Morrow
1976	20 Apr	Cascade	K.Schwartz
1976	23 Apr	Blue Lace	K.Schwartz
1976	28 Apr	Nevil	J.Taylor, R.Morrow, K.Schwartz
1976	12 May	William	K.Schwartz, R.Morrow
1976	3 Jun	No Entry	K.Schwartz, R.Morrow
1976	8 Jun	Zenana	K.Schwartz, R.Morrow
1976	8 Jun	Zenanos	C.Robinson, C.MacQueen
1976	31 Aug	Sods, Upleft	K.Schwartz and party
1976		Dog's Way	K.Schwartz
1976		Kyanite, Broos	J.Taylor, K.Schwartz
1976		Jewels	J.Taylor
1976		Curse	J.Taylor, A.Kimber
1976		Fribbles	J.Taylor, K.Schwartz
1976		Acceber	K.Schwartz
1977	Apr	Chalky Wall	D.Cuthbertson, M.Hamilton
1977	29 Jul	Diode	B.Sprunt, C.Hill

Top-roped prior to the lead.

1977		Tonis	T.Cardwell and party

FFA: M.Hall, E.Grindley 15 Apr 1978.

1978	Apr	Vampire Direct, Alt. Finish	E.Grindley and party
1978	15 Apr	Haul	M.Hall, E.Grindley
1978	22 Apr	No Entry	E.Grindley
1978	1 May	Versus	E.Grindley, R.Rodgers
1978	24 May	Pale Face	E.Grindley, C.Grindley
1978	24 May	Peg Route	E.Grindley
1978	9 Aug	Zephyr Street	K.Schwartz

Named in order to fit in the index of the guide without retyping!

1978	31 Aug	Atree	E.Grindley
1978		Rip	B.Sprunt

1978		Razor	B.Sprunt, A.Slater

1978 saw the publication of the second edition of Rock Climbs in Glen Nevis, published by Klaus Schwartz.

1979	14 Apr	Cigar	E.Grindley
1981	26 Apr	Pandy	E.Grindley, D.Meldrum, D.Gunn, J.Main
1981	10 May	Wee Joe	E.Grindley, D.Gunn, C.Grindley
1981	10 May	Puddy	D.Gunn, E.Grindley, C.Grindley
1981		Soap Suds	D.Cuthbertson, I.Sutherland
1981		High Street	D.Cuthbertson, A.Slater
1981	5 Aug	Vincent	D.Cuthbertson, I.Sykes

So named, because the rock architecture was thought to resemble a Van Gogh painting.

1981		Ring of Fire	D.Cuthbertson, D.Jamieson
1981		Risque Grapefruit	D.Jamieson, D.Cuthbertson
1981		Les Boys	D.Cuthbertson, D.Jamieson
1981		Sky Pilot	D.Cuthbertson
1981		Before the Flood	D.Cuthbertson, D.Jamieson
1981		Lucy Lime	D.Jamieson, D.Cuthbertson
1981		Quality Street	P.Whillance, M.Hamilton
1981		Black Magic, Bounty Hunters	D.Armstrong
1981		The Mint, Gobstopper Groove	A.Murray, M.Hamilton, P.Whillance
1981	12 Sep	Kaos	E.Grindley, P.Long
1981	13 Sep	Shergar	E.Grindley, C.Grindley, P.Long, G.Higginson
1981	13 Sep	Desmo	P.Long, C.Grindley, E.Grindley, G.Higginson
1981	25 Oct	Land Ahoy	E.Grindley, D.Gunn
1981	Oct	Close to the Wind	E.Grindley, D.Gunn
1981	Oct	Dying Crutchman	D.Gunn, D.Meldrum
1981		Tomag	M.Hamilton, J.Fantini
1982	Feb	Blockbuster	T.Swain

Two separate teams start to develop major crags around the Steall area.

1982	28 Mar	Sauer	E.Grindley, F.Gunn, D.Gunn, G.Reid
1982	3 Apr	Double or Quits	E.Grindley, D.Gunn
1982	5 Apr	Hun, Centrefold	E.Grindley, F.Gunn
1982	20 Apr	First Wave	E.Grindley, N.Williams

Opening gambit on what was to become one of the finest crags in the area.

1982	26 Apr	Edgehog	E.Grindley, N.Williams

Grindley's finest and most popular Extreme in the glen. It received its first on-sight solo from M.McGowan with a frightened crowd of onlookers.

1982	9 May	Ground Zero	E.Grindley, N.Williams, C.Grindley, F.Gunn
1982	19 May	Conscription	D.Cuthbertson, G.Latter
1982	19 May	All Our Yesterdays	D.Cuthbertson, G.Latter
1982	21 May	Cosmopolitan	D.Cuthbertson, G.Latter

Another technical testpiece that succumed after several attempts. It held a reputation for many years.

1982	22 May	Travellin' Man	D.Cuthbertson, G.Latter (alts)
1982	22 Jun	High 'n' Dry	G.Latter, D.Cuthbertson
1982	27 May	Plague of Blazes	E.Grindley, F.Gunn, N.Williams, W.Lawrie

| 1982 | May | In the Groove | D.Cuthbertson, G.Latter |
| | | | |

The first pitch was added by G.Latter, I.Campbell on 24 Jul 1984.

| 1982 | Jun | Pupil Power | N.Williams and Lochaber High School party |

Recorded with a blaze of publicity in the local rag.

1982		Spreadeagle, Slip Away	D.Cuthbertson, G.Latter
1983	25 Feb	Playaway	E.Grindley, N.Williams
1983	27 Mar	Shogun	E.Grindley, N.Williams
1983	Apr	The Handren Effect	D.Cuthbertson

Utilised a pre-placed hammered nut for protection. It was originally given E5 but is now considered to be E6. Over the period of 1982 and 1983, the jump to a higher standard of E6 in the glen came from Cuthbertson with his ascents of this route and Exocet (the first of this grade in the glen), although it took repeats some years later to verify this.

1983		Cubby's Route	D.Cuthbertson, J.Handren
1983	27 Apr	All's Fair	E.Grindley, N.Williams
1983	23 May	Bewsey Crack	E.Grindley, N.Williams
1983	30 May	Boteler Wall	E.Grindley, B.Owen
1983	May	Ziggy	N.Williams, A.Wielochowski
1983	1 Jun	Teenoso	E.Grindley (solo)
1983	2 Jun	Fly Direct Start	R.Treadwell, R.Shaw
1983	6 Jun	Social Democrack	N.Williams, E.Grindley
1983	8 Jun	Parisian Walkway	R.Donaldson (solo)
1983	11 Jun	Mini Cooper	W.Jeffrey, N.Williams, P.Hunter
1983	Jun	Frogs	A.Slater, R.Shaw
1983	7 Jul	Short Man's Walk About	D.Cuthbertson, G.Latter

Do the route to understand the name!

1983	9 Jul	The Singing Ringing Tree	D.Cuthbertson
1983	16 Jul	Bite the Dust	R.Lee, S.MacLean, G.Bones, K.MacDonald
1983	23 Jul	The Principle of Moments	G.Latter, I.Campbell
1983	25 Jul	Les Boys Direct Finish	G.Latter, I.Campbell
1983	31 Jul	Steallyard Blues	W.Jeffrey, N.Williams
1983	9 Aug	Think Vertical	E.Grindley, B.Owen

The route was a natural drainage line. Some ditching work at the top diverted the water and allowed a dry ascent.

| 1983 | 14 Aug | Crackattack | E.Grindley, B.Owen |
| 1983 | 20 Aug | Sisyphus | D.Gunn, E.Grindley |

Resulting from a failed attempt on the roof – later done on 26 Aug 1983.

| 1983 | 26 Aug | Going for Gold | E.Grindley |

A magnificent effort through a sizable roof crack.

| 1983 | 7 Sep | Earthstrip | D.Armstrong, A.Wright |

During 1983, The Cubby Hole, No Name, Ease Up, Two Into One, Doesn't Go, Ease On, Mini Mantel and Gibbon were climbed by N.Williams and partners.

1984	1 Apr	Mother's Day	K.Spence, R.Anderson
1984	28 Apr	Walter Wall	K.Spence, J.McKenzie
1984	Apr	On the Beach	M.Hamilton, R.Anderson (on sight)
1984	10 May	Caterpillar	D.Cuthbertson, E.Grindley
1984	May	Jodicus Grotticus	D.Cuthbertson

The first route on the crag to be named after a dog. RPs were pre-placed for protection, but they later fell out. Second ascent M.Lovat, G.Peel.

| 1984 | May | Romancing the Stone | K.Howett, M.Charlton |

1984	Jun	Dirty Tongue	A.Slater, A, Carmichael, R.Shaw
1984	Jun	Big Mickey, Stretcher Case	A.Slater, R.Shaw
1984	Jun	Just a Little Tease	D.Cuthbertson
1984	Jun	Sweet Little Mystery	D.Cuthbertson (solo)
1984	Jun	Where the Mood Takes Me	D.Cuthbertson (solo)
1984	Jun	Freddie Across the Mersey	D.Cuthbertson, D.Armstrong, S.Reid
1984	4 Jul	The Fascination Trap	D.Armstrong, D.Borthwick
1984	Jul	Le Midge	G.Latter, K.Johnstone
1984	Jul	Sabre	K.Johnstone, G.Latter

Later it had to be reclimbed after a large flake fell off – G.Latter 19 Jun 1986.

1984	Jul	Wavelet	K.Johnstone, G.Latter (both solo)
1984	25 Jul	Darkness on the Edge of Town	D.Armstrong, A.Wright
1984	Jul	Jahu	D.Cuthbertson (solo)
1984	3 Aug	Power in the Darkness	D.Armstrong
1984	Aug	Mo's Got Her Knickers in a Twist!	D.Cuthbertson, A.Moist
1984	Aug	Gawping Grockles	A.Moist, D.Carr
1984	23 Aug	The Fuzz	D.Armstrong (solo)
1984	Sep	Sue's Crack	A.Moist, A.Todd
1984	9 Sep	Teaser and the Firecat	D.Armstrong (solo)
1984		Ring of Fire Right-Hand	M.Hamilton
1984		Black Friday Right-Hand	D.Cuthbertson, J.Fantini, M.Lawrence
1984		White Rabbit, Orangeman	D.Orange
1984		Nasal Gully, A Bridge Too Far	I.Fisher, R.Lee, D.McShane, N.Williams
1984		Nostril, Cheek	I. Fisher, R.Lee, D.McShane, N.Williams
1985	6 Jan	The Beer Hunter	K.Howett, A.Moist
1985	14 Feb	A-Propa-Kiss-Now	K.Howett (on sold solo)
1985	Feb	Gregory's Crack	A.Moist, C.Henderson
1985	Feb	Self Control	N.Sharpe, A.Moist
1985	Feb	Cool Cookie	A.Moist, C.Henderson, M.Clarke, N.Sharpe
1985	16 Feb	Winter Blues	K.Howett, C.Henderson
1985	27 Feb	Easy Pickings	K.Howett, A.Moist, C.Henderson

As most of the harder remaining lines required cleaning by this time, it was rare to do first ascents on sight. This was one of a few that had been cleaned by other interested parties and so was 'easy pickings' for an on sight lead.

1985	28 Feb	Run for Home	K.Howett

A particularly productive start so early in the year to what developed as a bumper crop of new routes. It was also the start of a definite re-awakening of interest by a number of previously devoted activists. These early routes only just made it into the new guide book that was written by Ed Grindley and published by Cicerone Press later in 1985.

1985	7 Apr	Stuffed Monkey	G.Latter, W.Williamson
1985	21 Apr	Captain Kevlar	G.Latter, D.Cuthbertson

So named due to a runner used on the FA (or a character on the scene at the time?).

1985	20 Apr	Fool in the Rain	G.Latter (solo, in wellies)
1985	21 Apr	The Anniversary	D.Cuthbertson, G.Latter
1985	22 Apr	Washington	D.Cuthbertson, G.Latter
1985	23 Apr	Aquarian Rebels	D.Cuthbertson, G.Latter

Both Cuthbertson and Howett independently spent time cleaning the line and a race ensued for the prize.

1985	23 Apr	Mutant	D.Cuthbertson, G.Latter
1985	23 Apr	Rough Diamonds	G.Latter, D.Cuthbertson
1985	23 Apr	Hard Station	K.Howett, A.Moist, C.Henderson
1985	24 Apr	Quartzite Cruiser	G.Latter, D.Cuthbertson
1985	2 May	Tickled Pink	D.Cuthbertson, G.Latter
1985	2 May	Crinkle Cut	G.Latter, D.Cuthbertson
1985	4 May	Liquidator	P.Laughlan, M.MacRae
1985	10 May	Edgehog: The Extended Start	G.Latter, K.Howett
1985	11 May	Chimera	K.Howett
1985	11 May	Rats in Paradise	G.Latter
1985	11 May	The Amusement Arcade	D.Cuthbertson, G.Latter

Climbing in the gorge drew crowds of bemused tourists. In this case a change of footwear (from Fires to Superats) was accomplished on the small halfway footledge which must have added to the entertainment. An in situ nut runner was used on the lower wall for protection.

1985	12 May	The Gift	K.Howett, G.Latter, D.Cuthbertson
1985	15 May	The Sugar Puff Kid	D.Cuthbertson, G.Latter (both led)

Named in honour of Latter's eating habits

1985	19 May	Savage Cabbage	D.Cuthbertson, K.Howett

For the full effect it should be pronounced in a french accent like it's neighbour, Risque Grapefruit.

1985	19 May	Lullaby in Black	D.Cuthbertson, G.Latter
1985	20 May	Ugly Duckling	K.Howett, A.Moist
1985	20 May	If Looks Could Kill	D.Cuthbertson, G.Latter
1985	20 May	Diamond Delight	G.Latter, D.Cuthbertson
1985	21 May	Flight of the Snowgoose	K.Howett, G.Latter, D.Cuthbertson

The first use of tied-down skyhooks for protection in the Glen on an otherwise poorly protected line. Two hooks were used on the footledge below the crux. Howett nearly tested their holding power whilst in extremis near the top and a rope was thrown for help, but he reversed the moves unaided and completed the route without further backup.

1985	21 May	Reptile	D.Cuthbertson, K.Howett
1985	21 May	Sammy the Seal	D.Cuthbertson, G.Latter
1985	30 May	Spring Fever	D.Cuthbertson, K.Howett, C.Henderson
1985	31 May	Lame Beaver	K.Howett

Both strenuous and serious. A specially made Hex1 with Kevlar thread was used for the protection, but it partly cut through during falls, adding somewhat to the scare factor. Two rest points in the easier final crack were eliminated by D.Cuthbertson on the 25 May 1987. The third ascent (and first on-sight flash) came from M.Smith in 1994.

1985	16 Jun	Green Wellies	A.Todd, D.Carr
1985	20 Jun	The Edwardo Shuffle	D.Cuthbertson

"I have this vision of the man on a surf board with a scarf flowing in the wind..."

1985	13 Jul	Lord of the Midges	G.Latter, N.Sharpe
1985	14 Jul	The Amazing Adventures of ...	G.Latter

So named, as the belayer of the title had failed to rendezvous at the crag, and had instead crawled behind a boulder and fallen asleep!

1985	15 Jul	Midgiematosis	G.Latter, N.Donnelly
1985	Aug	Look no Book	R.Frew, A.McLeod
1985	19 Oct	Chugger	G.Latter, C.Henderson
1985	27 Oct	Stone Cold	G.Latter, D.Cuthbertson
1985	17 Nov	Fingertip Finale	G.Latter, D.Cuthbertson
1986	2 May	Simple Deduction	G.Latter

1986	2 May	Footnote	G.Latter
1986	30 May	The Quartzmaster	G.Latter, D.Griffiths, C.Bell
1986	3 Jun	Faceless	G.Latter, R.Lee, D.Cuthbertson
1986	11 Jun	The Counter Reactionary	G.Latter, E.Cameron
1986	13 Jun	The Dark Crystal	G.Latter

The finishing section was climbed separately by G.Latter on 29 Jul 1986 as The Final Scoop.

1986	16 Jun	Nowhere Near the Sea	G.Latter
1986	20 Jun	The Gallery	G.Latter
1986	25 Jun	Painted Face	G.Latter, R.Lee
1986	3 Jul	Nomad	G.Latter (solo)
1986	8 Jul	Jesus Christ Come on Down	M.McGowan, S.Yates
1986	9 Jul	Barndoor	K.Howett, A.Moist, G.Latter
1986	10 Jul	Dancing on the Edge of Existence	K.Howett, A.Moist

Named after the seconds' lifestyle. The variation up the edge by G.Latter and A.Nelson, 17 Jun 1988, meant the route also lived up to its name.

1986	12 Jul	Cruisability	G.Latter

One of the best natural lines in the glen.

1986	12 Jul	Straight Thinking	G.Latter, N.Sharpe
1986	12 July	Stage Fright	M.McGowan

The variation, Exit Stage Right was climbed in error of the original route in 1986 by C.Gilchrist.

1986	23 Jul	Wiggly Worms	G.Latter
1986	27 Jul	Femme Fatale	D.Cuthbertson

A very hard line, perhaps the hardest in this guide. Blind HB runner placements were practised on a top rope and a skyhook was also used for protection low down. The route has repulsed all on sight attempts so far.

1986	29 Jul	Psycho Cats	G.Latter, P.Farrell
1986	9 Aug	Lateral Thinking	G.Latter
1986	6 Sep	No Fear for the Pocketeer	G.Latter
1986	9 Sep	Dracula	G.Latter, R.Lee
1986	Sep	Sparkle in the Rain	M.McGowan, S.Yates
1986	2 Oct	Wall Games, Double Think	G.Latter
1987	19 Feb	The Swing of Things	G.Latter
1987	21 Feb	Assorted Gems	G.Latter, D.Griffiths
1987	21 Feb	Latter Day Saint	G.Lawrie, B.Wilson, P.Anderson
1987	3 Mar	Side Arms	G.Latter, K.Howett (both led)
1987	28 Mar	Running Scared	G.Latter

A variation was done on the second ascent immediately afterwards by M.McGowan.

1987	Apr	A Cut Above the Rest	M.McGowan (solo)
1987	Apr	Comfortably Numb	M.McGowan, S.McLean
1987	Apr	Frantic Across the Atlantic	M.McGowan, S.McLean, D.Griffiths
1987	19 May	Triode	D.Cuthbertson, A.de Clerk
1987	22 May	Liminality	D.Cuthbertson

A very hard addition. Second ascent by I.Cropley.

1987	May	The Nuns of Navarone	C.Gilchrist, J.Bain, C.Bell
1987	6 Jul	Lepidoptery	K.Howett, G.Latter (both led)

Amusingly, Howett failed to clip the peg (the only one he had placed on Scottish rock!) which was clipped for him by Latter. The peg has since fallen out.

1987	20 Jul	Jodicus Direct	M.McGowan

Climbed with ropes pre-clipped on abseil into a previous day's high point.

1987	Jul	A Spaceman Came Travelling	J.Williamson, S.McLean

1987	Jul	Enter and Remember	S.Bytheway, D.Orr
1987	29 Jul	After the Fire	G.Latter
1987	Jul	So Long and Thanks for all the Fish	A.de Klerk

Visitors to South Africa will learn that ADK is a climber of some note!

1987	8 Aug	Pieces of Eight	D.Griffiths, I.Griffiths

The name an intended reference to the Buccaneer, only the crag was named after the low-flying jets that come by at eye-level when on the crag.

1987	10 Aug	Viking's Day Out	N.Kirk
1987	19 Sep	Driving Ambition	A.Kelly, S.Bytheway
1987	Oct	Acappella	M.McGowan (solo)
1987	11 Oct	Centrepiece	K.Howett, D.Griffiths

Climbed on-sight with the use of a tied-down skyhook as well as a poor peg (placed by G.Latter). Latter tested the holding power of the skyhook during attempts, and made the second ascent immediately afterwards. The peg later fell out and the first ascent without it was nabbed by Mark Garthwaite in 1994, on sight.

1987	11 Oct	Juicy Lucy	G.Latter
1987	1 Nov	Quadrode, Cathode Smiles	K.Howett, G.Latter (both led)
1987	1 Nov	Bitter Days	K.Howett
1987	2 Nov	Overlode	K.Howett, P.Farrell
1987	6 Dec	Circus	D.Griffiths, C.Bell
1988	1 Mar	Epileptic in a bath tub	P.Farrell
1988	30 Apr	Parental Guidance, Tomsk Thumb	A.Nelson, K.Howett
1988	30 Apr	Rebecca	A.Nelson (solo)
1988	Apr	Desolation Angel	J.Williamson, C.Smith
1988	Apr	Blue Monday	C.Smith, J.Williamson
1988	7 May	Restless Natives	G.Latter, K.Howett, A.Nelson

Differing views on the use of skyhooks amongst the party meant the first pitch used one but the second pitch did not.

1988	9 May	Veinity Fair	A.Nelson, K.Howett
1988	10 May	Chiaroscuro	K.Howett, A.Nelson

One of the most serious routes in the glen.

1988	21 May	Rush	G.Szuca, C.Moody
1988	22 May	Son of a Bitch	M.Garthwaite, A.Wren, G.Szuca

Top-roped first. The team managed to make it from the crag into town in 15 minutes in order to record the route in the new routes book before closing time.

1988	22 May	Tectonic Man	A.Nelson
1988	22 May	Vertigo	A.Nelson, A.Hoppe
1988	28 May	Resurrection Shuffle	C.Bell, S.Lampard
1988	4 Jun	The First Cut	G.Latter
1988	4 Jun	Eliminator, Picnic, Barf	G.Szuca, P.Hyde
1988	8 Jun	Ex-Lax	G.Szuca, A.Moody
1988	18 Jun	Altitude Sickness	C.Moody, G.Szuca
1988	20 Jun	Solstice	G.Szuca, A.Nelson
1988	24 Jun	Midsummer Nightmare, Bog Crack	G.Szuca (solo)
1988	26 Jun	Strategic Midge Limitation Talks	I.Taylor, C.Moody
1988	Jun	Run to the Hills, Scorpion	A.Ravenhill, J.Prinn
1988	3 Jul	Forty Two	G.Latter, K.Howett
1988	Jul	Hedge of Insanatree	A.Ravenhill, S.Porter
1988	29 Oct	Blockage	D.Griffiths
1988		Dark Horse	S.Hill (solo)
1988		Apocalypse the Day Before Yesterday	P.Newton

1989	7 May	Fool's Gold	M.Gibb, G.Latter
1989	22 May	Lacerations	G.Latter (solo)
1989	23 May	Watermark	G.Latter
1989	1 Jun	Trick of the Tail	M.McGowan

Another much-eyed line but one that is often wet. A blow torch became resident at the crag to try and dry the line.

1989	11 Jun	Move It or Park It	M.McGowan
1989	3 Aug	Mice on the Riviera	G.Latter, P.Farrell
1989	9 Sep	Poor Man's Wimpabout	I.Taylor, A.Caren
1989		The Compost Heap that Time Forgot	S.Davidson (solo)
1990	Apr	Three Cracks Route	R.Wilson, S.Davidson
1990		Pink 'n' Trees	P.Newton, N.Martin

Practiced on a top rope prior to a lead.

| 1990 | Apr | Breathing Like a Drowning Man | C.Smith, A.Ravenhill |
| 1990 | Apr | The Short Straw | C.Smith |

Top-roped prior to a lead and the runners pre-placed.

1990	25 May	Digit Midget, Un-named	G.Szuca, A.Coish
1990	2 Jul	Around the Bend, Clam-Jam	J.Williamson, C.Smith
1990	2 Jul	Bananafishbones, Stratasphere	C.Smith, J.Williamson
1990	2 Jul	Hearth of Glass	C.Smith, J.Williamson
1990	9 Sep	Precious Cargo	S.MacLean (solo)

An impressive ascent attempted on sight. After abseil inspection for gear placements, it was soloed!

| 1990 | 26 Sep | Evil Eye | C.Smith, S.MacLean |

Top-roped first.

1991	5 May	Carpe Diem	G.Latter, K.Howett, G.Ettle
1991	30 Aug	No Porpoise	A.Ravenhill, A.Jummsame
1992	8 Apr	SNP	G.Szuca, G.Latter
1992	9 Apr	Pay No Poll Tax	G.Szuca, G.Latter
1992	9 Apr	The Gaza Strip	G.Latter, G.Szuca
1992	23 May	Virtual Reality	R.Anderson, D.McCallum, J.May

Pink-pointed with gear placed on the lead.

1992	30 May	Naetitherba'	G.Latter, T.Brannen, A.Tod
1992	May	Titter Ye Not	P.Thorburn (solo)
1992	21 Jul	Leopold	M.Hamilton

One of the best and hardest crack lines in Scotland. Its difficulty led Hamilton to pre-place the runners before climbing the route in pink-point style on the second day. Since then it has been partially retro-bolted as a sport route project that crosses it. First climbed in the 1970s by D.Knowles as Steall Hut Crag Crack (A3).

| 1993 | 14 Sep | The Dream of the Butterfly | G.Latter |

Numerous pegs were placed for protection on the crux traverse.

| 1993 | 19 Sep | Steall Appeal | M.Smith |

The first completed sport route in the glen, and the hardest of its type in Scotland. The route was bolted by another party.

| 1993 | 20 Sep | Arcadia | G.Latter |

Climbed in red point style.

1994	7 Jul	Singapore Crack	R.Stachan, A.Hammond
1994	Jul	Reflections	S.Kennedy, C.Grindley
1996	6 Apr	Gnork	K.M.Edgar, K.Schwartz
1996	6 May	The Trick is to Keep Breathing	G.Latter

Previously top-roped and climbed with many skyhooks for protection.

1997	22 Jul	Heading for the Howff, Weaver's Loom	A.Cameron, J.Stalker
1997	22 Jul	Mostly Harmless	D.Smith, D.Murray
1997	3 Aug	Little Blind Spider	A.Cameron, J.Stalker
1997	8 Aug	Infinite Improbability Drive	D.Smith, D.Murray

LOCH LINNHE AND LOCH LEVEN CRAGS

CREAG DUBH NA CAILLICH

All routes B.McDermott and party in 1985/6 with the following exceptions:

1986	21 Jul	The Big Tree	G.Latter, B.McDermott
1986	21 Jul	The Kiss of the Spiderwoman	G.Latter, B.McDermott

DUBH-GHLAC

1986	Feb	Animal's Route	M.Charlton, C.Henderson

CREAG MHOR

Left and Right-Hand Cracks were climbed by K.Spence, A.Fyffe (date unknown).

1978		Christie's Crack	K.Johnstone, D.Partridge
1990	10 Jun	Tao Mood	P.Potter, A.MacDonald

Top-roped prior to being led.

STAC AN EICH

1981	5 Oct	Original Route	E.Grindley, D.Gunn, N.Williams
1981	22 Oct	Gunslinger	E.Grindley, D.Gunn

So named, as the secod sat in slings en route!

1981	6 Nov	Marathon	E.Grindley, M.Hall
1981	14 Nov	Shuttlecock	E.Grindley, P.Long
1981	15 Nov	Red Fox	P.Long, E.Grindley, G.Libeks
1982	25 Mar	Old Fox	E.Grindley (solo)
1982	26 Mar	The Monument	E.Grindley
1984		Bill's Digger	D.Cuthbertson

An oft tried line. The hammered nut on the crux was placed by Grindley, but not hammered by him!

1985	19 May	Let Sleeping Dogs Lie	M.Hamilton, R.Anderson
1985	6 Jul	Bill's Digger's Fucked	C.Murray

Climbed with a runner an unspecified height up Marathon.

1986	6 Jan	The Leisure Trail	G.Latter
1986	10 Mar	Gunrunner	G.Latter, I.Campbell
1986	5 May	From Here to There	G.Latter
1986	8 May	Hallmark	G.Latter, D.Griffiths
1986	10 Jun	Gold Seal	G.Latter (solo)

KENTALLEN QUARRIES

The routes are not described in the text, but are included here for posterity.

1988	16 Oct	Furstenburg Hangover, Jagster	G.Szuca, A.Nelson
1988	16 Oct	Fairly Park	G.Szuca
1990	May	Creation Rebel	G.Szuca (solo)
1990	15 May	Sendoro Luminoso	G.Szuca, M.Thomson

CREAGAN-FAIRE FHAIBHIDH

1982		Barnacle, Cop Out	D.Gunn, R.Hamilton
1982		Fall Out, Prawn, Cocktail	R.Hamilton, D.Gunn
1982	10 May	Up Periscope	E.Grindley (solo)
1987	22 Jun	The Powerbulge	G.Latter, K.Howett (both led)

B-STATION BUTTRESS

1989	Twisting by the Pool	F.Coleman, P.Anderson.

TORR GARBH

A Bit Thin was climbed by F.Coleman. The route was top-roped, then led with a long sling on a pre-placed runner in the top crack.

DALLENS ROCK, APPIN

1991	6 May	The Golden Slab	S.Kennedy, C.Grindley
1991	12 May	Power of the West	S.Kennedy, C.Grindley
1991	3 Sep	Skywalker	S.Kennedy, D.Ritchie

THE BISHOP'S MANTLE, SEIL

1980	Jun	South Face	D.Hayter, P.Mallison
1982		North Face	D.Hayter, K.NIcholl
1982		Unnamed	D.Hayter, K.Nicholl
1987	22 Aug	North Face of the Shark's Tooth	G.Latter, I.Campbell

GLENFINNAN AND MALLAIG

THE RAILWAY BUTTRESS

1972		Locomotion	I.Sykes, W.Stitt
1973		Calop Junction, Absent Friends	I.Sykes, A.N.Other
1973		Humfibacket	I.Sykes, G.Smith
1984	27 May	Hunchback	E.Grindley, M.Ross
1984	8 Jul	Eegy Weegy	E.Grindley, D.Armstrong
1984	8 Jul	Danceclass	D.Armstrong, E.Grindley
1984	9 Jul	Don't Fear the Reaper	D.Armstrong, E.Grindley
1984	7 Aug	Pas de Deux, Reaper Direct	E.Grindley, D.Armstrong
1984	7 Aug	Scaredevil	D.Armstrong, E.Grindley
1984	9 Aug	Ghost Train	E.Grindley, D.Armstrong
1984	9 Aug	Wriggly Rib, Spearmint Slab	E.Grindley (solo)
1984	12 Aug	Even the Camels are Weird	D.Armstrong, E.Grindley
1984	12 Aug	Aosacko	E.Grindley, D.Armstrong (alts)
1984	12 Aug	Corner and Slab	E.Grindley, D.Armstrong
1984	Aug	Freestyle	K.MacDonald, R.Lee
1984	19 Aug	Cat People	D.Armstrong, A.Wright
1984	22 Aug	Silicon	D.Armstrong (solo)
1984	24 Aug	Overhang and Groove	E.Grindley (solo)
1984	24 Aug	Ramp and Crack	E.Grindley, A.Moist
1984	24 Aug	Manic Laughter, Night Games	D.Armstrong, A.Wright
1993	21 Aug	Falling Like a Stone	G.Szuca
1997	22 Jun	Cadbury Flake	P.Higginson, J.Lines
1997	22 Jun	Very Gneiss Wall	J.Lines, P.Higginson

CARN MHIC A' GHILLE-CHAIM

| 1986 | 30 Aug | Edge of Perfection, Carpet Bagger | G.E.Little, D.Saddler |
| 1989 | 22 Jul | Into the Light | G.Latter, G.E.Little |

Second pitch by K.Howett, G.E.Little on 27 Apr 1991.

| 1991 | 27 Apr | Smoke Screen | G.E.Little, K.Howett (alt) |

Second pitch by G.Latter, G.E.Little on 22 Jul 1989.

SGURR BHUIDHE, SOUTH WALL

1987	31 Aug	After the Dance, Before the Rain	G.E.Little, D.Saddler
1990	25 May	Dawn Patrol	G.E.Little, D.Saddler
1991	26 Apr	Going for the Jugular	R.Campbell, G.Latter

The first acensionists beat another interested party by a day.

CREAG MHOR BHRINICOIRE

1984		Grand Old Master	I.Sykes, I.Sutherland
1986	6 Jul	Penguin Monster	A.MacDonald, I.Sykes
1986	8 Jul	Nobs up North	A.Dunhill, M.Tolly
1987	2 Jun	West Coast Boys	G.Dady, A.Slater

Another line was recorded, though in fact not climbed on this occasion. Its ascent came in 1990 as Pump or Dump.

1987	27 May	Election Mania	A.MacDonald, G.Dady
1989		A Reflection, Invasion	C.Smith, J.Williamson
1989		Callanish, LJ, No Way Up	C.Smith, J.Williamson
1990		Pump and Dump	A.Ravenhill, C.Smith
1990		Far West	A.Todd, M.Graham
1993	6 Sep	Morar Magic	A.Ravenhill, H.Methold

CHARLIE'S CRAG

All routes by W.Anderson, J.Patterson

CHOCAHOLICS BUTTRESS

| 1997 | 22 Jun | Cadbury Flake | P.Higginson, J.Lines |

BOATHOUSE CRAG

| 1997 | 22 Jun | Very Gneiss Wall | J.Lines, P.Higginson |

BEINN ODHAR MHOR

1970	11 Oct	Mic	S.G.Crymble, K.Schwartz
1973		Egret	I.Sykes, I.Sutherland
1974		Eyrie	I.Sykes, I.Sutherland

MEALL DOIRE NA MNATHA

All routes by K.Schwartz, A.Gray and J.Mount in 1973.

STRATHNAIRN and SPEYSIDE

DUNTELCHAIG

Many routes were originally aided, including all on Dracula Buttress. Only the first free ascents of these routes are listed, with apologies.

1937	May	The Mica Chasm	K.A.Robertson, J.T.Walker
1937		Mica Arete	R.B.Frere
1937		Mica Chimney	R.B.Frere
1937		Mica Chimney Right Hand	R.B.Frere
1937	24 Jun	Drum	I.M.G., R.B.Frere
1937	24 Jun	Monolith Crack (descent)	I.M.G., R.B.Frere
1937	6 Nov	Inaccessible Crack	K.A.Robertson, R.B.Frere
1958		Sweeney's Crack	T.Sullivan
1962		Drumhead	Sykes, Pothecary, Hinde,Grant, Bell
1963		Swastika	J.Baines
1964		Top Corner	R.P.Bell, R.Todd
1964		Long Slab	D.Williamson
1966		Drumhead Direct	K.Anderson, J.Hunter, M.Allan
1967		Edir	K.Anderson, D.MacKenzie, D.Williamson, J.Jameson
1967		Banker's Doom	P.R.Walker, K.Anderson
1968		Triple Overhang	D.Williamson, A.Williamson
1969		Dracula	R.Brown
1976		Vampire	A.Liddell, M.Burrows-Smith
1978	Jul	Razor Flake (Zig-zag)	D.McCallum, J.MacKenzie
1978	Jul	Bent Peg	D.McCallum, J.MacKenzie

Possibly climbed first, around the same time, by C.Rowland, B.Ledingham.

1978		Monolith Recess (Ash Groove)	A.Liddell and party
1979	19 May	Anne Boleyn's Crack	J.MacKenzie, D.Butterfield, D.McCallum
1979	19 May	Eeny, Meeny, Miney, Mo	J.MacKenzie
1980	11 Apr	Slings (Maltese Cross)	D.McCallum

Possibly climbed first, around the same time, by A.Fyffe, S.Crymble.

1980s		Chasm Outside Route	C.Rowland, B.Ledingham
1980s		Sole Horror	C.Rowland
1980		Balrog (Hugh)	M Priestman, A Kassyk, D.McCallum
1981		Little Drummer Boy	A.Liddell, A.Fyffe

Drumstick Variation climbed by J.R.MacKenzie and C.Blunt-MacKenzie on 5 July 1992.

1982		Garlic	A.Liddell, M.Campbell
1982		Timpani Rib	A.Liddell, G.Liddell
1982		Misty Crack	A.Fyffe, A.Liddell
1982		Excavator	P.Savill
1983	Aug	Chasm Roof	D.McCallum, C.Fraser

Also climbed by M.Lawrence in the same year.

1983	6 Aug	Cyclops	D.McCallum
1984		Monolith Slab	A.Liddell
1987		Saville Row	P.Savill
1988		Eave	A.Nisbet, H.Geddes
1988		Outside Lane	A.Nisbet, B.Davison
1988		Girdle Traverse	A.Nisbet, S.Blagbrough
1990		Frankenstein	A.Nisbet, D.McCutcheon
1991	Aug	Wolfman	C.Forrest, R.Henderson

1994	Jul	The Percussion	A Liddell and Partners

Pitch 2 had been previously claimed as Drumskin by J.R.MacKenzie and C.Blunt-MacKenzie on 5 July 1992.

1995	7 Jul	Sare	I.Taylor
1995	17 Aug	Gearr	I.Taylor, R.Carlton
1996	11 Aug	Save the Trees	I.Taylor, D.Kennedy
1997	16 May	Bongo	S.J.Paget, A.Mullin
1997	26 Jun	Dragonfly	S.J.Paget, J.Munroe

DUNLICHITY CRAG

1980s		Four Finger Flake	S.Travers, J.Elliot
1980s		Garnish	S.Travers
1980s		Ivy's Slab and Chimney	S.Travers
1980s		Minder	S.Travers, H.Travers
1980s		Zig-Zag	S.Travers, H.Travers
1980s		The Vice	S.Travers

ASHIE FORT
All routes by D.W.Borthwick, O.Clem 7 Sep 1996

BRIN ROCK

1975		Treasure Island	R.McHardy, P.MacDonald
1984		Making Movies	A.Fyffe, A.Liddell
1984		The Block	A.Fyffe, A.Liddell
1984		Screen Test	A.Fyffe, K.Geddes
1985	Jul	The Gangplank (FFA)	A.Fyffe, A.Nisbet
1985	Jul	Pink Rib	A.Nisbet, A.Fyffe
1985	Jul	Turkish Cracks	A.Fyffe, J.Hepburn
1985	Aug	The Prow	A.Nisbet, S.Stewart
1985	Aug	Skytrain	A.Nisbet, D.Armitage
1985	Aug	Giant Flake	G.Ettle, S.Stewart
1985	Sep	Gold Digger	D.Dinwoodie, A.Nisbet
1986	14 Jun	The Wild Man	A.Nisbet, A.Cunningham
1986	14 Jun	Skytrain Direct	A.Cunningham, A.Nisbet
1986		Catweazle	J.Grosset, J.Lyall
1987		Catweazle Direct	J.Grosset, J.Kerr

TYNRICH SLABS

1982	1 Jun	Wrinkle	N.Lawford, P.Savill, F.Adams
1982	2 Jun	Scoops	P.Savill, N.Lawford, F.Adams
1982	23 May	Scorpion	N.Lawford, F.Adams, P.Savill
1982	16 Jun	Strewth	N.Lawford, F.Adams
1988		Puff Ball	A.Nisbet, B.Davison, H.Geddes
1988		Chanterelle	A.Nisbet, B.Davison, H.Geddes
1988		Trumpet of the Dead	B.Davison, A.Nisbet
1988		Blewit	A.Nisbet, B.Davison
1988		Slippery Jack	B.Davison, A.Nisbet
1990		Horn of Plenty	J.Lyall
1990		Boletus	J.Lyall
1993		Chocolate Truffle	J.Lyall

1993		Speechless	J.Lyall
1993		Playing Possum	J.Lyall
1996	Aug	Schist as a Newt	G.Lowe, I.Innes, D.Balfour

CONAGLEANN

1965		Dropout	K.Anderson, D.Williamson, J.Hunter
1966		Fanone	K.Anderson
1966		Foe	P.R.Walker
1966		Hushpuppy	J.Hunter
1966		Tipussip	K.Anderson, W.MacKenzie
1981	Aug	Gonzo	C.Rowland, B.Ledingham
1981		Molar	C.Rowland, B.Ledingham
1981		Toad's Arete	C.Rowland, B.Ledingham
1981		The Raven	C.Rowland, B.Ledingham
1981		Grande	C.Rowland, S.Cooper
1981		Black Slab, Ash Slab	C.Rowland, R.McHardy
1981		Hoody Climb	P.Nunn
1982		Tip Slab	C.Rowland, B.Ledingham
1982	4 Apr	Streaker	S.Travers, H.Travers
1982	12 Apr	Plumb	S.Travers, H.Travers
1982	18 Apr	Finger Arete	S.Travers, H.Travers
1982	25 Apr	Little and Large	S.Travers, I.Douglas
1982	May	Crack and Corner	S.Travers, H.Travers
1982	9 May	7 Up	S.Travers, H.Travers
1982	9 May	Adviser	B.Ledingham, S.Travers
1985		The Streak	C.Rowland, B.Ledingham
1985		The Grey Arete	C.Rowland, B.Ledingham
1986		Umbrella	P.Nunn, C.Rowland

HUNTLY'S CAVE

The details of the older routes were not recorded.

1970s		Pete's Wall	P.Boardman
1970		Lime Street	P.Livesey
1980		Bo-Po Crack	M.Lawrence
1986		Lime-Ade	A.Liddell and party
1987		Huntly's Jam	N.Sharpe
1988		Rentokil	A.Nisbet, T.Walker

BURNSIDE CRAG

All routes by K.Geddes, D.S.B.Wright, Aug 1986 except Grendel by S.Hill and Clear for Landing by A.Liddell, I.Peter, the same summer.

CREAG A' MHUILINN

All routes by S.Summers, R.Ferguson, Jun 1990.

FARLETTER

1983		Strike One	J.Lyall, S.Bowles
1983		Farrt	J.Lyall, S.Bowles
1985		Farr One	D.S.B.Wright, K.Geddes
1985	Jul	Too Farr for the Bear	A.Cunningham, A.Nisbet

1985	Jul	Farr Out	A.Nisbet, A.Cunningham
1985	Jul	Private Farr	A.Cunningham, A.Nisbet
1985	Jul	Yet so Farr	A.Cunningham, A.Nisbet
1985	Jul	The Art of Course Climbing	A.Nisbet, A.Cunningham
1985	Aug	Ceasefarr	A.Nisbet, K.Geddes
1986	Jul	Backwoodsman	A.Nisbet, K.Geddes
1986	Jul	Holiday Tricks	A.Nisbet, K.Geddes
1987		Farrplay	K.Geddes, A.Cunningham

Full name – If this is Farrplay, then I'm a Dead Man.

1988		The Master Farrter	A.Ross, M.Sutherland
1990		Liquid Quartz	M.Burrows-Smith (unsec)
1990		Links Fahren	M.Burrows-Smith, A.Cunningham
1990		Ausfahrt	A.Cunningham, M.Burrows-Smith
1990		Einfahrt	M.Burrows-Smith, S.Blagbrough
1990		The Farrter	M.Burrows-Smith, L.Healey
1990		Yet So Farther	M.Burrows-Smith, S.Blagbrough
1990		Holiday Tricks Direct	C.Forrest, R.Henderson
1990		Leeper Madness	M.Burrows-Smith, A.Fyffe
1990		Mighty Mouse	M.Burrows-Smith, A.Fyffe
1991		Farralaff	D.S.B.Wright, G.Ettle
1991	27 Aug	Farrthest South	D.S.B.Wright, R.Mansfield
1991	27 Aug	Farr Too High	R.Mansfield, D.S.B.Wright
1991	29 Aug	Farrouche	R.Mansfield (unseconded)

THE BADAN

1987	Jul	The Bad Uns	K.Geddes, D.S.B.Wright
1991	27 May	Vrotan	G.Ettle, D.S.B.Wright

KINGUSSIE

The details of the older routes were not recorded.

1980		Leftover	M.Burrows-Smith
1980		Bolt Ladder of the Flake	M.Burrows-Smith
1984		Central Wall	A.Liddell, G.Liddell
1988		Hole in One	B.Davison, A.Nisbet
1992		Bolt Revolt	C.Forrest, I.Dillon

CREAG DUBH AND LAGGAN

CREAG DUBH

Rib Direct was climbed by B.Halpin, T.Abbey, S.Tondeur, date unknown.

1959	Jul	Nutcracker Chimney	T.Sullivan, A Parkin
1959	Oct	Brute	T.Sullivan, N.Collingham
1962	Aug	Slanting Groove	M.Owen, D.Gregory
1964	Oct	Inbred	D.Haston, T.Gooding
1965	Mar	Tip Off	D.Bathgate, I.A McEacheran
1965	Apr	Tip Off Variation	A.Colvin, A McFarlane
1965	Apr	King Bee	D.Haston, J.Moriarty, A.Ewing
1965	Apr	Tree Hee	H.Small, J.Graham
1965	Apr	Tree Hee Variation	I.A.McEacheran, J.Knight, R.S.Burnet
1965	May	Negligee	I.A.McEacheran, R.S.Burnet
1965	May	Downtown Lunch	F.Harper, A.Ewing, A.McKeith

1965	May	Mount	D.Haston
1965	May	Muph Dive	D.Bathgate, R.K.Holt

FFA by M.Hamilton, A.Last, Sep 1977.

1965	May	Cuckold	D.Haston, J.Moriarty

FFA by P.Boardman in 1974.

1965	May	Gham	D.Haston, J.Heron
1965	May	Prak, Epar, Romp	D.Haston
1965	May	Erse	D.Haston, J.Moriarty

Pitches 3, 4 and 5 were added by D.Haston, J Heron. Aid was used up to and over the roof on Pitch 1. FFA by a variation to the right by MacDonald in 1974; FFA of the original is unknown.

1965	May	Migrane	I.A.McEacheran, A.McKeith
1965	May	Phellatio	A.Ewing, I.A.McEacheran

A direct finish was added by K.Crocket, C Stead in 1972 and is now the popular line.

1965	May	Mirador	I.A.McEacheran, J.Knight, R.S.Burnet
1965	May	Fred	A.McKeith, D.Haston.F.Harper, A.Ewing
1965	May	Gang Bang	F.Harper, A.McKeith

The Direct Start was added the same time by D.Haston and J.Moriarty.

1965	May	Jump so High	F.Harper, A.McKeith, A.Ewing

FFA by G.Shields and party in the early 1970s. A direct finish (now the normal line) was also added by Shields with aid. FFA: M.Hamilton and K.Spence in 1978.

1965	Jun	Hayripi	D.Haston, M.Galbraith
1965	Jun	Raven's Squawk	M.Harcus, G.Anderson
1965	Oct	Show Off	D.Bathgate, J.Renny

A variation start was climbed by D.Grey and Thompson, but was later superseded by the route Acrobat.

1965	Oct	Take Off	D.Bathgate, J.Renny
1965	Oct	Oui Oui	R.S.Burnet, A.McKeith
1965	Nov	Smirnoff	D.Bathgate, J.Brumfit
1965	Nov	Cunnulinctus	R.S.Burnet, A.McKeith
1965	Nov	Great Wall Girdle	D.Haston, R.N.Campbell
1965	Nov	Fiorella	F.Harper, A.McKeith, J.Knight
1965	Nov	Potato	J.Knight, A.McKeith
1966	Jan	Oui Oui	M.Galbraith, E.Woodcock

A winter ascent.

1966	21 May	Hungarian Hamstring	A.McKeith, R.Hart, A.Thompson
1966	Aug	Cockadoodlemoobahquack	A.McKeith and party
1966	Aug	Kneekers Off	J.Brumfit, B.Sproul
1967	May	Minge	A.McKeith, I.A.MacEacheran, W.Pryde

FFA by G.Shields and party in the early 1970s.

1966	25 Aug	Slabsville	A.McKeith and party
1966	Sep	King Bee Direct	K.Spence, R.Gough
1966	Sep	The Hill	K.Spence, J.Porteous
1966	Sep	Stoop so Low, Jump so High (Var)	K.Spence, J.Porteous

A direct finish was added to Stoop so Low by B.March and R.Smith in April 1972.

1966	Sep	Trampoline	J.Cunningham
1967/8		Sprawl Wall Girdle	K.Spence, J.Porteous
1970	10 Mar	Hornet	B.March, G.Cairns
1970	11 Apr	Porn	J.Porteous, M.Watson

1970	11 Apr	Line Up	I.Fulton, J.R.Houston
1970	Apr	Sweetness	B.March, F.Harper
1970	4 Apr	Route Toot Toot	D.Jenkins, C.Stead
1970	11 Apr	Tongue Twister	C.Stead, D.Jenkins
1971	13 Apr	Outspan	R.Barley, B.Griffiths
1971	27 Jun	Organ Grinder	K.V.Crocket, C.Stead

Later superceded by Ogan Grinder Variations.

1971	4 Sep	Mighty Piston	K.V.Crocket, I.Fulton
1971	10 Oct	L.M.F.	F.Harper, B.March
1971	Oct	Snoopy	B.March, C.Norris

FFA: G.Farquhar, K.Grennald 1988

1972	Apr	Scraping The Barrel	F.Harper, B.March
1972	Apr	Brass, Brazen	A.Fyffe, B.March
1972	Apr	Pshaw	F.Harper, B.March
1972	Apr	Zambesi, Niagara	G.Shields and party
1972	Apr	Mythical Wall	

Climbed the upper groove right of the corner of Brute which was later used by a direct ascent to give the Fuhrer.

1972	Apr	Felix	B.March, C.Rawlings

FFA: G.Farquhar, I.Marriott 21 May 1988.

1972	Apr	Sheath	R.G.Ross, H.Henderson, A.Walker
1976		Un Petit Mort	R.Baillie, M.B.Smith
1976	23 Jul	Sideshow, Run Free	D.Cuthbertson, D.Jameson
1976	24 Jul	Centrespread	D.Cuthbertson, D.Jameson
1976	9 Sep	Ticket to Ride, Men Only	D.Cuthbertson, A.Taylor
1976	10 Sep	Strapadictaemi	D.Cuthbertson, R.Anderson
1976	27 Oct	The Frustrations	D.Cuthbertson, A.Taylor
1976	11 Nov	Inbred Direct	D.Cuthbertson, R.Anderson
1976	12 Nov	Oddli	R.Anderson, D.Cuthbertson
1977	12 Sep	Breakaway	D.Cuthbertson, F.Allison
1977	19 Sep	Quickie, Ruff Licks	D.Cuthbertson, R.Anderson
1977	14 Oct	Muffin the Mule	D.Cuthbertson, D.Mullin
1977	15 Oct	Rising Damp	D.Cuthbertson, D.Mullin (alt)
1978	12 Oct	Case Dismissed	D.Cuthbertson, R.Anderson
1978	12 Oct	Pare	R.Anderson, A.McAllister
1978	13 Oct	Offspring	R.Anderson, M.Duff
1978	14 Oct	In Between Times	M.Duff, D.Cuthbertson, J.Small
1978	19 Oct	Easy Going	R.Anderson, A.McAllister
1979	16 Jun	Desire	D.Cuthbertson, I.F.Duckworth
1979	17 Jun	Fuhrer	D.Cuthbertson, I.F.Duckworth
1980	29 Sep	Instant Lemon	D.Jameson, D.Cuthbertson (alt)
1980	30 Jun	Instant Lemon Direct Start	D.Cuthbertson, P.Hunter, D.Jameson, C.Lees
1980	22 Oct	Acrobat	M.Duff, P.Barrass
1980	23 Oct	Succer	M.Duff, P.Barrass
1980	Oct	Bulger	D.Cuthbertson, T.Prentice
1980	Nov	Over the Hill	D.Cuthbertson, R.Kerr
1981		First Offence	D.Cuthbertson, R.Kerr
1981		Independence	D.Cuthbertson, R.Kerr, C.Fraser
1981		Ayatollah	D.Cuthbertson, R.Kerr, C.Fraser
1981		C'Est la Vie	M.Lawrence (Solo)
1981		Galaxy	D.Cuthbertson, M.Lawrence

1981		Separation	M.Lawrence, D.Cuthbertson
1981		Hands Off	M.Lawrence, D.Lawrence
1981		The Art of Relaxation	D.Cuthbertson, R.Williamson
1981		Footloose and Fancy Free	D.Cuthbertson, R.Williamson
1981		Organ Grinder Variation	D.Cuthbertson, R.Williamson
1981	6 Jun	Arch enemy, Probe	D.Cuthbertson, R.Anderson
1981	7 Jun	Silicosis	D.Cuthbertson, R.Anderson
1981	Jun	Jack The Lad, Goutes d'Eau	D.Cuthbertson, R.Anderson
1981	Jun	Featherlight, Cadillac	D.Cuthbertson, R.Anderson
1981	Jun	Gossamer	R.Anderson, D.Cuthbertson
1981	Jun	Acapulco, Hot to Trot	D.Cuthbertson, R.Anderson
1981	Jun	Wet Dreams	D.Cuthbertson, R.Anderson

Possibly climbed earlier with aid.

1981	Aug	Jump for Joy	D.Cuthbertson, R.Duncan, A.Taylor
1983	10 Aug	Black Shadow	M.Duff, T.Brindle
1983	10 Aug	Man on Fire	M.Duff, T.Brindle
1983	10 Aug	Ninja	M.Duff, T.Brindle
1983	10 Aug	The Snake	T.Brindle, M.Duff
1983	10 Aug	The Sting	T.Brindle, M.Duff
1983	11 Aug	Concealed Entrance	T.Brindle, M.Duff
1983	11 Aug	Free and Easy	M.Duff, T.Brindle
1983	18 Aug	Sense of Urgency	M.Duff, T.Brindle
1983	19 Aug	Mistaken Identity	T.Brindle, M.Duff
1983	28 Aug	Crazy Paving	M.Duff, A.Russell
1983	28 Aug	Pattern of Violence	M.Duff (unseconded)
1983	29 Aug	The Force	M.Duff, A.Russell
1984	20 Aug	Orinoco	A.Fyffe, M.Seaton
1985	16 Jun	Heather Wall	G.Latter, C.Henderson
1985	7 Jun	Most Girls Do	S.Richardson, R.Webb
1985	23 Oct	Colder than a Hooker's Heart	D.Cuthbertson, C.Henderson, G.Latter
1985	23 Oct	Nobody's Fault but Mine	G.Latter

The second failed to follow on this girdle traverse.

1986	17 Jul	Legover	R.Sharpe, A.Moist
1986	21 Sep	Jade	G.Nicoll, J.Hotchkis
1986	Sep	Apathizer	G.Livingston, W.Todd
1986	11 Oct	Warmer than a Badger's Bum	R.Anderson, M.Fowler
1986		Kiwi	R.Treadwell, D.Williams
1987	May	The Final Solution	S.Monks, W.Todd

A superb addition. Monks beat the locals to the FA by a matter of days.

1987	Aug	Bratach Uaine	G.Livingston, A.Cunningham

An excellent find.

1987		Turf at the Top	S.Aisthorpe, J.Lyall
1988	21 May	Harder than your Husband	G.Farquhar, I.Marriot
1988		Not Before Time	N.Shepherd, D.Douglas
1988		Ground Control	D.Griffiths, I.Griffiths
1989	May	Snotrag	G.Farquhar, C.Carolan
1990	May	Zygote	J.Kerr, R.Mansfield
1990	May	Jezebel	R.Mansfield, J.Kerr
1990	May	Serendipity	J.Kerr, R.Mansfield
1991	Aug	Straight Line	A.Nisbet, J.Lyall
1991	Aug	Thyme	J.Lyall, A.Nisbet

1991	Aug	Take Three	A.Nisbet, J.Lyall
1991	Sep	Cockquack	A.Nisbet
1991	Sep	On Guard	A.Nisbet, R.Henderson
1991	Sep	The Badger Direct	A.Nisbet, R.Henderson
1991	Sep	The Bum Direct	A.Nisbet, R.Henderson
1991	Sep	Niagara direct start	A.Nisbet, J.Lyall
1991	Sep	Unlawful Behaviour	C.Forrest, G.Ettle
1991	Sep	Jailbreak	C.Forrest, G.Ettle
1991		This One	P.Thorburn, G.Latter
1992		Cross Leaved Heath	C.Forrest
1994	9 Jul	Cream Dream	C.Pettigrew, R.Renwick
1994	2 Sep	King Tubby And The Fat Boys Rap	R.Mansfield, I Sherrington

CREAGAN SOILLEIR

1989	May	Skylarking	J.Lyall
1989	May	Flypast	J.Lyall
1989	May	The Coroner	J.Lyall
1989	May	Culture Vulture	J.Lyall
1989	May	Magical Ring	J.Lyall, E.Pirie
1989	May	Laggan Behind	J.Lyall, E.Pirie
1989	May	Badenoch Beckons	J.Lyall, E.Pirie
1989	May	Thistle Crack	J.Lyall, E.Pirie
1989	May	Cracking	J.Lyall, E.Pirie
1989	Sep	Ring of Truth	S.Aisthorpe (unseconded)
1989	Sep	Caledonian Crack	J.Lyall, S.Aisthorpe
1990	Sep	Eternal Optimist	A.Nisbet, J.Lyall
1990	Sep	Sanction Busters	J.Lyall, A.Nisbet

BINNEIN SHUAS

1964	May	The Fortress	T.Patey, R.Ford, M.Stewart
1967		West Chimney, Brocken Gully	G.N.Hunter, D.F.Lang
1967	Apr	Hidden Gully	G.N.Hunter, D.F.Lang
1967	24 Jun	Ardverikie Wall, Merry Down	G.N.Hunter, D.F.Lang
1967	25 Jun	Kubla Khan	G.N.Hunter, D.F.Lang
1967	15 Jul	Criss, Cross	D.F.Lang, G.N.Hunter
1967	16 Jul	The Keep	D.F.Lang, G.N.Hunter, M.D.Main

An alternative start was added 21 June 1996 by G.Latter and R.Kerr.

1967	Jun	Fly Paper	D.F.Lang, G.N.Hunter
1967	17 Sep	Blaeberry Grooves, Cube Wall, Hairline Grooves	D.F.Lang, G.N.Hunter
1968	Jun	Usquebaugh	G.N.Lang, D.F.Hunter
1968	24 May	Soft Shoe Shuffle	G.N.Hunter, D.F.Lang

The variation was climbed by I.Taylor, A.Carren and R.Turner on 27 May 1990.

1968	25 May	Whiplash	D.F.Lang, G.N.Hunter
1969	May	Tip Top	J.McDowell, Todd
1969	May	Differential	J.McDowell, Todd
1969	May	Eastern Chimney	J.McDowell, Todd
1970	Jul	The Fortress Direct	R.Carrington, J.R.Marshall
1971	26 Jul	Crisscross Edge	D.Regan, K.Schwartz
1971	28 Jul	Near Miss	M.Horsburgh, D.Regan, K.Schwartz
1972	8 Jul	Left Foot First	B.Dunn, C.Higgins

A long, long girdle of the main face – guess the direction!

1976	15 Aug	Whipped Cream	D.Baker, M.Smith
1976	11 Sep	Hurricane	C.Ogilvy, C.Stock
1980		Un-named	J.Lyall, E.Pirie
1982	10 Jan	Foxtrot (Winter)	J.Jeffrey, S.Kennedy, C.Macleod, M.Sclater
1983	30 Jul	Delayed Attack	G.Goddard

Those involved with the line were sworn to secrecy but when Bill Birkett came up to do it with D.Lylle on 26 Aug 1983, he found he was too slow and only got the second ascent.

1984	17 May	Storming the Bastille (1PA)	M.A.Charlton, A.A.Moist

Charlton returned later and freed the roof of the foot sling used for aid.

1984	27 May	Ardanfreaky	M.A.Charlton, A.A.Moist, J.Griffiths

Both this and Storming the Bastille were climbed on sight by Charlton and were the first of a harder batch of routes on The Bastion.

1985	11 Aug	Motte	G.Muhlemann, S.Richardson
1987		Eastern Chimney (winter)	K.Howett, A.A.Moist
1987		Scotch on the Rocks (winter)	M.Charlton, R.Stewart

A winter line close to Usquebaugh.

1988		Wallachian Prince	K.Howett, A.Nelson

Vlad The Impaler would have liked this one!

1980s		Cowberry Wall	C.Forrest, K.Davis
1990	27 May	The Perils of Perseus	I.Taylor, A.Carren, R.Turner
1992	17 Jun	Use of Weapons	G.Farquhar, C.Carolan
1993	9 May	Native Stones	N.Kempe, D.Lang

The founder member of the 'Binnein Shuas Appreciation Society' makes a welcome comback after 26 years.

1993	14 Aug	Comriach	A.Tibbs, A.Mathewson
1993	6 Jun	Tairnearan Tar As	I.Taylor, R.Campbell
1994	22 May	Far East Chimney	N.Kempe, D.Lang
1994	11 Jun	Turning a Blind Eye	R.Campbell, P.Thorburn
1995	3 Jan	A Lethal Affair (winter)	S.Allan, M.Atkins
1995	5 Jul	Bog Myrtle Trip	R.Campbell, P.Thorburn
1995	31 Jul	Wild Mountain Thyme	N.Craig, G.Latter, R.Campbell

Climbed on sight, the line having been cleaned some years before by another suitor.

1996	30 Aug	Rubaiyat	G.Latter, J.Hartley

DIRC MHOR

1966	23 Aug	Holy Smoke	A.McKeith and party
1980	25 Jul	Slowhand	A.Fyffe, K.Geddes
1980	1 Aug	Working Class Hero	A.Fyffe, K Geddes, A.Liddell
1981	23 Aug	Positive Earth	M.Burrows Smith, A.Fyffe
1994	16 Jul	Fanfare for the Common Man	G.E.Little, K.Howett (alt)

The start of the Dirc Mhor renaissance. A first attempt failed due to the wind (an ever present hazard here) and the cold.

1994	30 Jul	The Scent of a Woman	K.Howett, G.E.Little

'The perfume of a friend followed us all the way to the top.'

1994	30 Jul	Carry on up the Kyber	G.E.Little, K.Howett
1994	31 Jul	After Many a Summer	G.E.Little, K.Howett
1994	31 Jul	No Way Out	G.E.Little, K.Howett
1994	11 Aug	A Deep Green Peace	K.Howett, G.E.Little
1994	13 Aug	Murderous Pursuit	K.Howett, J Horrocks
1994	13 Aug	Schist Hot	A.Banks, G.Ridge
1994	28 Aug	Spurlash	K.Howett

1994	22 Aug	Crowberry Crank	G.E.Little, K.Howett
1994	17 Sep	Whitecap Direct	G.E.Little, K.Howett (alt)
1994	25 Sep	Galileo's Gambol	K.Howett, G.E.Little
1995	24 Jun	The Man with the Child in his Eyes	K.Howett, G.E.Little (alt)
1995	25 Jun	Dry Roasted	G.Ridge, J Horrocks
1995	25 Jun	Scorched Earth	J Horrocks, K.Howett
1995	13 Aug	Breaking the Wind	K.Howett, L.Hughes
1995	13 Aug	Bournville	G.Nicoll, J.Hotchkiss

Climbed on-sight. Most other recent additions needed cleaning.

1996	9 Jul	Close to the Wind	G.Latter
1996	14 Sep	Gullible's Travels	N.Kempe, M.Dales
1996	14 Sep	Working on the Hoof, Dust Devil	K.Howett, K.Ross

CREAG DOIRE NA H-ACHLAISE

| 1989 | 7 May | Centenary Wall | M.Slesser, I.Smart |

Crocket, McEwan, Richardson and Walker (SMC) did some routes here prior to this one but did not record them.

| 1997 | 20 Jul | Quartz Boss, Zagaboot | R.Anderson, C.Anderson |

STRATHTAY and STRATH TUMMEL

CRAIG VARR

All early routes were climbed by various people from Rannoch School at Dell and Stirling University's Outdoor centre at Crosscraigs, apart from Mutton, Pork, Grouse, Avenue, Black Rod (M.Duff, L.Brims 23 May 1983); Macman, Stratafear, Shakin' Not Stirred (K.Howett, S.Harrison 27 Jul 1994).

BONSKEID CRAG

Full first ascent details are unknown, although Ian Rowe was one of its discoverers (in 1965) and its leading pioneer, whilst Pat Mellor and Peter Macdonald also had a hand in it.

| 1972 | | Johnny Apollo | D.Hamilton, I.G.Rowe |

WEEM CRAGS

1997	8 Mar	Brass Monkeys	G.Ridge
1997	9 Mar	Caledonia Dreaming	N.Shepherd
1997	22 Mar	Batweeman	I.Watson
1997	22 Mar	The Watchtower	C.Miln
1997	24 Mar	The Chemical Generation	C.Miln
1997	29 Mar	The End of Silence	C.Miln
1997	30 Mar	Faithless	G.Ridge
1997	31 Mar	On the Tick List	N.Shepherd
1997	5 Apr	100 Ways to be a Good Girl	J.Horrocks
1997	10 Apr	The Last Temptation	G.Ridge, J.Horrocks
1997	12 Apr	Confession of Faith	J.Horrocks
1997	12 Apr	Forbidden Fruit	I.Watson
1997	13 Apr	Mannpower	D.Pert
1997	13 Apr	High Pitched Scream	N.Shepherd
1997	13 Apr	The Screaming Weem	G.Ridge
1997	20 Apr	President Shhean Connery	C.Miln
1997	20 Apr	The Republic of Scotland	C.Miln
1997	26 Apr	Don't Fear the Reaper	G.Ridge

1997	29 Apr	Crushed by the Wheels of Industry	G.Ridge
1997	25 May	The Long Good Friday	I.Watson
1997	29 May	Drop Dead Gorgeous	N.Shepherd
1997	31 May	The Glass Ceiling	G.Ridge
1997	31 May	Alien Artifact	N.Shepherd
1997	22 Jun	Left on the Shelf	R.Anderson
1997	13 Jul	Right in the Face	R.Anderson
1997	Jul	Justice	C.Miln
1997	26 Jul	Looking for a Rainbow	M.Nicoll, G.Nicoll
1997	2 Sep	Strong Signal	G.Nicoll, K.Howett

Climbed on sight.

1997	4 Sep	Communication Breakdown	K.Howett, L.Hughes
1997	4 Sep	The Detector Van	G.Nicoll, K.Howett
1997	Jul	Kissing the Witch	J.Horrocks

A sport route, later climbed in part with natural gear by L.Hughes and K.Howett as The Choice of a New Generation. The bolts remain in place.

1997	15 Sep	Pawn Channel	L.Hughes, K.Howett
1997	16 Sep	Static in the Air	K.Howett, L.Hughes
1997	18 Sep	Wired for Sound	G.Nicoll, K.Howett
1997	18 Sep	Moving the Aerial	K.Howett, G.Nicoll, A.Todd

Climbed on sight.

CLUNY ROCK

| 1987 | 29 Aug | Tartan, Tae the Oaks | D.Donoghue, C.Moody, L Roberts |
| 1987 | 6 Sep | Shortbread, Domino | W.Hood, C.Moody, I.Taylor |

CREAG NA H-EIGHE

1989	Mar	Rabbit Run	G.Penny
1989	Mar	Wee Brahmer, Woodworm	G.Penny, D.Black
1989	Mar	Jaggy Bunnets, Jugs	G.Penny, D.Black
1989	Apr	'A Votre Sante' Dickie	D.Rennie, R.Gatehouse
1989	May	Just A Pech	D.Rennie, G.Penny
1989	Jun	Separation	G.Penny, D.Rennie
1989	Jun	Raptor's Chimney	D.Rennie, G.Penny
1989	Jun	Heather Wall	G.Penny
1990	May	Wee Arete	D.Rennie, C.Wallace
1989		Hunt the Gunman	S.Downie, D.Cassidy

There were numerous contenders for the first ascent in the 1990s, as it is the best route here. However Downie and Cassidy got in first.

| 1992 | 5 Sep | Cohen's Climb | G.Cohen |
| 1992 | 13 Sep | Raptor's Chimney Direct Start | N.Holmes, W.Jeffrey |

Possibly done by P.Gribbon in 1960.

| 1993 | 27 Jun | Doctor Squeal | B.Kerr, M.Boyle |
| 1993 | 27 Jun | Picnic Parade | B.Kerr, M.Boyle |

Top-roped by other parties at about the same time.

| 1993 | | The Sleeping Sickness | P.Thorburn, R.Campbell |

CRAIG A BARNS

POLNEY CRAG

| 1957 | | Twisted Rib | R.N.Campbell |

Direct Finish by P.Brian in 1959.

1957		Consolation Corner	P.Brian
1957		Kestrel Crack	R.N.Campbell
1958		Ivy Crack	P.Brian
1959		Beech Wall	R.N.Campbell
1959		Bollard Buttress	R.N.Campbell
1959		Terminal Buttress	R.N.Campbell
1959		Wriggle	R.N.Campbell
1959		Hoggs Hindquarters	R.N.Campbell
1960		Myopic's Corner	I.G.Rowe

The first ascent of the direct version was by A.Taylor.

| 1960 | | Springboard | R.N.Campbell |

The direct version was climbed by D.Bathgate with 2PA. FFA: D.Jameson 1978. A left-hand finish was recorded by B.Ankers in 1988.

| 1960 | | Polney Girdle Traverse | R.N.Campbell |
| 1960 | | Piker's Progress | R.N Campbell |

Other Piker's variations were later superceded by Twilight.

1960		The Groove	R.Smith
1960		The Rut	N.MacNiven
1960		Holly Tree Groove	R.N.Campbell
1960		Recess Route	J.Proom
1960		The Creep	R.N.Campbell
1960		Cuticle Crack	P.Brian
1960		Crescent	R.N.Campbell
1960		Bollard Buttress Direct	P.Brian
1961		The Chute	R.N.Campbell
1961		The End	R.N.Campbell
1961		Left-Hand Crack	N.MacNiven (aid)

FFA: J.Mackenzie in 1974.

1961		Right Hand Crack	N.MacNiven
1961		The Trap	N.MacNiven
1961		Poison Ivy	R.N.Campbell

Variation finish by R.N.Campbell.

1965		Airy Arete	A.McKeith
1966	Apr	Cuticle Creek	I.G.Rowe, P MacDonald
1967	3 Jun	Coathanger (A3)	J.R.Dempster, K.J.Martin

Later bolted in part by I.Cropley in 1991 to give The Vibes.

1967	Jul	The Way Through	K.Spence, R.Sharp
1969		Piker's Progress Direct	I.G.Rowe
1969	8 Dec	Spirochaete	J.Camerson, C, Norris
1971	13 Mar	Carpet Beater	C.Norris, A.Moore
1976	Jun	The Beginning	D.Cuthbertson, M.Hamilton

Top-roped previously by D.Cuthbertson

1978	Nov	Wriggle Direct	D.Cuthbertson, R.Anderson
1978	21 Oct	Pop	M.Duff, A.Kelso
1979	23 Aug	Scram 79	P.Hunter, C.Lees
1979	Sep	The Porker	K.Spence, M.Hamilton
1979	Sep	Psoriasis	A.Taylor (solo)
1980		Hot Tips	D.Cuthbertson, R.Anderson

Previously aided as Ivy Arete.

1980	May	Mottled Rib	D.Cuthbertson, G.Saxon
1980	Jun	Dynamo	R.Anderson, D.Cuthbertson
1980	Jun	The Excuse	D.Cuthbertson, R.Anderson

| 1980 | Aug | The Duel | P.Hunter, C.Lees |

The original route traversed a flake out right to finish. Steve Hill made the direct variation using a peg runner and the flake has since disappeared rendering the original defunct.

| 1980 | Aug | Barefoot | D.Cuthbertson, P.Hunter |
| 1980 | Sep | Live Wire | M.Duff, P.Barrass |

So named as a fall saw Duff brush the ledge below on rope stretch making the final lead of the crux a very scary experience.

1980	Oct	Helter Skelter	A.Taylor, R.Anderson, K.Spence
1980	Nov	Poison Arete	D.Cuthbertson, T.Prentice, I.Duckworth
1980	Nov	Left-Hand Edge	D.Cuthbertson
1980	Nov	Nicotine Rush	R.Kerr, D.Cuthbertson
1980	Nov	Twilight	D.Cuthbertson, R.Kerr
1983	15 May	Gitanes	M.Duff, L.Brims
1983	25 Jun	Space Scuttle	A.Brindle, M.Duff
1983	20 Aug	Turbo	M.Duff
1986		Monopod	G.Nicoll, J.Naismith
1987	28 Apr	Sideline	N.Shepherd, R Worth

Climbed initially with a peg runner. G.Farquhar recorded an ascent by bridging up the tree to miss the crux. Both tree and peg are now defunct and the first recorded ascent without either was made by K.Howett in 1994 after top-rope practice. A direct start, named Sharp End, was added on 7 July 1997 by G.Lennox after top-rope practice.

| 1990 | | Granola Head | D.McCallum |
| 1991 | | The Vibes | I.Cropley |

The bolts of both the above routes were removed at one stage but replaced after general consensus agreed the venue as a suitable place for sport routes.

1992	Apr	Eschebaum	D.Hamilton, C.Becker
1992		Katie Morag's First Steps	B.Ankers, C.Fettes
1994	10 Sep	The Mound of Venus	G.Ridge, K.Howett

The belayer became very attached to a nearby tree.

| 1994 | 23 Sep | Crash Test Dummies | K.Howett (unseconded) |

The expected second never arrived due to a traffic accident.

| 1996 | Aug | The Chopping Block | N.Shepherd |

LOVER'S LEAP

| 1959 | | Direct Route | R.A.Hockey, J.Proom |

A direct start was added in 1960 by R.Campbell.

| 1960s | | Ash Tree Wall | I.G.Rowe |
| 1960s | | Central Route | I.G.Rowe |

Variation start by G.Farquhar in 1970s.

1977	3 Jul	Jungle Jim	R.Baker, A.McCord
1982	11 Apr	Twister, Hedghog	M.Duff, P.Boyle
1982	12 Apr	Worms	M.Duff (solo)
1983	25 Jun	Bullet, Little Gem	M.Duff, A.Brindle

The first pitch of Bullet was climbed by G.Farqhar in the 1960's.

| 1996 | 23 May | Bullet Direct Start | G.Nicoll |

EVEN LOWER CAVE CRAG

| 1987 | 6 Jul | Just for Laughs | A.Leary, M.Macrae, D.Cassidy |
| 1988 | | Alternative Comedy | R.Kirkwood, A.Leary |

LOWER CAVE CRAG

1959		Cherry Tree Ridge	R.N.Campbell

Direct finish added by R.A.Hockey, J.Proom.

1959		Civer (Aid)	I.G.Rowe

FFA: M.Hamilton in 1977.

1959		The Stank	G.and R.Farquhar

Climbed with 2 pegs on pitch 2. FFA: M.Coustan in 1974.

1959		Hood	R.N.Campbell

The Direct finish was added by B.Robertson in 1963.

1959		Fuck Face	D.Haston
1959		Grot	R.N.Campbell
1959		Lower Cave Crag Girdle Traverse	R.N.Campbell
1960		Cludge	R.N.Campbell
1965		Harelip	R.N.Campbell

Later superseded by Cabaret.

1976	3 Oct	Paramours Rib	B.Clarke, G.Rooney
1977	26 Nov	Kaituma	A.Taylor, R.Anderson, M.Duff
1978	12 Dec	The Stripper	M.Duff, R.Anderson
1979	22 Apr	Tremendous Applause	M.Duff, R.Anderson
1979	23 Apr	Dhias	M.Duff, R.Anderson
1979	22 Apr	Dram	M.Duff, R.Anderson
1979	6 May	Shikari Rib/Geronimo	P.Hunter, S.Drummond
1979	16 Jun	Caberet	R.Anderson, R.Bruce, M.Duff
1979	Sep	In the Shrubbery	D.Cuthbertson, R.Anderson
1980	Sep	Wot Gorilla	N.Morrison, T.Kay
1981	18 May	Secret Affair	M.Duff, L.Brims
1986	13 Sep	Stay Hungry	R.Anderson, M.Hamilton

A sport route was produced just to its right and Stay Hungry itself was retro-bolted. The bolts were later removed and Lower Cave Crag accepted as a bolt-free venue.

UPPER CAVE CRAG

1957	Noddy	P.Brian
1957	The Ramp	P.Brian
1959	Flook	R.N.Campbell
1959	Left Edge	R.N.Campbell
1959	Crutch	A.Wightman
1959	Squirm	N.MacNiven

FFA: M.Hamilton, A.Taylor, 1976.

1960	Coffin Corner	P.Smith

A wedged tent peg bore witness to a possible prior ascent by unknown Ferranti Club members.

1960	Corpse	N.MacNiven

The line was attempted by R.Campbell but he had to be helped off with a top rope one move below the top. He foolishly told MacNiven who climbed it using 3 pegs for aid. FFA: M.Hamilton, A.Taylor in 1976. A left-hand finish was added in 1980.

1960	Squirm Direct	D.Bathgate

Graded A3 (5PA). The direct finish was added in 1969 by J.Porteous. FFA: M.Hamilton, A.Taylor in 1976.

1960	Gnome	B.Robertson

FFA: M.Couston, 1974.

1960		Coffin Arete	G.Farquhar, R.Farquhar

FFA: as High Performance by D.Cuthbertson 1978. Climbed on sight, it was Scotland's first pitch to receive the 6b technical grade.

1960		Mousetrap	I.G.Rowe

FFA: D.Cuthbertson 1979. Climbed over two days and initially given 6c.

1963		Rat Race	B.Robertson, J.MacLean

FFA: (pitch 1) M.Hamilton 1976, then finished direct with 1PA. At the time this was one of Scotland's hardest free climbs and a major breakthrough. FFA: (pitch 2) D.Jameson and party during the first ascent of Warfarin, 1978. The first complete on sight free ascent went to visiting American M.Graham, 1978.

1966		Rat Race Direct	I.G.Rowe, D.S.B.Wright

FFA: D.Cuthbertson, K Johnstone, 1980.

1969		Ratcatcher	A.Petit, K.J.Martin

Climbed as an aid route at A3. FFA: D.Cuthbertson, M.Hamilton, 1976

1969	4 Oct	Green Cheese	K.J.Martin

An aid route. Climbed partially free by Alan Petit. FFA: 'In Loving Memory' D.Cuthbertson, M.Lawrence, 1981. The route waited 7 years for an on sight ascent when its true grade was confirmed at E6.

1969	8 Dec	Fall Out	M.Forbes, G.Millar

Climbed on aid at A3. FFA: D.Cuthbertson, G.Latter, 1982. The original free route on the steep central wall, using a mixture of natural gear and old bolts from the aided ascent.

1972		Hang Out	M.Forbes, G.Millar

Aided (5PA). FFA: M.Hamilton, D.Cuthbertson, D.Jameson, 1976.

1974		Sidewinder	D.Brown, R.Anderson, D.Cuthbertson

1976	Jun	Tumbleweed	D.Jameson, D.Cuthbertson

The first ascensionist fell from the final moves clutching handfulls of heather.

1976	Oct	Death's Head	D.Cuthbertson, A.Taylor, M.Hamilton
1977	Mar	Marjory Razorblade	D.Cuthbertson, M.Hamilton
1978		High Performance	D.Cuthbertson

A free ascent of Coffin Arete.

1978	5 Sep	Warfarin	D.Jameson, G.Nicoll, M.Duff

They freed the origional second pitch of Rat Race in the process.

1978	10 Oct	Tombstone	D.Cuthbertson, M.Duff
1978	5 Nov	Stand Clear	M.Duff, R.Anderson, G.Clarke
1978		Epitaph	P.Hunter, C.Lees
1978	21 Nov	Lilly Langtry	M.Duff, R.Anderson
1978	Nov	Summerdays	D.Cuthbertson, R.Anderson
1979	11 Mar	Morningside Warm Up	P.Hunter, C.Lees
1979	21 May	Evening Hot Line	P.Hunter, S.Drummond
1979	21 May	Hot Line Direct	P.Hunter, S.Drummond
1979	24 Jun	Morbidezza	D.Cuthbertson

Graded at E4 at the time, but actually regarded as one of Scotland's first E5s. Second ascent by J. (Spider) MacKenzie.

1979	5 Sep	Gotterdammerung	P.Hunter, R.Williamson

Top roped prior to an ascent, with a peg runner. Climbed without the peg by D.Cuthbertson.

1979	Sep	Voie de l'Amie	D.Cuthbertson, R.Anderson, M.Duff
1980	Apr	Lady Charlotte	D.Cuthbertson (led) with M.Duff (Pitch 1), K.Johnstone (pitch 2).

An impressive blank-looking wall succumbs. The original start was further left from the now popular way. Cuthbertson returned in 1987 to add a direct version.

1980	24 Apr	Pied Piper	D.Cuthbertson, M.Duff
1980	19 May	Sexy Lady	M.Duff, W.Wright

Duff took some very long falls onto a hand-placed peg which pulled out when the second fell on it!

1980	Sep	Laughing Gnome	D.Cuthbertson, D.MacCallum
1980	Sep	Hos	D.MacCallum, R.Williamson
1981	18 May	Secret Affair	M.Duff, L.Brims
1981		In Loving Memory	D.Cuthbertson

A free ascent of an old aid route called Green Cheese.

1983		Sore Fingers	M.Wilkins (solo)
1986	Jul	Rattle Yer Dags	D.MacCallum

The first modern placement of a bolt for protection on a Scottish cliff, replacing old bolts from an aided ascent. The route started and finished partway up the crag. It was flashed on the second ascent by M.Hamilton, and later superseded by sport routes such as Marlina.

1986	3 Aug	Marlina	D.Cuthbertson

Two bolts were placed for a direct ascent up the steep wall. Some natural gear was also necessary.

1986	Sep	Marlina Left-Hand	M.Hamilton

The variation was climbed utilising only the bolts placed in the original route. Extra bolts were placed on this and the common start to both lines by S.Lewis on 13 Sep 1986, then red pointed to produce the most popular version.

1986	21 Sep	Fall Out Direct	M.Hamilton

Climbed over two days with new bolts.

1986	11 Nov	The Crossing	G.Latter
1986	11 Nov	Baled Out	R.Bruce

Climbed with a rest that was later dispensed with by M.McGowan.

1987	Apr	The Silk Purse	G.Livingston

An extra bolt prolonged the agony of doing Fall Out Direct to produce the hardest sport route on the crag. Second ascent by D.Cuthbertson.

1987	8 Jul	Ultima Necat	M.McGowan

A direct route up the wall above Marlina using a poor peg runner, later replaced by a bolt.

1987		All Passion Spent	M.McGowan

Originally climbed by E.Cameron using 2 bolt runners and named Cushionfoot Stomp.The bolts were eliminated on the second ascent by M.McGowan and the route renamed. Later in 1995 bolts were replaced on a slightly different finish, but again removed.

1988	31 Aug	Necrophilia	G.Farquhar

An excellent effort climbed on sight.

1990	7 Oct	Post Mortem	G.Farquhar, C Carolan

Climbed with the protection of 2 peg runners before another interested party were going to bolt it.

1991	4 Apr	One Size Fits All	G.Farquhar, C.Carolan

Another on-sight effort from Grant.

1992		Hamish Teddy's Excellent Adventure	D.MacCallum, J.May, R.Anderson
1995	18 Mar	Father Figure	G.Ridge, C.Ridge
1995	25 Mar	Six Fours-Les Plage	G.Ridge, C.Ridge
1995	26 Mar	Fear of the Dark	J.Horrocks, G.Ridge
1995	28 Jun	Sweaty Time Blues	K.Howett, G.Ridge
1995	4 Jul	Chopping and Changing	G.Ridge, J.Horrocks
1995	15 Jul	Working up a Sweat	K.Howett, G.Nicoll
1995	13 May	Ring Piece	P.Thorburn, R.Campbell, G.Latter

| 1996 | 24 Mar | Method Man | L.Hughes, T.Legget |
| 1996 | 5 Apr | Generous Offering | K.Howett, G.Ridge |

NEWTYLE QUARRY

| 1979 | 11 Sep | Slateford Road | M.Duff, G.Clarke |

Top roped previously.

1979	24 Sep	Marguerita	M.Duff, R.Kerr
1979	27 Sep	Counting Out Time	M.Duff, J.Handren
1980		Atomic (1PA)	M.Duff, A.Russel, B.Stitt

FFA: D.McCallum in 1981.

| 1980 | 31 Aug | Raspberries | M.Duff, A.Russell |
| 1981 | May | Spandau Ballet | D.McCallum, J.Handren, R.Anderson |

The most popular route in the quarry. A flake fell off the crux in 1982 and a further ascent followed by T.Brindle and M.Duff in 1983.

1981	7 Jun	Soft Shoe Shuffle	D.McCallum, J.Handren
1981	Jul	Pulse	M.Duff, D.McCallum, C.Barlow, L.Duff
1981	18 Jul	Just Gentleman	M.Duff, A.Russell
1983	7 Sep	Flashdance	M.Duff, H.Brindle
1986	Sep	Compulsive Gambler	S.Stewart, C.A.M.Smith

The second ascent by G.Farquhar followed immediately afterwards.

| 1997 | 3 Jun | Pantile Headlap | G.Nicoll, M.Nicoll |

CRAIG LAGGAN

1978	12 Jun	Misconception	Strickland, Owen, Dowds
1978	20 Jun	Goliath's Grandad	Strickland, Owen
1978	20 Jun	Larceny	Owen, Strickland
1978	13 Aug	Grandad's Groove	Cheesman, Owen

A harder start was later added by M.Duff, G.Hornby.

1978	13 Aug	Convergance	Owen, Cheesman
1980	12 Oct	Rainbow Warrior	M.Duff, G.Hornby
1980	13 Oct	Chrysalids, Snare	M.Duff, G.Hornby
1980	13 Oct	Trouble with Lichen	G.Hornby, M.Duff
1980	13 Oct	Nomad	G.Hornby
1980	15 Oct	Rib Cage, Power Play	M.Duff, G.Hornby
1980	15 Oct	Wiper	G.Hornby, M.Duff
1980	15 Oct	Spare Rib	G.Hornby
1980	26 Oct	General Woundwort, Lettuce	M.Duff, R.Anderson
1990	27 May	Spare Rib Direct	T.MacDonald (solo)
1990	27 May	Razor Flake	T.MacDonald (solo)
1995	9 Aug	Sirius	S.Hardie (solo)

CRAIG RUENSHIN

| 1968 | | Victoria's Chimney, The Huge, Larch Crack | J.MacKenzie, R.Lambert |
| 1995 | | Eye of Newt | G.Nicoll |

STRATHEARN AND STRATHYRE

GLEN LEDNOCK

CREAG NA H-IOLAIRE

1979	6 May	Sultans of Swing	N.Morrison, R.Stewart, B.Hogg
1979	6 May	Premiere	N.Morrison, R.Stewart, B.Hogg
1979	6 May	Tigger	N.Morrison, B.Hogg
1979	25 May	Juniors Jinx	I.Duckworth, N Morrison
1979	25 May	The Strangler	I.Duckworth, N.Morrison
1979		Deuxieme	I.Duckworth (solo)
1979		Right-Hand Groove	I.Duckworth (solo)
1979	29 May	Black September	N.Morrison
1979	23 Sep	Strategies for Survival	N.Morrison, I.Duckworth, B.Duncan
1979	19 Sep	Get a Grip	N.Morrison
1979	19 Sep	By the Way	N.Morison, R.Stewart, B.Hogg
1979	19 Sep	Oddball	R.Stewart, N.Morrison
1979		Sultan's Direct	C.Calow, B.Hogg
1980		Cranium Wall	I.Duckworth, C.Calow
1980	10 Jun	Jessicated	I.Duckworth, N.Morrison
1980		Disco Dancer	I.Duckworth
1980	2 Oct	Disco Duck	N.Morrison
1980	2 Oct	Scarey Monsters	N.Morrison, B.Hogg
1981		Diamond Cutter	K.Spence, J.MacKenzie
1981		No Cruise	J.MacKenzie, K.Spence
1983	Jul	Perishing	K.Spence, D.McCallum
1988	9 May	Bear Cage	A.Tibbs, R.McGuire
1992	18 Jun	Sidewinder	K.Howett, D.Douglas
1994	Jul	Cranium Wall Direct	G.Lenox, C.Adam
1995		Time for a Sharp Exit	A.Thow, B.Chalton
1995	1 May	Pleasure Cruise, Dying Breed	G.Lennox, C.Adam
1995	6 May	Rucking with Rosie	C.Adam, D.Parr
1995	30 May	Power Pinch	G.Lennox, D.Alexander, C.Adam
1995	16 Sep	Lenny's Jinx	D.Alexander, G.Lennox

BALNACOUL CASTLE

1971	Jun	Castle Crawl	J.Monan, F.Binning
1971	Jun	Carcase Wall	R.Campbell, J.Monan, P.Murray-Rust

Direct Finish added in 1974 by unknown members of The Squirrels and Rosyth Naval personnel.

1972	May	Spare Rib	R.N.Campbell, I.Thomson
1973	10 Oct	Moonbeam	I.Conway, T.Connelly
1973	17 Oct	Percy Thrower	D.Baker, T.Connelly
1974	31 Mar	Grafter	D.Baker, I.Conway
1974	31 Mar	Moonshadow	I.Conway, D.Baker
1974	3 Apr	Humdinger	I.Conway, D.Baker
1974	6 Apr	Barnstormer	I.Conway, D.Baker
1974	7 Apr	Little Brahma	I.Conway, D.Baker

The Direct Finish was added by N.Morrison.

| 1974 | 10 Apr | Moonraker | I.Conway, T.Connelly |

1974	15 May	The Great Crack (1PA)	I.Conway

An impressive ascent, Conway succeding where many had failed. FFA: E.Grindley, I.Duckworth, May 1975.

1974	12 Jun	Lunar Groove	I.Conway, D.Baker
1974	Jun	Sweat	I.Conway
1974	Jun	Dividing Chimney	J.Porteous, R.MacDonald
1975	Jun	The Chancers	E.Grindley, E.Brookes
1978	8 Apr	No Place for a Wendy	M.Hamilton

One of the best climbs in the glen. Originally climbed in two pitches.

1979	11 Jun	Piggie's Paradise	D.Cuthbertson, I.Duckworth, N.Morrison
1979	11 Jun	Gabrielle	D.Cuthbertson

Originally named Grooved Arete.

1980	29 Jun	Les Alpiniste Deshabilles	N.Morrison, T.Kay
1985	20 Jul	Wendy's Day Out	G.Muhlemann, S.Richardson
1984	4 Aug	Jungle Warfare	S.Richardson, R.Everett
1992	Jul	Central Groove	R.Campbell

Thought to be the free ascent of a previously named route climbed entirely on aid, but in fact it was not the same.

1993	Jul	Pole-axed	R.Campbell, I.Taylor
1996	28 Apr	Goldie	L.Hughes, K.Howett
1996	2 Jun	Drunk in Charge	G.Lennox, C.Adam
1996	4 Jun	Hormone Warrior	L.Hughes, K.Howett

Climbed on sight by G.Lennox and C.Adam on 2 Jun 1996 with a point of direct aid and named Pump up the Jam. The free ascent followed (again on sight) by L.Hughes and K.Howett after the line had been gardened by the first ascensionists.

1996	4 Jun	Bruised and Battered	K.Howett, L.Hughes
1996	4 Jun	Pump up the Groove	G.Lennox, C.Adam

Climbed on sight with lots of rests to allow cleaning.

1996	7 Jun	Feet Don't Fail Me Now	C.Adam, G.Lennox
1996	8 Jun	Optical Illusion	C.Adam, G.Lennox
1996	19 Jun	Zig and Zag, Bridget Midget	G.Lennox, C.Adam
1996	18 Jul	International Colouring-in Contest	L.Hughes, K.Howett
1996	18 Jul	Hide and Sneak	K.Howett
1996	25 Jul	Rough Cut	G.Lennox, T.Rankin

Climbed on sight with several rest points.

1996	25 Jul	White Lines	D.Parr, C.Adam
1996	15 Aug	Huckleberry Thin	L.Hughes, K.Howett
1997	9 Jul	No Digidy	L.Hughes, A.Gould
1997	13 Jul	Diesel Power	L.Hughes, K.Howett
1997	20 Jul	Solutions to a Small Problem	K.Howett, L.Hughes

GLEN OGLE

BEINN LEABHAIN

1990	13 May	Ex Officio	G.E.Little, R.G.Reid

CREAG NAN CUILEANN

1991	11 May	Pruner's Groove	G.E.Little, K.Howett, T.Prentice
1991	11 May	Poison Ivy	K.Howett, T.Prentice
1991	3 Aug	Mind Bogle	K.Howett (unseconded)
1991	3 Aug	The Harder They Come	T.Prentice, K.Howett

1992 13 Jun The Bigger They Fall   R.Campbell, R.Anderson
Climbed jointly. Both climbers led and placed gear in some of the pitch but neither did so to all of it.
1992 24 Aug Merlyn's Flight   K.Howett (unseconded)
This was the start of the development of climbing in the glen that everyone travels through on their way to Glen Coe, although further action involved the drill.

THE SPORT ROUTES

1992	4 Jun	Sugar and Spice	R.Campbell, R.Anderson

Not a sport route!

1992	20 Jul	Metal Guru	R.Anderson
1992	12 Jul	Children of the Revelution	R.Anderson
1993	8 May	Easy Over	R.Anderson
1993		Midge Patrol	C.Anderson
1993		Wristy Business	R.Anderson
1993		Trossachs Trundler	M.Smith
1993		Slave to the Rythum	R.Anderson
1993		Rum Ration	D.McCallum
1993		Blithe Spirit	R.Anderson
1993		Get a Grip	R.Anderson
1993		Off the Beaten Track	P.Thorburn
1993		Cut Loose	R.Anderson
1993	24 May	After the Flood	G.Ridge
1993		Chain Lightning	R.Anderson
1993		Spiral Tribe	D.McCallum
1993	5 Jun	Arc of a Diver	R.Anderson
1993	7 Jun	Eat Y'self Fitter	G.Ridge
1993	12 Jun	Old Wives' Tail	N.Shepherd
1993	12 Jun	Waiting for a Train	G.Ridge
1993	13 Jun	One in the Eye for Stickmen	N.Shepherd

The name derived from the fact that it was the first route on The Diamond that didn't require the use of an enormous clip-stick for the first bolt!

1993	13 Jun	The Pack Horse	N.Shepherd
1993	29 Jun	Paradise Road	G.Ridge
1993	22 Jun	Horrid	R.Maguire
1993	26 Jun	Gotta Sin to be Saved	G.Ridge
1993	28 Jun	Short Sharp Shocked	J.Horrocks
1993	Jun	Speedfreak	G.Ridge

The record for travel from Dundee to Lochearnhead gets reduced every visit as regular evening sorties turn the twisting road into the Scottish equivelent to the Indie 500.

1993	3 Jul	Gross Indecency	R.Anderson
1993	4 Jul	Raspberry Beret	C.Anderson
1993	5 Jul	Hive of Industry	N.Shepherd
1993	10 Jul	Scaramanga	N.Shepherd

This remains unrepeated due to the extra 5 minutes walking involved to reach it.

1993	10 Jul	Ship Ahoy	C.Anderson
1993	17 Jul	Fight Fire With Fire	N.Shepherd
1993	25 Jul	The Bends	R.Anderson
1993	Jul	Maniaxe	A.Banks

Named after another prominent Ogle activist was seen with first an ice axe, then a spade hanging from his harness.

1993	Jul	The Guilt Trip	A.Banks

1994		The Asteriod routes	R.Hutton and friends
1994		Weigh Anchor	R.Anderson
1994		Hang Free	R.Anderson
1994		Digital Quartz	I.Pitcairn
1994		Climb and Punishment	R.Anderson
1994		Cauldron of Spite	C.Anderson
1994		Stone Junky, Dirt Digger	R.Anderson
1994		That Sinking Feeling	R.Anderson
1994		The Drowning Pool	R.Anderson
1994		Mona Sleaza	C.Anderson
1994		Overkill, Overlord, Over the Top	R.Anderson
1994	May	Frigging in the Rigging	G.Ridge

1994 saw the rush for routes really begin and the Dundee team were making Alpine-style starts at weekends to beat the Edinburgh team in staking their lines. These early starts also allowed climbing to be had in the sun on The Dark Side!

1994	21 May	Face the Heat, Ultaviolet	N.Shepherd
1994	21 May	Outshined, Burnt Offerings	G.Ridge
1994	22 May	Burn Baby Burn, Burn It Up	G.Ridge
1994	22 May	Infrarete, Under the Same Sun	N.Shepherd
1994	28 May	Don't Pass Me By, Havering Skate, Infinite Gravity	N.Shepherd
1994	29 May	Nitrogen	N.Shepherd
1994	11 Jun	Rush, The Edge of Ecstacy	N.Shepherd

The micro-route boom of Glen Ogle!

1994	Jun	Satan's Slaves	G.Ridge
1994	Jun	Under Where?	G.Ridge
1994	Jun	Far Beyond Driven	G.Ridge
1994	Jun	XX	G.Ridge
1994	Jun	Under Mind	G.Ridge
1994	Jun	Hyperhyper	G.Ridge
1994	Jun	Driven to Distraction	G.Ridge
1994	Jun	Carsonagenic	G.Ridge

Neil Carsons just misses a flash ascent of Off the Beaten Track.

1994	Jun	Hanging Out the Smalls	G.Ridge
1994	2 Jul	Chocaholics, Hot Chocolate	N.Shepherd
1994	30 Jul	Fingers of Fudge, Half Covered	N.Shepherd
1994	Jul	Voodoo Ray	N.Shepherd
1994	Jul	Don't Fight the Feeling	G.Ridge

Bolted and climbed in the rain and grossly undergraded initially.

1994	Jul	Debt of Pain	G.Ridge
1994	Jul	Chimera	J.Horrocks
1994	Jul	Sudden Alchemy	J.Horrocks
1994	Jul	Beggar's Banquet	G.Ridge
1994	Jul	Sorry Tess	G.Ridge
1994	Jul	The Greenhouse Defect	G.Ridge
1994	6 Aug	The Age Old Problem Rears its Ugly Head	G.Ridge

At this point the Dundee team calculate the amount they have spent on petrol, discover Cambus O' May Quarry on Deeside and the Edinburgh team find new haunts. New routing in Glen Ogle slows to a trickle.

1995	28 Apr	Hold the Press	G.Ridge

1995	5 May	Recreational Chemistry, Raving Lunatics	N.Shepherd
1995	6 May	Restless Souls	C.Anderson
1995		Submersion	R.Anderson
1996	15 Sep	Pullover	R.Anderson

CREAG MAC RANAICH

1994	Aug	Sidewinder	R.Campbell
1995	20 May	Toiler on the Sea	P.Thorburn, R.Campbell
1995	28 Jun	Charge!	P.Thorburn, R.Campbell
1996	3 Aug	Complicity	P.Thorburn

A major new crag is found from the man with wings and bendy bones, Paul (The Stork) Thorburn – watch this space!

STRATHYRE

CREAG NAN SPEIREAG AND CRAIGRUIE

1993		An Dialtaig	P.Thorburn
1994		Dirty Deeds	G.Ridge

BLEATER'S WALL and THE BIGG WALL

1993	2 May	Skin Up	G.Ridge, C Ridge, K.Howett
1993	2 May	The Old Boy Network	G.Ridge, C.Ridge
1993	3 May	Bleating Heart	K.Howett, G.Ridge

On the way to the crag, a lamb takes a liking to George and follows him around for the rest of the day.

1993	15 Aug	Scruff	K.Howett, S.Harrison
1993	15 Aug	Wondr'ing Aloud	S.Harrison (solo)
1993	24 Oct	Flapping Around	K.Howett, G.Ridge
1993	26 Oct	Escape from Drudgery	K.Howett, G.Ridge
1993	30 Oct	Guisers and Ghouls	G.Ridge, K.Howett
1993	30 Oct	The Slippery Slope	G.Ridge, K.Howett, S.Smith
1993	30 Oct	The Blind Buddha ...	A.Banks, G.Ridge

STRATHYRE CRAG

1993	Oct	Static Discharge, Power Surge	R.Anderson
1993	24 Oct	Electrodynamics	R.Anderson
1993	7 Nov	Short Circuit	R.Anderson
1994	30 Apr	High Tension Lead	P.Thorburn
1994	1 May	Power Sink	R.Anderson
1994	1 May	Clam Chowder	G.Ridge
1994	May	Bridging the Gap	R.Anderson
1994	May	Spark Thug	R.Anderson
1994	21 May	Circuit Breaker, Cracking the Lines	R.Anderson
1996	14 Sep	All Electric, Crossed Wire	R.Anderson

Index of Routes

THE GLEN NEVIS CRAGS

To Fort William

Am Mam Buidhe

Leith Aire

Achriabhach

Lower Falls of Nevis

P

P

1	Creag an Fhithich	7	Buccaneer Crag
2	Polldubh Crags	8	Boot Hill Crag
3	Upper Polldubh	9	Creag Uamh Shomhairle
4	Scimitar Buttress	10	Car Park Crag
5	Barrel Buttress	11	Gorge Crag
6	Whale Rock	12	The Gorge Wall